TIANJIN COSMOPOLIS

Columbia Studies in International and Global History

COLUMBIA STUDIES IN INTERNATIONAL AND GLOBAL HISTORY

Cemil Aydin, Timothy Nunan, and Dominic Sachsenmaier, Series Editors

This series presents some of the finest and most innovative work coming out of the current landscapes of international and global historical scholarship. Grounded in empirical research, these titles transcend the usual area boundaries and address how history can help us understand contemporary problems, including poverty, inequality, power, political violence, and accountability beyond the nation-state. The series covers processes of flows, exchanges, and entanglements—and moments of blockage, friction, and fracture—not only between "the West" and "the Rest" but also among parts of what has variously been dubbed the "Third World" or the "Global South." Scholarship in international and global history remains indispensable for a better sense of current complex regional and global economic transformations. Such approaches are vital in understanding the making of our present world.

Jie-Hyun Lim, trans. Megan Sungyoon, *Victimhood Nationalism: History and Memory in a Global Age*

Sandrine Kott, *A World More Equal: An Internationalist Perspective on the Cold War*

Julia Hauser, *A Taste for Purity: An Entangled History of Vegetarianism*

Hayrettin Yücesoy, *Disenchanting the Caliphate: A History of Secular Political Thought in the Early Abbasid Empire*

Anne Irfan, *Refuge and Resistance: Palestinians and the International Refugee System*

Michael Francis Laffan, *Under Empire: Muslim Lives and Loyalties Across the Indian Ocean World, 1775–1945*

Eva-Maria Muschik, *Building States: The United Nations, Development, and Decolonization, 1945–1965*

Jessica Namakkal, *Unsettling Utopia: The Making and Unmaking of French India*

Michael Christopher Low, *Imperial Mecca: Ottoman Arabia and the Indian Ocean Hajj*

Nicole CuUnjieng Aboitiz, *Asian Place, Filipino Nation: A Global Intellectual History of the Philippine Revolution, 1887–1912*

Mona L. Siegel, *Peace on Our Terms: The Global Battle for Women's Rights After the First World War*

Raja Adal, *Beauty in the Age of Empire: Japan, Egypt, and the Global History of Aesthetic Education*

Ulbe Bosma, *The Making of a Periphery: How Island Southeast Asia Became a Mass Exporter of Labor*

Perrin Selcer, *The UN and the Postwar Origins of the Global Environment: From World Community to Spaceship Earth*

Dominic Sachsenmaier, *Global Entanglements of a Man Who Never Traveled: A Seventeenth-Century Chinese Christian and His Conflicted Worlds*

For a complete list of books in the series, please see the Columbia University Press website.

Tianjin Cosmopolis

AN ALTERNATIVE HISTORY OF GLOBALIZATION

Pierre Singaravélou

Translated by
Stephen W. Sawyer

Columbia University Press
New York

Columbia University Press
Publishers Since 1893
New York Chichester, West Sussex
cup.columbia.edu

Library of Congress Cataloging-in-Publication Data
Names: Singaravélou, Pierre, author. | Sawyer, Stephen W., 1974– translator.
Title: Tianjin cosmopolis : an alternative history of globalization / Pierre Singaravélou ; translated by Stephen W. Sawyer.
Other titles: Tianjin cosmopolis. English | Alternative history of globalization
Description: New York : Columbia University Press, [2025] | Series: Columbia studies in international and global history | "Originally published as "Tianjin Cosmopolis: Une autre histoire de la mondialisation" © Editions du Seuil, 2017." | Includes bibliographical references and index.
Identifiers: LCCN 2024024685 (print) | LCCN 2024024686 (ebook) | ISBN 9780231192002 (hardback) | ISBN 9780231192019 (trade paperback) | ISBN 9780231549608 (ebook)
Subjects: LCSH: Globalization—China—Tianjin—History—20th century. | Cosmopolitanism—China—Tianjin—History—20th century. | City planning—China—Tianjin—History—20th century. | Tianjin (China)—History—20th century. | Tianjin (China)—History—Siege, 1900. | Tianjin (China)—Politics and government—20th century. | China—Foreign relations—20th century.
Classification: LCC DS796.T557 S5613 2025 (print) | LCC DS796.T557 (ebook) | DDC 305.896/338507300904—dc23/eng/20240808

LC record available at https://lccn.loc.gov/2024024685
LC ebook record available at https://lccn.loc.gov/2024024686

Printed and bound by CPI Group (UK) Ltd, Croydon, CR0 4YY

Cover design: Milenda Nan Ok Lee
Cover image: Wikimedia Commons

From now on I shall describe the cities and you will tell me if they exist and are as I have conceived them.

—KUBLAI KHAN TO MARCO POLO
IN ITALO CALVINO, *INVISIBLE CITIES*

Figure 0.0 Map of Tianjin by Feng Qihuang, 1899. Courtesy of the Library of Congress, Geography and Map Division, G7824.T5A3 1899 .F4

Contents

TIANJIN COSMOPOLIS

INTRODUCTION

Ten Empires on the Head of Pin

A Situated History of Imperial Globalization

I always go to Tientsin by train. There are soldiers from all the nations that have troops in China in the same car. We try to start a conversation; we speak the Chinese *sabir*, that is, the few words of Chinese that every soldier has learned in the country. When accompanied with expressive gestures, we manage to make ourselves more or less understood. Though on occasion you ask for tobacco and your interlocutor passes you the salt.

—LÉON SILBERMANN

When we entered the ruins of the city, the smell of burning was replaced by a singular odor that we call the Chinese smell. It is a smell of grease, aromas, and mud, distinct from all the good and bad smells known in our country: that's why we consider it Chinese.

—GIUSEPPE MESSEROTTI BENVENUTI

. . . perhaps because the Chinese case is exemplary, or perhaps because the sinologist is exemplary. (This is a very important problem when one reads a work: one tends to attribute the singularity of a description to the singularity of the country, but it may be due to the singularity of the analyst).

—PIERRE BOURDIEU

During the Universal Exhibition of 1900 in Paris, the "rue des Nations" along the Seine was home to a veritable anthology of architectural styles and technology from countries around the world. At the same moment, some 13,000 *li* (5,184 mi/8,343 km) away, the same utopia of universalism and the dream of an ideal city molded by science and industry was taking concrete form in the Chinese city of Tianjin. According to a commonplace of the early twentieth century, Tianjin was a *cosmopolis* where the great powers of the planet fought, exchanged, and coinhabited.[1] Contrary to the rue des Nations, the vestiges of these diverse origins are still visible today in a megalopolis whose municipality has invested in the legacy of foreign imperialism. Indeed, Tianjin is a *hapax legomenon* in the history of the contemporary world: Ten imperial powers were concurrently present in the agglomeration through the foreign concessions they acquired following a series of wars in East Asia, including the Second Opium War (British, French, and American concessions in 1861), the Sino-Japanese War (German concessions in 1895 and Japanese in 1898), and the Boxer War (Russian concessions in 1900, Italian in 1901, Austro-Hungarian and Belgian in 1902).

Why was the world's gaze fixed upon Tianjin? The city is strategically situated near the Bohai Gulf on the principal access route to Beijing. A garrison town that controlled access to the capital since the fifteenth century, after the Second Opium War (1856–1860) the city became the country's second economic center behind Shanghai and a warehouse that supplied the capital via the Grand Canal. Tianjin also constituted the most important political and intellectual center after Beijing. At once close to the Imperial Court and distant enough (87 mi/140 km) to benefit from a more "liberal" environment favoring commerce, cultural production, and political activity, the city held a particular attraction for foreigners. Last, it was the true diplomatic capital of China. The two most powerful men of state of the empire lived and worked there from the middle of the nineteenth century to the beginning of the twentieth: Generals Li Hongzhang and Yuan Shikai, who led the political group of pro-Western "modernizers" at the Court. As these two dynamic political figures show, the Chinese government was not merely subject to foreign imperialism. In fact, it had originally created concessions to distance the foreign powers from territories under full Chinese sovereignty. It was then that modernizing Chinese elites voluntarily transformed Tianjin into a privileged space of interaction and dialogue with foreign powers.

Today Tianjin is almost unknown to "Westerners," though it was one of the most cosmopolitan metropolises in the world at the beginning of the twentieth century. Where else could one encounter Chinese, Manchus, French, Britons, Americans, Germans, Japanese, Russians, Belgians, Italians, Austro-Hungarians, Canadians, Danes, Norwegians, Australians, Vietnamese, Mongolians, Tamils, Rajput, Punjabis, Koreans, Filipinos, Ashkenazi Jews, Ottomans, Greeks, and expatriates of all types? The city was transformed by the Boxer War into a microcosm of the world where small and great powers constantly interacted, frequently cooperated, rivaled one another, and occasionally came to blows. Tianjin thus represents an exceptional observatory for international relations at the turn of the twentieth century, a moment when expeditions into China and the military occupation of Tianjin pushed the great powers to become at once partners and competitors. Beneath these interimperial rivalries there were also tensions on the ground among national elites, as well as between civilian and military personnel. Innumerable transnational social interactions took place alongside the interstate relations between Allies, reinforcing and sometimes counteracting them.

China: A colonial empire like any other?

Nineteenth-century China has long been presented by historians as an aging, isolated, and inward-looking empire whose opening to foreigners was forced by Western imperialism.[2] In the second half of the nineteenth century, foreign powers encountered a Chinese Empire ruled since the mid-seventeenth century by a foreign ethnic minority, the Manchus, who had imposed their power over the Han majority.[3] With the help of a vast administration and literate elite, the emperor (*Tianzi*) of the Qing dynasty reigned over twenty-two provinces, themselves composed of several prefectures, each made up of different districts. In every district, magistrates administered a muddle of judicial, economic, and religious affairs. Within this system the Manchu emperors pursued an expansionist policy: in 1750, China imposed its hegemony on all nations on its northern border, established relations with the Russian Empire, and integrated the Southeast Asian states into its tributary system. The Qing's imperial politics relied on the organization of a modern state, founded on the coordinated use of economic, technical, and ideological resources. Its army, through which it governed, bore a greater resemblance to the Ottoman, Russian, or Austro-Hungarian armed forces than those of the Ming dynasty: a highly mobile cavalry with artillery, firearms, and effective logistics. The empire's economy expanded rapidly in the eighteenth century with highly developed irrigation systems and transport networks. At the same time, the Chinese emperors entertained universalist ambitions: toward the end of the century, Qianlong was persuaded that Qing domination could be expanded over all peoples sufficiently civilized to appreciate it.[4] Thus Europe and the United States hardly had a monopoly over universalism and colonial aspirations. In the eighteenth century, Chinese emperors built tremendous gardens representing the world with the help of European architects in the old summer palace, replete with pavilions and objects from different countries of Europe. This universalist ambition pushed the emperor at the end of the eighteenth century to engage in costly and risky military operations on the empire's margins, initiatives that emptied the Qing's coffers at the beginning of the nineteenth century and contributed to its social and political difficulties.

Qing China therefore expanded its borders and simultaneously constantly interacted with foreigners according to the doctrine of the three concentric circles of the empire: the first circle included the population directly under imperial control; the second circle included peoples paying occasional tribute; the third circle was the realm of barbarians with no relations to China.[5] To the south and the east, the two first circles included the vassal states of Korea and Nepal. To the north and the west China cooperated pacifically with its neighbor, Russia. It maintained contact with states farther afield, with peoples who gave off strong odors and dressed bizarrely, "savage men" likened to animals. The Chinese emperors were also surrounded by a few Jesuit priests, who played a decisive role as diplomatic and scientific advisors, even as they decided to maintain a certain distance and to keep the great majority of these foreigners in reserved areas. It was this practice that birthed the idea of the concession. From the middle of the eighteenth century, Chinese authorities adopted what they referred to as the Canton system, in which commerce with Europeans was concentrated exclusively in the southern port of the empire. The emperor authorized the foreign merchants, who usually belonged to the British East India Company, to come to Canton from October to March after having received permission in Macao. The Europeans and the Indians (Parsis) were required to use Chinese mediators, the Cohong, who paid high taxes to the imperial government. The commercial activities of Canton grew rapidly at the end of the eighteenth and beginning of the nineteenth century under the development of British demand for tea as well as silk and porcelain. To restore a negative trade balance, the British sold opium to the Chinese. In 1839, when the Chinese decided to put an end to this trade for economic and health reasons, Great Britain attacked Canton and occupied Shanghai.

As a result of the First Opium War (1839–1842), the British established an initial foreign concession in Shanghai in the 1840s. The concessions then developed along the Anglo-Indian model: a port, docks, depots, a Bund, social and sporting clubs, racetracks, impressive buildings supported by imposing columns, and so forth.[6] The foreigners benefited from extraterritorial privileges. The great "open ports" of China constituted one of the principal hubs for Asian commercial networks, "at once points of contact between the internal and the world market, poles of development for the domestic economy, and points of contact and exchange between western economy and culture and those of Asian states."[7] Thanks to its size and the density of its population, China was no doubt able to constrain the imperial powers into modifying their colonial practices. The concession was clearly different from a colony in that it was defined as an original contractual solution that formally respected Chinese sovereignty. At the end of the century, the powers were engaged in the "breakup of China" as they accumulated new privileges in the form of concessions, land leases, railroads, and the exploitation of mines and state loans.[8] The Middle Kingdom included forty-five cities or ports that were officially open to foreign commerce in 1899.

The paradoxical development of foreign concessions in Tianjin

Located thirty-one miles (50 km) from the sea, Tianjin is a relatively recent city within China's urban development. The city's development would seem to have depended on the Hai River (or Peiho River, "white river," owing to its appearance in winter), which regularly devastated the city with flooding while also considerably enriching the area through river commerce. In this city, alternatively hit by floods and droughts, managing water became crucial. A simple garrison town in the tenth century, it became the administrative center of a district (*hsien*) when the Mongols arrived and established the capital in Beijing in 1272.[9] This little fortified city expanded from the beginning of the fifteenth century with the displacement of the main capital from Beijing to Nanjing by the Yongle Emperor, who hoped to assert better control over the natural resources of the north and the northern border. Tianjin served to protect Beijing from threats to the city, guaranteeing its provision in grain and controlling the Grand Canal. The city became a central depot and site for the salt trade in the northern half of China.[10] Tianjin's commercial activities benefited from its situation at the confluence of land routes, the Hai River, and the Grand Canal. Indeed, it was a cosmopolitan center long before the arrival of the Europeans.[11] The city was first described by Dutch diplomats (1655) and then by the British

Lord Macartney (1793) and Lord Amherst (1816) as a prosperous economic site that transmitted important natural resources in the north of China and the production coming up from the fertile south toward the capital.[12] The region around the city, Zhili (Hebei), was constituted as a province in 1669, and the economic growth of Tianjin helped elevate it to the rank of prefectural seat (*fu*) in 1726. In 1842, the district of Tianjin included, outside the walled city itself, three cities and 399 villages for a total of 442,292 inhabitants.[13]

The British hoped to make Tianjin the base for their expansion of settlements into the north of China. In 1860, after the failure of Macartney's and Amherst's diplomatic missions, a Franco-British military expedition opened Tianjin by force to foreign trade. Two decades after the creation of foreign concessions in Shanghai at the end of the First Opium War, the creation of a foreign concession in Tianjin resulted in Chinese military defeat during the Second Opium War. The Beijing Convention of October 18, 1860, authorized foreigners to reside in Tianjin. The Chinese government leased land to the British, French, and Americans in perpetuity. The Chinese allowed them to settle somewhat less than two miles (3 km) south of the city, on the territory of the village named Zizhulin (forest of violet bamboo), where the first three concessions on the left bank of the Hai River were created. Despite the European military victory, the Chinese cordoned off the foreigners in the swamplands alongside refuse dumps and cemeteries. Nonetheless, the foreigners understood the advantages of being on the edges of the river at Zizhulin, where the boats could easily maneuver and take anchor.

The borders of the concessions were decided jointly by two French and British officers: Lieutenant Admiral Augustin Trève, provisional consul of France to Tianjin, and Captain Charles George Gordon, commander of the Royal Engineers, who would become one of the most famous heroes of the British empire.[14] The foreign officers needed to negotiate the terms of compensation for the Chinese property owners with the vice minister of the court of justice. The British concession was seventy-six acres (31 ha); the French held sixty acres (24 ha), and the Americans held twenty-two acres (9 ha). The Methodist minister John Innocent recounted the foundational act of the concessions thirty years later, highlighting the promethean role of Charles Gordon, a veritable *Rex*, in the etymological sense of the term:

> The British Settlement was a long stretch of vegetable gardens, with here and there a cluster of squalid mud houses a little west of what is now Victoria Road; and thence to Taku Road, chiefly fields of kao-liang and pools, with a few burial grounds.[15] This rude area Gordon penciled out into a bund, roads, and lots for buildings, and on the plan he carefully elaborated the lots that were subsequently sold to the highest bidders in August, 1861, on conditions precisely defined.[16]

The British and French consuls subleased the lots for ninety-nine years to European renters. The regulations for the concessions stipulated that the European property owners pay an annual "rent," half of which was transferred to the Chinese government and the other half for urban development in the concession. Article 11 of the "Regulation pertaining to land management in the French Concession of Tientsin," from June 2, 1861, established that "the French or those protected by the French, who will have been in legal possession of lots they have requested will be held to pay as a perpetual rent, a sum of 2000 copper cash coins [*sapèques*] per 665 m_2 [*mou*], half of which must be transferred to the Public Treasury of China for the benefit of the Chinese government, and the other half deposited with the French Consulate to fund the rebuilding of roads and digging waterways."[17] The British, whose concession was further away from the walled city, paid a smaller annual rent of 1,500 copper cash coins per 7,165 square feet (665 m^2, or 1,500 cash coins per *mou*). Foreign residents participated in the investments for the development of the concession, notably the costs of drainage, construction, paving, maintenance, streetlights, and the creation of recreational areas, and so on. French, British, and Chinese therefore forged an original system for cofinancing the concessions' urban development. From as early as 1861, urban and territorial planning was part of the accord between the Chinese and the powers that held the concession. A major road cut through and structured the development of the concessions while also leaving room for national identity and characteristics. From north to south, the rue de France became Victoria Road and was then extended at the beginning of the twentieth century into the Kaiser Wilhelm Strasse in the German concession. It was forbidden to "build in a Chinese style," and even at the beginning to sell parcels of land to Chinese inhabitants.[18] Elected municipal councils governed the concessions and pursued their urban planning objectives.

Over the first two years the concessions developed slowly. Outside of the allied forces, only thirteen foreigners resided there in 1861, no more than a few representatives of the trade houses and missionaries, who built the first buildings.[19] Indeed, most foreigners, traders, and missionaries preferred to live in the Chinese city outside the concessions to be closer to their clients and their customers. In fact, between 1860 and 1900 the French concession was French in name only. It was above all a little Catholic kingdom, a haven for missionary congregations (Lazarists, Jesuits, Daughters of Charity) that rented and occupied the quasi-totality of the territory as early as 1865 (see figure 0.0).

> Except for two Russians and a Swiss, who purchased sizeable lots along the river, no French buyer has come forward. So the consul solicited Lazarist and Jesuit missionaries to help conserve for France the memory of the victories of Chang-Kia-Ouan and Palikao (1860). The two orders understood and thus acquired three quarters of the French concession of Tien-Tsin. Little by little, Misters Batouieff, Startzef and Loup constructed; the Fathers as well.[20]

The French and the British were always minorities amid the foreign population of their respective concessions, which remained extremely cosmopolitan. In 1869, outside the concession near the walled city, the missionaries inaugurated the church of Notre-Dame-des-Victoires, a neo-romanesque Albigensian edifice that commemorated the expedition of 1860 thanks to the financing of the Lazarists and a call for donations from Catholics of the metropole. France fulfilled its mission as a protective power for Catholics in China.[21] This extensive missionary presence did not lead to a massive evangelization of the Zhili population, since there were only a few thousand Catholics out of the two million inhabitants of the district of Tianjin at the end of the nineteenth century. Nonetheless, the activism of the congregations and the rumors that surrounded them (notably regarding the death of children in the concession's Catholic orphanages) generated tension between a portion of the local Chinese population and the missionaries. On June 21, 1870, a shot fired by the French consul that killed a Chinese civil servant unleashed the famous "Tientsin Massacre," during which churches were destroyed and the diplomat Henri Fontanier, three priests, ten Daughters of Charity, local Chinese converted to Christianity, and three Russians who were mistaken for Frenchmen were killed. These murders and the ambiguities surrounding the Chinese authorities, who attempted to use the popular uprising to control the foreign presence, provoked strong diplomatic tensions between France and China.[22] France forced China to pay indemnities and to send diplomat Chung How, under the aegis of the Imperial Commissioner, to offer an official apology to Adolphe Thiers in November 1871. The massacre of 1870 pushed the Europeans to a small "exodus" of the walled city toward the zones under Franco-British control.[23] The concessions, which had 112 foreigners in 1866, were home to 262 in 1879 and 612 in 1890. The most dynamic concession was the British, even if, in fact, it was a rather small personal colony in the hands of a magnate of German origin, Gustav Detring, who owned more than 90 percent of the concession's territory.[24] The United States never clearly delimited nor planned the territory it was ceded, becoming an area of lawlessness that escaped both the control of American and Chinese authorities. The local Chinese and foreigners could hide there to escape the different jurisdictions. The United States returned the territory of their concession to China in October 1880 with the guarantee that they would be able to recover it later if they so desired. Until the end of the nineteenth century, the foreign concessions were not developed and were essentially populated by religious figures and civil servants. One contemporary wrote: "Just as the foreign city is tiny, and you can cover its entirety in 30 minutes, it is also sparsely inhabited: 600 to 700 Europeans and Americans make it their home. About half of them are missionaries; the other half are consuls and consulate staff, bank employees, Chinese government officials (customs, railways, etc.), professors (naval and military schools, etc.), doctors, ship owners, and especially merchants."[25]

A diplomatic capital and matrix for Chinese "modernity?"

Outside of these two concessions, Tianjin resembled an ordinary Chinese city of the second half of the nineteenth century. This is true to such an extent that, in most histories of contemporary China, it is almost entirely forgotten.[26] And yet the city played a determining role in the self-strengthening movement at the end of the Qing.[27] Tianjin's importance grew rapidly following the Second Opium War when the imperial government transferred the capital from the province of Zhili to Tianjin after being previously located in Baoding. Tianjin became home to the commissariat of the northern ports in 1870.[28] The viceroy of Zhili (*Zhili zongdu*) was then, according to imperial protocol, the first of the general governors and the most powerful statesman of the empire between 1868 and 1912: Zeng Guofan, Li Hongzhang, and Yuan Shikai.[29]

Traditionally, Chinese diplomacy was the responsibility of different administrations, the Ministry of Rites, the department managing borders, and the viceroys of the bordering and coastal regions. In 1861 the government founded the Zongli headquarters to centralize foreign affairs in Beijing. For the fifteen years that followed the Second Opium War, the Chinese government offered the pretext that the emperor was a minor in order to prevent foreign diplomats from accessing the Imperial Court and meeting the sovereign. This allowed the Chinese to avoid the obligation of foreigners to prostrate before the Son of Heaven, which foreigners would have considered humiliating. Nonetheless, as early as 1870, it was Tianjin—a city which has not been sufficiently studied by specialists of diplomatic history—that served as the diplomatic capital of China.[30] The Zongli headquarters was de facto moved there, since the head of Chinese foreign policy at the end of the nineteenth century was Li Hongzhang, named viceroy of the province of Zhili in order to reestablish order in Tianjin following the massacre of 1870. "He is the true minister of foreign affairs," wrote the American pedagogue Charles Tenney at the time.

The foreign consuls residing in Beijing since 1861 were forced to move to Tianjin to meet Chinese dignitaries, who also hosted foreign sovereigns during official ceremonies, such as the visit of the Hawaiian king in 1881. Between the Second Opium War and the Boxer Rebellion, more than half of the international treaties were signed in the city's concessions (twelve of twenty-three): the treaty with the United States (1858), Great Britain (1858), France (1858), Portugal (1862), Denmark (1863), the Netherlands (1863), Spain (1864), Japan (1871), Peru (1874), Brazil (1881), and France (1884, an accord, and 1885, a treaty).

Treaty negotiations and signing ceremonies most commonly took place at the Astor Hotel, the first Chinese grand hotel, founded in 1863 in the British concession by British Methodist missionary John Innocent.[31] The profits of the establishment were used primarily to finance the activity of the missions. The very name of the hotel manifests the link between Western and Chinese cultures: foreign visitors saw it as the patronym of a family of notables known in Great Britain and the United States, while its transcription in the Chinese characters *li*, *shun*, and *de* expressed the Confucian concept of "power of reason."[32] European shareholders close to Li Hongzhang then bought the hotel, including the German Gustav Detring, president of the Municipal Council in the British concession, who became at the same time the main shareholder of the Astor (1878), the Chinese customs commissioner of Tianjin (1877),[33] and the main diplomatic adviser to Li Hongzhang. As a result, Detring negotiated the peace with the French at the end of the Sino-French war of 1884–85 and represented the Chinese emperor to the Japanese government. By working through a foreign power, the Chinese were able to maintain their dignity in the face of the failures and humiliations imposed by the victorious Japanese and French forces. In 1881 the commissioner of British customs Robert Hart effectively summarized the central role that the Westerners had attributed to Gustav Detring: "The German commissioner had become Li's man and is for the moment more go-ahead than any other man in China. . . . Li is the man for the moment and D. is at his right hand."[34] A haven of peace, the Astor Hotel was the place par excellence for urban modernity and internationalization in China. It may be interpreted as the microcosm in the heart of the miniature world reproduced in Tianjin, where the representatives of the different concessionary powers such as the Portuguese, Danish, Dutch, and Spanish diplomats did business in the 1860s. Twenty-two foreign consuls resided in Tianjin in 1900 and the Astor was even home to some diplomats: the first consulate of Japan, Germany, Canada, and the United States (until 1929), even though the Americans, in theory, had their own concession.[35] This establishment served as a neutral space that offered the most modern communication infrastructures. No doubt one of the first telephones installed in China served the hotel in 1879, thanks to the personal support of Li Hongzhang.[36] Rebuilt to three stories in 1886 with forty rooms and four suites, the Astor was the most imposing and luxurious building within the foreign concessions at the turn of the century, becoming the symbol of the city. The practice of diplomacy in Tianjin allowed them to negotiate more freely while at the same time benefitting from the status of extraterritoriality of the concession and symbolically preserving the dignity of the emperor residing in Beijing where only four treaties were signed between 1858 and 1900. The concession played a central role in distancing and cordoning off the foreign powers.

Between 1870 and 1900, under the leadership of Li Hongzhang and his foreign councilors, Tianjin became an incubator and a showcase for Chinese "modernity." The first public postal system was introduced in Tianjin in March 1878 by Li Hongzhang with the help of customs commissioners Robert Hart and Gustav Detring, who imported the first copies of the famous dragon stamp.[37] Thanks to Li Hongzhang, Tianjin was still at the center of the first great project to introduce the telegraph in China. Though it was ultimately Ding Richang, viceroy of Fujian, who installed the first Chinese telegraphic cable in Taiwan in 1877, Li, fully aware of the power of this new communication for diplomatic and military affairs, conceived of a veritable development program for this technology. For strategic reasons he began by building a line between Tianjin and the Taku Fort in 1879. The viceroy succeeded in convincing the emperor to support the installation of the telegraph in China and to make Tianjin the center of the network. As early as 1880, the new imperial telegraph office was set up there, as well as a telegraph school to teach Chinese students how to use the network. The 955-mile (1,537 km) line connecting Tianjin to Shanghai was started in April 1881 and completed eight months later. In 1882 the line between Tianjin and Tongzhou was finished, followed by a tremendous boom in the installation of telegraphic lines across China. Li Hongzhang ceded the right to use these lines to private companies under the control of the imperial administration of Tianjin.[38] The new network, reserved for social elites who could afford fifteen cents per character for a telegram sent to Shanghai, also provided the opportunity to develop the press in Tianjin and Shanghai. Li Hongzhang also transformed Tianjin into a pioneering city for railroads. Struck by Charles Denby Sr.'s exhibition in Tianjin on the construction of trains in the United States, the viceroy envisaged the construction of a railroad line between Tianjin and Taku and then between Tianjin and Beijing.[39] Following the opening of the coal mine in Kaiping in 1878, the first commercial line in China connected the mining region in Tangshan to Tianjin in 1888 and was then extended to Taku in 1890 and Beijing in 1898 by the British Imperial Railways of the North China Company.[40]

> The first Chinese locomotive was assembled in the workshops of Kaiping and from there the railway line that was to lead to the next canal . . . the coals destined for the military arsenal created by Li Hong-tchang in Tientsin. The transport by waterways was stopped every winter by ice. Li Hong-tchang finally obtained the authorization

> to continue the railroad intended only for the service of the mines to Tientsin. Mr. Kinder discreetly added a few wagons for the personnel. The status quo was thus gradually overcome, and permission was finally obtained to run fast trains for passengers.[41]

The first true Chinese train station was built in Tianjin, then moved to the riverside in 1891, where it was the scene of clashes first between Allies and Boxers and then between the powers.

Tianjin became a site of military experimentation for the Qing Empire in the context of political reforms known as the "self-strengthening movement" of 1860–90. "China surpasses all western countries except in armaments," Li Hongzhang supposedly declared, set on making his city the heart of a Chinese military revival.[42] As a result, Tianjin hosted the first modern arms industry in China alongside the Fuzhou Arsenal, which was completed in 1869.[43] Indeed, the Tianjin Arsenal, founded in 1867 and reorganized in 1875, was made up of the Eastern Arsenal, which produced powder and munitions, and the Western Arsenal, which produced war machines.[44] Li Hongzhang also founded a naval academy there in 1880. In October of that year the city shined thanks to its construction of the first Chinese submarine.[45] In 1885, Li created the first "modern" military academy, while Zhang Zhidong, viceroy of Liangguang, founded a similar institution in Canton in 1887.[46] In these schools the German instructors formed the Chinese cadets in the Western art of war: they studied mathematics, geography, astronomy, military strategy, and German in textbooks translated into Chinese.[47]

At the same time, Western-style higher education was quickly taking off in Tianjin. The first medical school in China was founded there in 1881 as part of the hospital created by the British missionary J. Kenneth Mackenzie of the London Mission Society and Li Hongzhang in 1880.[48] The first modern Chinese university, the University of Peiyang, was founded in 1895 following the humiliating defeat by Japan under the impetus of American missionary and pedagogue Charles Tenney and based on the American model. The first professors received their diplomas from Harvard and Stanford, also employing German pedagogy in the classroom. Following upon the demands of the missionaries set up in Beijing and Shanghai, the Young Men's Christian Association (YMCA) sent David William Lyon to China. He preferred to settle in Tianjin in 1895 thanks to the extensive development of Western educational institutions. The YMCA then spread throughout the rest of China from its center in Tianjin, promoting as early as 1896 the physical education of young Chinese based on athletics. Four years later, after James Naismith invented basketball in the United States, Lyon introduced the sport into China long before it arrived in Europe. The sport progressively became central to the city's cultural identity. From 1896 onward Lyon organized the first basketball lessons.[49] Before the American pedagogues, the British created the first Chinese soccer/football club in Tianjin in 1884, three years before Shanghai.[50] These practices, presented as vectors for the expansion of "muscular Christianity," were rapidly appropriated by the non-Christian population. Tianjin, the door to so-called modern sports, became the sports capital of the empire.

Table tennis, or ping-pong, was introduced into Tianjin for the first time in China in 1901.[51] It was popular among foreigners in the city even as the game remained almost unknown in the rest of the world, as a Belgian entrepreneur wrote in a postcard to his family back home (figure 0.1):

> Here in all the European houses a little game of tennis is played in the living room which is very amusing. It consists of a net placed on a large table, two rackets covered with a stretched drumhead and celluloid balls. A net is placed in the middle of the table and the game is played as on a court, the table being the limit of the game and each player is placed at one of the ends. This game is all the rage here. It should be sold in Brussels in toy stores.[52]

Tianjin and the modernization policy considerably reinforced the political position of Li Hongzhang, who had been weakened by the Chinese defeat in the Sino-Japanese War. He returned to grace with the defeat of the Boxers, as was emphasized by the photographer James Ricalton, who nicknamed him the "Bismarck of the Orient." "The most famous man in China, the ablest statesman in Asia, the second richest man in the world and one of the most widely known figures of history."[53] Following the magisterial work of John K. Fairbank, historians have tended to present the nineteenth century as an extended period of agony for the Chinese state, incapable of dealing with internal revolts and international wars. Yet Li Hongzhang's biography shows that a portion of the Chinese elites were able to respond effectively to the challenges of internationalization.[54]

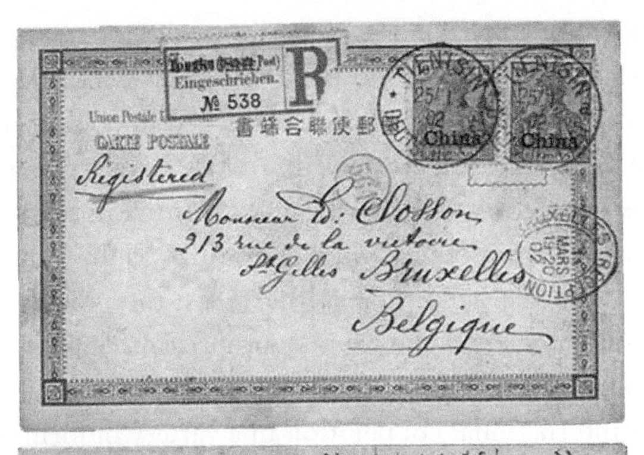

Figure 0.1 Postcard from Mr. Chosson sent from Tianjin to his family living in Brussels, January 22, 1902. Lausanne International Table Tennis Federation.

Tianjin 1900, a touchstone of imperial globalization

Despite these profound transformations, the city remained ignored by foreigners, who merely passed by in the style of Jules Verne's character Claudius Bombarnac, who announced: "We stayed only fifteen minutes in Tientsin."[55] The Boxer War changed everything. During the summer of 1900 it seemed to transform the city from top to bottom. Tianjin suffered a destructive siege and a bloody massacre. The Allies established a new international military government to administer and modernize the Chinese city and its environs. In just a few days the provincial city was transformed into a global city where population from throughout the West and Asia seemed for a time to cohabitate and exchange in the wake of merciless fighting. Violent and peaceful exchanges proliferated; the circulation of individuals and ideas accelerated. During this brief episode, the limited space of Tianjin seemed to contain an entire world, including its processes of integration and its multiple contradictions. In little more than two years the most powerful nations on the planet attacked the oldest empire, colonizing and decolonizing this tiny portion of its territory, massacring and "civilizing" its population, devastating and planning its territory.

Tianjin in 1900 thus offers a window into turn-of-the-century imperial globalization. From the beginning of the 1880s, the process of territorial expansion through different modes of appropriation (colonies, protectorates, concessions, military occupation, and so on) took place alongside the movement for international cooperation in a variety of forms (diplomatic, development of international law, creation of international organizations, and so forth).[56] In Tianjin in 1900 these two phenomena converged and were institutionalized with the founding of an international military government, the ephemeral form of political globalization, twenty years before the League of Nations. Under this Provisional Government, the number of concessions increased from four (only two of which were effectively developed) on the right bank to eight on both sides of the Hai River. The appropriation of territory became the object of a unique colonial experience in China and the rest of the world. The joint movement of colonization and internationalization resulted as much from cooperation as competition between the great powers. British hegemony was diminishing; Germany, Russia, the United States, and Japan were rising. At the same time, France maintained the second largest world empire. Overall, the situation in Tianjin reflected the oligarchical system composed of six powers, none of which were able to dominate coalitions between the others. This book focuses on the Provisional Government, this unprecedented international experience that transformed the Chinese city into a veritable laboratory for regional planning as well as administrative, police, and hygienic modernity.

As an object of study, Tianjin requires two shifts for understanding the history of imperial globalization. On the one hand, a general history of globalization gains texture from situated case studies, which have been relatively rare outside of a few monographs on cosmopolitan cities at the turn of the century.[57] In the second half of the nineteenth century, local powers played a determinant role in opening cities to the international circulation of shared models of city management.[58] Tianjin constitutes a key link in the chain of this global history of municipal authorities. It offers a unique terrain of investigation: at once global in the diversity of actors, modest in its exiguity within the Chinese territory, and temporally circumscribed by the brevity of the Provisional Government. This first international mega-production of the twentieth century developed within a precise unit of time (1900–1902), space (Tianjin and its hinterland), and action (the politics of the provisional government). The contemporary city of Tianjin, a "terrain of mediation" par excellence, was born of the meetings, concrete needs to exchange, dialogues, negotiations, confrontations, and staging of a diverse set of interactions in the eyes of the rest of the world.[59] The territory of Tianjin contained multiple borders, interstices, and enclaves. Indeed, this city represented an interface between contiguous spaces, national loyalties, and varied social practices (political, juridical, military, linguistic, and so on). It was therefore the theater of innumerable interactions and international circulations, multiple conflicts between jurisdictions and interimperial borders. The study of the division of the city between the great powers may, we hope, complement the recent—and important—work on the scramble for China.[60]

The history of Tianjin also invites us to decenter our dominant narratives on the history of nineteenth-century globalization, which have tended to focus on the role of British imperial expansion in the process of global economic and cultural integration. Apart from a few pioneering works by Richard Drayton and James R. Fichter,[61] the studies on "anglobalization," the "British world," the "anglosphere," or the "angloworld" have tended to avoid the transimperial dimension of globalization in Africa, the Antilles, or in Asia. Imperial globalization in Tianjin was not only the product of ancient and new Western colonial powers but also resulted from the expansion of Japan and the actions of Asian merchant communities.[62] In Tianjin, globalization must be more accurately studied as a process of "coproduction" rather than the pure and simple "westernization" of a territory and a population. This work also focuses on the role played by the Chinese in this "coproduction" of urban "modernity" in Tianjin at the turn of the century. It attempts to reproduce the capacity for action and invention, accommodation, and resistance among the Chinese in the face of foreign incursion. The ambition here is to offer an account of colonization in China, which was marginal in relation to the rest of the territory but remains of singular interest for imperial history more broadly.

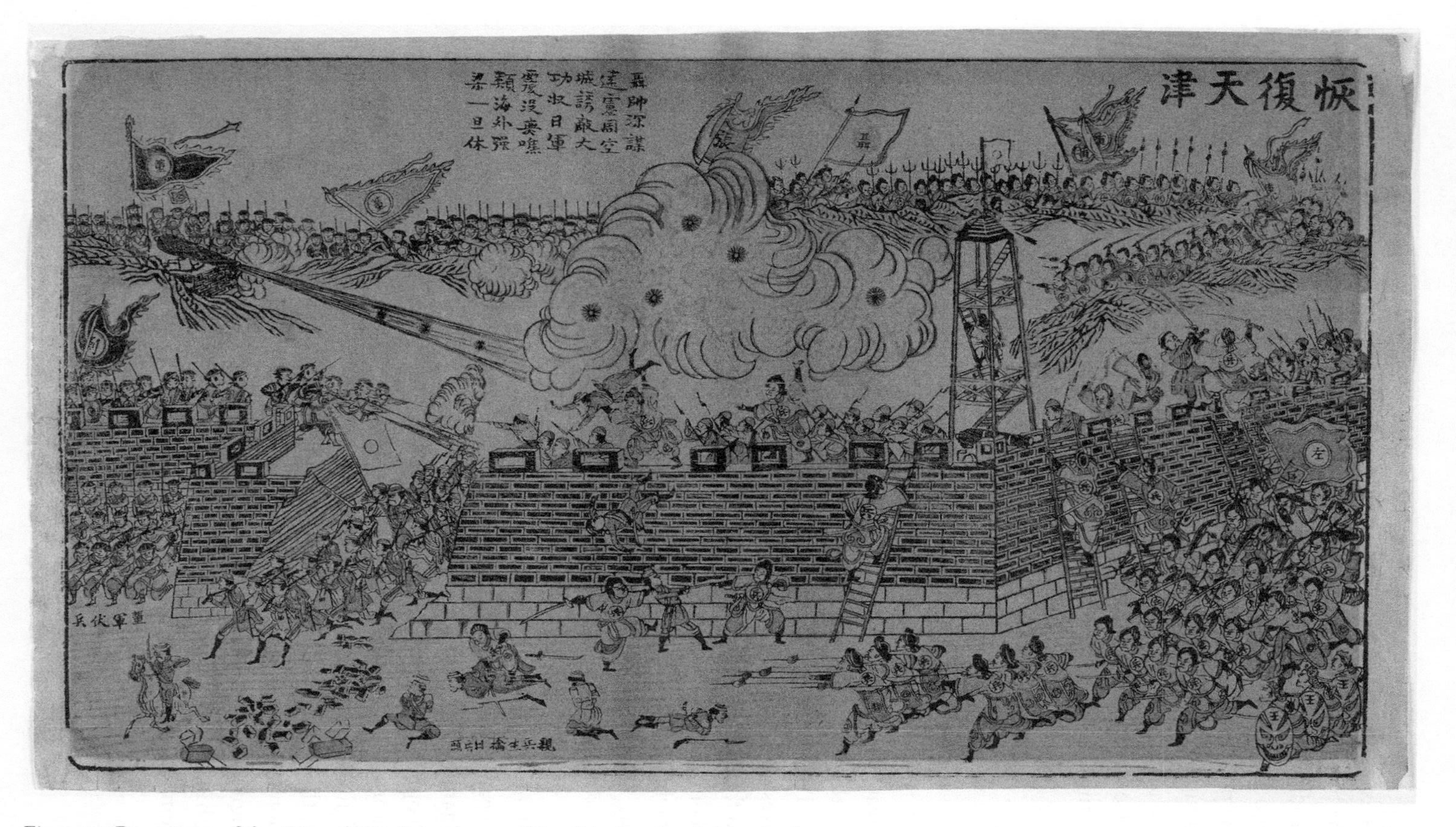

Figure 1.1 Recapture of the City of Tianjin, ca. 1900. Woodblock print: ink and color on paper. Harvard Art Museums, Cambridge, MA. © Harvard Art Museums/Art Resource, New York.

CHAPTER I

"Pandemonium"

The Siege, the Battle, and the Sacking

We Boxers have come to Tientsin to kill all foreign devils and protect the Manchu dynasty. Above, there is the Empress Dowager on our side and below there is Junglu. The soldiers of Yulu and Yuhien [governors of Shantung and Chihli] are all our men. When we have finished killing in Tientsin, we shall go to Peking. All the officials high and low will welcome us. Whoever is afraid let him quickly escape for his life.

—BOXER MANIFESTO, MARCH 30, 1900

These soldiers who disembark barefooted in the sand and cry out in a multitude of languages seem to be amusing themselves. What they are doing is referred to as a "pacified take over" and could even be considered a festival of universal union and universal concord—while, to the contrary, not far away in Tientsin and around Pekin, everything is in ruin and cadavers are everywhere.

—PIERRE LOTI IN NING-HAÏ
(IN THE BOHAI GULF), OCTOBER 3, 1900

Such was the siege of Tientsin. From a military point of view, it was incontestably the most significant of the entire war presently going on in China. From the frequency of combat to the violence of the bombing, from the number of people engaged to the magnitude of the final action, the siege represented the greatest effort and the highest death toll in the Allied battles. Europe was hypnotized by the blocked legations in Pekin and so paid less attention to the dangers in the concessions of Tientsin. It seems right for us to bring them to people's attention.

—"JOURNAL OF THE SIEGE OF TIENTSIN,"
LA REVUE DE PARIS, JANUARY 15, 1902

Starting in the autumn of 1898, the Boxers (*yihetuan*) formed their "militias united in righteousness" to attack the Christians and foreigners in Shandong and Zhili provinces. In the spring of 1900, the Boxers benefited from the benevolence of the Empress Dowager Cixi and part of the Imperial Court in being allowed to enter the capital, defended by about 130,000 imperial guards. In the face of this menace, the representatives of the Allied powers asked the Qing government to combat the Boxers and direct warships toward Taku in proximity of Tianjin to put pressure on Chinese authorities.[1] In the absence of a reaction on the part of the Imperial Court, the Allies decided on May 30 to increase the number of soldiers in the northeast of China and most notably in the capital. Between May 31 and June 2, four hundred soldiers were sent to Beijing where the attacks against the foreigners steadily increased. On June 10, one thousand and then two thousand soldiers under the command of Admiral Seymour marched on Beijing, where the chancellor of the Japanese Embassy, Akira Sugimaya, was assassinated the next day by Chinese soldiers in the Gansu Army under the leadership of the pro-Boxer general Dong Fuxiang. The heated debate within the court between the pro-Boxers (Prince Duan) and anti-Boxers (Ronglu) did not establish a clear direction for the government, which attempted until the last moment to appease the Allies and the popular movement in China. Finally, on June 13, the Empress Dowager seemed to have decided to fight against the Boxers, who were generating more and more trouble in the capital. The following day she ordered Li Hongzhang back to Beijing to negotiate with the representatives of the Allied powers. However, on June 16 the Chinese government tried to convince the foreigners to repatriate their troops to Tianjin, and the next day, fearing that the Seymour Column, then sixty-some miles (100 km) from the capital, would take control of Beijing, ordered the viceroy of Zhili to halt his advance. On June 17 the Allies took the Taku Forts. On June 19 the Empress Dowager ordered the foreigners to leave Beijing for Tianjin within twenty-four hours under threat of losing protection by Chinese authorities. The next day the German minister Ketteler was assassinated while on his way to negotiations at the Zongli headquarters (*yamen*). The foreigners then fell back into their legations, and the famous siege began.

The city of world war

In collective memory as well as in the traditional historiography, this sequence of events in Beijing has served to illustrate the Boxer War and the international expedition that brought it to an end.[2] But the excessive focus on the "heroic" resistance of the besieged, crowned by a stunning Allied victory in the capital, as well as the capacity to transform the military failures into glorious exploits (the Seymour Column) have no doubt served to mask the complexity of the power relations on the ground and the difficulties met by the foreign troops. Another siege of at least equivalent importance has been almost completely forgotten, even though it provides a better understanding of the complexities of this "world war" in northeast China.[3] The study of the occupation of the walled city of Tianjin by the Boxers, the siege of the concessions, and the Battle of Tianjin on July 13–14, 1900, a major historical event largely underestimated by historians, demonstrates the city's importance. Indeed, it reveals a city transformed into a veritable Commune in revolt, the capacities for resistance, the effectiveness of the Chinese troops, the profound divisions among the Allied powers and the Chinese, as well as the ambiguities of the civilizing mission of the "Christian powers." The meager interest among historians in the confrontations in Tianjin have been magnified by the ignorance over the violent event that followed: the sacking of the city—including massacres and pillaging—that crystallized into a veritable war of religions between Boxers and Christian crusaders. "Pandemonium," a capital in flames, these were the words used to describe Tianjin by Henry Savage-Landor in 1900 as unimaginable horrors combined with palpable chaos.

Tianjin, the revolutionary capital of the Boxers and the Red Lanterns?

Before becoming a hellish city for besieged foreigners and massacred Chinese, Tianjin was a kind of "paradise" for the Boxers as unemployed boatmen, dockworkers, rickshaw drivers, and sedan bearers, along with refugees, peddlers, thieves, veterans, prostitutes, and adolescents on the verge of bankruptcy, flocked in from neighboring provinces. Multiple factors—economic, meteorological, political, and sociological—all contributed to making the walled city a Boxer capital, the rallying point and site for expressing aspirations of autonomy. The repeated floods of the Yellow River (Huang He) in the 1890s and the great draught of 1899 brought numerous refugees, who interpreted the natural disasters as divine punishment on the province of Zhili. At the same time, the reduction in traffic on the Grand Canal, resulting in part from the development of the railroads in 1897, generated high unemployment among boatmen and dockworkers. Finally, tens of thousands of soldiers from the imperial army were stationed there during the Sino-Japanese War of 1894–1895, after brutalizing the local population and pillaging the city. At the end of the conflict, numerous veterans joined the bands of brigands and vagabonds (*hunhunr*), who began to take control of portions of the city. A number of these men then participated actively in the Boxer movement on the side of the *hunhunr*, whom they instrumentalized to hide their illegal activities. As a result, the two principal leaders of the Boxers in Tianjin emerged out of these socio-professional milieus marked by the war, unemployment, and the disruptions brought on by modern technologies: Cao Futian was a former soldier turned bandit, while Zhang Decheng had been a boatman on the canal.

At the beginning of June 1900, the streets of the walled city of Tianjin gradually passed into the hands of gangs (*tuan*) of Boxers, often operating independently of one another. The Boxers called each other "brother-disciple" (*shixiong*) and "sister-disciple" (*shijie*), traditionally students of the same martial arts master.[4] The most talented acquired the status of gang leader. In Tianjin, each group of Boxers gathered around an altar (*tan*) or a designated temple. One of the principal headquarters of the Boxers was set up in the Luzu Tang Temple dedicated to the cult of Lu Dongbing, a Tang dynasty poet who became one of the eight immortals: transformed in 1985 into the Boxer Memorial, it is today the only museum in China dedicated to the history of the period. The members of each gang lived together frugally, abstaining from alcohol, tobacco, meat, and relations with women, which they considered had corrupted the purity necessary to exercise supernatural powers. They shared their pittance equally as well as the fruits of their predations.

The singularity of the Boxer's occupation of Tianjin resided in the omnipresence, and perhaps omnipotence, of adolescent groups and young women—the famous Red Lanterns (*Hongdeng zhao*)—in the streets of the city. The French doctor Depasse remarked that certain towns and cities of Zhili, in April and May 1900 "elected fifteen- or sixteen-year-old children as supreme leaders, who adults follow blindly and venerate like saints."[5] In Tianjin young Chinese women played a key role. These unmarried adolescents, less than seventeen years old, were reputed to fly in the night to burn the houses of foreigners in their home country, notably Japan. Possessing extraordinary powers, they were guided by Lin Hei'er, a magician better known under the name Sacred Mother of the Yellow Lotus (Huan Lian Shengmu). She accompanied her father, a traveling acrobat, and from her youngest years learned martial arts and opera.[6] She married the eldest son of the boatman Li You and lived, like several future Boxers, on a boat on the Grand Canal.[7] In the spring of 1900, the imprisonment of her father-in-law, who had been accused of offending foreigners, marked the beginning of her awakening and political action. When the Boxers settled in their neighborhood in the beginning of June, Lin Hei'er joined the group of women, who organized the night of processions with red paper lanterns. She quickly rose to lead the movement thanks to her great physical capacities and her knowledge of popular traditions. Lin Hei'er was joined by her sister-in-law, Huang Sangu. Dressed in red from head to toe with a remarkable scarf and a purple fan, the Red Lanterns purified the Chinese streets with ritual dances, chanting incantations and burning incense. They used these processions to burn the buildings that represented foreign presence: churches, schools, hospitals, and the like. These nighttime gatherings were also designed to rally—in a literal sense—the local Chinese population by going to meet them and striking fear in the hearts of the adversaries, who witnessed a giant red blaze lighting up the sky from the roofs of the concessions: "At times, in the alcoves and corners of the streets and squares, it is easy for us to see long parades of red lanterns passing by, fixed on top of large bamboos, and everywhere that this sinister parade stops for a moment, a new fire immediately breaks out. These gloomy processions of Boxers snake through the city."[8] Finally, the Red Lanterns participated in keeping public order, collecting information on the enemy, organizing provisions, tending to the wounded, and sometimes taking up arms to fight. In Tianjin, Boxerism offered some young women the opportunity to escape the Confucian patriarchy, prearranged marriages, or the grip of their mothers-in-law. The Red Lanterns refused to bind their feet or wear traditional hairstyles and chose instead to fill the public spaces of the city.[9] Parents struggled to impose a curfew on their daughters, who joined the Red Lanterns every evening.

The head of the Boxers, Zhang Decheng, quickly seized on the interest of this movement of young women and encouraged Lin Hei'er to organize the Red Lanterns of Tianjin. A growing share of the population worshiped her as a goddess, covered her with alms and bowed to her, worshiping her in temples across the city. She set up an altar for the Boxers on a salt transportation ship on the Grand Canal with a flag marked "Sacred Mother of the Yellow Lotus." They tended to the sick and drafted battle plans on the boat.[10]

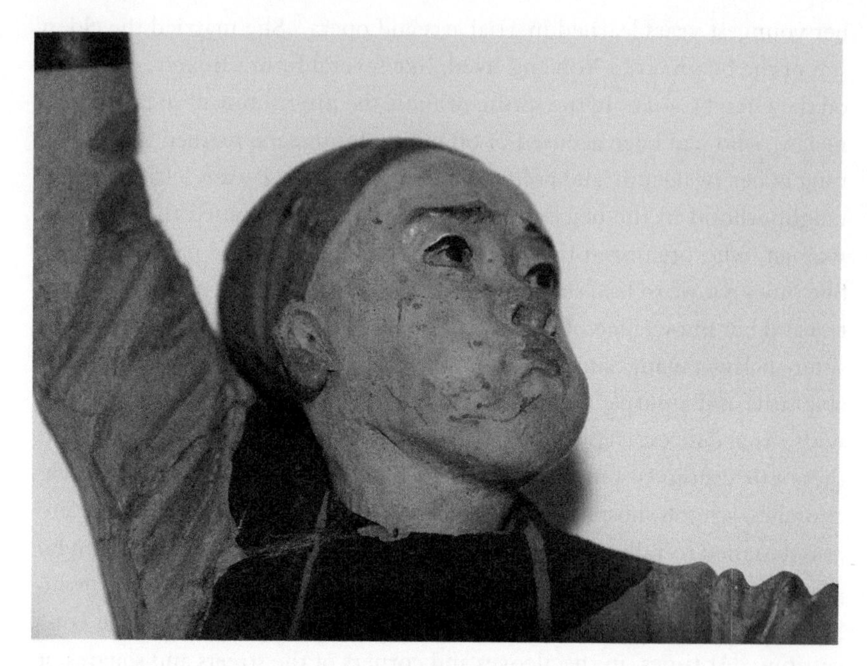

Figure 1.2 B011345. A clay figure of a Boxer, probably made around 1901 in Tianjin. The figure represents an iconic Boxer, marked visually by a yellow, black, or red turban. *Australian Museum, photo by Dr. Stan Florek.*

The viceroy of Zhili and his entourage—treasurer Ting Yong, magistrate Ting Mao, *daotai* Tan Wenhuan, and head of security Xu—were all favorable to the Boxers and the Red Lanterns in mid-June, while foreign diplomats, wrongfully convinced that the provincial authorities supported them, planned to take refuge on a British ship.[11] At the same time, Lin Hei'er was in her own offices to profit from the protection of its propitiatory virtues. She entered in great pomp in a sedan chair, honored with the rite of the nine prostrations by the viceroy. From the middle of June, they requisitioned the Qing administration to provide provisions, money, and weapons to the Boxers.

Boxers and Red Lanterns sought prosperity and regenerations by eliminating the scapegoats responsible for their misfortune, which they attributed to Christians and foreigners. Tianjin and its concessions constituted a privileged target because the agglomerations symbolized, more than any other city in the northeast, the process of "westernization" imposed on the

Chinese. The Boxers clearly stated their motivations and their military objectives in the tracts distributed in Tianjin since the beginning of 1900: "We Boxers have come to Tientsin to kill all foreign devils and protect the Manchu dynasty. Above, there is the Empress Dowager on our side and below there is Junglu. The soldiers of Yulu and Yuhien [governors of Shantung and Chihli] are all our men. When we have finished killing in Tientsin, we shall go to Peking. All the officials high and low will welcome us. Whoever is afraid let him quickly escape for his life."[12]

At the beginning of June, the Boxers put up red posters throughout the walled city and in the concessions, promising the destruction of churches on the anniversary of the demolition of the cathedral in 1870.[13] They referred to foreigners as the "big hairy ones" (*da maozi*), the native Christians as the "subaltern hairy ones" (*er maozi*). The term *san maozi* was reserved for those who used objects of foreign origin and Chinese dignitaries who, like Li Hongzhang, maintained good relations with foreigners.[14] On June 14 they began looting portions of the walled city, burning churches on the outskirts of the city and the houses of their compatriots converted to Christianity. These uncontrolled fires sometimes spread to the Chinese residential neighborhoods.[15] The next day, the Boxers attacked the Chinese administrative buildings that symbolized foreign influence such as the Imperial Telegraph Company and the customs office. They also purified themselves by attacking all the inhabitants wearing foreign clothes and possessing foreign objects: watches, clocks, matches, umbrellas, lamps, mirrors, etc. This practice also partly explained the military "primitivism" that led the Boxers to fight their foreign opponents without firearms.[16] This interdiction also concerned language itself since those unable to speak Chinese were assaulted and vocabulary itself was transformed. For example, the term "rickshaw"—translated in Chinese as "transportation of the Eastern Ocean"—was banished.[17] The rickshaw was of Japanese origin (*jinrikisha*), developed in the 1870s in Tokyo, and then rapidly spread to Singapore, China, and India. It was renamed "transportation of the Great Peace" to avoid the taboo term *yang* (ocean), which was of foreign significance. The rickshaw offers a clear demonstration of the Boxers' ambivalent attitude toward foreign objects, since there were approximately eight thousand of them crowding the city. Their drivers, known to be fighters and to have swollen the ranks of the Boxers, were themselves the fruit of Asian globalization at the end of the nineteenth century. New ideograms were created, notably for the character *yang*:

"The character for yang itself, which has a water radical on its left-hand side, was given a fire radical on its right to show that the foreigners were now between fire and water."[18] Shop owners banished the character *yang* from their signs.

From mid-June to mid-July Tianjin became a magical city. Seasoned Boxers were able to appear in multiple places at once, make themselves invisible, breathe fire, swallow swords, command rain, and raise the dead.[19] They declared themselves invulnerable to blades and bullets thanks to the mastery of a new martial art in which spirits took possession of their bodies, making them invincible. One of the Boxers preferred techniques was hypnosis, induced no doubt through the consumption of small portions of mercury sulfide. Nonetheless, such pretentions of invincibility contributed to a growing deception among the faithful, as demonstrated by the anonymous observer in *A Month in Tianjin*: "If there were dead and wounded in the Boxer militias, the Masters would not permit people to weep for them, nor to burn paper money. . . . 'So-and-so has become a spirit,' they would say. 'What is the use of weeping?' At first, people obediently did as they were told, but, as the deaths and injuries increased, many disobeyed and cursed the Masters for their lack of magic, which had merely destroyed men's lives."[20] The Boxers justified their failures by affirming that invulnerability was reserved for the purest men and women. To secure their authority and increase their influence, the head Boxers also mobilized popular polytheism by invoking, for example, the Jade Emperor of Taoism, using rhetorical techniques, wearing costumes, employing techniques of Chinese theater, and drawing inspiration from characters in fairy tales (Sun Wukong, Zhuge Liang, and Guan Gong) and popular operas (Xiang Yu and Huang Tianba). They carefully organized spectacular performances destined to impress inhabitants and rally them to the Boxer's cause. The leaders performed the burning of churches with incantations, crying out *Shao! Shao!* (Burn! Burn!) with pyromaniac accomplices, who simultaneously ignited fires inside the religious buildings.[21] The leader Zhang Decheng secretly buried a knife in the ground and declared the neighborhood dangerous. His acolytes then dug the knife up by accident, revealing an imminent threat to the shocked residents.

As opposed to Beijing, where the Boxers were often drafted into the standing Qing army, in Tianjin they maintained their independence and had their own leaders. They were more organized and more disciplined than anywhere else in China.[22] The arrival of General Nie Shicheng, considered one of their fiercest adversaries, led to complaints and exacerbated the tensions between the Boxers and the regular soldiers. In the walled city the Boxers enjoyed official authority—at once conquered by the leaders and delegated by the viceroy—founded on a favorable balance of power that allowed them to assert themselves before Chinese civil servants, forcing them to leave their sedan chairs and remove their hats to show their respectful submission when they crossed paths.[23] Certain witnesses recounted that the high civil servants should have given up their costumes and their "mandarin scarf" upon the Boxer's request.[24] Tianjin was transformed into an insurrectional commune in June 1900. The *daotai* of the customs and the district magistrates took refuge in the viceroy's headquarters.[25] The Boxers pillaged the imperial arsenal and liberated the criminals for the prisons. The Red Lanterns did not hesitate to stop a ship of Li Hongzhang's son, who suffered the supreme humiliation of submitting to a woman.[26] By declaring themselves speakers on behalf of the poor and forgotten, by concretely appropriating a portion of power, by running into battle without hesitation, the Red Lanterns, even more than their masculine counterparts, seemed to momentarily subvert the Confucian social order and the Qing political regime. For a month in Tianjin the Boxer movement—at once a war and a rebellion—fought the foreign powers while also calling the authority of the imperial administration into question.

The spectacular siege of the concessions: Chinese domination and interallied tensions

After taking possession of the walled city, the Boxers attacked the concessions as symbols of foreign imperialism. This understudied siege included diverse actors, some of whom have been misinterpreted by historians, who have based their accounts on the seminal work of Otto Rasmussen. Rasmussen attributed to the Boxers engagements that were in fact initiated by Chinese regular soldiers.[27] The Boxers slowly but surely gained ground in the concessions, appropriating territory by surrounding the chimneys of the outlying houses with bands of red cotton. In the city's surroundings, the sporadic combats opposed the Japanese and Russian soldiers to the Chinese. The foreigners fell back into the French and British concessions on the right bank of the Hai River and around the train station on the left bank of the river, where the deadliest battles took place, to protect the eastern flank of the concessions and the communication routes toward Taku and the ocean. The experienced general Nie Shicheng ("Nieh") commanded the regular Chinese army. He had fought the Europeans during the Sino-French War of 1885 and the Japanese during the Sino-Japanese war of 1894–95. More than ten thousand imperial soldiers and sixty-some pieces of modern artillery peacefully encircled the concessions: "the arms were extremely varied, siege canons, canons for open countryside, for the mountains, machine guns, etc., the most perfected models of German and English origin."[28] Admiral Yeh of Tianjin maintained excellent relations with the Krupp family, who in April 1900 delivered arms to the garrisons specifically made for Tianjin such as gunpowder designed to resist extreme variations in temperature characteristic of Zhili Province as well as a smokeless variety in order to prevent the enemy from locating the cannons. Chinese soldiers were also positioned in the train station to protect foreigners, much to the surprise of the officers disembarking in Tianjin.[29] In the concessions, four hundred foreign civilian men and three hundred women and children had access to nine guns and approximately two thousand soldiers, as well as one hundred and sixty French sailors and four hundred foreign soldiers in Beijing and two thousand soldiers from the Seymour column between Tianjin and the capital.[30] In the face of such a weak defense, the French consul, Gustave du Chaylard, offered Russian and Japanese troops the possibility of being housed in the French concession, where the battle lines were to be drawn against the Chinese. The French defended Paris Street and Tientsin Street, the Japanese defended the quai de France downstream of the railroad bridge, and the Russians defended the bridge itself and the train station. On June 14 a train arrived from Port Arthur (Lushunkou) bringing Russian soldiers to join Admiral Seymour, Beijing, and the legations. But in the face of the mounting violence against Christians in the Chinese city, they remained in Tianjin to protect the concessions. "They declare emphatically that, had not 14,000 Russian troops arrived at Tientsin in the nick of time, Tientsin would have been overrun by the Chinese and every foreigner in the place would most likely have been slaughtered. Happily things did not come to that pass."[31] It was in these counterfactual terms that two of the foreign engineers, employed by the imperial railway, attempted to demonstrate the importance of the Russian intervention. Faced with the deployment of allied naval forces assembled in front of Taku, the Chinese imperial army set up "electric mines" on June 15 in the Hai River to prevent an offensive on Tianjin and Beijing.

During the night of June 15 to 16 the Boxers took up positions in the southern and southeastern suburbs of the city about a thousand feet (300 m) from the French concession and fired on the houses on multiple occasions during the night. Three Russian soldiers lost their lives. It was later discovered that the assailants were not Boxers but Chinese soldiers "who came to the walled city to fire on the outposts without leaders, training, or orders, only because they had access to guns and ammunition."[32] Immediately following the first night of combat, some inhabitants watched the siege like a giant spectacle. At 4:00 a.m. a stunned French officer encountered at the end of the "railroad" street near the front "a group of strange figures, who were walking among the trees and, to his great surprise, a few women in morning robes were also there watching with little theater binoculars." This surprise was exacerbated by the sense that they were faced with "a military comedy" against poorly trained and ill-armed Boxers.[33]

Figure 1.3 Lou Hoover, wife of Herbert Hoover, at the end of June 1900 in Tianjin. Herbert Hoover Presidential Library.

At night during the battles, civilians constructed barricades with openings for their guns made from bags of rice and sugar.[34] The twenty-six-year-old engineer Herbert Hoover took control of organizing the defense at the head of a militia of some three hundred civilians.[35] His wife, Lou (figure 1.3), also demonstrated her courage when she rode her bicycle through the concessions under fire with a Mauser on her belt, caring for the wounded and standing guard at night.[36] The couple was entirely aware of the power of the media and took care to welcome a dozen war correspondents on the ground floor of their beautiful home, where the journalists could benefit from their fifteen servants.[37] The making of this future American president into a hero began in the living room of his home where journalists from across the world inundated their newspapers with the glories of the Hoovers.

Faced with the threat of the Boxers, who were by definition enemies of the Western educational model, Charles Tenney decided to arm the students at the Imperial University and turn them into a veritable defensive force. With the massive arrival of foreign soldiers, however, and their "incredible ignorance and [illegible: stupidity?] regarding all things Chinese," there was the danger that they could "confound the students and Boxers." As a result, Tenney decided to disarm the students.[38] The missionaries played an important role in the defense of the concessions. For example, Rev. Charles F. Grammon had been a former American teacher employed by the Chinese imperial forces and specialized in arms and munitions; he then converted to become a representative of the American Bible Society in Tianjin. He explained that "they got so accustomed to enjoy[ing] the sound of the bullets and listened to them with much pleasure. A missionary woman disappeared one day during the most terrific fire, and when she returned it was discovered that she had made a reconnoiter of the outposts and could describe the whole situation. She was asked how she dared to go out in such a shower of bullets, and she replied nonchalantly, 'Oh, they were only little ones.'"[39] On June 16 the concessions seemed emptied of a large part of the Chinese who resided and worked there, creating a sudden increase in the cost of living as one Chinese from the French concession ironically noted: "Almost all the natives fled. All the stores in Zizhulin have stopped their activities, and their storefronts are closed. The cooks have escaped, and many foreigners are crying out for food because of the refusal of indigenous boys to remain in the concession. A bathtub of water costs ten cents, and a rickshaw from here to the station half a dollar!"[40] And so began the exodus of Chinese merchants toward the walled city, many of whom were stripped of everything they owned as they left the concessions.

The commanding officer of the French forces, Alexis Daoulas, regretted the absence of communication among the Allied powers from the first day of the siege: "Already today I have the clear impression in this moment of imminent danger that everyone is only thinking of him or herself and keeping the information they have for themselves."[41] Diplomats and officers were interested above all in defending the interests of the Allied powers, who disliked one another on occasion and above all were in constant rivalry: long-standing rivals such as France and Britain and new ones such as France and Germany, or Japan and Russia in the western Pacific, Britain and Russia in Central Asia, and so forth. The coalition was fragile at best. It was therefore out of a desire to prevent the Americans and the British from establishing a strategic position that the French navy set up the Imperial School of Medicine on Taku Road, that was in direct contact with the outlying Chinese neighborhoods. Luck was certainly on their side: the director of the school, Doctor Depasse, had been a childhood friend of Commander Daoulas and greeted him warmly. The medical school provided at once an exceptional site for observing the plain that separated the walled city from the concessions as well as a vast hospital for French and Russian wounded. The hospital functioned for a month thanks to two French doctors, Depasse and Houillon, as well as two Russians. The other wounded were also cared for in the German Club and the British Club in the British concession, which had been reconverted into military hospitals. On the night of June 16 to 17 the Boxers burned the cathedral in the northwest of the walled city. The gripping "spectacle" was watched by foreigners atop the roofs in the concessions. Slowly realizing that General Nie and the twelve thousand soldiers were doing nothing to fight off the Boxers, the foreigners began preparing for a veritable war with China. The foreign troops were given the order to fire on anything that moved around the concessions and on the left bank of the Hai River. On June 17 Consul Gustave du Chaylard proclaimed his own territorial ambitions in the middle of the siege: "Later when we have brought China back to reason, which will no doubt happen quickly, I will take advantage of the current troubles to expand into the area adjacent to the concession and we will build a superb tree-lined boulevard."[42] The French commander was surprised by such preoccupations in a time of war, but was seduced by the "confidence and energy" of the consul. He accepted therefore the burning of the Chinese neighborhood to the west of the rue de France, which had been slated for expansion, to remove any obstacles to future planning. They did not hesitate to use dynamite to raze to the ground a venerable set of three pagodas in the Chinese territory, which would have hindered the expansion of the French concession, since according to Consul Chaylard, "the Chinese never rebuild what has been totally destroyed."[43] The soldiers were unable to control the gigantic fire that destroyed part of the French concession in addition to the Chinese suburbs. The fires caused by foreigners and especially by the bombardments and Chinese spies were in fact the main threat to the concessions.[44] The first Chinese cannon shots from the left bank bombarded the concessions and slowly the foreigners became aware that they had to face, in addition to the Boxers, portions of the imperial army. How may this outbreak of hostilities on June 17 be explained? The Chinese soldiers, who until then had protected the concessions from possible Boxer assaults, began to bombard the concessions upon learning that the Allied fleet, against the advice of the American Admiral Kempff, had attacked the Taku Forts the day before. They targeted the strategic buildings of the concessions, including the Tientsin Native City Water Works Company and the gas station.[45] Three hundred women and children took refuge in the basements of the Hotel de la Poste in the French concession, in the Astor Hotel, and in the cellars of Gordon Hall in the British concession.[46] Some foreign bourgeoisie, who considered leaving Tianjin without understanding the military situation, provoked mockery by the soldiers: "The fugitives' idea of taking all their affairs with them, in such a moment of crisis, was humorous. It was necessary, in some cases, to discuss at length to convince them to abandon their piano and their beautiful chest of drawers to the compassion of the Chinese."[47] Foreign troops tried to react amidst the bombing. The Russians sent three companies in search of enemy artillery, and German soldiers, on the left bank of the Hai River, seized the Chinese military academy and its innumerable crates of new Mausers imported from Germany. The next day, imperial infantry attacked the Russians at the railway station, reinforced by French and British troops. The foreign troops took shelter in trenches and, against all expectations, managed to repel the attackers thanks to the unanticipated return of the Russian companies that took the Chinese troops by surprise. The Russians lost eighteen soldiers and the French three men. In the opposing camp, the Sacred Mother of the Red Lanterns coordinated the logistics and the care of the wounded.[48] At the end of the day, the Chinese had cut all railway, telegraphic, and telephone communications with Taku. The inhabitants of the foreign concessions were isolated from the rest of world and left to their own fears and anxieties.

On June 19 Beijing learned that Taku had been taken by foreign armies and the Boxers had begun their siege. At Tianjin, a flood of devastating shells rained down on the concessions from the walled city and the Chinese forts, so much so that a British officer, formerly in the Transvaal during its siege by the Boers, claimed that the "severity and accuracy of the Chinese shelling the past week exceeded that of the Boer bombardment at Ladysmith."[49] The witnesses highlighted the extraordinary effectiveness of Chinese artillery: "The defenders of Tien-Tsin are barely holding their positions under deadly fire from Krupp batteries. . . . The reading of the first telegrams from Tien-Tsin is no less suggestive. Almost all of them contain a sentence, repeated every day, whose terms vary, but whose meaning is always the same: 'The Chinese fire is of an astonishing precision! The Chinese batteries seem admirably served!' "[50] Fires broke out everywhere, and Allied soldiers saw on the roof of the French municipality a Chinese individual waving a red flag to guide the bombardments. The building was hit by a projectile soon afterward. The precision of the Chinese fire from nearly 1.9 miles (3,000 m) away from the occupied buildings suggests that the imperial artillery maintained an effective network of spies within the concessions. Paranoia gripped those under siege, who suspected their servants of collaborating with the attackers. The foreigners learned from the French consul that the Chinese regulars were preparing to cross the Hai River the following night to attack the concessions. In front of them, the Chinese soldiers had already begun to fire on foreigners from the huge piles of salt, connected by a telephone or telegraph line that allowed them to inform the Chinese headquarters of the movement of foreign troops. The exhaustion of the reserves pushed the soldiers to prepare large pots of a disgusting black broth that made military rations look like gourmet food.[51] A British resident, James Watts, and three Russian Cossacks were charged with reconnecting with Taku to search for food and reinforcements.[52] The Allies immediately hurried five hundred soldiers to Tianjin. On June 20 the firing on the French concession continued, and the British consulate offered to house Gustave du Chaylard along with his personnel in the British concession. But the consul refused to be the host of a foreign power: "As long as there is a stone standing and a sailor fighting in the French concession, I will stay here. My place is next to the French flag."[53] On June 21 in Beijing, the empress noted the attack on the Allies in Taku and finally clearly chose sides. She officially declared war on the foreign powers and stigmatized those foreigners, who "over the last thirty years have benefited from China's tolerance to invade our territory, walk over our people, and makes claims on our riches. Each concession made by China has only increased their pursuit of violence. They have oppressed peaceful citizens and insulted our gods and religious leaders. . . . And at the same time that they refer to themselves as 'civilized states,' they continue to act in total disdain for what is right, acting only through military force."[54]

In Tianjin, the Russian and British artillery attempted in vain to respond to Chinese fire. After having surprised the spies, who were sending signals from the roofs of the telegraphic school and the French consulate, Commander Daoulas fired all the Chinese servants of the French municipality. The "more or less Christian" servants were housed in religious institutions and "all the Chinese who were walking in the streets without signed authorization were to be arrested and imprisoned for interrogation."[55] The British arrested Chang, superintendent of mines, for having communicated with the enemy through carrier pigeons, as well as Tong, the head of the train station, for having thwarted the movements of the Allied powers' military forces.[56] Nonetheless, life continued on as possible. Each evening, the French officers went to Doctor Depasse's home to listen to the fashionable French hits by Paulus and Yvette Guilbert on his gramophone. But these small pleasures were reserved for elites and hardly masked the desperation that gripped the population and led them to charge men with executing women and children within the concessions to prevent them from falling into the hands of the assailants if an expeditionary force did not succeed in "liberating" Tianjin.[57] The following day, the besieged received bad news from the Beijing legations: the Europeans were to leave within twenty-four hours. General Ma's reinforcements and his ten thousand men as well as the Seymour Column had taken refuge in the arsenal of the village of Siku 6.2 miles (10 km) north of Tianjin. At the same time, they were relieved to learn that Allied reinforcements were coming in from Taku.[58] Two thousand Russians with four cannons, three hundred British, three hundred Germans, and one hundred Americans entered the concessions on June 23, accompanied by celebrations among the foreign residents. The Allied powers decided to send two contingents of soldiers to help the Seymour Column. Composed of British, Germans, French, and Japanese, these reinforcements managed to enter Tianjin without any problem on the morning of June 26, to the great astonishment of the officers in the concessions: "It would have been easy, in fact, for the Tien-Tsin forts to annihilate the Allied forces on June 26, when the Seymour column, with its endless numbers of wounded, and the Russian forces that had rescued it, came under Chinese cannon fire on their way from the Siku arsenal to the foreign concessions. It is not yet clear why the bombing, which had been going on for nine days and would continue for another eighteen days, stopped that day."[59] Drinking water was increasingly in short supply due to the low number of filters and the lack of time to boil water from the river, where dead Chinese and animals were accumulating. On June 28 the bombings intensified, and the next day foreigners prepared for an impending Chinese attack that never took place. "Three times during the day, we have been warned that we are going to fall under a general attack. We have made our arrangements and . . . nothing comes."[60]

The dissent between the different foreign troops continued June 29 as they renewed their pillaging in the concessions. British soldiers emptied shops on the rue de France, Russians pillaged a German house across the street from the French consulate, and so forth. The quarrels between civilians and the military increased, as the anecdote recounted by Lou Hoover suggests:

> We had a cow, famous and influential in the community, which cow was the mother of a promising calf. One day the cow was stolen and Mr. Hoover set out to find her. With three or four friends and half a dozen attendant Chinese boys he took out the tiny calf one night and by the light of a lantern led the little orphan, bleating for its mother, about the streets of the town. Finally, as they passed in front of the barracks of the German contingent of the international defending army, there came, from within, an answering moo, and Mr. Hoover, addressing the sentry, demanded his cow. The sentry made no move to comply, but, summoning all his *Wörterbuch* English, countered with the inquiry: "Is that the calf of the cow inside?" Upon receiving an affirmative reply to his Ollendorff question, he calmly declared, "Also, then, calf outside must join itself to cow inside." And thereupon by aid of a suggestive manipulation of his bayonet, he confiscated the calf, and sent Mr. Hoover home empty-handed.[61]

In the opposing camp Chinese soldiers deserted after each engagement, trying to avoid the Boxers and the imperial soldiers. In the French consulate on June 30, Jean Ruffi de Pontevès and the Baroness d'Anthouard, wife of a French diplomat en route from Japan to Peking, sympathetically conjectured on the international rivalries that prevented any coordinated offensive from taking the walled city.

> "Why don't our troops attack the Chinese city right now?" the Baroness d'Anthouard asked me.
>
> You know better than I, Madame; for you know the European concert better than I do. Here—as elsewhere—the musicians do not play in harmony: the Russian general wants to play the Tartar March alone on the left bank; the British admiral prefers to dance an English Polka on the right bank; and the Japanese general plays a "shamisen" . . . while the French take the blow on the front lines.[62]

On July 1 the river was secured, and the French civilians left the concession at 4:00 p.m. to take refuge in Taku. A few minutes later a battalion of marine infantry and a battery of naval artillery from Tonkin entered the French concession, completely exhausted before the combat even began: "We will no longer be the tiny handful of men who are ignored, a tiny troop of French drowned in foreign soldiers."[63] Vietnamese soldiers joined the Indian troops. The Mongols of the Russian army and the Japanese military fought against the Chinese enemy in a veritable Asian war. Forced to recognize this fact, Western officers saluted the courage and altruism of the Japanese military, who systematically came to the aid of foreign forces: "It must be noted that the brave little Japanese are always the first to confront the danger and come to our aid, and it is always with their accustomed pleasantness that they offer their help, asking if their presence bothers us or not." On July 2 the Chinese batteries continued to fire on the concessions, causing multiple deaths, most notably among the French and the Russians. On July 3 the Russians decided to take on the Chinese batteries of Lutai in the northeast of the city and were replaced at the train station by a hundred French, a hundred Japanese, and a hundred British soldiers. The Allied powers approved this Russian initiative while at the same time regretting that "they did not concert with the international troops for this operation"[64] as the Japanese officers were doing. On July 4 violent combat against the Chinese broke out in the trenches around the train station, during which the French lost eight soldiers and the Japanese twenty, or one-fifth of their troops on the ground. The Allies held and the next day communications with Taku were reestablished along the Hai River. French artillery bombarded the headquarters (*yamen*) of the viceroy of Zhili, which was partially burned. On July 7 British artillery destroyed a portion of the Western Arsenal. Meanwhile, the commanders studied plans for taking the Chinese city. The British and the Japanese took the Western Arsenal on July 8. They were quickly forced to abandon it to the Chinese however because they had destroyed the northern wall of the arsenal, exposing it to Chinese artillery fire coming from the southern wall of the Chinese city. The second infantry battalion of the French navy and another battery of artillery under the command of Colonel Charles-Baltazar de Pélacot arrived in Tianjin on July 9. But when the French commander announced his decision to repatriate the French navy, Doctor Depasse, the general consul, and the French community mobilized to stay in the French concession:

> The reason was that scenes of disorder and cases of looting had been reported since the soldiers arrived. For these men who lacked everything, food, clothing, objects of all kinds, the temptation was strong to stock up on necessities from half-destroyed, and sometimes even abandoned, houses. Moreover, the example had been set for them by the soldiers of other nations. Some merchants complained about the attitude of certain soldiers. It must be acknowledged to the contrary that since the beginning of the siege, the sailors, without any sense of pride or vain fatuity, had maintained perfect conduct and dress, which everyone in Tien-Tsin recognizes.[65]

Colonel de Pélacot ceded to the pressure and kept fifty navy shipmen in the concession. Outside these tensions within the same army, the divisions between the Western powers remained strong. Still, on July 9, the Russians, contrary to the British, the Americans, and the Japanese, refused to follow Major General Yasumasa Fukushima's command when he pushed for an attack on the Chinese units to the southwest of Tianjin.[66] On July 11 a third confrontation opposed the Chinese and the Allies near the train station. More than 150 Allied soldiers were killed in the trenches.[67] Fortunately for the foreign troops the Chinese did not push their advantage, but the Allied powers sustained numerous deaths: seventy Japanese, twenty-two British, twelve French.[68]

Over the next days the French commander solemnly asked his foreign counterparts to coordinate to bring an end to the siege. The month of siege and its numerous consequences were characterized by the absence of any unified international command and poor communication and coordination between the allied troops and different army corps: "One will quickly notice the lack of sequence, the bizarre disjointedness within the history of this siege. . . . This lack of clear sequencing faithfully translates the incoherence and the absolute lack of unity that characterized the international movements."[69]

The forgotten battle: An unexpected Asian victory?

Contemporaries experienced this forgotten battle as a major event. From the beginning of July the foreign officers each devised plans for a major assault to take back the walled city and transform it into a logistical base necessary for the conquest of Beijing. Above all they required reliable topographical information, pushing all the commanders to search desperately for maps of Tianjin:

> The ship captain passed by and asked if we had a map of the Chinese city, which we would soon have to attack and attempt to bring under our control. Well, no, we did not possess one; it would, of course, have been most valuable to us in the circumstances we were going through; but no one, so far, had been able to provide us with one or even give us sufficient information to enable us to establish one in a rough way. Our friends in Tien-Tsin were so far from suspecting the possibility of the hostilities they never worried about gathering knowledge of the immense city that spread out over the plain three kilometers from us. Accustomed, moreover, to seeing their Chinese "compradors" taking the time to come to their offices in the concession, they rarely went to the walled city and, when they did, their journey was generally at night and in sedan chairs, so they could give us no useful advice, much less military intelligence.[70]

The French officers found the plans for the city in the houses of Catholic missionaries, who produced "exact and careful" representations and communicated information on "the best ways to access the mysterious Chinese city." Another topographical source was a map Hoover drew by hand on the spot along with multiple sketches (figure 1.4) that allowed the soldiers to orient themselves during the siege and prepare the assault. Hoover's sketches contained strategic details that did not appear on the maps produced at the end of the nineteenth and beginning of the twentieth century by the Chinese or foreigners, like the immense piles of salt on which Chinese gunmen and communications were placed. Only the Japanese military possessed their own cartographic documentation, which they carefully updated throughout the conflict: "These little Japanese, looking placid and indifferent, are the only ones who know the exact topography of the place. . . . The lower ranks are provided with a map of Tien-Tsin that I have often seen them consult and annotate."[71] They were the only ones to know and understand the deep divisions within the Chinese headquarters thanks to the linguistic and cultural proximity but also the effectiveness of their

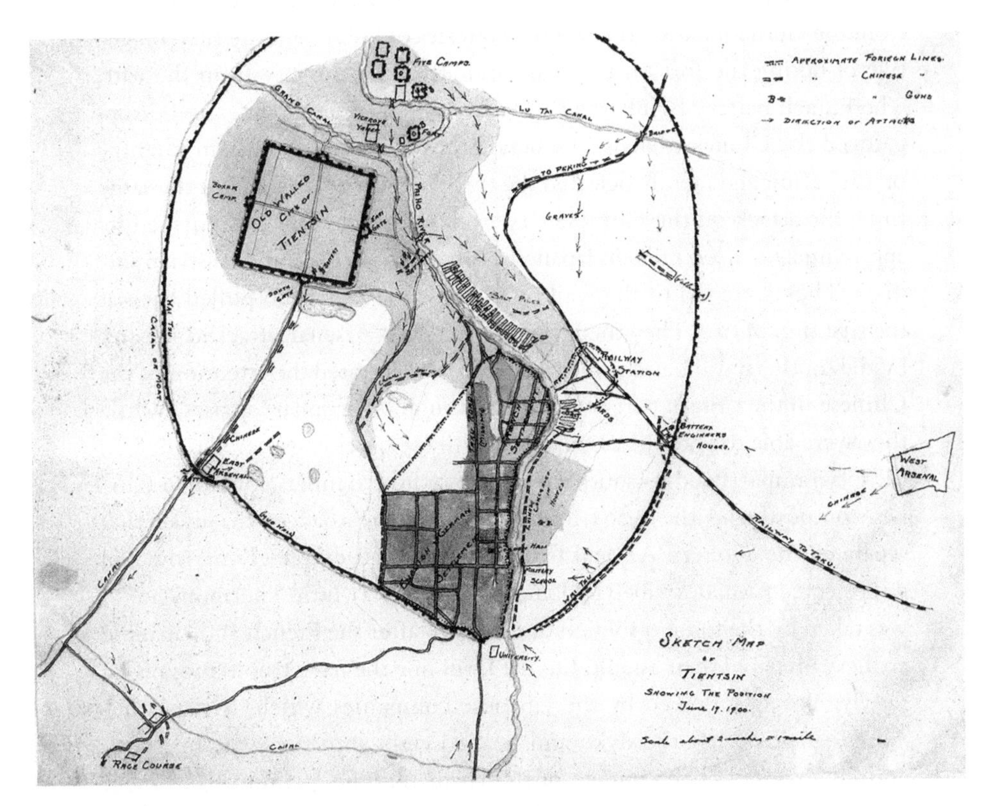

Figure 1.4. Map of Tianjin by Herbert Hoover, early July 1900. Herbert Hoover Presidential Library.

intelligence services. As early as July 4, the Japanese officers perfectly communicated in English, raising the possibility of a "general attack" on the Chinese front combined with a movement on the walled city.[72]

In mid-July the balance of power was reestablished. The Allied troops, approximately fourteen thousand men, were numerous enough to envisage an assault on the walled city defended by twenty thousand to thirty thousand Chinese.[73] The council of superior officers fixed the date of July 13, and General Dorward, who had been in India and Jamaica, was designated commanding general. The assault was complicated from the beginning by the thickness of the walls and the number of Chinese soldiers. At 4:00 a.m. on July 13 the Allies simultaneously attacked the Chinese city from the south and the great fort of the Hai River bend (Black Fort) and the batteries of Lutai from the west. On the left bank, from the Eastern Arsenal, four battalions of Siberian infantry and two batteries of Russian artillery, along with a battery of French artillery and a company from the German navy, attacked the batteries of Lutai with the final objective of taking the fort on the bend and attacking the city from the east. The French battery bombarded a massive depot of gunpowder and disorganized the Chinese defense. General Stoessel launched Russian infantry on the assault and rapidly defeated the three batteries of Lutai.[74] At the same time, the attack on the Chinese city from the right bank was pursued by approximately 3,500 French, Japanese, American, British, and Austrian soldiers. They were led to the wall by Herbert Hoover, who pulled back at the first sign of fire. They then took the Western Arsenal, attacked the city by the southern wall, and simultaneously concentrated the attention of the Chinese in the eastern part of the city through diversionary tactics. While they were able to take the arsenal, the Chinese quickly gathered to defend the city ramparts and its southern suburbs whose hamlets contained Chinese outposts and the 4,265-foot (1,300 m)-long road of the dyke that separated the Western Arsenal from the city. This extremely narrow and unprotected path, described by James Ricalton as a "little Thermopylae,"[75] was taken by the foreign soldiers at 8:00 a.m. after the French and Japanese artillery prepared their assault. On the front line the navy troops progressed slowly, closely followed by the Japanese companies which, to the other Allies' surprise, left the dyke and headed right into the swampy plain, entirely exposed. The courage of the Japanese, who lost numerous men, inspired the admiration of the Allied soldiers. The Americans spread out into the marsh to the left of the dyke behind the Franco-Japanese line while the British remained in reserve behind. In less than an hour, the infantry of the French navy had established their position in the suburbs, about a thousand feet (300 m) from the walled city, where the houses and the streets began. At 10:00 a.m. the commanders ordered the men to stop advancing and to retrench until nightfall; the soldiers benefited to gather food and reserves and evacuate the wounded and the dead. The Japanese once again showed their effectiveness: "The superior organization of the Japanese has shown itself once again in these circumstances. Their able medical service enabled them to pick up in two hours the three hundred men lying on the battlefield and evacuate them in a field ambulance installed behind the arsenal."[76] On the evening of July 13 the assault was pushed back, and the Allies suffered 750 wounded or dead (390 Japanese, 180 Russians, 132 French, and 50-odd British, Americans, and Germans). The battle was not sufficiently prepared, nor was the territory sufficiently studied, and there remained the challenge of taking the city and its wall, which was thirteen to sixteen feet (4–5 m) thick and nineteen feet (6 m) high. Captain Barnes and the men of his Chinese Regiment observed the troop movements from the roof in the concessions. The outcome of the battle seemed uncertain to them: "The gunfire [of the Chinese artillery] never abated enough for the Allies to have a chance to arrive at the ramparts . . . it was . . . a sad day, resulting from the gloomy parade of wounded British, Americans, and Japanese in stretchers, in carts, in rickshaws, and limping painfully, each telling his own story of desperate fighting among the ruins."[77] James Ricalton, looking out from his house, offered a more definitive conclusion: "It is defeat."[78]

In the early evening, the commanders united in an interallied council and proposed retreat under the cover of night. General Fukushima was firmly opposed and proposed to pull American and British soldiers and reinforce the position of the Japanese so that they could push through the hole in the southern door.[79] On July 14, a little after 3:00 a.m., squadrons of Japanese torpedo sailors set off with their explosive-filled wagons, placed in front of the southern gate of the city. The fuse was extinguished twice.[80] Finally a Japanese engineer officer sacrificed his life, reminiscent of the *kamikaze* a half century later: "matches in hand, he ran forward and lit the powder. The explosion immediately reduced the man and the door to bits."[81] The Japanese could thus charge and take sole possession of the door until the early morning. The Allies entered the city that the regular soldiers had fled through the northern door during the night.[82] By default, the Allied powers, like the Chinese, perfectly illustrated the principle of Sun Tzu: "When you surround an army, leave an outlet free,"[83] thus dissuading the besieged combatants from fighting vigorously to their death. Indeed, most of the Boxers disappeared during the night at the beginning of the battle.[84] The Japanese troops crossed the walled city, planted a flag at the solar clock, and attacked through the north gate of the fort on the bend, which was simultaneously attacked by the Russians. The symbol of Chinese power was taken without difficulty. It is no doubt the Japanese victory, due to their initiative and their maneuvers, that explains in part why the Battle of Tianjin was forgotten in Western military history. Even specialists have not lingered on the subject. David Silbey dedicates only ten lines in *The Boxer Rebellion* to it as opposed to the seventy-seventy lines dedicated to the difficulties met by American soldiers of the Ninth Infantry Regiment at the same moment.[85] The Chinese strategy of continuous bombardment and isolation of the concessions through the conquest of the train station considerably weakened and slowed the Allies but proved incapable of countering the offensive coordinated by the Allies and especially the Japanese on July 14. This unexpected victory is most thoroughly explained through the profound divisions among the Chinese. In Tianjin "the regular troops and the Boxers cordially hated each other," wrote Herbert Hoover, and regularly confronted one another during the pillages perpetuated by the Boxers in the walled city in late June. General Nie Shicheng may have killed up to three thousand Boxers during the siege of the concessions.[86] Disavowed by the Imperial Court, perhaps briefly imprisoned in the walled city, the Chinese general let himself be killed in combat on July 9.[87] His successor, General Ma Yukun, equally anti-Boxer according to Hoover, also used a Maxim gun to eliminate many thousands of Boxers at the end of the siege. In the end, on July 13 only seven thousand Chinese combatants, some portion of which were demobilized, took part in the fight against eight thousand soldiers on the side of the Allied powers.[88]

The confrontations around Tianjin may not simply be understood as a war between the Chinese and foreigners. Indeed, Chinese fought alongside the Allied powers, notably the indigenous Christian militias, the Chinese soldiers of the British Chinese Regiment from Weihaiwei, and a few men from the Chinese regiment of Jiaozhou alongside the Germans. George Weulersse signaled their propensity to desert during the siege, but we do not have enough sources to confirm this information.[89] And, more

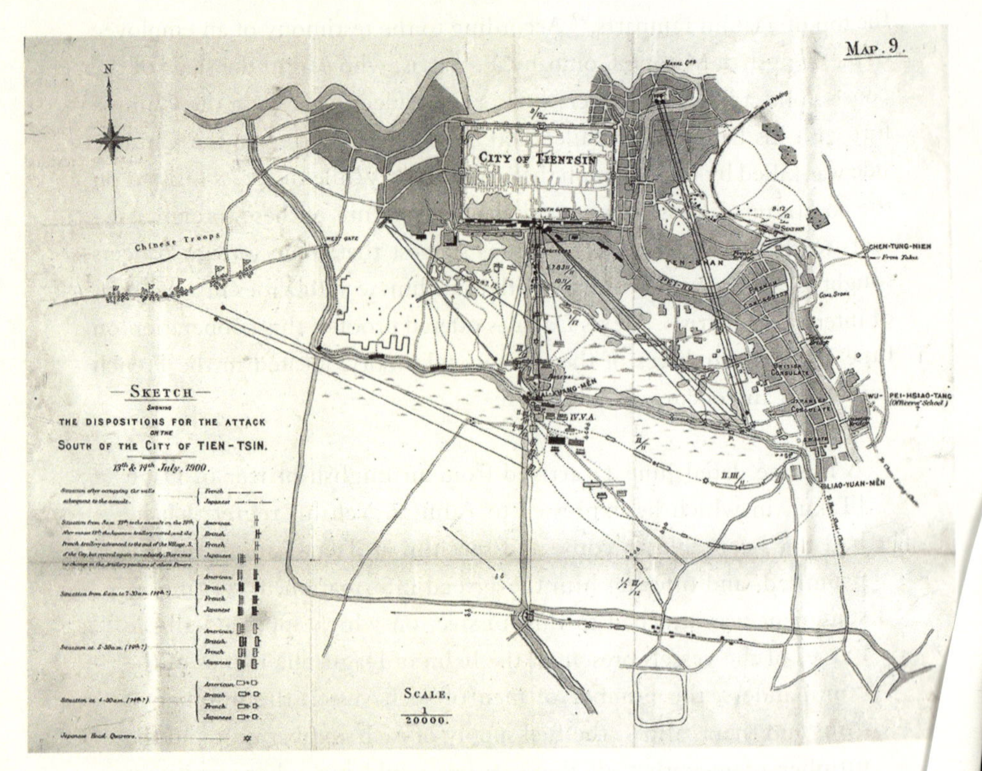

Figure 1.5 A British military map of Tianjin, July 1900. National Archives, WO 32/6148.

surprisingly, the foreign military seemed to continue to serve in the impe-rial army during the siege and the Battle of Tianjin. It might have been a rumor spread by the European press in order reassure themselves tha China was incapable of such military prowess without outside help "Well-placed observers claim that the march of operations around Tier Tsin reveals the presence, at the head of the Chinese masses, not of a Tu or a Boxer or a military mandarin of any kind, but of an organizatio mind and an energetic will such as only Westerners possess."[90] In the e of many besieged, the artillery shots seemed too precise to be the wor the Chinese. It was said that eight Russian artillery instructors han the cannons and the threat of Chinese bayonets. In speaking of the nese Regiment, Captain Barnes even explained that it was foreign lery in the service of the Chinese at Taku who fell back on the city. Allied soldiers did indeed see foreigners on numerous occasions—G and Russian instructors—handling the cannons and the machine g

the top of Tianjin ramparts.[92] According to the testimony of an employee of the Tongshan Mining Company, F. Harris, who was in the siege of the concessions, a Russian artillery officer succeeded in escaping the Chinese fort with his hands tied, while a foreign artillery officer on the Chinese side was killed by the Allies on the city walls.[93] While the press insisted on the constraints imposed upon and even the torture of these foreign assistants to the Chinese, other witnesses suggest that some foreign officers sought to "cooperate" willingly with the Chinese authorities in a moment of international crisis. Alexis Daoulas offered proof of this cooperation on June 20 in the archives of the Chinese admiralty, located in the French concession and occupied by his men:

> A missive dated June 13 arrived from an English officer of Dagu [Taku], in which he expressed to Admiral Yeh his regret that he had not been able to come and see him at Tien-Tsin, as he had promised, and offering him the agreed information in writing. A statement was attached to this missive, on which appeared all the names of the vessels present at the helm of Dagu, the names of the commanders, the number of men of each vessel, the number of guns and their caliber, the fuel supply of each combat unit and the number of men that all these vessels could put ashore, without offloading too much and hindering their possible departure. One small fact suggests just how accurate this information was and how meticulously it was recorded: the name of the commander of the *Descartes* is crossed out in pencil, by the hand of the Chinese secretary, and replaced with that of the new captain. This is the only error in this account.[94]

Clearly the battle of Tianjin was a singular event that exceeded the ordinary framework of war in a colonial context: mastery of intelligence techniques, symmetry of technological capacity, and an almost equivalent number of combatants made the outcome uncertain. The disorganization that followed the Japanese assault explains the difference concerning the number of victims, between six thousand and ten thousand deaths on the Chinese side and the eight hundred to two thousand wounded on the side of the Allies.[95] But the figures concerning the indigenous population were nothing compared to the massacre that was to come.

The other massacre: Shared memory, practices of carnage, and typologies of looting

The walled city became a living hell for the Chinese, immortalized by the gripping photography of the globe-trotting James Ricalton. As soon as they entered the city the Allies unleashed a veritable carnage. From the tops of the ramparts they fired randomly and without mercy on civilians, including many women and children, who fled the city through the northern and western gates. "We have shot every Chinese within reach,"[96] wrote a German soldier to his parents residing in Berlin. Wealthy families were able to escape the city by taking the Grand Canal toward the west. The less well-off took refuge in the northwest of the walled city in the Muslim neighborhood. Knowing that the Allies considered the monotheists to be against the Boxers, numerous Chinese converted instantly to Islam.[97] The city was literally in flames. On July 15 witnesses counted more than fifty fires burning in the city. Soldiers of all nationalities participated in the massacres, though the Americans and especially the Japanese would seem to have avoided committing such atrocities: "The international forces, except the Japanese, be it noted, burned half of Tien-Tsin and looted the city from end to end."[98] Extreme violence was attributed to the Russians in French, British, and Japanese sources. They were accused of cruelly massacring three hundred women and children and burning the bodies in a junk.[99] Articles in the American press stigmatized the French soldiers, who "assassinated left and right."[100] Herbert Hoover attested to their ferocity: "The French and the Russian soldiers did nothing but kill Chinese women and girls or what amounted to the same thing. They outraged them and there is nothing left for an outraged Chinese woman but suicide."[101] Numerous Chinese women preferred suicide over rape and murder. Similarly, the viceroy, Yu Lu, took his own life to escape the horrors that might have been inflicted on him by foreign military or administrative sanction by the imperial government. Lin Hei'er was arrested and executed by the Allies. The rapes committed by the strangers seemed to bother some Japanese officers, who instead brought Japanese prostitutes to China to limit the violent behavior. These massacres and rapes also solicited the reprobation of a portion of the metropolitan journalists, who considered the violence counterproductive since it reinforced the Boxers, increased mistrust toward the foreign powers, and threatened the traders who were the primary partners of foreigners in Tianjin:

> The coolies who were killed in the bay were not Boxers, otherwise they would not have been there working for foreign merchants. The moral of that lesson is, "become Boxers." The men, women, and children killed in villages by the Russians were not Boxers. They stayed behind because they trusted the foreigner. The moral of the killing of these people was "trust not the foreigner." When Tien-Tsin was burned and plundered, it was not the Boxers or the Imperial troops, or the Manchus, or anybody responsible for the anti-foreign movement who suffered, but the merchants who did business with the foreigner, the solid men who opposed the movement. Who got the bulk of the plunder of Tien-Tsin but the mass of Chinese coolies, the riff-raff of the city, who carried off tons of stuff that did not belong to them—the very lowest class of Chinese, among whom the Boxers find their strongest recruiting on the ground? The moral of the looting of Tien-Tsin was, "The foreigner rewarded his enemy and punished his friend."[102]

How can we explain this massacre of the population over several days, targeting not only unarmed soldiers but also noncombatant men, women, and children? How did the actors justify these practices, which were killed in conflicts between "civilized" nations? Far from being fortuitous, this paroxysmal violence proceeded in part from the construction of the Chinese as a "total enemy."[103] Many Allied combatants broke away from the rules of war by refusing the Chinese, who were all assimilated to Boxers, the qualification of regular soldiers. The female combatants of the Red Lanterns and the adolescents, who formed the ranks of the Boxers, reinforced their idea that this was a total war. Situated within the tradition of colonial conflicts of the nineteenth century, they considered the Chinese to be morally and physically inferior. Tianjin and the province of Zhili were thus considered to be territories that needed to be "pacified," where any distinction between military and civilian was erased. This uncontrollable violence may also be understood through the siege mentality of the foreign powers. For months, numerous cases of espionage, either true or fictive, fed the idea that all the Chinese regulars and Boxers were potential enemies. They also had in mind the recent images of the foreigners

Figure 1.6 Photograph of the southern gate of the walled city of Tianjin by James Ricalton, July 14, 1900. © Granger Historical Picture Archive/Alamy Stock Photo.

decapitated by Boxers in Zhili during the month of June. So the massacre in Tianjin was not the unfortunate consequence of war but its climax, its ultimate objective. The colonial experience and the context are insufficient to explain this hyperviolence. It was explicitly recommended by Kaiser Wilhelm II during his speech to the troops, who left for China at the end of June from Bremerhaven: "Advance toward the enemy and crush him! Show no mercy! Take no prisoners! Whoever falls into your hands shall die. A thousand years ago, King Attila's Huns made a name for themselves that still resounds today in memories and tales. May the German name acquire the same reputation in China, so that never again will a Chinese man dare look sideways at a German."[104]

This crusade ideology on the part of Christian powers was relayed on the ground by certain officers such as the ideas attributed to a Russian commander before taking the city: "'It will be necessary to destroy Tien-Tsin.' . . .'We must give these beggars a lesson.'"[105] The Allied soldiers wanted to punish the Chinese to purge "the murderous bombings and the cruel anxiety of the last month" that they imposed in their siege of the concessions.[106] The sack of Tianjin was explicitly conceived and interpreted as a privileged moment in the Boxer War, designed to mark the Chinese imagination spectacularly and durably.[107]

Indeed, the massacre of thousands of civilians echoed two others: the imaginary massacre of the foreigners in the Beijing legations in the beginning of July 1900 and the previous "massacre" of 1870. The besieged in the concessions, deprived of all communication with Beijing from June 22, believed for several weeks, as did journalists from all over the world, that the foreigners of the legations had been exterminated.[108] Different reports as well as foreign and Chinese articles drafted in Tianjin and Shanghai related the "greatest crime of the century," the storming of the legations by the Boxers and the Chinese regulars during the first days of July, in all of its goriest details: "It is only left to hope that in the final rush of the murderous hordes, the men of the legation had time to slay with their own hands their womenkind and children."[109] The lion's share of these alarmist rumors were fed by Li Hongzhang, who sought to weaken the pro-Boxers within the Imperial Court and who controlled the only telegraph that still functioned in the area.[110] However, the date of the storming of the legations varied depending on the correspondents between July 1 and July 6, according to the *New York Times*, or even July 7 if we consider the news transmitted by the viceroy of Shandong, Yuan Shikai, to the British consul general in Shanghai. All this information was inaccurate and focused on filling the gaping absence of news coming from Beijing while numerous correspondents in Tianjin and Shanghai attempted to fill their "China" column. And when the Allies took the walled city, they attempted to avenge the compatriots, who had supposedly been assassinated in the capital. Rumors even circulated about the massacre of 1,500 foreigners in Tianjin by the Boxers, who supposedly took over in the concessions on June 21. This information, which had been announced in a message from Shanghai, founded on Japanese sources and published in western newspapers on

June 22, was contradicted the next day by military authorities.[111] In early summer 1900, the virtual deaths were far more numerous than the victims accounted for by the foreign powers. Indeed, the Allied powers attempted to minimize the number of Chinese deaths in the Tianjin massacre. Reactivating the collective memory of another "massacre" no doubt contributed to the celebration of the Allied soldiers and the Boxers. The assassination of twenty foreigners on June 21, 1870, in Tianjin provoked a global emotional response in the international press. The event, known to the world as the "massacre of Tientsin," remained present in the minds of contemporaries. Hence George Weulersse wrote during his stay in Zhili: "We remember with great anxiety that 30 years ago, almost day for day, was the massacre of Tientsin! (June 21, 1870)."[112] On the opposing side, since the beginning of June, the leaders of the Boxers declared their intention to burn the church of Notre-Dame-des-Victoires built in 1869. They put their strategy into action earlier than planned on June 15 at 11:00 p.m., burning the church and destroying the tombs of the assassinated missionaries in 1870 and dispersing the remains.[113] It was not so much the number of dead as the media coverage and its political mobilization that created the event. Hence the massacre of thousands or even tens of thousands of Chinese civilians in Tianjin in July 1900 has been eclipsed by echoes of "the massacre" of tens of foreigners in 1870.[114]

"As soon as the work of carnage was over soldiers and civilians devoted themselves methodically to looting."[115] Banks and lenders lost their funds, shops were emptied, and private property was destroyed in the name of "the fruits of victory."[116] The soldiers commandeered rickshaws to transport their booty (see figure 1.7). The scenes echoed past events once again: the sacking of the summer palace in 1860, symbolized by the "Peking dog" named "Looty" in honor of the looting and offered to Queen Victoria by the British officers.[117] The Allies justified the sacking by insisting that they were satisfied with saving goods from the flames that had been left behind by the Boxers and the Chinese regulars.[118] The foreign residents of the concessions who knew the labyrinthine streets of the city well went directly to the most promising parts of the city: the palace of the viceroy of Zhili and the salt commissioner, the mint, and the jewelry and jade stores. The foreign soldiers, who were not satisfied to merely sack the walled city, also pillaged a portion of the concessions. The head of Tianjin customs Mr. Drew, declared: "Next to our enemies who endeavoured to kill us preserve me from our protectors who have looted our houses."[119] The

Figure 1.7 The looting of Tianjin. Gordon Browne, "The Crisis in China, the Looting of Tientsin by Chinese and Foreigners," *The Graphic*, September 22, 1900 (© Bridgeman).

soldiers behaved as if they were on conquered territory. They were defended by their officers such as the British Captain Bayly, who openly demonstrated his contempt for the civilians he had nicknamed "cave worms" and "cave rats" and considered deserving of punishment for their passivity during the siege. The missionaries also participated in the pillaging, claiming to confiscate goods as an indemnity for the tragedies suffered by Christians during the siege and more generally throughout Zhili and Shandong provinces. Above all, the looters seemed to want to bring "souvenirs" and mementos back to metropolitan France: "It can certainly be said that 75% of the looting by soldiers was not carried out for the love of profit but simply to obtain souvenirs."[120]

Each nationality accused the other of more devastation when in fact they all participated in the sacking in different ways, provoking different national typologies of looting. Contrary to the celebratory articles of the American press that lauded the morality of its citizens and despite the interdiction by General Adna Chaffee, the Americans committed the same acts by focusing on gold and silver. The psychology of the American soldiers seemed oriented toward business: "When he opened his mouth, money was his only topic of discussion, and when he couldn't talk about it, he remained silent."[121] Debonair and generous, they quickly became popular with other nationalities who were struck by their pronounced taste for firearms: the Americans were thus delighted to be put in charge of guarding the arsenal

of the walled city near the south gate. The British, after having hunted birds and ducks to ensure a proper meal, took an interest in silk and silver jewelry. The French seemed interested in anything without value: old clothes to wear themselves, cotton pajamas, edible products, or tobacco. On July 14 Savage-Landor, strolling through the heart of the walled city, was encouraged by a French soldier:

> "Go ahead! Help yourself! There's plenty to go around!"
>
> "Of what?" I asked, cautiously, deducing from their excitement that he had found gold or silver ingots.
>
> "Go ahead, I tell you. It's ham, don't you see? Ham! And it's excellent!"[122]

Most surprising of all, the French soldiers proposed to share their comestible booty with the British, contradicting for once on the battlefield the supposed animosity between the two armies. The generosity and solidarity between foreign soldiers broke with their cruelty toward the "indigenous" population. The Russian soldiers, coming primarily from Siberia, were considered particularly brutal and yet appreciated the jewelry, bracelets, rings, watches, perfumes, and furs that were a specialty of Tianjin, and above all the music boxes that played airs from European operas such as *La Traviata* or popular Chinese songs. The Russians justified the looting based on their military culture and economy. When a French officer showed surprise at the theft committed by the Cossacks in the shops of the French concessions, a Siberian officer responded with a smile: "Don't blame them, Captain, sir! The only love the state shows to our Cossacks is their uniform, their weapons and their horses. Their pay is nil, and their food, which you justly judge so primitive, makes it excusable—when it does no harm to anyone, which is the case today—to try to procure from time to time a small supplement."[123] The Japanese, including the regular soldiers, were distinguished once again by their more measured behavior, their artistry, and their refined taste for Chinese arts compared to the generalized vandalism of foreigners: porcelains, engravings, scrolls of old paint, and rare bronzes were the focus of their attention. And it was not uncommon to witness surreal scenes in the midst of the carnage such as graceful Japanese soldiers, contemplating a vase, reflected on its materials, the artist who painted it, the period, and the style, even trying to guess its age.[124] The Japanese were also pragmatic when it came to selecting objects that were easy to return home, including foreign-made watches—of which there were many in Tianjin—that were not destroyed by the Boxers or instruments and music boxes. In principle the Japanese were strongly opposed to the looting of private homes: "When General Fukushima, of the Japanese army, came to one of the commanders of the Christian nations to say, 'it is not right that private property should be plundered in this way,' well might the Christian commander afterward have said: 'It was hard for me, a Christian, to have to listen to such words from a Japanese and not have a word to answer.'"[125] Similarly, when Japanese soldiers seized a million taels of silver belonging to the Chinese imperial treasury, they entrusted it to the care of U.S. troops in order to protect it from Allied greed. The description of the looting in Tianjin leaves one wondering about the permanence of certain stereotypes, reinforced by the copresence of different nationalities, where each seems to both overplay and suffer from its national habitus. Finally, the Chinese, including many Buddhist monks, also plundered the walled city and hunted for treasures buried by the inhabitants.

The looting would seem to be a paradoxical moment of "globalization." All the foreigners—military and civilian—as well as the Chinese mixed during this moment, which was ripe for conflict as well as mutual aid and exchange of loot. Thus, on July 15, in the shop of a rich pawnbroker in the walled city, Chinese from different social classes came together with Americans, British, Australians, Pashtuns, Punjabis, Weihaiwei Chinese, French, Annamites, Russians, Mongols, Germans, and Austrians belonging to different military corps (navy, infantry, cavalry, artillery, engineers, transport, health service).[126] Each foreigner had a gun or rifle, and the Chinese were on the lookout for corpses; the sharing was carried out in an indescribable hubbub but without any noticeable clashes. The military authorities notably organized an auction at Temperance Hall where a whole range of objects were displayed, purchased, and exchanged. The Allies proceeded along the same lines after taking Peking, organizing sales within the British legation and the Northern cathedral.[127] Some looted objects from Tianjin then circulated around the world, notably in Europe, Russia, and the United States. Toward the end of September 1900 a part of the plunder from the walled city was seized in San Francisco in 150 undeclared cases and transported to the hospital boat *Solace* with numerous "cases of silks and curios addressed to persons all over the United States."[128] The looting in Tianjin and Beijing contributed to the emergence of an international Chinese art market at the beginning of the twentieth century.

The military authorities slowly regained control. After giving the soldiers free reign on July 14–15, which were entirely devoted to plundering, the allied officers decided on July 16 to "loot the looters."[129] British guards on Taku Road entered the concessions of the walled city, confiscated the soldiers' and foreign civilians' loot. These goods were then redistributed among the wounded soldiers or sold in auction.[130] The commanders took more strict measures on July 17: the foot soldiers, as opposed to the officers, were not authorized to transport loot outside the walled city, while the Japanese placed guards in front of certain houses to prevent further losses. Only the French command refused to put an end to the looting. A francophone American succeeded in crossing the British blockade by passing as a Frenchman. Several soldiers and civilians hid or buried loot to be recovered in the future.[131]

The Chinese inhabitants did not passively endure these foreign military predations and aggressions. As we have seen, they participated actively in the looting. In addition, many fled as the walled city was emptied of most of its population in the days following the defeat. To escape the carnage those who remained adopted a variety of strategies of self-presentation. Many Chinese wore medals or a cross around their necks, shouting toward the foreigners in different languages, "I'm Catholic, I'm Catholic."[132] The Chinese wrote approximate Japanese, French, English, or German phrases on the doors of houses, wore signs around their necks, or carried white or nationally colored flags of certain Allies: "Japan," "Friend of Civilization," "Subjected to the Western powers and Japan," "Spare me great Japan," "French protection," "Vive la France," "Friend of England inside, please do not kill me," etc.[133] These messages were drafted by the old Chinese employees in the foreign companies of the city.[134] Nine-tenths of the flags had a Japanese symbol; 4 percent had the French tricolor; 4 percent were German; 1 percent carried the colors of the United States and Britain.[135] These last two flags were less common within the population since they were difficult to reproduce, and Great Britain and the United States had the reputation among Chinese elites of having been weakened by the Boer War and the American war in the Philippines. One may be surprised that the Chinese did not imitate Russian flags, since they had been present in Zhili for some time. The Siberian soldiers inspired too much fear to be credited with any benevolence. The French seemed to benefit from the favors of many inhabitants wearing the sign "France." For the most part, however, the messages were addressed to the Japanese because of their cultural and linguistic proximity, which facilitated written communication. They were also drawn to the Japanese because of the role they had played in the victory of July 4, which made it the conquering nation, as well as undoubtedly the Japanese soldiers' respect for the local population as they protected certain buildings and buried the dead. Gustave du Chaylard, who traveled through the walled city on July 16, offered another explanation that revealed the activism of the Japanese in these circumstances: "The Japanese have given the majority of the population small flags of their nationality under whose protection they move freely. This measure increases their influence and ensures them a preponderance against which we must be wary."[136] Presumably coproduced by the Chinese and the Allies, this system of control functioned in the weeks following the capture of the city: all Chinese without a flag, sign, or pass were instinctively shot down or at best imprisoned.

After the victory of July 14, the Allied troops remained in Tianjin for three weeks to rest, recuperate, and resupply before marching on to Beijing.[137] Under the pressure of defeat and the Han viceroys of the center and the south of China (Li Hongzhang, Yuan Shikai, Liu Kunyi, and Zhang Zhidong), who refused to wage war on the strangers and preserved peace in their provinces, the Manchu Imperial Court decided to moderate its position: the bombing of the legations stopped, and the empress asked Li Hongzhang to negotiate with the Allies.

This contingent victory no doubt dissimulated the effectiveness of the Chinese military, which had proven itself through a range of techniques including the flooding of the adversaries' trenches, gathering intelligence behind enemy lines, cartography, communication by signal and telegraph, and modern armaments (stable and smokeless powder, torpedoes, mines, and so on).[138] Forgotten in contemporary historiography, the siege and the Battle of Tianjin seem to mark a turning point in the conflict, the moment when the course of the Boxer War could have been altered. Had the Allied forces been pushed back to the sea or at least been durably stalled, the outcome could have been different.[139] The taking of Tianjin as a logistical and strategic center made the "liberation" of the Beijing legations possible. The month of combat constituted a paradoxical global event. Mediatized around

the world thanks to on-site correspondents, the combat was quickly forgotten and entirely eclipsed by the march on Beijing and the taking of the capital. With it also disappeared its outcome, the massacre of the population of Tianjin. This city was indeed a hell on earth—"Pandemonium"—that the Chinese as well as the foreigners hoped to forget.

"When I left Tientsin on August 14 the town was still in a state of anarchy," wrote Herbert Hoover.[140] Pierre Loti described on October 14 "the immense desolation of a city with cyclopean walls, which is now only a heap of rubble and corpses."[141] The walled city was largely destroyed by fire, and the concessions were said to have taken nearly sixty thousand shells during the siege.[142] Even putting the impact of the deluge of fire into perspective—we know, for example, that during the Crimean War, in the middle of the nineteenth century, only one bullet in a thousand reached its objective—it is undeniable that the major part of the French concession was destroyed and that the entire agglomeration had to be rebuilt.[143]

During these months of conflict, the "Westerners" hardly dominated. The concessions were saved several times by Russian troops, and the Japanese alone achieved victory. They earned the Allies' respect in battle and imposed themselves on a part of the population as a benevolent power. Contrary to appearances, the war in Tianjin did not end on July 14, 1900. The Chinese—Boxers and former regulars—in the streets of the city and in the surrounding areas continued for long months to use other means to fiercely resist the foreigners. The "battle history" must therefore be inscribed within a medium duration of the "history of the campaign," from the beginnings of the siege to the withdrawal of foreign troops, to highlight the complexity and the diversity of the military interactions.[144] Slowly, however, life returned to normal in Tianjin, and, three months after taking the city, the small Chinese vendors took the place of foreign looters:

> In certain neighborhoods, the Chinese, especially marauders and the depraved, little by little returned after their great flight to set up open-air bazaars in the beautiful sunshine of that autumn Sunday, among the gray dust of the demolitions and the ashes, to sell to the soldiers' things gathered from the ruins, vases, silk dresses, furs. And there were so many of these soldiers and so many uniforms of all kinds on the road, so many presenting their weapons, that one's arm grew tired amidst efforts to return the continuous military salutes received passing through this extraordinary Babel.[145]

Indeed, the war of 1900 brutally globalized the city, internationalizing its government, dividing its territory into nine concessions, and concentrating in one place soldiers from around the world. An eyewitness offered a rich and precise description:

> From the moment the God of Armies (Deus Sabaoth) brought the torch to this land of Cockaigne, the ladies took refuge in Japan or Shanghai and the streets, instead of offering elegance and goods for their faces offered little more than uniforms from all the races of Europe and Asia. We discovered next to the uninspired blue canvas outfits, which added nothing to the military "chic" of the infantry and the navy artillery, the half-European half-Asian khaki suit of our Annamites. The English had imported, alongside sailors from the landing companies, the whole range of colors of Hindustani, Gurkhas, Nepalese, Bengali, and Sikhs, who, with their long skinny legs and pirate faces, hardly brought honor to their gracious Queen. They had been parked on the wastelands on the tracks outside the mud wall. The Consulate was guarded by soldiers of the Chinese regiment of Wei-Hai-Wei, dressed in khaki canvas with a straw hat and raised brim placed on his head. The Germans, dressed in khaki canvas, also wore straw hats, fully equipped with abundant new equipment, as they maneuvered and marched to the sound of fife and small flat drums, as if in a Prussian garrison. One group was stationed in the university of Mr. Detring; the other camped on the abandoned lands of the concession. The Americans were distributed throughout the *godowns* of the English city and in their evangelical missions.[146] An outpost camped at the corner of rue Saint-Louis, in front of the Hong Kong Shanghai Banking Corporation, which it protected. The Italians housed their *bersaglieri* almost everywhere. Near the house where I lived, they had rented an enclosure from the Jesuits for their cavalry and had gathered a hundred donkeys, who spent the night lamenting the boredom of sleeping under the stars and working for the "devils of the sea." The Japanese lodged around the Consulate and the stopover service located in its outbuildings. The Russians were scattered along the line from Tong-Kou to Yangcun. Their only concentrated groups occupied the Military School and the Grand Arsenal, established by Li Hung Chang, in the eastern plain of Tianjin, about two kilometers away. They quietly moved all its rich

equipment to the workshops in Port-Arthur. It was not uncommon to meet, at the same time, in the same street, a squad of large Hindu Rajpoots, made even taller by their turbans and their flame throwers, a band of Sikhs riding small donkeys, mules, poorly maintained horses or lazily dragging long hand carriages, a line of Chinese, naked to the waist and covered with sweat, pushing their wheelbarrows with big wheels sometimes loaded with a thousand kilos. The confrontation was complete when a detachment of small Japanese men arrived, stocky, playful looking, beardless, with round bags on their backs, rifles on their shoulders, dressed in white, with a small bayonet as long as a knife hitting their backs to the rhythm of their steps, or a troop of Americans, tall, well-sculpted men, walking solidly, or well-saddled, feet in the stirrups with a leather hood, topped with a felt hat dimpled in the middle, and stamped with a copper insignia, sometimes decorated with a toothbrush as a cockade, bridge pants mounted high on a black shirt, and strapped with a belt lined with nickel-plated cartridges.[147]

Figure 2.1 The official government headquarters (*yamen*) of the viceroy of Zhili transformed into the Provisional Government's headquarters, 1900. "Boxer Rebellion 1900: Military Operations In and Around Peking," National Archives, CO 1069/422, "China 2."

CHAPTER II

The Invention of an International Government

Foreign Military Bureaucracy or Chinese Democracy by Petition?

In any case, the way is open to conflicts of authority, distribution of power and national interests that are further complicated by questions of persons and rank: consuls, ministers, plenipotentiaries and, more rarely, chief generals, will thus from time to time be a cause of embarrassment for the Provisional Government of Tientsin, often a very great embarrassment. Some will resent the high cost of membership but will see its authority grow in spite of itself.

—CHARLES CONDAMY

Sharp rivalry between the Allied powers prevented the formation of a unified command of the coalition forces. On the eve of the battle of Tianjin on July 12, 1900, the British refused the creation of a war council composed of the command from each power, proposed by the Russian Minister of Foreign Affairs. Each of the Allied powers had their own handicap in their claims to provide a commander in chief. The Americans were a young imperial power. The Austro-Hungarians and the Italians did not have a sufficient presence in China. The Russians and the Japanese were omnipresent and decisive but neutralized one another through local rivalries, and France was focused on southern China. Great Britain, the primary imperial power, was the natural candidate but suffered at that moment from difficulties in southern Africa created by the Boers and the spectacular military failure of the Seymour Column.[1] Their relative hegemony in Asia pushed the other Allies to mistrust and undermine them. There remained the Germans, who hoped to obtain the general command to avenge the assassination of Baron von Ketteler and affirm their international ambitions. Kaiser Wilhelm II personally requested the support of Tsar Nicolas II, who accepted in order to weaken his British rival. Thanks to this support, Wilhelm II decided unilaterally, in early August, to name his close friend and former commander in chief, Marshal Alfred von Waldersee, Allied supreme commander for the international expeditionary forces. Officially the British prime minister, Salisbury, accepted and began to envisage a new alliance with the Japanese to counterbalance the cooperation between Russia and Germany. Nonetheless, the Allied powers made it clear that the troops needed to maintain their autonomy regarding the commander in chief.[2] As a result, the march on Beijing began on August 5 in disorderly fashion without a unified international command and ended by the taking of the capital on August 15. Marshal von Waldersee and the expeditionary force arrived in China after the battle in September 1900, and the commander in chief was forced to constantly negotiate with the other commanders. Each power on its own could create an alliance with whomever it chose and, notably, sign separate treaties with the Chinese government.

The foreign armies acted independently of one another in Zhili Province. However, they acted in concert in Tianjin the day after taking the city to establish a provisional military government that would administer and reconstruct the Chinese city and its suburbs, which had been largely destroyed by the conflicts. Oddly, this short and extremely dense political experience (July 1900–August 1902) has been ignored by historians, except for the pathbreaking works of Otto Rasmussen and Lewis Bernstein,[3] even though it is undoubtedly the first multinational government in modern history, at the head of a hierarchized and cosmopolitan municipal administration. The new government gained the "plenipotentiary powers" granted to the commanders of the Allied troops. That is, they possessed an "absolute authority" over the territory to fulfill a series of missions: reestablishing public order threatened by the Boxers and the *hunhunr* brigands, promoting public health that had been severely degraded by the massacres and epidemics, facilitating the life of the troops and the inhabitants through urban and regional planning, inventorying and guaranteeing public and private properties, preventing famine in the development of a system of social aid. It administered the *hsien*, the Tianjin district, that is, the Chinese city and its surrounding areas up to the mud wall, except for the foreign concessions, the arsenals, barracks and military camps, railroad lines and telegraph lines already managed by the Allied forces.[4]

By taking on the title of "government" as opposed to "municipality" or "commune" or "administration," the new organization officially announced its political and administrative ambitions. Nonetheless, this form of ostensibly unprecedented international military government seemed difficult to define clearly from the outset. Was it an "imported state" in the form of a military occupation or an imperial apparatus of the metropole states?[5] What foreign

models were mobilized to conceive of this administration? W
degree of autonomy of the Council of the Provisional Gover
regard to the chancellery and the military command? Was this g
effectively international in its composition and its exercise of p
international character of this organization should not erase the
and transformations of Chinese administrative practices. It is no
the context of Tianjin to consider the Allies to have operated, a
tially, from within the cameralist tradition of the Qing more than
radical reform from outside it. We must therefore examine how t
"civil servants" adapted and at times adopted administrative practi
most imposing "bureaucracy" in the world with 40,000 Mandarin
commanding more than 1.2 million secretaries and 500,000 agen
experience would no doubt have been impossible without the activ
pation of a foreign elite of experts in Chinese public affairs and n
Chinese, who constituted most of the government agents.

A cosmopolitan bureaucracy in a Chinese framework

The foundation of an international and provisional governmen

The first signs of tension between the Allies appeared when the comm
decided to name a governor general at the head of the new intern
government founded on July 16, 1900. The French preferred the Ru
who had been privileged partners with the French since the secret co
tion of 1892, which had saved the French concession by defending again
attacks of the Chinese troops.[7] The British, however, had no intenti
serving under a foreign command, much less a "non-Western" one, Ru
or Japanese. Moreover, the French recalled that during the siege, the B
distinguished themselves by refusing to bombard the walled city unde
pretext that some British businesses might suffer.[8] The Allies condemned
conciliatory attitude of the British, who seemed to want to go out on t
own. Unable to agree on a governor, the foreign powers adopted the unpr
edented formula of creating an international council within the Provisio
Government, proposed by Admiral Alexeieff.[9] It was first constituted b
triumvirate with a Russian, British, and Japanese general placed at the he
of the government: "We are already envisaging serious difficulties in
functioning," wrote the French consul to Minister Delcassé.[10]

The council held its first meeting as the executive arm of the government on July 30 at 10:00 a.m. in the headquarters (*yamen*) of the viceroy of Zhili Province.[11] The Chinese administration was distributed into three corners of the government building: the viceroy was located in the north, the mandarin civil offices in the east, the mandarin military offices in the west, organized according to the popular expression: "Those in the east govern our lives, those in the west govern our death."[12] Contrary to the African and Asian colonizers, the Powers did not build a government palace ex nihilo. Instead, they settled in a local building, inscribing their action in continuity with the Chinese powers just as the foreign dynasty of the Manchus took power in the majority Han empire. The international administration immediately occupied its offices in the prestigious offices of the viceroy and were satisfied to substitute the former "*yamen* of the viceroy," an expression that was now forbidden, with a new name for the government (*dutong yamen*).[13] In October 1900 Pierre Loti provided a worried description of the palace guarded by "stone monsters" and foreign soldiers:

> At the end of the destroyed city, near the high walls, in front of the palace of the viceroys where we went to see the goddesses, Chinese in cangues were lined up along the wall, with signs explaining their misdeeds.[14] Two figures guarded the gates with bayonets, one American, the other Japanese, next to the old stone monsters with horrible grins that, in Chinese fashion, watched crouching on either side of the threshold. There was nothing sumptuous about this palace of decrepitude and dust, which we crossed distractedly; nor was there anything great about it. It was the real, very old China, grimacing and hostile; monsters in profusion, made of marble, broken earthenware, worm-eaten wood, falling from obsolescence in the courtyards, or threatening the edge of the roofs; awful shapes were everywhere sketched under the ashes attesting to the effacement of time; one witnessed horns, claws, forked tongues and big, shady eyes. And in sadly walled courtyards, a few late season roses, still bloomed, under hundred-year-old trees.[15]

The members of the council attempted to distinguish between the new and the old while at the same time insisting on administrative continuities: the headquarters of the international government was required to,

like the other public buildings as well as the ships that belonged to it, display a new flag. This rectangular flag with a yellow background and the English acronym T.P.G. (Tientsin Provisional Government, in one of the three official languages of the government) in black, explicitly reproduced the color code of the Chinese empire and the Qing dynasty. In principle only the imperial family could use these colors for its clothes and buildings. This was not the first modern—that is, rectangular—flag used in China. At the beginning of the 1880s Li Hongzhang drew inspiration from the foreign models to progressively abandon the triangular flag and adopt a rectangular one. He then encouraged the Empress Cixi to choose a national flag for the Manchu dynasty, promulgated in 1888 and used from 1900 onward, apparently just prior to the usage of the Provisional Government's flag. Similarly, the council ordered the making of a bilingual "Chinese seal," written in the two other official languages of the government (French and Chinese), for use by the district heads and their services to legitimate and render more visible their action in the eyes of the notables and Chinese elites.[16]

In the first government's months in office, the Allies took possession of all the buildings and terrains belonging to the Chinese administration, including the private property of the high civil servants of the Qing regime, much like the highly symbolic headquarters (*yamen*) of Li Hongzhang occupied by the new administration on January 11, 1901. The foreign civil servants did not hesitate to continue the Chinese administrative tradition in the manner of agents of the treasury. Their paystubs followed the Chinese calendar year, and for the Chinese New Year the council closed the Provisional Government offices to mark the solemn occasion between February 18–21, 1901. Finally, when a fire ravaged a portion of the Provisional Government's headquarters, the council took care to have the buildings rebuilt "in a Chinese style, on the old foundations."[17]

In addition to pursuing continuity with Chinese imperial power, the government officially affirmed its "provisional" character the day after the capture of the city to reassure the Chinese authorities and distinguish this "humanitarian intervention" from a vulgar colonial expedition. But in the months that followed, the council affirmed its authority and considered the possibility of removing the term "provisional" (Chan Hsing Kuan Li) in its title when making official proclamations. Its members considered that this epithet tended to "diminish the prestige of the Provisional Government in the eyes of the Chinese and those they were addressing." Charles

Tenney, the "Chinese secretary," that is, the secretary of Chinese affairs, categorically opposed the proposition, which he argued could give the impression that "foreign control over the city of Tientsin would be permanent," and in turn provoke grave political and social disturbances. The government remained officially "provisional" until its dissolution two years later. The temporary character was quickly enhanced by the uncertainty that reigned over the foreign administration. Indeed, the civil servants elaborated and attempted to put into place policies without knowing how things would function in the months that followed. This existential anxiety, which remained imperceptible within the official proclamations, pervades the administrative correspondence. Hence, when Charles Tenney began his six-month leave in September 1901, the council imagined the possibility that the government would no longer exist when he returned to Tianjin, and therefore arranged to pay his salary in advance. It is possible to imagine that many of the employees within the administration struggled with such uncertainty.[18]

A council of power and seat of interimperial rivalries

Contrary to what historians of Tianjin have suggested, the council was not a consensual creation that immediately welcomed representatives from the eight powerful allies.[19] From the start the Provisional Government suffered critiques by military and consular authorities. General Voyron, commander of the French troops, officially complained that France was not mentioned in the proclamation establishing the government, "a fact that will tend to weaken the influence of France in the city's protection."[20] To appease the French, the council henceforth forbid the mention of the nationality of members, named "governors," in all following proclamations. More problematic, a part of the consular corps followed the French to protest that they had not been officially informed of the foundation of a provisional military government. It was indeed necessary to wait more than two months after its creation for the council to consider it necessary to address an official message to the foreign consuls of Tianjin through its secretary general: "The secretary general is charged with sending the Council's regrets to the leader of the consular corps for not having announced to the consuls, due to the tremendous number of occupations, the fact that it had been established. The Council now desires to do so and to ensure the consular corps of its desire to maintain cordial relations."[21]

The council was originally composed of three members—Russian Colonel (then General) Vogak, British Colonel Bower, and Japanese Colonel Aoki—who were chosen by the command of the Allies and held identical powers as well as "absolute independence."[22] The Russian command was the centerpiece of the council, the only member who, despite multiple absences, continued through the final dissolution of the government. According to an interlocutor whom he met in June 1900, he possessed the social qualities and linguistic competencies that were indispensable in a cosmopolitan context: "Colonel Vogak served as personal interpreter for all of us, and I could not help but admire the stunning facility with which he grasped so many diverse languages, transmitting the slightest desires of each individual to the others. It was truly for me, over the course of an entire hour, a tremendous subject of envy and reminded me, in practical terms, of an old maxim that was dear to one of my professors: 'we are as many men as we speak foreign languages.' "[23] The council administered the goods of the Chinese government, established all the regulations concerning the walled city and fixed the tax rates. The other Allied powers hoped to obtain a seat on the council to participate directly in the decision-making process. The negotiations began in October with General Voyron, who forbade soldiers from participating in the international administration if a French representative was not integrated into the council. The general even attempted to force the council's hand by removing the French soldiers sent to police the Chinese city and, as a result, provoking "a rise in crime, that had been diminishing."[24]

Following the lead of the French command, Marshal von Waldersee and General von Lessel demanded on October 11 the appointment of a German representative, Major von Falkenhayn. The council did not immediately respond and asked for instructions from the Allied commanders. Count von Waldersee understood the necessity of finding agreement with French and American generals to formulate on October 20 a common request in the name of the three powers, which was then presented to the Russian, Japanese, British, Italian, and Austrian commanders. They accepted the request: the German Major von Falkenhayn, the American Colonel Foote, and the French member, whose appointment General Voyron delayed, were authorized to integrate the council.[25]

This enlargement provoked the interest of the commander of the Italian forces in China, Admiral Candiani, who asked for a seat for his country in late November. General Voyron had no objection, but the American General Chaffee's position was more ambivalent: in the name of the general principle of the "equality of nations," he consented to the admission of the Italian representative, but also wrote that he considered the number of members of the council to be sufficient. Adept in these circumstances, Admiral Count Rudolf Montecuccoli, commander of the Austro-Hungarian troops, did not object either as long as there was also an Austrian representative. First Lieutenant Valli was thus ready to join the council. But he then opposed the appointment of a lower-ranking officer to government posts and refused on principal the appointment of an eighth Austrian member. The Italian command found a solution by designating a superior officer, Lieutenant Commander Casanuova, a member of the council. The same problem reemerged in January 1902 when General Sucillon sought to replace Colonel Arlabosse with a lower-ranking officer, Captain Jullian, a deputy chief of staff from the Occupation Brigade. The French commander's proposal met the approval of British General Creagh but ran up against the opposition of Major General von Rohrscheidt and the Japanese Colonel Akiyama, who were committed to the appointment of a superior officer. In this context of Allied tensions, the conference of commanders, brought together on February 5, 1901, found a solution for integrating the French candidate while also respecting military protocol: "The Council may arrange its functions so that it does not have to give orders to senior officers." From this moment forward, Captain Jullian supervised the Department of Public Works while also serving as the intermediary for the other members of the council when it gave instructions to the heads of service and the heads of the districts.[26]

At the same moment when Italy was applying pressure to join the council, the United States was looking to leave. As early as September 29, 1900, Colonel Samuel Sumner, caught up in the withdrawal of American troops, unilaterally announced the exit of his soldiers from the Chinese city on October 8. The American representative to the council, Colonel Morris C. Foote, notified the Provisional Government of the departure of his country's representative at the end of April 1901 before leaving the council on May 10, as American troops were withdrawing from northern China. From this point forward, the secretary general of the government, American citizen Charles Denby Jr., officially represented the interests of his country to the council and maintained the connection with the Beijing legation for "all affairs of importance for the US government." The Russian representative remained conscious of the Russian territorial ambitions in Tianjin and adopted a different strategy. Kept away by other military obligations from June 1901, General Vogak insisted that he be considered a full-fledged member of the council and that his name appear on all official proclamations until the government's dissolution.[27]

The council members attempted early on to ease the international tensions that threatened the Provisional Government. Following on the proposition of Major von Falkenhayn, an ad hoc committee was named to develop a reform proposal for the council's functioning. The report, which recommended a rotating presidency of their meetings, was adopted: following the alphabetical order of the nations, their representatives succeeded one after the other in presiding over each session. The government defined itself through this new regulation as an international representative organization with the division of powers over time decided by alphabetical order: "The direction must not remain in the hands of one member for more than one session." The president of the session directed the votes and the debates, examined the requests, and signed the arrest warrants and the executive orders. Each member received an annual salary of 1,500 pounds sterling.[28] They also had a private secretary and personal control over a department of the Provisional Government from which they received a report prior to each session. These different services came together to put into place a governmental policy over the territory under its jurisdiction.

National officials in the service of an international government: Experts within the departments and districts

Between September and November 1900 the government created a number of administrative services for the city: a general chancellery of the council (which then became a secretary general), of safety (then policy), health (then sanitation), treasury, judiciary, military (which was quickly abandoned), the Chinese secretariat, public works, the office of public supplies and food, and the office of registration for goods and property.[29] The offices of the viceroy of Zhili were previously divided into ten departments (*liu fang*): human resources, revenues, rites, war, punishment, work, taxes, reception, and distribution of documents, and the justice and the salt department.[30] Each department of the Provisional Government had its own chief and multiple deputies as well as foreign military or civilian employees with annual salaries between eight hundred, six hundred, and three hundred pounds respectively. The council then succeeded in imposing on civil servants the payment of their salaries in Mexican dollars, the most common currency in Tianjin. But in March 1902 the mobilization of the heads of the service, notably through a petition, allowed all foreign civil servants—except for members of the council, who were supposed to set an example—to be once again paid in sterling, a more prized currency.

The distribution of the management of the department was partially determined based on "national genius," that is, the technical competencies of each Allied power: the secretary general (Charles Denby Jr.), who coordinated the action of the administration, and the head of the judiciary administration (Walter Scott Emens) were American; the chief of police (Guy Henry Gaston Mockler) was British; the treasurer (Carl Rump) was German; the head of the health service (Doctor René Depasse) was French; the Chinese secretary, originally attributed to an American (Charles Tenney) who was deeply knowledgeable about Chinese culture, was then given to the "Orientals," a Japanese civil servant (S. Nishigori) and his Russian deputy (Mr. Brackmann). The council did not hesitate to recruit foreigners, that is, individuals not from the Allied countries, such as the Dane Albert de Linde and his deputy and the Norwegian Benjamin Wegner Nørregaard, who directed the service of public works. A few Chinese intermediaries occupied the key posts of deputies to the secretary general (Y. K. Lee), the head deputy of the health service (Doctor Soo Hao Doong), and the "comprador of the government" (Lo), who, thanks to his indispensable function as broker, cleverly negotiated a particularly high salary (2,400 taels per year). The rarity of competencies and human resources could on occasion push the council to institutionalize a form of professional polyvalence. Hence, W. H. Smith served as deputy magistrate in the morning and treasury account auditor in the afternoon.

These heads of service and the deputies possessed all the technical competency required. Certified with university diplomas, they formed a veritable government of experts. The Allies recruited the best foreign specialists, most of whom were considered "Sinophiles" and who had already demonstrated their talents before the Boxer War: engineers, diplomats, doctors, pedagogues, and the like often came from the social and university elite, and almost all were familiar with Chinese language and culture. A minority were born in China, such as Walter Scott Emens. Some participated in Freemasonry in China (James Bromley Eames, Walter Scott Emens). Born at the end of the 1850s and the beginning of the 1860s, these men belonged to a generation which prior to 1900 had been in the service of Li Hongzhang, viceroy of Zhili and high dignitary of the Imperial Court, as a private doctor, preceptor to his children, military instructor to his armies, diplomatic advisor, and manager or engineer of the imperial railroads.[31] They constituted the indispensable civilian element for the military men within the council and were no doubt during this period among the most knowledgeable Westerners in China.

The two pillars of the government were Secretary General Charles Denby Jr. (1861, Evansville, Indiana–1938, Washington, D.C.) and Chinese Secretary Charles Tenney. Born into a wealthy American family, grandson of a senator on his mother's side, son of an ambassador to China and nephew of the secretary of the navy, Denby studied at Princeton and then accompanied his father in 1885 to the Beijing legation as second secretary and then first secretary (1894–1897). Charles Denby was a specialist in Chinese language and culture. He married Martha Dalzell Orr (1895) and pursued his business interests in the Chinese capital between 1897 and 1900. The mastermind behind the negotiations between China and Japan during the first Sino-Japanese War and author of the project of the Treaty of Shimonoseki, which put an end to the conflict, Denby then pushed for great support on the part of the United States to Chinese missionaries in the context of the growing tensions at the end of the century.[32]

The Chinese secretary, Charles Daniel Tenney (1857, Boston, Massachusetts–1930, Palo Alto, California) was educated at Dartmouth College, where he received his BA (1878) and his master's degree (1879), then later an Honorary Doctorate of Laws (LLD) in 1900. In 1886 Tenney founded the Anglo-Chinese School, where he served as principal until 1895.[33] In 1887 he became preceptor of the two sons and grandson of Li Hongzhang, whom he had come to know. He published several schoolbooks: *Tenney's English Lessons* (1890), *Tenney's English Grammar* (1892), and *Geography of Asia* (1898). In 1895 the Chinese government offered to transform the Anglo-Chinese School into the Imperial University of Tianjin (Peiyang University), the first Western-style public institution of higher education in China, of which he became the first president.

The Imperial University of Tianjin educated multiple civil government officers. Noah Fields Drake (1864–1945) was among the first professors recruited to the new institution. Having earned an engineering degree at the University of Arkansas (1888), he worked for four years for the Geological Survey of Texas and Arkansas and then for the U.S. Geological Survey. He entered Stanford University in 1893 and obtained a doctorate in geology in 1897. The following year, Charles Tenney appointed him professor of geology and mining at the Imperial University of Tianjin. He became surveyor for the Provisional Government on September 24, 1900, before the department of public works was created the following November. The legal counsel of the Provisional Government, the British lawyer James Bromley Eames, had previously been professor of law at the Imperial University of Tianjin.

Doctor René Depasse (1862–1901) was a leading doctor of the colonies and a fervent Sinophile. He participated in the Asian military campaigns of Formosa, Fuzhou, and the Pescadores before serving as doctor to the Navy of Tonkin in Cochinchina and Cambodia. He was then granted leave to serve as doctor to the French legation in Beijing, after which he became professor of medicine at the Imperial School of Medicine of Tianjin founded by Li Hongzhang and directed by Dr. Lin Luen Fai Lu. At the same time, he served as private doctor to the viceroy of Zhili, caring for Li after an attempted assassination in Shimonoseki in 1895. He enjoyed a reputation as an expert on the region, as attested to by his old friend Alexis Daoulas, whom he met by accident in Tianjin at the end of June 1900: "Dr. Depasse is, in fact, one of the Europeans who knows China best, he speaks the language very well, and the imperial government has long since appointed him director of the School of Chinese Medicine in Tien-Tsin. He fulfills, in the opinion of all, this difficult mission with perfect tact, a rare consciousness and a science that everyone here recognizes very deeply." The French doctor behaved heroically during the siege and succumbed in January 1901 to an illness contracted "as a result of the fatigues of war and the privations of the siege."[34]

The head of the legal service, Walter Scott Emens, was born in Shanghai in 1857 and had been the representative of an American trading company in Tianjin. Since he had lived there his entire life, he knew the language as well as Chinese imperial law. He married Elizabeth Scott Farnham (1882), with whom he had three children. He died of a heart attack in Shanghai in 1919.

The head of the service of public works was the Danish engineer Albert de Linde (1857–1934). He held a doctorate (1884) and had stayed in Siam

(Thailand) in 1884, where he was employed in the Department of Bridges and Roads in Bangkok. In 1887 he entered the service of the Russian government to develop telegraph lines. In 1888–89 he directed the construction of a factory of oil gas in Tianjin. After a mission on the Yellow River in 1889, he was charged with intervening in the context of the floods that struck Zhili and the Shanxi in 1890. In 1892 he began serving as engineer to the imperial Chinese railroads. In 1892 Albert de Linde married Margaret McLeish, who was seventeen and the daughter of a well-known figure in the city, William McLeish. He participated in the construction of a water supply system in Tianjin in 1896–97 before being tasked in 1898–1900 with redirecting the Hai River. His deputy within the services of public works of the Provisional Government, the Norwegian Benjamin Wegner Nørregaard (1861–1935), also worked for the Chinese imperial railroads between 1896 and 1900 after having completed his education as an officer and entering the Norwegian army as a captain in 1881.[35]

The treasurer of the government, Carl Rump, was born in Hamburg in 1860 and completed his studies at the central gymnasium of the city and then in Heidelberg. He arrived in China in 1881, where he first worked for the German business Meyer & Co, and then in 1897 he started working for the Asiatische Bank of Tianjin. The banker actively participated in the concessions' defense and the taking of the Chinese city before he was recruited by the Allies.

Finally, some information is available regarding the head of the police, Major Guy Henry Mockler, born in 1866 in Great Britain and educated at the Royal Military College. Among the department heads was also the chief of the Tianjin station, Major Whittal, from the British contingent in Hyderabad, who was "perhaps the most famous man in Northern China." Fluent in English, Russian, French, and German, he embodied the prototype of an efficient international civil servant, capable of managing daily troop transports and conflicts between different nationalities.[36]

These officials directed their administrations while at the same time devising projects to improve public policies, for example, on the "nature and method of tax collection," the procedures to be followed by the judge, or the "organization of the indigenous police in the villages." Some of them were businessmen (Charles Denby, Walter Scott Emens, Carl Rump), while others had family ties to the economic interests of Tianjin (Albert de Linde) before they took on public service. These leaders collaborated on an almost daily basis with the two magnates of the city: Gustav Detring and his nephew Constantin von Hanneken who, without having any official role, acted regularly on behalf of the government.

A German with British citizenship, Detring (1842–1913) decided at twenty-three to dedicate his life to the service of the Chinese government and Li Hongzhang, to whom he would become the principal foreign advisor. As the Chinese customs commissioner in Tianjin for nearly twenty-five years, he acquired numerous properties and buildings in the city to become the largest property owner in the British concession, where he served as the head municipal magistrate. His businesses, including the Traction and Lighting Syndicate, which he presided over, actively participated in the regional and urban policy and planning initiated by the Provisional Government. His daughter married a military engineer in Tianjin, Constantin von Hanneken (1854–1925, Tianjin), the son of a Prussian general, who served for a brief period in the German army before becoming a military advisor in the service of Li Hongzhang (1879–1887), building the great fortress of Port Arthur in Manchuria and notably participating in the battle of the Yalu River in the Sino-Japanese War of 1894–95, after which he was named admiral in the Chinese fleet. In 1899 he became a businessman in Tianjin, where he developed industrial fabrics, constituted one of the most beautiful collections of Chinese porcelain in the world. He became one of the leading figures in the public works of the Provisional Government.[37]

Alongside proficient Sinophiles and Chinese language experts were the officers appointed to the head of each district. Following the extension of the territory under the jurisdiction of the government out to the Gulf of Bohai and 15.5 miles (25 km) to the west and northwest of the Chinese city, the council decided at the beginning of February 1901 to adopt a new "regulation" to divide the territory into five distinct districts, each under their own head. They consisted of the inner city of Tianjin inside the city walls; the district of Tongku to the east; to the west, the district of Chunliangcheng, which was approximately twenty-two miles (35 km) wide; the district of North Tientsin, which spread up to nearly ten miles (16 km) north of the city; and South Tientsin. The council distributed the direction of the districts among the French, British, Japanese, and the Germans.[38] The Russians showed no particular interest, the Americans were leaving and uninterested, but the Italians expressed their regret through the Colonel Carioni that no district had been given to them. The council directly controlled the district of the walled city and delegated authority to the heads of the four other districts in the domains of police, judiciary, and fiscal nese. . . . Among these workers, these coolies, there were men of conditions, sons of poor and former rich ruined by the war, but all ally hungry. . . . In the morning, the coolies who wanted to work ne to the barracks yard. They would crouch on their heels, knees ve the ground and huddle together tightly to warm each other. e officers divided them into groups by work site and each of them eived an attendance sheet that they gave to the *cail* [indigenous eman] in the evening in exchange for their wages. In order to id fraud, the model of the cards varied from day to day.[42]

treated by the government agents, in the administrative documents olies were anonymous and simply referred to by number, for exam- oolie no 1 from the train station," whose house was mercilessly con- d by the government and transformed into police headquarters.[43] e foreign administration also relied on indigenous managers. The adors, intellectual elites, secretaries, writers, assistants, accountants, ors, booksellers, and clerks ensured the daily tasks that were neces- r government services. The number of official interpreters for the nment constituted a category in itself. In April 1902 there were thirty- official interpreters for the government as well as several temporary reters with no trace in the records. The Provisional Government thus shed a clear continuity with Chinese administrative practices by hir- some cases more than ten times the official number of employees ly declared.[44] Contrary to appearances, interpreters already played a n the offices of provincial viceroys as translators from local dialects ndarin, which was the language of the civil servants. The govern- hired Japanese interpreters fluent in Chinese. They held extensive , which on some occasions they abused, as demonstrated in the rous judicial affairs in which the interpreters were involved when they accused of extorsion in the villages. Targeted by the inhabitants when eements arose, some interpreters were the object of articles of denun- n in the Chinese press before being sent before a tribunal or govern- The "Chinese experts" were also mobilized to resolve the technical ems concerning public works and fiscal questions. Hence, in early 1901 the indigenous specialists were sent to the heads of the districts p "classify boutiques according to their taxes."[45]

e salaries of the Chinese employees varied depending on seniority roximity with foreigners. But overall, except for comprador Lo, they

questions. Each head of district was aided by a Ch
more deputy officials on horseback, a few lowe
served as police inspectors, and ten to twenty *sowar*
formed the "military police." These men in the fie
ing and aware of local constraints while enjoying
and providing a precious relay to the council for
what was happening on the ground. The head of
ngcheng thus proposed to the council a new taxatio
was submitted to the other heads of districts and
government before being adopted. The heads o
the council's meetings, as the prefects and the m
the viceroy of Zhili.[39]

The Chinese foundations of a foreign ad

Outside the foreign managers, the Provisional G
through a whole range of intermediaries and in
agents. Interpreters, "boys" and "coolies" as wel
formed an indispensable corps for the functioning
even if they remain less visible in the archives.[40] In
were not satisfied with just retooling the symbolic
rial Chinese power (palace, flag, seal, and the lik
employees who had worked in the official headqu
men and messengers, laundrymen, cooks, and aides
served as guards, doormen, jailkeepers, and so forth
bles and the horses of foreign officers and official
grooms: the members of the council owned and pai
Boys ran the government mess, and about fifteen
palace courtyards. In addition, there were thousand
tributed to the Provisional Government's public wo
not hesitate to systematically requisition prisoners se
to clean the headquarters, demolish buildings or bu

> The work "grinded away," we watched it being
> enous people, because all the soldiers, except for
> cial workers, had become bosses who encourag
> people by kicking them in the legs. We employe

were far lower than those of their foreign counterparts. Hence, a Japanese interpreter made more. However, the Chinese mobilized for higher pay, starting with the "indigenous officers" who, in early November 1900, managed to increase their annual salary from $180 to $600, an increase of more than 300 percent. The following year the head of the judicial service increased his interpreters' pay by 50 percent. The establishment of the Provisional Government and the presence of Allied troops led to an increase in the labor costs to such a degree that by March 1901 the "civilian community complained that the high prices paid by the military authorities made these employees' demands exorbitant." Following numerous recriminations by the Chinese employers and the foreigners, notably in the concessions, the Chinese secretary attempted to organize the labor market by elaborating a proposal for a salary grid for coolies, domestic servants, and Chinese employees. At the end of six months of negotiations, the council succeeded in convincing all the public and private workers (Allied commanders, foreign consuls, the administration of the railroads, and Chinese businessmen) to adopt a new wage of twenty to twenty-five cents per day for "coolies" and thirty to thirty-five cents per day for "workers."[46]

While introducing a new form of government of experts, this administration also depended on less formal and vernacular forms of knowledge. What were its relationships with the indigenous population and what were its capacities to represent them and take their requests into consideration?

Democracy by petition?

The Provisional Government founded its legitimacy on its respect for one guiding principle: the right to petition, that is, the capacity of Chinese inhabitants and foreigners of a given jurisdiction to call upon public powers to present a complaint or request intervention on a personal affair or a measure of general interest. In the European political tradition, the petition was considered a technique of democratic participation. Within the Provisional Government, this practice occupied a fundamental—even invasive—place in everyday administration at the same time that it was presented by civil servants as an instrument introduced by a foreign power that was well-meaning and designed to ensure the local population's well-being.

The petition system, or permanent reform

At the end of December 1900 a box for petitions was installed in front of the small entryway of the Provisional Government's headquarters. Starting in February 1901, each local district headquarters had its own box to better cover the entire territory of the jurisdiction. Each day, according to a preestablished order, a member of the council collected the contents and brought the petitions to the council's chamber to be counted, classified, and dated. While these petitions have disappeared, we know that the member of the council was supposed to register his own name, date, number of the petition, its subject, as well as the name and place of the petitioner's residence. They were then treated by the Chinese secretary and his assistants, who translated and summarized their contents before returning them to the council's chamber, which decided on each case brought to its attention. The decision, or in some cases the measure adopted by the council, was to be verified in the register by the head of the secretariat.[47]

In this system of daily interactions between the indigenous population and the foreign administration, the Chinese secretary served as an intermediary. The Japanese, who enjoyed the reputation of being closer to the local Chinese population, played a decisive role in the office of the Chinese secretariat. The department was supervised by a Japanese member of the council—Colonel Aoki and then Colonel Harada—who relied on Nishigori, Tenney's deputy, who became interim Chinese secretary from September 1901 to April 1902 and then official head of the Chinese secretariat after May 1902. As we will see, for questions relating to police and justice Tenney and Nishigori tirelessly defended Chinese interests. Hence, they opposed the council's proposal to tax the petitions, officially designed to fill the government's coffers, but no doubt also to discourage the increasing number of petitions that could climb to more than ten per day. Indeed, some of the inhabitants did not hesitate to send numerous petitions on the same subject. For example, regarding a petition on the "confiscation of petrol," the council ordered the petitioner to "no longer trouble the Provisional Government on this matter" and declared "that it would no longer consider any petitions on this subject."[48]

Thanks to their proximity with the local Chinese population, the Chinese secretariat was regularly suspected of taking their side against the members of the council. When Tenney defended some Chinese who insisted they had been attacked by German soldiers, the government advisors reproached him in the absence of proof and mere oral witnesses who sided with local population and sidestepped the council by directly addressing Count von Waldersee through the mediation of the British Colonel Bower. The council reminded them of the "civilian" character of the Chinese secretariat and therefore officially reprimanded Tenney, who was forced to communicate all information he possessed to the council. After receiving the information, the council decided that it was false and should not have been communicated on "official departmental letterhead" used for reports. In a context of strong interimperial rivalries, the council paid careful attention to the foreign troops and the instrumentalization to which they could be subject. Therefore, the council denied the Chinese secretariat the right "to open the boxes of written petitions" and demanded following an investigation in 1901 that dishonest or misleading petitioners be punished. A few days later the Italian commander demanded that the Chinese who submitted "false accusations" against his troops be punished. One year later the government published a notice that all anonymous petitions would be ignored.[49]

From this point onward the council took care to rationalize and improve the petition system by regularly controlling the procedure. At the beginning of March 1901, the members examined the petition registers and noticed that they were not up to date. The council ordered that they be updated daily and transmitted to all the services of the government, and that each petition be sent to the appropriate department. The Chinese secretary responded that his office was facing difficulties in treating them because of the number of daily arrivals in the offices. The council restated its instructions and requested that the follow-up to each petition be noted in the registers. The members regretted on a few occasions the lack of reactivity of the service heads, who didn't keep updated registers. On March 25 twenty-six petitions addressed to the public works office and six letters to the Department of Justice received no response, according to the service's register. Unable to get better results, on November 11 the council ordered the heads of the service to return all the petitions with a description of the actions taken, which would then be noted in the book of petitions by the head of the secretariat. This obligation was renewed regularly within the administration between the different services and posed a problem most notably with the disappearance of certain documents and numerous "irregularities." The council then obliged the Chinese secretariat to send the petitions to the various services and districts in certified registered envelopes.[50]

Despite the bureaucratic and political problems posed by treating a growing number of petitions, the system proved to be indispensable for the functioning of the government services and its legitimacy as an authority that protected the population. Chinese could send a petition to the government as long as they had someone able to write. As a result, the local Chinese notables seemed to control the contents of the requests. The government also received petitions from foreigners such as the lawyer Allen, whose tone was considered offensive enough that the letter was returned without commentary. Among the authors of the petitions, one finds a few women such as Hung, a concubine to Yang, who was opposed to a real estate transaction that she was being forced to pursue. The success of petitioning among the population was such that the Chinese secretary was forced to refuse to consider the petitions from villages outside the Provisional Government's jurisdiction and have them sent to officers in the Chinese administration. This is why, in spite of the many practical constraints and the opinion of the secretary of Chinese affairs Nishigori, who wanted to close the petition boxes on August 1, 1902, the council insisted the government receive them until August 12, three days before the retrocession of the city to Chinese authorities. The next day the Chinese secretariat was charged with informing the petitioner that henceforth they needed to address the "Chinese authorities."[51]

Reinventing Chinese administrative practices: Petitions and "worthy notables"

The foreign government therefore seemed to hand power over to the Chinese authorities without great difficulty. And for good reason: without saying a word about it in administrative documents and official proclamations, the foreign military and civil servants were inspired by an old Chinese tradition, the petition or reprimand addressed to the emperor. This Chinese political practice fascinated the Allies even more because it constituted a precedent to what was, in the collective "Western" imagination then and now, a European invention rooted in medieval English petitions and French *cahiers de doléances*. In fact, another foreign power present in Tianjin also had an ancient petitioning tradition. In Japan, as early as 646,

Emperor Kotoku ordered the installation of a petition box. This system reappeared in the sixteenth century, before being instituted in 1759 and definitively abandoned in 1873 by the Meiji government, which intended to centralize the administration.[52]

This Japanese procedure, which had only recently disappeared, grew out of a Chinese political tradition. A system of complaints and petitions appeared early in China, first informally during the Zhou dynasty and then progressively developing under the Han and the Sui dynasties until it was institutionalized for the first time under the Tang dynasty.[53] The procedure developed considerably over the course of these centuries.[54] Under the Jin dynasty, anyone could strike a drum set up for this purpose next to the office headquarters to express his discontent. In 436, under the Northern Wei dynasty, to remedy the obstruction and the corruption of administrative officials, the possibility of calling out an incompetent local administrator by sending a petition to superior authorities was established. The Empress Wu Zetian of the Tang dynasty installed the first petition box (*guihan*) in China in 686.[55] At first, the box's function was to collect information from spies and informers about the enemies of the imperial power, but it soon received many complaints and recommendations. After 756 the struggle against corruption and censorship meant it was forbidden to civil servants outside of those designated to do so to open the box and handle the petitions. In fact, the Provisional Government had adopted these ancient Chinese practices for its own purposes.

The system allowed the imperial power to gather a sense of public opinion, to limit critiques, and to prevent possible rebellion. But the effectiveness of this "institution of remonstrance" (*jian*) depended largely on the goodwill of the Chinese emperors, who were more or less enlightened.[56] Léon Vandermeersch argues that since it declined under the Mongols (the Yuan dynasty) because of a strengthening of the emperor's powers, this institution was not "democratic." In his view, the petition would appear to be more of an obligation than a right, in conformity with Confucian principles: "What the Prince does well, encourage; what he does poorly, reprimand."[57] There may nonetheless be something of an imperial model inherited from the Zhou and the Han that maintained proximity with the people and a privileged framework for interactions between the administrative elites and the population. This political culture resulted, according to Fang Qiang, from the "populist" ideal of the early Han, who reinforced the *minben* principle of the Zhou. The Confucian concept of the *minben*, in which the people were the foundation of the state, authorized and encouraged the exercise of the petition as a heavenly or natural right.[58] While this system did not in itself constitute a democratic regime, it did force one to revisit the paradigm of despotism often attributed to imperial China.

This system functioned thanks to the active participation of literary elites and rural notables, who filtered and relayed the population's requests. In each district the magistrate depended on the local elites to distribute and collect the tax as well as to maintain order.[59] Once again, without making it explicit, the Provisional Government reappropriated the indigenous administrative regime. The Chinese notables, named *shentung* in the archival documents, formed the body of intermediaries, who managed conflicts, collected taxes, planned district areas, recruited "indigenous police," and fought against the brigands and the Boxers. It was the *shendong*, the "local administrative elites," who took on an increasingly important role in nineteenth-century China:

> Everyone could identify these men—a small core of local leaders with power to mobilize their communities at large for any and all forms of social, political, or economic activity. Many gentry managers were degree holders, but this was not an absolute prerequisite for entry into this locally defined functional elite. Literacy and wealth seemed far more important. . . . Thus, our picture of local-level elite society in late Qing Jiangnan is that of domination by a small, self-contained group of prominent families, engaged not only in landownership and degree seeking but also in assuming a multitude of new local managerial roles.[60]

After the end of the Ming dynasty local notables began to take on these public responsibilities openly as they acquired increased social prestige even as they were distinct from the traditionally imposed tasks. They also played a role in education under the control of the magistrature.[61] The *shendong* captured the emergence of a "sphere of public activity" between the imperial state and "private" society in the second half of the nineteenth century.[62]

The Council of the Provisional Government decided, at the beginning of February 1901, to institutionalize the role of the *shendong* by organizing over the following two weeks in each village of the jurisdiction the election of three notables, who were "responsible for peace and order in the village."

These notables, who remain almost entirely absent from the Provisional Government archives, turned out to be omnipresent in daily life, as demonstrated by the reward procedure put in place in April 1902 by the foreign administration to thank the "worthy notables" in the context of returning the city to Chinese authorities. On this occasion, the head of the government police and the heads of all the districts needed to provide the council with a list of *shendong*, who were zealous government servants. The head of South Tientsin considered that only thirty-one *shendong* were worthy to receive payment from the council out of 395 notables in the district. The head of Chunliangcheng counted four notables in his circumscription, who merited a recompense while the head of the Tongku recommended nine.[63]

Once the definitive list of "worthy notables" was established at the end of June 1902, the council reflected extensively on how to properly compensate them. The Chinese secretariat needed to informally solicit the opinion of the Chinese authorities: Would they be in favor of a payment or awarding medals to the *shendong*? In his report, Nishigori stated that the Chinese administration did not object to awarding medals, but in his opinion the government should not give bonuses to notables, which might put collaborators in a difficult situation after the Tianjin handover. Under these conditions, the council was satisfied with giving the heads of the districts the responsibility of thanking the notables in their jurisdictions for "their faithful and precious service." The *shendong*, like some foreign civil servants, feared retribution after the Tianjin handover. In the district of Chunliangcheng, "the village of Wei Chia Mo Tou is in danger of being attacked by brigands after the dissolution of the government because of the services it has rendered to foreign authorities." To avoid this risk, the council asked French troops to protect the village and at the same time inform the Chinese authorities of the threat. From the opposite perspective, on August 11, 1902, a portion of the notables of the walled city invited members of the council to a grand dinner in the building of the guild of Shanxi to celebrate the handover of the city.[64]

An exemplary government? Corruption and the promotion of administrative ethics

The council demonstrated consistent interest in the probity, effectiveness, and impartiality of its agents. Violence and irregularities were constant following the taking of the city and its members were conscious of the necessity of establishing a series of regulations and duties to manage the administration and the conduct of its foreign and Chinese agents, notably in their relationships to the inhabitants. In this period of intense construction of the state apparatus, ethical conduct was necessary to instill confidence and secure the inhabitants' support. It needed to be legible and visible to the indigenous population through their public declarations as well as the sanctions inflicted upon the prevaricators and the thieves.

The Provisional Government presented itself as an exemplary administration in all areas (use of authority, battling corruption, procurements, public-private relations, conflicts of interest, contracts with itself, avoiding the peddling of influence). The council officially proclaimed that "all abuse of power on the part of the police agents will be severely punished." The duty of probity and attention to government agents constituted a counterpart to the inhabitants' duty of obedience as sworn police officers and civil servants, a list of which was officially published in each district. In addition, the council decided to combat corruption by prohibiting government officers and officials from receiving gifts of any kind from Chinese citizens. This indigenous practice was "severely discouraged" except for gifts in the form of fruit or flowers, which were tolerated. The foreigners nonetheless continued to benefit from the gifts by the population, and the council was forced to sanction any regulatory infractions. This practice was not—despite the council's insistence—the mere prerogative of the local Chinese population. For example, a rich French businessman, Philippot, who was heavily involved in the siege of the concessions, offered a rowboat and a tugboat to the Provisional Government, whose fleet was destroyed, hopeful of attaining in exchange one of the numerous government contracts. The secretary general responded that he could not accept the gift despite its great utility. Other reform proposals failed. For example, when the British General Creagh considered that the salaries of the members of the council and the employees of the Provisional Government were too high and requested a reduction, the council ignored his requests.[65]

The polyvalence of the professional activities and the blurring of boundaries between the public and the private led to numerous conflicts of interest. Indeed, a number of civil servants also had private activities, such as the government surveyor Noah Fields Drake, who designed the official map of Tianjin. The original belonged to the government, but lithographic copies were made and sold by Drake at a price that he determined. The head of the treasury, Carl Rump, directed at the same time the branch of the Deutsch-Asiatische Bank in Tianjin until November 1, 1901, after which he worked solely for the Provisional Government. This situation created conflicts of interest with his mission that the Provisional Government seemed willing to accept. When Rump chose a privileged partnership to complete financial operations, he naturally chose the Deutsch-Asiatische Bank, and the council said nothing. The same went for Lo, comprador of the Provisional Government, who also oversaw the Russian-Chinese Bank. Similarly, James Bromley Eames, the primary legal advisor to the government, worked at the same time as a private secretary to the British Colonel Bower, his protector, and as a lawyer to different Chinese clients (notably salt merchants) and foreigners (Herbert Hoover, for example). Conflicts of interest could be controlled through the transparency of information concerning professional activities of government agents. This polyvalence could at times be considered an advantage within certain negotiations, such as the somewhat surreal intervention after the fact of Eames, who pleaded the case of the Chinese Engineering and Mining Company. The company had hoped to obtain permission to buy a fort northwest of Taku from the council, which was supposed to defend its interests. A few weeks later the council agreed to allow Eames to represent both the Provisional Government and the Electric Traction Co. and to prepare a contract between the two clients. Finally, James B. Eames and his colleague, the lawyer Kent, were able to plea before the council, which was transformed into an appeals court for the occasion to defend the interests of the local Chinese bank Tung Tai Hao against four of its debtors. These practices were pursued despite government injunctions that demanded its agents consider themselves "above all civil servants to the Provisional government and that their duties were derived from this occupation over all others." The construction of a public service therefore took shape through a slow and unstable process.[66]

The government also attempted to limit conflicts of interest and set up legal limits to the acquisition of public contracts. After April 1901 the contracts needed to be granted to the best bidder with fifteen days' notice. The American Colonel Morris C. Foote intended to go further by proposing the same day that all contracts first be presented to the council and approved by a majority of its members, and above all that it ensure against any pursuit of illegal interest and thus contracts with themselves: "I further propose that there should be no contracts or purchases or sales, of any real importance, in connection with trading houses or companies, of which a member of the Council, or a department head of the Provisional Government, would be a member or have an interest." The council could only agree with the principle behind this measure, but it insisted on the difficulties of its execution. We will see to what extent the principal businessmen of Tianjin maintained close ties with the government. The council was satisfied with submitting all the bids to the treasury. In June 1902, in the context of tensions between the Allied powers, the treasury established public contracts without taking into consideration the contractor's nationality: "The Provisional Government will require that, when contracts are made, they will be awarded by public tender, and to the contractor, of whatever nationality, who will offer the most favorable terms."[67]

In the context of this policy for government reform, the foreigners never evoked the Chinese administrative model that, outside the meritocratic recruitment of civil servants through exam since the Qin dynasty (3rd century BCE), developed its own techniques of control and its own code of good conduct. For example, there was the principle of avoidance that forbade—since the Sui at the end of the sixth century—the nomination of a civil servant to a position in connection to one's region of origin. Under the Qing, anyone who had a familial connection (father, uncle, brother, grandparents, nephew, cousins, in-laws) could not serve as officers in the same local or provincial administration. Civil servants were regularly moved from one position to another. These different rules sought not only to fight against corruption but also to prevent civil servants from creating cliques within certain provinces or imperial administrations. While there is no trace of mutual references between these two administrative traditions in the sources, one is nonetheless struck by the structural similarities in their discourses and the bureaucratic reforms traditionally produced by the Chinese elites and, under the Provisional Government, by the foreign civil servants.

Such a policy supporting the local Chinese population was no doubt the product of "indigenophilia" that took root in the colonies at the beginning of the twentieth century, following the declaration of Queen Wilhelmina who, in 1901, demanded that the Netherlands ethically recognize the well-being of the colonized population in the Dutch Indies. In France it was necessary to wait until the 1930s for the École Coloniale to offer courses on administrative ethics entitled "Duties of the Colonial Administrator."[68] We will see in the following chapters that the representatives of the foreign powers rivaled each other's initiatives to stage the benevolent and civilizing nature of their international power, not hesitating to experiment with new techniques of social engineering.

This unprecedented form of international governance was distinct in its dual mission, which was both civil and military. The government was clearly military to the extent that it was represented by soldiers from the ground all the way up to the "International Military Commission," which was the council. Hence, the Colonel Arlabosse celebrated his colleagues on the council, explaining that these officers "were animated by a common spirit of military duty, both vast and impartial" and that they constituted the military foundation of what he considered a political success. "I affirm that it is our qualities as soldiers, our common origins, that have facilitated the task at hand."[69] The council hardly held infinite power: the conflicts within the Provisional Government were decided by the Allied commanders in accord with the Consular Corps.[70] The civilians were in large part new to the administrative services that employed the best experts in Chinese affairs (engineers, diplomats, pedagogues, businessmen, doctors, and so forth). This cohabitation was not always without conflict, as demonstrated by the foreign soldiers, who refused to salute employees, betraying their apparent disrespect for the civil servants in the Provisional Government's headquarters. The council considered that it was impossible "to order the soldiers to salute individuals in civilian dress."[71]

However, despite the appearance of being an absolute novelty, this international government was in many ways quite Chinese. The Allies relied on local elites, the *shendong*, who probably suffered much less from foreign occupation than from the domination of the Boxers. The Provisional Government brought together civilians and military just as the viceroy's headquarters had done and continued the formalities of the administration of the viceroy of Zhili (his own name, palace, flag, seal, and so on). It recruited Li Hongzhang's former advisors, who became the main architects of the reforms of the Provisional Government. It sought the consent of the indigenous population and based its legitimacy on Chinese political practices: the use of Chinese notables and the petition system. This practice was then updated in the form of *xinfang* by the Chinese Communists in the 1930s and then officially by the Maoist regime from 1951 onward.[72]

Figure 3.1 Japanese soldiers accompanying a Chinese prisoner in Tianjin in 1900. "Boxer Rebellion 1900: Military Operations in and Around Peking," National Archives, CO 1069/422, "China 2."

CHAPTER III

"Bringing Order to Chaos"

Police Practices, Legal Repression, and Social Protection

One sees uniforms everywhere; national gendarmes and London police officers direct the traffic of rickshaws and keep them in line: I am tempted to show my pass and cut the line to the braided agents who assist these cosmopolitan police. Not to mention that we are in the middle of the capital where there are civilians with hats and, a startling phenomenon, white women walking with combed and flowery hairstyles like one would see in our shop windows; General Linevitch's car is decorated with beige skirts, circulating around and around to complete this image of Europe. Amidst so many splendors China is forgotten.

—*LIBERTÉ*, FEBRUARY 20, 1902

The entire city has been invaded and taken over by soldiers from all the civilized nations. Everywhere reigns the most complete disorder and waste . . . and troops continue to arrive! There are already 100,000 . . .

—JEAN JADOT, SEPTEMBER 24, 1900

The Chinese realize that the officers are there on their behalf; they cowardly follow us, denounce our jokes, and manifest hostility against us. . . . We would have avenged ourselves, if the length of the day and the clarity of the night had not prevented us from upsetting the indigenous city as we did in winter. Around this time, edicts of pacification were published, and caravans, accompanied by bizarre fanfares, brought gifts to General Voyron and the French Consul, who accepted them. This complacency towards the chiefs and the hostility towards the soldiers irritated us and our bad mood could be seen in our performance.

—JACQUES GRANDIN, 1902

The Boxer War did not come to an end on August 15, 1900, with the taking of Beijing.[1] Chinese resistance continued in the form of a guerrilla war in the countryside of Zhili Province between the capital and Tianjin. After being subdued by Chinese authorities, a time of pacification came for the Allied powers. As in the wars of colonization, the appropriation of the territory under the Provisional Government's jurisdiction was achieved through the brutal subjugation of the indigenous population. If one believes the Allied powers' account, they successfully introduced a police force and rule of law in China during this time. Indeed, since the end of the nineteenth century and until very recently, researchers have described the Chinese Empire as being under the control of local customs and not under the rule of law, which was proper to the West.[2] As Jérôme Bourgon has suggested, there reigned "a tenacious skepticism among sinologists and comparativists regarding the aptitude of the Chinese to produce rational norms distinct from ritualism."[3] Without jurists or juridical science, Chinese society was supposedly governed by disciplinary and bureaucratic regimes.[4] Pierre-Étienne Will, to the contrary, has demonstrated the deep tradition of rationalization within the Mandarin administration and Jérôme Bourgon has set out with others to reveal the wealth and diversity of forms of right and Chinese juridical practice.[5] The intrusion of foreign powers and the creation of concessions did not introduce an unprecedented juridical complexity: as a multiethnic empire, China possessed its own ancient tradition of juridical pluralism.[6] In the districts of the Chinese empire, justice was delivered within some 1650 local courts by magistrates who performed at the same time economic, administrative, and religious functions.[7] From a Eurocentric perspective, we could say that a separation of powers did not exist in China. Since the third century BCE, each dynasty promulgated a new code of laws until the publication of the Qing Code in 1740. These texts provided punishments for every sort of crime imaginable based on the social status of the accused.[8] At the same time, most of the trials did not take place in tribunals but were resolved by heads of family, the clan, the village, or the guild that judged according to diverse customs and moral principles.[9] In Confucian culture, recourse to state justice was a necessary evil or a last resort.[10]

An indigenous society without police or rule of law? Vernacular modes of social regulation and the invention of a new public order

Until the beginning of the twentieth century on the other hand, there was no police force as such, in the sense of civilian or military forces that maintain public order. Indeed, there was no distinction between the use of force against foreign aggressors and the repression of the emperor's subjects. The role of the police was generally taken on informally by the head of the family, and by extension, the representatives of the clan and the community that formed the units of economic production and social control. Hence, in Tianjin, the government controlled the population through the *baojia*, a system of surveillance and mutual responsibility that depended on the actions of the members of each community and the agents charged with this function.[11] The wealthy salt merchants recruited "honorable" brigands, *hunhunr*, who controlled the city streets.[12] This system for maintaining public order was critiqued extensively throughout the nineteenth century because of the growth of corruption that impacted its agents.[13] In this area as well, the Sino-Japanese War generated a new awareness and an initial one-time experiment was attempted in Changsha (Hunan) in June 1897 by Huang Junxian, the provincial minister of justice, and in Beijing in 1901.[14] Yuan Shikai introduced modern police for the first time into China in Baoding, the capital of Zhili Province next to Tianjin, in May 1902 and then adopted the first system of police patrols in Tianjin a few months later.[15] In this official history of the police recounted since the pioneering works of Stephen MacKinnon, researchers have ignored the Provisional Government's experiments with policing.[16]

The Provisional Government established as early as the summer of 1900 an "international police force" and a "Chinese police force" that was to "reestablish order and security" in the city and its jurisdictions.[17] Usage of the term *police* in the minds of the superior officers of the council must have suggested the benevolent character of the foreign forces whose constant mission was to protect the civil population and, in so doing, to confirm the Allied powers' official line that the Boxer War was simply a Chinese conflict. For the first time in the history of China, a city was controlled by specifically designated police officers, who were distributed across the eight police districts of the territory under the jurisdiction of the Provisional Government. At the same time, the Provisional Government established a new judicial system under the council that acted at once as a court of appeals and the sole legislator: "the minutes of the Council were always considered to have been debated and to have force of law."[18] The Allies attempted to respond to the challenges of "pacification"—end the war and effectively manage the territory—by relying on a powerful police corps and repressive justice while also developing social control over the population. This is how the Provisional Government attempted to ensure the submission and solicit the consent, if not the support, of the indigenous population.

The war continues: New and old problems of public security

The day after taking the city, the sources of insecurity were numerous and at times unexpected. Not only did the war continue for months in Zhili, but other troubles threatened the new order that the Provisional Government attempted to put in place. During this period of great confusion not all the brigands were Chinese, and the general uncertainty favored the multiplications and usurpations of identity as well as the use of counterfeits that destabilized the international authorities.

Boxers or brigands, war or disorder?

After the Boxers' retreat from the city, violence continued in the eastern part of the city and in the rest of the jurisdiction. The council attempted to calm the disorder, which by its very "nature gave the Provisional Government a bad reputation." The state of war continued despite the idealist propaganda of the Allies. The military operations continued throughout the city with attempts to fire artillery—notably from Taku Road above the German concession—regularly interrupting people's daily lives. Pierre Loti was surprised during his trip to Tianjin in October 1900 that the government agents, including police inspectors and Allied officers were necessarily accompanied by at least three foreign soldiers during patrols or missions in their jurisdictions.[19]

In August the police stopped and decapitated numerous Chinese, who were assumed to be Boxers based on testimonies of the inhabitants and foreign soldiers. Nonetheless, after September the term "Boxers" tended to disappear from military discourse in favor of "brigands" and "thieves." This new lexicon confirmed the absence of a state of war in the province and justified the creation of a simple police force. Only the missionaries, such as G. W. Verity, continued to use this terminology. Verity continued to observe the Boxers' movements in the southwest of the jurisdiction as did the regular Chinese police forces engaged in the district of Tsang-chou Chien during the Boxer repression, like General Mei. To put down the groups of Boxers on the margins of the jurisdiction, the council depended on the army of the Qing state, which also used the opportunity to reassert their authority. At the end of 1900 the "bandits" moved out to the territory surrounding Tianjin, and "pirates" infested the Hai River. At the same time, during the months that followed the taking of the city, the line between Boxerism and banditism was fluid. For example, a brigand named "Hot Iron" (*Re Tie*), lived in the west of the walled city and joined the Boxers for a few weeks before abandoning his red scarf and becoming a bandit again after the fall of Tianjin.[20]

The government attempted to respond to these "organized gangs" by disarming the Chinese population. As early as its first meeting on July 30, 1900, the council ordered the Chinese within the walled city to bring their weapons to the police headquarters nearest to them within three days. From that point on, anyone in possession of guns was "severely punished." Since these measures proved ineffective, the government demanded a few weeks later that inhabitants of the jurisdiction give up all "guns, pistols, knives, bayonets, swords, and munitions" in their possession within five days, under penalty of decapitation. In addition, it seized all the houses where weapons were found. A few weeks later, the government forbid the sale and use of firecrackers widely enjoyed by the Chinese. Thousands of weapons were destroyed to limit their circulation in the region and the metal was auctioned off for the benefit of the Provisional Government. Only regular Chinese soldiers escaped these highly restrictive regulations: their weapons, confiscated during their stay in the territory under the jurisdiction of the Provisional Government, could be recovered when they left.[21]

Dangerous foreigners: Soldiers, deserters, and adventurers

With the sacking and massacre of a portion of the inhabitants, Tianjin became a "Far East" city where all foreigners carried a weapon to "protect" themselves from the "Boxers" and "bandits." A variety of weapons circulated among the soldiers, the United States being reputed to be the most liberal purveyor, according to one French soldier: "We spent some time with the American soldiers, they were 'troublemakers' who ignored all discipline, drank to excess and sold their weapons to drink more. With our small savings, we bought their revolvers from them for two piastres, which were admirable weapons."[22] The military entertained themselves by eradicating the stray dogs that the council, from its first meeting, decided to remove by any means necessary. The soldiers, motivated by the reward offered for each "dead" canine, engaged in a veritable intraurban hunt during which a Chinese woman was killed by an American soldier. The council reacted by prohibiting the practice, arguing that it represented a "danger to public safety." Faced with growing disorder, the government prohibited foreign soldiers from entering the Chinese city without specific orders. But when the chief of police asked the council to forbid foreign soldiers from carrying their weapons off duty, the council opposed the proposal, which contravened the customs of certain armies. Instead, he merely denied guns and ammunition to Zhili missionaries who organized their defense. After two long weeks of intense looting, the time had come for the council to establish a semblance of legality by investigating the damage done by foreign soldiers at Chinese expense. This first official recognition of the problem was the direct result of a letter sent by the commander of the American troops demanding information on the July events. A long and complex judicial process then began, at the end of which a few people were poorly compensated. The international police force tried to impose its monopoly of coercion on the local population by forbidding foreign soldiers to search for Chinese in the streets and at the gates, starting on August 8, 1900. From then on, only the police had a right to control them.

Three weeks later, the council forbid the allied troops from requisitioning horses, mules, and wagons, "since business was returning to normal in the city."[23] But the violence and crimes perpetrated by the Allied soldiers continued in Tianjin and the neighboring villages, regularly rekindling the horrific scenes of the July 1900 massacre. Some French soldiers even boasted of their life of looting, rape, and gratuitous violence:

> One did not grow soft over there. They were looking for money, not for emotions. So they went straight at the Chinese: "You want to die, my good man, well take this! And *bam* a bullet and the individual, still smiling, fell in a corner of the hovel. Everything was turned upside down and searched through, and one never found anything anyway; if these people had money, they hid it well. I tend to believe they did not have any; the mandarins had already taken it all. I was told that the Chinese dislike death by bayonet: it seems that their good

god does not receive them in his Paradise when they bring him their torn skin. I was told that over there, and I didn't bother to check if it was true. In the scenes of looting and burning, I noticed yet another sign of courage concerning the women. We had started a fire in a corner of a village, from which bullets and even arrows had been shot; some of the houses were set on fire, we searched the others. In a hut, some comrades and I were lucky enough to get our hands on a beautiful young girl. We tried to molest her, but the mother tore her away from our brutalities, dragged her towards the end of the village, which was burning, and threw herself into the flames with her. They were savages, every population we visited were savages and became more and more so the closer we went toward the Great Wall.[24]

The soldier's stunningly cold account of the events also reveals a curiosity about those they encountered, a sense of observation, a form of recognition of the virtues of the enemy, combined with an objectification of the Chinese, which was no doubt due to the contemporary state of mind. For the soldier Jacques Grandin, the "savages" were the others, the Chinese civilians and then the Russians and the Germans, who managed to be even more feared by the local population than the French: "The Germans brutalized them even more than we did, and the Russians, not content with merely mistreating them, cut off their ears."[25] The Cossacks, whose offences also included numerous rapes, were the subject of several detailed reports written by the Provisional Government's chief of police. The international police even arrested two Russian soldiers and handed them over to the Russian chief of staff, Admiral Alexeieff, who, under pressure from other commanders, ordered an investigation before imprisoning them. Other complaints of violence and insults were lodged against the Russian soldiers in the weeks that followed, but without further investigation. The Russians certainly were not the only ones to commit grave abuses. Indian soldiers of the British army were regularly incriminated by petitions denouncing their "bad conduct" in the vicinity of Tianjin, in the district of North Tientsin, in Siku, Yangcun, and Wang Chia Kou. Despite reminders from the British staff, petitions against the Indians continued to pour in until early 1902. Complaints against French soldiers were also common, especially in the North Tientsin district, but they amounted to nothing. Thus, when villagers in Hankou sent a petition to the Provisional Government to complain about the criminal behavior of French soldiers, the investigation conducted by Japanese Captain Satō concluded that the accusations were probably false and "had no other reason to exist than the fear they [the villagers] felt when they saw them [the French soldiers]." And when the offences were proven to be true, the military hierarchy took care not to punish those responsible. On April 1, 1901, in response to the numerous assaults committed by French soldiers in the Chinese city, the chief of police merely confined the troops after 6:00 p.m. The Japanese soldiers, who enjoyed a better reputation among the local population, were also the subject of some complaints. When the Council of the Provisional Government received a report from the chief of South Tientsin with complaints from several villages about the Japanese troops, he stated bluntly "that he attached little importance to this report, which was based solely on the testimony of Chinese witnesses." When Italian soldiers were accused of looting the village of Lu-Chuang-Tsze, killing a man and wounding a woman in their home for no apparent reason, the matter was handed over from the chief of police to the commander of the Italian troops without any action being taken. Petitions accused the German soldiers of regularly attacking villages, ransacking Chinese graves, and offending the population. But, as always, the Allied commanders had the last word, despite the Provisional Government's desire to render justice to its citizens: when the notables of Siao Liu Chuang reproached the German soldiers for having burned down their village, General von Lessel considered the accusations unfounded and "unsupported by any evidence." The Chinese almost never won their case through petitions against the soldiers. As a result, some villagers adopted other less peaceful forms of resistance. Thus, as early as October 1900 German soldiers were regularly attacked by villagers, and foreign troops fell under fire from houses in the villages. At the end of 1901 the military authorities tried to control and curb the violence of the soldiers by lecturing them and repressing actions taken against the local population: "Discipline was severely imposed upon us. One day, we were told that the Chinese were men like any other and that it was forbidden to mistreat them, to plunder them, etc. We had probably gone too far. Some senior officers were then ostensibly less harsh on the natives than on their soldiers."[26] According to Jacques Grandin, at the end of 1901, every week, about thirty French soldiers were sent to the war council, which punished those who had committed the crimes, some of whom were controlled through a disciplinary brigade organized at Yangcun.

Contrary to appearances, and to what the many accounts suggest, not all foreign soldiers harbored hatred toward a dehumanized Chinese population. Many troops, probably a few hundred, left their posts after the Allied victory to join the Qing camp or simply to settle incognito in Chinese villages. This fact no doubt explains one of the great mysteries contained within the minutes of the Council of the Provisional Government, which attests almost every week to the disappearance of foreign—most notably French, German, and British—soldiers. The Provisional Government issued search warrants which carefully avoided the term "deserter:" "The *Lagerkommandant* Hoffmann of the German troops reports that a German soldier has been missing since October 18, 1900, and requests the assistance of the local police to find him."[27] This relatively common practice suggests the development of actual networks of desertion, as witnessed by Japanese merchants who provided civilian clothing to British soldiers in the summer of 1901. Chinese interpreters were other intermediaries who incited and facilitated desertion on behalf of the Qing government from May 1901 onward. To do so, these recruiting agents skillfully identified the soldiers, who had been most subject to punishment, to encourage them to desert and join the regular Chinese army: "They came to the barracks gate, waited for the men, took them for a walk, provided them with money, and bought them drinks. About 80 soldiers in a few months ran away from the garrison with their rifles, cartridges, and bags."[28] Others fled to Chinese villages, like seven who took refuge in a hamlet south of Baoding, where they lived like locals. When the French military authorities located the deserters, they formed a patrol made up of their former comrades to avoid a bloodbath and facilitate negotiations. The fugitives were thus allowed to return to their unit without being punished, while the leader was brought before the council of war and sentenced to two years in prison. Some foreigners, having become officers in the Qing army, ended up returning to their former garrison in Tianjin because they were unaccustomed to "native life." The military authorities were again lenient with their valuable troops. Only those soldiers considered to have become irreversibly Chinese were severely punished, such as the infantrymen who had become "Chinese traders," wearing robes and braids, and who were immediately arrested and imprisoned. Deserters could also pose a direct threat to both the Allied powers and the Qing army. International armed gangs made up of foreign veterans tore through Zhili Province outside the Provisional Government's jurisdiction, such as the "deserters of different nationalities committing depredations between Peking and Tianjin," who forced the German soldiers to withdraw and the British cavalry to intervene.[29]

Like these deserters, many foreigners tried their luck at illegal enterprises. While the Boxers gradually disappeared from the scene, sources suggest that these foreign brigands from all over the world soon became omnipresent. The former magistrate of Ching hsien complained of two "American soldiers" accompanied by three Chinese who claimed to be sent by the Provisional Government and tried to extort money by "intimidating" the population.[30] The council sent a detachment of U.S. soldiers to apprehend the suspects, who fled south without their nationality being verified. Almost every week Chinese coolies were robbed of their daily pay by "freebooters of all nationalities."[31] Four Americans, accompanied by five Chinese, robbed the villagers of Ching Hai hsien. U.S. Colonel Foote ordered their arrest with the help of the village elders. A well-organized band of "Japanese pirates" and their flotilla of flagless junks operated on the Hai River during the summer of 1900 before being arrested, modestly described by the chief of police as "Japanese coolies." These brigands did not disappear, however, as evidenced by attacks on ships, particularly customs ships, in early 1901. A few weeks later, a case of arms trafficking—cane swords with concealed blades that were all the rage during the prohibition period—organized by Japanese subjects appeared in the local news.[32]

These foreign brigands were mainly involved in arms trafficking, such as the Frenchman Heliès de Kerangar, who tried to bribe prison guards in the Chinese city to obtain arms, or a British man named Woods who tried to bribe the chief guard to get three thousand Springfield rifles. Honest Tianjin trading houses were also involved in arms trafficking, such as Walte & Co., a German company that illegally supplied a gun repair store in the village of Shang Kou Tsung, South Tientsin District, with "broken weapons" (gun parts)—from the Siku arsenal—theoretically destroyed on behalf of the German troops.[33]

Europeans were accused of having been the Boxers' accomplices. A certain Macdonald, son of a hotel owner in Tianjin, was accused by Wang Teng-chen and Chou Chun-yen, Chinese Christians from the village of Ching Hai hsien, of having been bribed by the Boxers in exchange for 3,000 taels to participate in the persecution of Christians during the summer of 1900. His nationality—British or Chinese—being uncertain,

Macdonald was arrested before being brought to justice.[34] A similar problem of identification arose when St. Clair Damon was arrested in October 1901 for having fired a revolver on Taku Road while intoxicated. The prisoner claimed to be an American citizen, but the U.S. consul did not recognize him as such. The police chief proposed "deportation," but the council preferred to ask all consuls in Tianjin if he was one of their nationals. The consuls of the United States, Great Britain, France, Italy, the Netherlands, Russia, Belgium, Germany, and Japan declared that St. Clair Damon was not under their jurisdiction. Finally he declared that he was Danish and therefore under the jurisdiction of the Russian consul protecting the citizens of Denmark. Faced with the skepticism of the Russian diplomat, the council removed the stateless man by financing his transfer to Shanghai on condition that he not return to Tianjin. The city attracted numerous adventurers such as Victor Pain, a French citizen who came from Nagasaki after a stay in Cochinchina. In September 1901 he was hired as a "works manager" by the Provisional Government, which dismissed him soon after. Pain then went to Beijing. His troubles with the gendarmerie prompted the French minister in China to have him sent to Saigon at the expense of the French consul in Tianjin. The latter refused to take charge of his passage after learning through a letter from the attorney general of the republic in Saigon that he had been arrested in the city for attempted murder under the name of Félix Gachet: "with these few pieces of information your Excellency will understand that I had no desire to attract Victor Pain to Tientsin where the presence of too many individuals of this kind, already causes me enough difficulties."[35]

To the brigands, who were nationals of the Allied powers, were added the "indigenous" adventurers of the colonies. Two armed Indians associated with the Chinese, claiming to serve the Provisional Government, persecuted villagers near the Machang Dam in August. Other Indian civilians of "corrupt morals," who were active in the underworld, were condemned to be "deported" before escaping from prison. A man named Rosario, a "native of the Philippines," was sent back to Shanghai by the chief of police for having raped several prostitutes, raising concern within the government's health department. The U.S. consul refused to pay for the "deportation" of this "American subject of the Philippines," and it was once again up to the Provisional Government to handle his deportation. A few hundred Koreans resided in Tianjin, some of whom made a living from various trafficking activities. The international police regularly repatriated "dishonorable" nationals and adventurers "without the means to support themselves" to Korea: fifteen Koreans were expelled three times from July through August 1901 alone.[36]

While the government easily rid itself of Asians with a "bad reputation," it had difficulty sending away Western and Japanese adventurers. When the chief of police decided to tackle the problems of "foreign adventurers found traveling with arms within the jurisdiction of the Provisional Government" in the summer of 1901 and demanded that they be arrested and "removed by sea" from Tianjin, the consular corps, represented by the British, retorted that this proposal presented so many legal difficulties that it was impossible to agree to it. This failure of the policy of controlling "Western" foreigners partly explains the criminality and insecurity that prevailed until the dissolution of the Provisional Government: a "gang of foreign thieves" associated with the Chinese was still rampant in the region of Hsin Hai hsien during the summer of 1902.[37]

These foreign adventurers could deftly play the role of intermediaries between the local population and the Provisional Government. Thus, the Japanese convinced the Wang Chia Kou notables to hire them as "agents" to officially represent the village's interests to the Allies. For lack of resources and for greater efficiency, the government subcontracted repression to village militias, including the one in Wang Chia Kou, where, during one of the clashes, the inhabitants killed a Boxer and seized 4,100 taels from him, which they sent to the Provisional Government as a sign of "goodwill." The Japanese agents demanded that 1,000 taels extorted by agents of the Methodist mission be returned to the villagers and asked for details on the use of the 4,100 taels sent to the council. The council replied curtly that it did not recognize any foreign agents representing the villages and that it did not have to justify the use of its subsidies. The government inquired about the identity of these "agents" and passed them on to the Japanese consul, but in the end it could not prevent them from selling their services to the Chinese villagers.[38]

Local demands and international protection

The Provisional Government claimed to exercise legitimate power rooted in the rule of law, fundamental principles of justice, and, in practice, the consideration of petitions submitted by the population. The Allies repeatedly proclaimed that the inhabitants could bring complaints and disputes to the Provisional Government, which would "give them help and protection in all circumstances, and to which they owed strict obedience in return."[39]

In this particularly violent and troubled period, some notables and villagers quickly understood the advantage of asking the government to protect their villages from the Boxers, Chinese brigands, deserters, foreign thieves, and looting by Allied soldiers. Protection was a major issue in the rivalries between the different powers that coexisted in Zhili Province (that is, the Provisional Government, the Qing army, and Chinese brigands). Armed Chinese extorted money in the villages "under the pretext of protection," such as two men named Hsieh and Liang denounced by the missionary J. A. Slimmon of the London Missionary Society. Some inhabitants turned to those they considered responsible for their situation, like the regular Chinese army or two Chinese whose family had been murdered and whose house was pillaged by Boxers south of Tsang Chou. They sent a petition to the Provisional Government in the hopes it would write to General Mei on their behalf to expose their grievances and obtain reparations. In such a delicate matter, the Provisional Government asked them to contact the Chinese authorities directly. For their part, the Chinese generals wished to lead the repression of the Boxers and Chinese brigands themselves in certain villages bordering on the jurisdiction of the Provisional Government. General Mei also wished to compensate the Chinese missionaries and Christians residing there. The council agreed to this request and endorsed a strategy of reoccupation by Chinese troops of certain villages near the border of the jurisdiction.[40]

Numerous petitions from villages outside its jurisdiction requested the Provisional Government's protection as early as August 1900, and the Provisional Government used these petitions to support its request to the Allied commanders to extend its territory. Villages outside the jurisdiction proclaimed themselves members of the North Tientsin district to benefit from government protection. Villages in the neighboring districts sent petitions to the council during the two years of the Provisional Government's rule. The Provisional Government was tempted to intervene each time but was forced to entrust these investigations to Chinese magistrates or to the commanders of the allied forces, who were responsible for policing outside its territory. In some cases, the village communities adopted even more refined strategies of attaching themselves to a district whose administration was considered more benevolent: for example, the village of Yang Chia Chuang submitted a petition to be transferred from the district of Chunliangcheng to one of the police districts of the Chinese city.[41]

While some Chinese preferred to escape foreign jurisdiction, such as Fu Yung Ho, who claimed to have been arrested by international police outside the territory of the Provisional Government, many village elders near the "French Pond" sought government protection against thieves. Other village communities were even more enterprising, such as Shih Ko Chuang, northwest of Tianjin, who asked the government's secretary general for permission to hire two "Indians" to reinforce the "local police." The council feared creating a precedent that would be costly in terms of men and so refused to comply with this request. The council then confirmed its decision to withdraw its soldiers while assuring them that it would send frequent patrols to the village. Sometimes the activism of village notables proved more effective: the villagers of Pan Kou, in the district of Chunliangcheng, who repeatedly asked the French soldiers to open a post next to their village, won their case. Similarly, the great merchants of Tianjin mobilized so that the government would employ "armed native boats and cavalry to suppress the brigands." The council took it upon itself to protect the Chinese merchants beyond its jurisdiction by asking the Chinese magistrates of the neighboring districts to guarantee the safety of the city's merchants.[42]

At the end of August 1900 the Provisional Government decided to defend the Chinese coolies who were being bullied and abused by their foreign employers. It was a question not only of ensuring respect for the fundamental rights of these workers, who, in the words of the council, should not be "forced against their will," but also of guaranteeing the proper functioning of the labor market. To do this, the council offered to provide the necessary labor to the major employers—the Allied armies. The representatives of the commanders informed the chief of police each day at noon how many coolies they wanted to have the next day and where the government should transport them. Henceforth, the coolies did not hesitate to address the government representatives in case of violence or dispute, like the eight laborers who, carrying water every day to the British guards at the western gate of the city, complained they had not been paid. The government was declared in the right by the British military authorities. Foreign soldiers frequently assaulted and robbed the coolies, especially in Ma Chia Kou. The council ordered the establishment of a twenty-man police station in which "as far as possible each nationality was represented" to protect the "indigenous" workers. These policemen also patrolled every day from 5:00 p.m. to midnight for "the protection of passers-by." The multinational character of the police force was a response to the need to control, and even apprehend, the soldiers of the various international powers present in Tianjin.[43]

In the end, the Allies, voluntarily or not, justified the creation and maintenance of this new protection system by the insecurity generated by their own troops or former soldiers. In response, the village communities, for their part, sometimes had an astonishing capacity for action: petitions, self-protection, requests for foreign soldiers, and so on. The new social order established by the Provisional Government could be challenged by other, more subversive forms of accommodation to foreign domination.

The reign of forgery, or the appropriation of power by local populations: Identity, offices, and money

In this period of uncertainty and confusion, when the government was trying to establish its authority and build its legitimacy, many Chinese as well as foreigners transgressed "social and professional boundaries" to acquire positions and the power associated with them.[44] Political crises encouraged the appropriation of the symbols of the Provisional Government (letterhead, mandates, flags, business cards, uniforms, and so on), which constituted a source of power or protection.

In parallel to the European deserters, who dressed in Chinese clothes, some Chinese wore military uniforms to pass for foreigners. Thus, three of them, one of them armed and disguised as a foreign soldier, with a paper presented as a "warrant from the Provisional Government to arrest Boxers," extorted money from the villagers in October 1900. They were arrested in early November 1900, imprisoned as numbers 455, 456, and 457, and beheaded. It turns out that these brigands had been officially working for the U.S. military authorities and that the alleged government warrant was a paper signed by Lieutenant Coleman authorizing them to buy livestock for U.S. troops. This was not an isolated case. The Chinese criminals understood the profit to be made from the political shift in Tianjin. Thus, General Mei arrested three Chinese who "claimed to have been granted authority from the Provisional Government to arrest the Boxers, and who presented a paper as proof of this authority." When the general cooperatively offered to hand over these usurpers to the Provisional Government, the Allied officers authorized him to "do with them as he pleased." Several Chinese Christians claimed to be acting on behalf of the Provisional Government to collect monetary compensation for the damage caused by the Boxers, especially to missionary properties. Again, these were often Chinese who interacted with foreigners, in this case missionaries of the American Methodist Mission who had sent agents to the villages to demand compensation. Similarly, several Chinese interpreters, claiming to represent the Provisional Government or the military authorities, took advantage of their position as indispensable intermediaries between the natives and the Allies to extort money from villagers. Following numerous reports on this subject, the council declared these "requests for money made in the name of the Provisional Government" to be fraudulent and invited the citizens to denounce the perpetrators.[45]

These usurpations produced a multiplication of counterfeit papers, false signatures, and the manufacture of forged seals. A certain Lui Huan Chang, from the village of Wu Ching hsien, made "forged letters and proclamations," presented as official acts of the Provisional Government. Chinese people sold "counterfeit certificates" to the villagers to ensure their protection. In addition, forgeries of the seal of the Provisional Government circulated in the jurisdiction to the point that, only ten months after the establishment of the new power, the council decided to fight against them by adopting a new "method of engraving." Faced with the difficulty of accomplishing this task in Tianjin, the head of the secretariat first commissioned the contractor Kelly & Walsh to order relief seals from Tokyo for all the Provisional Government's departments and districts. Without any news of this directive, the council ordered steel seals in relief from Great Britain, which finally made it possible to distinguish authentic acts from forgeries. This practice was not limited to criminals, as shown by the case that agitated the financial world of Tianjin in June 1902. Chinese banks used the signature of the German company Carlovitz & Co. on petitions addressed to the authorities, without the knowledge of its managers. On the river, local boatmen and bargemen flew foreign flags without the authorization of the military authorities. Faced with this multiplication of flags on the Hai River, the chief of the "river police" finally prohibited this practice at the end of September 1901: only junks whose captain had a consular or military certificate were authorized to fly the flag of their nationality or of the Provisional Government. These practices of usurpation continued until the government's dissolution. Thus, during the night of July 14–15, 1902, a band of heavily armed Chinese thieves, pursued by the international police, took refuge in the houses adjoining the palace of Li Hongzhang. They were arrested there in possession of business cards that presented them as employees of the Provisional Government's headquarters.[46]

Counterfeit currency was of great concern to the Provisional Government. Faced with an influx of forged Chinese currency, the government proclaimed a ban on counterfeiting at the end of December 1900. The skill and imagination of counterfeiters were not limited to Chinese money, since they also manufactured foreign currencies such as Japanese banknotes, which then circulated in northern China. Colonel Akiyama, commander of the Japanese troops, obtained the prohibition of these banknotes from the council, apparently without much effect. A few months later the British consul general complained about the massive circulation of counterfeit dollars. The government seemed to identify the source of these "counterfeit dollars" south of the city, in the Tongku district, but since it was unable to stop them, it had to be satisfied with informing customs authorities in Canton and Shanghai.[47]

The production and trafficking of counterfeit money sometimes circulated thanks to cosmopolitan networks: the American Walter B. Tuttle played a decisive role in the aftermath of the capture of the city. The "counterfeiters" were able to benefit from unexpected institutional support of rival authorities within the Provisional Government. Thus, the chief of police noted that one of the main sources of the monetary influx came from the French concession, whose consul received a monthly license of one hundred dollars from the manufacturers. The chief of police identified the names of seven Chinese counterfeiters and apprehended them according to standard procedure: the council had to present an arrest warrant to the consul of the concession. However, Henri Leduc, the French consul who succeeded Gustave du Chaylard in 1902, chose to protect these craftsmen to whom he had provided licenses. He obtained the support of the French ambassador to Beijing for this protection. Leduc informed the council that the mandate issued by the Provisional Government was not valid. The council replied that "the minting of money by private individuals is illegal." In the face of such resolve, but nonetheless sure of himself, the consul invoked the custom of the French concession, where his predecessor had authorized the minting of coins "for the general good." The council deferred to the Allied commanders-in-chief to settle the dispute, recalling that the Provisional Government had always forbidden the minting of money, that its police force was fighting against any such practice by the Chinese and foreign brigands, and that it could not tolerate a foreign concession legally authorizing this practice, which was the reserve of recognized states. Field Marshal von Waldersee then asked the French minister to stop minting money in the French concession: the French legation forced the consul to comply.[48]

Counterfeit money flooded the markets of Tianjin. The international police struggled to dismantle the sites of production in the jurisdiction, let alone in the villages beyond its borders where counterfeiters set up shop to escape the control of the international police. The North Tientsin district chief succeeded in arresting eleven counterfeiters in the village of Sun Chia Chuang, as well as a police officer, who was clearly complicit in obstructing the investigation. The council also imposed a collective fine of $700 on the village. The district chiefs apprehended more and more Chinese in possession of counterfeit money. As a result, the chief of police proposed to the council that individuals carrying counterfeit money should no longer be arrested: the government "decided to take no further action on this matter, and to let the merchants protect themselves." Following discussions between the government treasurer and representatives of Chinese banks to improve the fight against the circulation of counterfeit money, in March 1902 the government banned the public sale of counterfeit cash coins in the jurisdiction and ordered, by virtue of the "imperial edict of the 23rd of the 12th moon," that counterfeit coins withdrawn from circulation be replaced with new ones. Believing it was doing the right thing, the government aroused the ire of the city's money changers, who understood much, if not most, of the currency in circulation at the time was "counterfeit" from the government's point of view. They sent a collective petition to the council asking that this counterfeit currency not be withdrawn so as not to disrupt trade. The government reassured the city's financial actors that it did not seek to remove this money but rather prohibit its distribution in the city, before finally giving up its project to substitute "good money" for "bad money."[49]

In addition to the extensive number of counterfeit cash coins circulating in Tianjin throughout the period, there were countless worthless bills issued by banks without a sufficient guarantee of funds. In addition, the coins considered genuine by the government were not properly titled. The city's merchants asked the council to create a "testing office" to guarantee the accuracy of the silver alloy used to make taels. This depreciation of silver also worried Chinese bankers who asked the government for compensation for the decrease in the value of the deposited funds. The Provisional Government refused to accept this responsibility and referred the local economic actors to the Chinese imperial government, which traditionally dealt with monetary matters. However, it did accede to the traders' request by opening a "testing office" within the government's Treasury Bank, which was responsible for verifying the quality of the currency. From September 1901 onward the inhabitants were obliged to bring their money to the office, at the risk of a fine of 500 taels, and any holder of undeclared money of inferior quality was liable to a fine of the same amount. The devaluation of the tael and the cash coin continued to worry merchants. In early February 1902 fifty-eight stores in Tianjin petitioned the council in Chinese and English to establish a fixed exchange rate between the tael and the dollar, since the high price of the latter made "business difficult." When there was no response, the merchants renewed their request a month later. Finally, the treasurer of the Provisional Government gave in to pressure from the bankers and refused to adopt a fixed exchange rate that would undermine the "freedom of the banks" for the sole benefit of the merchants. The Provisional Government had close ties with certain Chinese banks, with whom it was able to open accounts, as did the international police department, which had an account in an "indigenous bank."[50]

In the realm of money, which remained the reserve of the state, the Provisional Government, despite its great ambitions, never overstepped its prerogatives and the Qing imperial administration maintained its sovereignty in the matter. In December 1900 the former Chinese director of the mint asked the Provisional Government for permission to resume minting in the Eastern Arsenal. The council refused. When a man named Mou, who wished to mint outside the western gate, returned two weeks later, the government turned him down despite serious assurances. The Allied commanders entrusted the Provisional Government with the machines for minting silver and copper coins that were in the Eastern Arsenal. It repaired the machines, replacing the bronze coins "stolen by the Chinese" with coins made in Tianjin and other elements ordered from

Germany. But he was careful not to circulate them: the thorny question of creating a "new currency" or "subsidiary currency" was consistently postponed. In December 1901 the Chinese administration renewed its request, this time through the mediation of Arnhold, Karberg & Co. which was introduced to the members of the council. But they once again refused to sell the minting equipment. The Chinese authorities changed their strategy at the beginning of 1902, and it was Viceroy Yuan Shikai who personally asked the council to hand over the machines to one of his two representatives, either the customs *daotai* Tang Shaoyi or the honorary *daotai* Wang. The council agreed to satisfy this new strongman of the empire on condition that the equipment was not assembled and used within the Provisional Government's jurisdiction. And a few months later, when, without waiting for the scheduled dissolution of the foreign power, *daotai* Chang asked the council for permission to establish a mint in Tianjin, he was refused by the government, which intended to enforce its decisions and preserve the exercise of its sovereignty for another two months.[51]

The question of forgery is crucial for several reasons. Forgery, in its multiple forms, constituted a mode of accommodation but also often of contestation of Allied domination. The usurpation of offices, in a period of political and military crisis, reveals how individuals may "concretely produce the institution that produces them": the Provisional Government was indeed built for two years from above, against competing authorities (consular powers, military commands, the Chinese imperial administration), and from below, against these numerous usurpers.[52] But usurpation and counterfeiting was a category imposed from the point of view of Provisional Government officials and Allied soldiers. For the local population it was a tool for appropriating power and part of an ancient vernacular cultural practice (false dates, false genealogies, false texts of abdication, false coins, false proclamations, and so forth) that required specific expertise and knowledge.[53] The boundary between what was false or authentic was both relative and shifting and depended on the balance of power between the Provisional Government and the local population. The latter thus succeeded in imposing the false cash coins on the former. We are therefore compelled to consider the relationship of the different actors to the question of authenticity, which for the Chinese "resides in the spirit and not in things."[54]

Techniques of law enforcement

The government attempted to respond to these challenges by establishing different types of police and a new judicial system.

"International police," "local police," and secret agents

The police were at the heart of the Provisional Government's policy, as reflected in the new international police station located symbolically and strategically in the central tower of City.[55] The territory under its jurisdiction was divided into eight police districts: four in the Chinese city, representing four rectangles that joined at the tower, and four outside that radiated out from the four gates of the city. In the walled city, the British controlled the northwestern district, the Japanese the northeastern, the French the southwestern, and the United States, followed by the Italians, the southeastern.[56] The German soldiers were too few in Tianjin, while the Russian military preferred to concentrate on the outer districts.

As soon as it took office, the council was careful to distinguish its new police force from the soldiers omnipresent in the jurisdiction by granting them specific uniforms and by wearing metal badges with Chinese and Arabic numerals. The government established police stations at all key points such as the railway station, where at least twenty men were permanently stationed, and placed a Chinese agent, with two guns, in front of each of the city's banks. The police were also responsible for facilitating the movement of vehicles and pedestrians: dozens of posters written in French, English, German, and Chinese ordered the population to drive on the left ("Keep Left") following the British model and forbade "brisk pacing." The council even regulated the width of loads carried on wheelbarrows. Despite the regulations and the efforts of government agents, traffic in the city remained congested. The police department issued the passes and passports needed to enter and leave the city and the jurisdiction, as well as the licenses that allowed boats to navigate on the Hai River. However, it was not until March 1901 that the Provisional Government succeeded in imposing its monopoly on issuing permits and passes to the natives on the Allied military authorities. The police were charged with investigating deaths "from causes other than natural." Thus, when a young married woman committed suicide in April 1902, the chief of police in North Tientsin wrote a report explaining that there was nothing suspicious about the disappearance.[57]

In August 1900 the new international police force consisted of 850 soldiers seconded from the various Allied contingents: 350 Russian troops, 200 Japanese, 100 French, 100 British, and 100 American. The council ensured that the "various nationalities" were represented in the police force, and its chief put forward this argument when he proposed hiring several Australian sailors as police inspectors in the city. Faced with the tensions between the various Allied troops, the police force was probably less "international" than it appeared. Indeed, the chief of police and the district chiefs were pragmatic and often favored grouping police officers by nationality. The district chief of Chunliangcheng, for example, asked for fifteen more Indian soldiers, "preferably from the same army as those already there, in order to prevent the complications that might arise from mixing nationalities." In addition, some powers showed less goodwill in this cooperation: thus, barely a few days after the creation of the new police force, General Frey, commander of the French troops, reduced the detachment from one hundred to sixty men. At the same time as this partial disengagement, a new power, Germany, contributed one hundred men to the international police force. A month later, the number of troops increased again, without the French participating in the collective effort, but with the addition of one hundred Italian infantrymen, eighty German infantrymen and twenty cavalrymen, twenty American cavalrymen, and twenty British cavalrymen. Tianjin then had about 1,100 foreign police officers. However, from the beginning of 1901, the number of officers decreased due to the gradual withdrawal of Allied troops from China and the rise of new demands as new concessions developed in Tianjin. In January the Russians withdrew their entire police force, and the Italians reduced their numbers by more than 20 percent before the Japanese announced at the end of February that they too were withdrawing some of their police. In the spring of 1901 the Allied commanders decided to replace as many foreign troops as possible with Chinese.[58]

Following the suggestion of the commander of the German troops, the government created a special police force to monitor the river. In November 1900 it obtained from the Italian commander, who was in favor of greater involvement on the part of his troops in law enforcement, that he put at its disposal an officer and fifty sailors. But it was not until the summer of 1901 that this new river police force, led by Captain Denti, was actually mobilized. It was made up of soldiers from the Italian navy and some sixty Chinese police officers, and was equipped with eight junks costing $700 each, a steamboat costing $5,000, and horses to patrol the banks of the river.[59] The river police, composed of equal numbers of foreign and Chinese police officers, patrolled not only the Hai River but also the Grand Canal to monitor the operation of the bridges, oversee river development, and combat increasing piracy and robbery that led to a decrease in commercial traffic.[60] In order to better control the river, the council divided the police into five posts established at the Provisional Government's headquarters and along the river, at Chan Chai Wan (North Tientsin district), Yang Liu Ching (South Tientsin district), Chunliangcheng (Chunliangcheng district), and Peitangho (Tongku district). At the beginning of 1902 the government provided new means to the river police, whose activity continued to grow: from then on, nine junks, each crewed by five Chinese sailors and an Italian sailor, methodically traveled the waterways of the jurisdiction thanks to a clever patrol system: "two junks will make the service from Tientsin to Lao-Mou-Tien, one junk will make the service from Tientsin to Yang Liu Ching, one junk will make the service from Tientsin to Yang Kia Chwang, three junks will make the service from Yang Kia Chwang to Ko-Ku, one junk will make the service from Ko-Ku, upstream of Tongku." In addition, five sampans, each manned by an Italian sailor and a Chinese policeman, were responsible for policing the bridges, and two steamers manned by Italians carried out inspection and enforcement missions. The expansion of the river police worried some district chiefs, who were unhappy about its actions—especially arrests—in their districts. For example, the chief of police of South Tientsin asked to be consulted beforehand and demanded the release of three Chinese arrested by the Italian sailors. He won his case with the council. The district chiefs were in fact responsible for directing police operations outside the walled city. Each one could count on about fifty European soldiers and a variable number of "indigenous" policemen. Thus, the Tongku district had two German cavalrymen, two German noncommissioned officers, fifteen German soldiers, four Japanese cavalrymen, fifteen Japanese infantrymen, and three *sowars*, or Indian cavalrymen.[61]

The Chinese played a crucial, indispensable role in the new police. The government leaders, including the Chinese secretary and the chief of police, wanted to involve the local notables in the creation of the new police force from the start. The treasurer proposed that the merchants and "bourgeois" of the city pay subscriptions to finance the organization of an "indigenous police force." The council agreed, providing that no coercion was exercised on the Chinese elites. For some reason, three days later the government withdrew the law and ordered that the project be cofinanced, presumably out of fear that it would create government dependence on the local elites. But it retained the plan to create a Chinese police force and instructed the district chiefs to visit their constituencies and inform the notables of each village of the number of men to be hired in the "indigenous police force." The Chinese police, in the city and districts, differed from the international police. Its commander, H. R. Stewart, wore a silver star, and his men wore a special uniform. The Chinese policemen were equipped with Springfield rifles of poor quality and five rounds of ammunition "to defend themselves against the attacks of brigands." These local officers were designated by their numbers like the prisoners.[62]

Each district was divided into several police sections and was controlled by a foreign police inspector, who relied on a few foreign mounted policemen and two Chinese sub-inspectors. In addition, in each village the notables recruited men in "the proportion of one man for every twenty dwellings." They wore the name of their village and a number in Chinese and Latin characters on their chest. They were paid five piasters per month; their pay and equipment were the responsibility of each village, which paid the required sum to the district chief. The local elders, or the *shendong*, also financed the housing and lighting costs of the Chinese policemen, but the government ordered the policemen not to ask for anything else from the inhabitants, to limit corruption. A public proclamation gave the villagers the names of the police officers and were ordered to obey them. At the same time, the government declared that any abuse of power by the Chinese police would be severely punished and that they were forbidden to receive gifts from the population. The "indigenous police" in each village were visited at least twice a week by the police sub-inspectors and once by the section inspectors. The "indigenous" police allowed the Allies to control the entire territory through patrols established in each locality by the district chief, "such that the agents of a locality may put themselves in communication with those of neighboring localities and all parts of the country without exception are traversed by patrols."[63]

When in late 1901 district chiefs considered the "indigenous police" incapable of responding to the frequent assaults of brigands in some villages, the government accepted the proposal of the chief of South Tientsin to arm the village population of Yang Liu Ching and Wang Chia Chuang. The district chief then distributed "certificates," badges, and weapons to the men of fighting age. This example of a village community being armed by the occupiers was undoubtedly exceptional, but it was part of the logic of developing "Chinese police" out of an older system of protection. In the field, the boundaries between "Chinese police" and private militia could be tenuous, as illustrated by the creation of a "district police force with brigands" by a notable in the Chunliangcheng district: the international police arrested the armed men, beheaded them on the spot, and brought the notable to justice. In some villages in the jurisdiction, "local armed guards," the old village militias, with or without the blessing of the Provisional Government, continued between 1900 and 1902, despite the expansion of the new police. This was a process of "doubling up" perfectly described by Georges Balandier in some of the French colonies in sub-Saharan Africa, where certain local institutions remained in place alongside the development of new colonial infrastructures. Under these conditions, the chiefs sometimes had difficulty taking possession of their districts: the chief of Chunliangcheng had to wait until March 1902 to create police stations in his district, which replaced "the old police force, originally organized by the notables."[64]

The effectiveness of the Provisional Government's police force depended largely on its Chinese informants and secret agents. The police chief had a network of informants to identify Boxers and brigands in the jurisdiction. He recruited his agents through public proclamations inviting the population to participate in surveillance: rewards were offered "to those who provide indications on the traffic of weapons or on the existence of brigands." The council gave instructions to the heads of departments and districts to recruit informers who were rewarded according to the services rendered. The government remained discreet about the use of its "secret agents," who were generally absent from administrative documentation. They sometimes appeared under the name of "special agents" or under the expression "secret police," in an account book under "miscellaneous expenses" of the Department of Justice. However, the payment of native informers and "secret agents" represented one of the main items in the police budget.[65]

Often highly paid informants helped district chiefs solve cases of robbery, extortion, and murder. One informant received $200 from Major Ducat for helping to dismantle an organization of river thieves. Faced with the generosity of the district chiefs, whose results were partly linked to the efficiency of their agents, the council became increasingly thrifty to the point of categorically refusing to offer rewards in the spring of 1902: the informer who enabled the river police to arrest a man named Chang Erh in possession of a Mauser did not obtain the promised reward of $50.[66]

The police chief's agents intercepted native correspondence, which was translated by the Chinese secretary's department before being presented to the council. The government subcontracted some police investigations to informants, but not without difficulty. For example, a certain Liang Jui Tang had a "certificate," valid for thirty days, to search for Boxers and guns in the city. He had to provide evidence to support his accusations and could not make the arrests himself. He received $50 for each significant discovery of firearms. Two weeks later, the Chinese secretary accused Liang Jui Tang of having lent his "license to denounce the Boxers and search for weapons" to other Chinese. These people caused numerous disturbances in the city and were arrested. The "certificate" was canceled, and the protagonists were brought before the government court. The Chinese secretary repeatedly alerted government officers about the criminal behavior of certain secret agents such as Tai Lao, employed by the district chief, Major Ducat, even though he was considered "a dangerous man." All in all, local Chinese secret agents were considered by the council to be a necessary evil. The government officers depended heavily on their information while being wary of their power of influence: "The chief of the Tongku district is authorized to hire another interpreter and several secret agents of the police, but with regard to the latter, his attention is called to the danger that there always exists when employing Chinese in functions of this kind."[67]

A complex judicial architecture

The Provisional Government was vested with judicial power to exact fines on the Chinese, confiscate their property, imprison, or sentence them to death. Regarding foreign civilians and military personnel, the government only exercised police powers: violators of the rules laid down by the council were arrested and then handed over to the consular or military authorities responsible for them within twenty-four hours. A magistrate, assisted by a private interpreter, directed the government's judicial service and presided over the court. It was possible "exceptionally" to appeal the magistrate's sentences to the Council of the Provisional Government, which made the final decision. The members of the council thus concentrated all the powers of the executive, legislative, and judicial branches, like Chinese judges.[68]

The district chiefs, each of whom headed a court, heard civil cases in which the amount in dispute did not exceed $20, and then as of April 1901, $200. They also acted as magistrates in criminal cases not involving a fine of more than $50, a month's caning, two months' imprisonment, or twenty-five strokes of the rod. The district chief was to encourage the settlement of disputes out of court and could, except in important cases, release suspects on bail. More serious cases were referred "urgently" to the court of justice of the Provisional Government, which also served as the court of appeals for the district chief's judgments. The Tianjin justice department could decide to hold a trial in the court of the Provisional Government or send the head of the judicial department to try the case in the district court. District chiefs sometimes bypassed the chain of command in the judicial pyramid, such as Major Ducat who as head of Chunliangcheng district took the decision to behead a wounded Chinese brigand. While the council approved of the principle of execution, it thoroughly disapproved of Ducat's initiative since "the only authority by which a prisoner can be executed is by that of the Council." Internal tensions within the government undermined the judicial service. Relations between the magistracy and the members of the council grew tense in the spring of 1901, as shown by mutual calls to order. When the head of the judicial service drew the council's attention to processing an appeal on a case of piracy in Tongku, the latter retorted, without going into details, that he "should devote more time to his official duties," undoubtedly implying that the judge's commercial activities kept him too busy. The magistrate and the chief of police also had a difficult relationship, sometimes to the point of challenging one another. For example, the latter, without prior discussion, released Chinese prisoners from the former's prison, under the pretext that the suspects should be kept in a "detention house," separate from the prison for Chinese convicts. Following several disputes, the magistrate officially challenged the police chief's right to criticize the court's judgments and convinced the council to issue "a general order that no department or district should criticize another except in a communication to the Council." This intervention did not seem to calm relations between the department heads. A few months later, the chief of police complained to the council that the magistrate made his decisions by "annotating in pencil on the margin" of the reports. The council then ordered the magistrate to write his "decision in ink and sign it."[69]

The judicial service of the government multiplied the number of judged cases. In June 1901 alone, 282 criminal cases and 201 civil cases were tried. The development of judicial activities pushed the government magistrate to propose that the court's operations should be financed by the litigants through a fee of one dollar for each hearing, to which should be added a registration fee according to the amount requested by the plaintiff ($2 if the amount was less than $500, $5 between $500 and $1,000, and one percent of the amount when it exceeded $1,000). This tax made it possible to socially select the plaintiffs and thus reduce the number of applicants. In fact, from the beginning of 1901, the district chiefs complained about the congestion in the judicial system, especially at the level of the head of the department, who was unable to handle the numerous appeals that were accumulating from the districts. The government tried to relieve congestion by assigning the Chinese secretary to handle "trivial civil cases" that the magistrate did not have time to deal with. However, the head of the judicial service remained jealous of his prerogatives and convinced the council to abandon this reform two days later. And the district chiefs complained again about "the accumulation of judicial cases that await a decision by the magistrate of the Provisional Government."[70]

This judicial practice resulted in prison overcrowding. The Provisional Government ordered the construction of a large prison in September 1901, which began the following November for the modest sum of 800 taels. The prison, run by the British chief George Williams and his Dutch deputy Ernst Yunger, also employed a "Chinese doctor," who was in permanent residence. Smaller prisons were then built in the districts. In each village, the government also encouraged the construction of a depository for suspects guarded by the Chinese police. The arrested individuals had to be taken within thirty-six hours to the district capital. However, the district chiefs had to administer justice with very few resources. The Provisional Government declared itself unable to finance the purchase of "instruments of repression" such as canoes, so Captain Satō, the Japanese officer in charge of North Tientsin, was forced to improvise with the help of the craftsmen of his district.[71]

Prison inflation also resulted from norm inflation. Not only did the council produce abundant and binding regulations, but the district chiefs were themselves legislators, in the manner of the "emperors without a scepter," the French colonial administrators studied by William B. Cohen. For example, the chief of North Tientsin proposed several regulations for "bird hunters." This proliferation of legal texts under the Provisional Government was de facto a continuation of the Qing administrative tradition, where, especially during the reign of Emperor Guangxu (1875–1908), jurists struggled to master the complexity of the teeming codes and administrative jurisprudence.[72]

Repressive and expedited justice?

From the outset, the government's justice system was extraordinarily repressive. The American general Chaffee indicated the rule of law and order that prevailed in 1900–1901: "It is safe to say that where one real Boxer has been killed since the capture of Pekin, fifty harmless coolies or labourers on the farms, including not a few women and children, have been slain. The Boxer element is largely mixed with the mass of the population, and by slaying a lot one or more Boxers might be taken in."[73] In Tianjin, the new judicial system allowed the war to continue by the same means. From the outset, the council devised a pedagogy of public execution: each one was the subject of a public proclamation and a government "executioner" was dispatched to the scene. The executions had to be a big event in the villages or in Tianjin, and the decapitated heads were exhibited for ten days in places "where they had been known" with a "notice of their crime" underneath.[74] The members of the council conceived of the sentences imposed as "a warning to others:" the decapitation was intended to instill fear and thus a form of collective intimidation. Numerous professional and amateur photographers ensured the publicity of these executions, which recalled the barbarity of Chinese customs in the Western imagination.[75] However, faced with the enthusiasm of foreigners and some Chinese, the council prohibited civilians from taking photographs at public executions in September 1901. The thieves were also exposed to the vindictiveness of the population: Li Erh and Yang San, guilty of theft on a railway construction site, were taken to the scene of their crime, where they were placed in the cangue for three days under the gaze of their former colleagues. They each received twenty-five lashings of bamboo on the construction site before being sent to forced labor for eighteen and twenty-four months respectively, where they were inflicted with another twenty-five lashings of bamboo per week for three months. Anyone resembling a Boxer or a bandit was eradicated, and the government tried to control closely the Chinese "corporations" and "societies" "whose members, by their clothing or the way they addressed each other, resembled Boxers." Aware of the importance of the social fabric of Tianjin, the police kept a register of all societies, "secret or not." The registration of associations became a condition of their legal existence and of government authorization.[76]

The Chinese found in possession of arms and ammunition in the territory of the jurisdiction were, without further trial, sentenced to death by the council and beheaded at the place of their arrest. In the end, it was often only the council member on duty in the headquarters, Lin Hei'er, who ordered the immediate beheading. Many so-called pirates and brigands were executed in this way. The possession of a weapon was the decisive factor: thus, when Lieutenant von Mutius, replacing the district chief of Chunliangcheng, arrested three members of a well-known band of robbers in Ta Sun Chuang, the council ordered the beheading of two armed robbers and sentenced the unarmed individual to one year of hard labor. The astonishing disproportion of the sentences was designed to demonstrate the absolute prohibition to carry a weapon. Thus, the council administered the same capital punishment the during the same session for the Chinese man arrested for possession of a weapon he did not use, a man guilty of armed robbery and a man who committed murder. And when eight suspects were apprehended near Hsiao Chan, the seven men carrying weapons were beheaded and the eighth "unarmed at the time of his arrest" was released.[77]

The justice system of the interim government operated as if the Chinese could not be completely innocent. Thus, a man arrested for theft in the Tongku district, against whom no evidence or testimony could be given, was released but subjected to a judicial control requiring him to report daily to the police station. Similarly, when the guilt of a man named Li San, accused of murder in 1900, could not be proven, the magistrate nevertheless sentenced him to one year of hard labor. When a prisoner accused of murder by Captain Satō was found not guilty by the magistrate—a rare occurrence—the acquittal was necessarily suspicious, and Major von Falkenhayn, a member of the council who supervised the police, initiated his own investigation. At the same time, the justice system proved intractable with perpetrators of minor offenses: Chinese sentenced to more than one month in prison were marked to facilitate their identification and, from the spring of 1902, prisoners sentenced to more than four months had their heads shaved and their "tails" cut off, officially as a sanitary measure but also as further punishment.[78]

However, several factors combined to limit the arbitrary nature of the Provisional Government's justice. The competition between the different jurisdictions induced a mutual control to the benefit of the Chinese. Thus, the chief of police, after an investigation, released two Chinese accused by the French consul of illegally levying taxes. In addition, from September 1901 onward, the council gradually tried to ensure that the punishments for the same offences were identical throughout the jurisdiction.[79]

Government judges took into consideration the suspect's reputation. During the first year, a highly subjective "bad reputation" was enough to condemn a suspect. On the other hand, from the end of 1901 a "good reputation" became a determining criterion for the judges. Thus, a Chinese man, prisoner 199, who was found armed at the Tianjin train station was spared because of certificates guaranteeing his "good reputation" and his past as a contractor in the service of German troops. He got off lightly with a fine of $25 and the confiscation of his weapon. A "good reputation" ultimately permitted a generous interpretation of the offences committed and thus made it possible to exonerate postmortem a man killed while opening his door to a thug. After originally being an accomplice, his family obtained the status of victims. The Chinese administrative authorities also intervened, as in the case of the magistrate from Ching Hai hsien, a locality near the jurisdiction, who attested to the "good reputation" of Li Ching Tang, Kao Ma Tzu, and Kao Te Tzu (prisoners 222, 223, and 225) arrested for robbery. In the end, the council ordered their release. Reputation could motivate the council to pardon them, and following the intervention of the chief of justice and the head of the Tongku district, it commuted the death sentence of Ma Te Li, convicted of murder, to two years of hard labor "since he had a good reputation and was not a hardened criminal." At the same time, a "bad reputation" was no longer sufficient to justify a conviction. The prisoners Ko San and Co Ssu, "well known to be robbers," were acquitted because of insufficient evidence against them.[80]

The magistrate and the chief of police showed more tolerance for travelers from outside the jurisdiction: they released armed Chinese, who had come in junks through the Grand Canal, "because they had traveled a great distance and had weapons for the protection of their cargo." From this point on Chinese civilians going to Tianjin had to deposit their weapons at a police station, which they could retrieve with a receipt when leaving the jurisdiction. The police chief and the magistrate also debated the definition of a weapon, such as a cannon hidden on a junk, which the captain was allowed to have, "since the cannon was not of such a nature that it could be considered a weapon."[81]

From January 1902 onward, faced with the inflation of prisoners and the prospect of the dissolution of the government, the chief of police lobbied the magistrate for "the release of prisoners and the reduction of sentences for good behavior." Enforcement became more lenient and took account of extenuating circumstances. Li Tsung San, convicted of armed extortion, escaped the death penalty thanks to his "youth," which was invoked by the magistrate. An old man accused of possessing two swords in his house was found guilty but, "because of his age and feebleness," his death sentence was commuted by the council to one year in prison. General Vogak, a prominent member of the council, stated in April 1902 that "the time has come to mitigate the rigors of this regulation." Another mitigating circumstance was self-defense, which allowed the perpetrator of the homicide to be exempted from prosecution. The council was careful not to automatically impose collective sentences and began to examine individual responsibility. The magistrate was now concerned with prevention, and when in June 1902 police officers discovered cartridges and rifle barrels in the house of a blacksmith, the craftsman, whose "good intentions" were taken into consideration, was not beheaded but simply fined "as a warning to others." The tone adopted by the council would seem to have evolved. When the following month it recommended the population not eat melon to prevent the risk of cholera, he took care to specify that he did not foresee any sanctions for those who would not comply with this proclamation. In 1902, not only were there more and more acquittals, but the magistrate was also concerned about the fate of the weak, such as a young girl, kidnapped in Shandong and transported to Tianjin, who was returned to her mother. As the handover of the city approached, the government even allowed itself to question the severity of its previous judicial decisions. Thus, the prisoner Huang Fy Yo, sentenced to death as a brigand, who had not been executed because of the negligence of the administration, saw his sentence commuted to two years of hard labor in consideration of the "delay in the execution of this sentence." This easing of punishment in criminal cases aroused some discontent, especially among foreigners. The large British import-export firm Butterfield & Swire complained to the council about the way justice was administered in the Tongku district: "A gang leader caught looting on board the [ship] Sheng King was sentenced to only two months in prison." The government seems to have been unresponsive to the demands of the foreign community for increased repression.[82]

The whole population benefited from this reform of the government's policy, especially for daily trafficking. From December 1, 1901, the Chinese were authorized to use the streets of the city and the suburbs after 10 p.m. on condition that they carried a lighted lantern, with the police immediately arresting any recalcitrants. At the end of July 1902, on the recommendation of the chief of police, the council abolished this obligation. In June 1902, the magistrate considered that the complaint of the German company Melchers & Co. against a Chinese company, accused of having infringed a monopoly on a certain species of indigo, was inadmissible.[83]

The middle of 1901 seemed to mark a turning point for the government, as it increasingly sought to combat corruption among its officials and promote exemplary justice and policing. The fight against corruption was even an issue in the rivalry between the council and the French consul, who accused two Chinese government police officers (Nos. 672 and 687) of extorting money from a local trader in the French concession. The magistrate cleared the government officers and stated that "this accusation was made to cover up an illegal practice by a certain Chinese man in the said concession." Police officers no longer hesitated to bring their own men accused of extortion or theft to justice. The government jailed a Chinese policeman, who was an accomplice of a banker and claimed to have been robbed. The chief of the river police recommended that one of his officers, number 57, be shot for extorting money. The council finally sentenced him to one year of hard labor and fifty lashings of bamboo. In accordance with the council's recommendations, the aim was to show the people that government agents were not above the law. Chang Wang Liu, a sergeant of the sanitary police, was convicted of extortion and given twenty lashings of bamboo before being subjected to thirty days of caning, escorted through the streets by two Chinese agents, and then two years of hard labor.

The government was anxious to prove its goodwill and its promptness toward the population, to which it claimed to be listening. Two police sub-inspectors accused of extortion by villagers were thus immediately brought before the government court. The government was determined to make an example of them, since even before the court decision, the council declared that "the sentence that will be pronounced by the judge will be posted in all the police stations of the Provisional Government's jurisdiction." Judged guilty, they were sentenced to one year of hard labor. This ostensibly exemplary decision was marred the following week by the intervention of villagers, who sent petitions to defend the two sub-inspectors they believed had been unjustly convicted. The government did not respond to these petitions, which undermines the image of swift and effective justice. The government attempted to discipline its police officers by heavily punishing any breach of ethics. The council directly exercised this disciplinary justice, bypassing the magistrates, to directly control all government agents. Two police officers who used a porter as a sentry to replace them were not only dismissed but punished with fifty lashes and sentenced to six months in prison. In the event of an offense, the government agent immediately reverted to being an ordinary Chinese whose body was to be severely punished. A native policeman, who frequented gambling houses was arrested, dismissed, and sentenced to six months' hard labor. Foreign officers did not escape administrative punishment but were exempted from corporal punishment. Thus, Mr. Truchet and Mr. Jungers, deputies to the chief jailer, were successively dismissed for drunkenness. But the complaints concerning the foreign policemen never succeeded, such as the one concerning the Italian sailors accused by Jardine, Matheson & Co. of extortion when one of their cargo ships passed through Hsian Cheng on October 13, 1901. Foreign military personnel were exclusively dependent on their command, while foreign civilians were protected by their consul.[84]

Starting in the middle of 1901, "missteps" became an object of concern for the government. The magistrate investigated the case of the "murder" of a notable by Italian river police officers. Ultimately, the foreign police officers were not investigated. Under the leadership of Major Ducat, the government wanted to compensate the victims of illegitimate police violence. For example, the government paid $30 in "compensation" to the family of a Chinese man of "good character" killed by a German soldier, who thought he was apprehending a thief. These compensations gave rise to subtle justification. Thus, when Lieutenant Hall's policemen killed two Chinese who were not robbers, Major Ducat requested compensation for the families of the two innocents. The council authorized a compensation of $50 for the family of the man killed by a stray bullet, while it refused to give anything to the family of "the man killed while opening a door for one of the brigands." The chief of North Tianjin asked for an indemnity for the widow of a notable of Peitsang, murdered on May 23, 1902, by a member of a band of brigands whose leader he had helped to arrest. The council agreed to grant $100 to his family and directed the district chief to attend the *shendong*'s funeral in person. But when the district chief asked for $300 in compensation for the notable's family, the council refused, informing him that it "considers the incident closed." The district chiefs in the field understood better than the council members the need to protect and reward Chinese notables, informers, and agents.[85]

The government also instituted a system of assistance for the families of its officers killed in the line of duty. When a sepoy was killed in Chunliangcheng while attempting to apprehend a brigand, the council proposed to offer "as much [compensation] as the government treasury will allow" after inquiring with General Creagh about the family situation of this Indian soldier, who left a widow and an aged father in India. After discussion, the council decided that the "suitable sum" was $400, the equivalent in rupees being transferred to India. This transimperial welfare assistance became effective six months later when the deputy commissioner of the Ludhiana district in Punjab acknowledged receipt of a consignment of 572 rupees for the widow of the sepoy. Families of Chinese agents killed in the line of duty were usually compensated up to $100. The compensation could be less when the death was "indirectly" related to the individual's service, as in the case of policeman No. 60, who oversaw searching for corpses in the river and died of cholera: his family received only $25. This sum may seem derisory in comparison with the compensation provided to the families of dead or injured foreign soldiers, such as the Italian sailor Sessa, who received $3,500 from the government for his injuries while on duty. However, the Chinese families of agents working for the Allies seemed to have integrated the principle of employer responsibility, to the point of sometimes taking the initiative to address the government directly on this subject. The parents of a young worker killed during the destruction of the Hsin Cheng forts requested compensation from the district chief of Chunliangcheng, who referred them to the project manager, a private contractor, who oversaw employee safety.[86]

The members of the council believed that police and judicial repression could be accompanied by a policy of social assistance which should contribute to maintaining public order.

Disciplining the destitute: The fight against begging and the creation of "poor houses"

The heads of the government were convinced that poverty led to increased crime. The fight against unemployment and the promotion of agriculture therefore represented a tool for "pacification" in the region where the socio-economic situation was catastrophic in the aftermath of the city's capture: "The crops had, in fact, been destroyed by the Europeans and the stock of harvested rice seized by them."[87] This idea was first formulated by the U.S. consul, who advocated encouraging farmers to sow the fields around Tianjin. The Council of the Provisional Government then ordered district chiefs to issue proclamations throughout the jurisdiction to let Chinese farmers know they would be protected by the police if they resumed cultivating their land. To revive livestock farming and in response to numerous petitions from villagers, the council prohibited soldiers and police from seizing animals from Chinese farmers. When, for security reasons, General Lorne Campbell, who was responsible for the Provisional Government's communications, demanded the prohibition of crops on railroad embankments that were above a certain height, the council complied while pointing out that this decision "would leave a bad impression; that it might force the farmers near the line to participate in robberies." Campbell was compelled to reassure him that it was not a matter of preventing the land from being cultivated but of preventing any illegal action.[88]

The government officers seemed convinced of the benefits of work to counteract brigandage: thus the head of North Tianjin warned the council that the men of the villages of his district were leaving to look for work in Tianjin and that "if they can find it they will undoubtedly remain honest."[89] The government fixed the wages of the workers and coolies in the jurisdiction, originally adopted in order to reduce the "extraordinarily high wages introduced by the foreign armies."[90] These fixed earnings granted a living wage to the workers of Tianjin: fifteen Mexican cents per day with rice, and thirty cents per day without rice. In view of the high rents that discouraged coolies from settling in Tianjin, the government even ordered the construction, at its own expense, of several "cheap" housing units for the workers of the Provisional Government on the site of Fort No. 13. This innovative project was part of the recent dynamic of the international "workers' housing" movement, which held its first congress in Paris in 1889.[91]

As soon as it took office, the council was concerned with reducing the number of indigents, considered a source of public disorder, by mobilizing them for public works: during the winter, poor people were forced to build the quay along the river. The London Missionary Society and Chinese charities regularly raised the government's awareness of this problem, notably through the intervention of Charles Tenney. In September 1901 the government established a first asylum for the poor in the buildings abandoned by the French troops in the city. At the beginning of October, the prefect's offices were in turn transformed into "poor houses" for the modest sum of $1,040. Faced with the influx of indigents, the government founded new ones in 1902, transforming a large building into an asylum for $1,000.[92]

In January 1902 the government adopted a more coercive policy to empty the streets and fill these new institutions. Following Colonel Harada's proposal, the council decided to expel all nonhandicapped beggars from Tianjin "on the first day of the first moon of the Chinese New Year." Similarly, beggars, old men, and handicapped who remained in Tianjin were to reside compulsorily in the poor houses. After sorting out the poor and confining the destitute, the Chinese secretary suggested that they should undergo a medical examination to offer an alternative to the "beggars capable of working:" either leave the city or work for the government. The Public Works Department thus recruited some of its workforce from among the "beggars" in the government's asylums, particularly for the demolition of the Chinese forts. However, the government was kind enough to offer coffins to the "beggars" who died during forced labor. The government offered a food ration of five cents per person, provided clothing and wooden cots, and forbade the residents to go outside. The poorhouses were in fact part of the prison system set up by the council. In fact, the "beggars" paid their own expenses: two-thirds of their income was returned to the government, and one-third was kept for their benefit. The government instituted a specific tariff of punishments for disciplinary infractions. A French doctor, Dr. Brunet, specifically assigned to the poorhouses, assisted by three "native" nurses, tended to the health of this precious workforce. Here, as in other areas, the Provisional Government's policy had some similarities to Chinese social practices: Tianjin was in fact the seat of several indigenous poorhouses (Yu ying tang, Kuang jan tang, and Yu li tang) administered and financed by the merchant guilds and the *shendong*. The Chinese secretary decided to impose the workhouse model on the Chinese settlements. They could remain under the control of the local notables on condition that their able-bodied poor be made available to the government. In return, as a token of goodwill, the Chinese secretary obtained that the widows' asylum occupied by Italian troops be returned to the Chinese charitable society to which it belonged before the city was taken. We do not have any specific figures, but the government leaders seem to have been satisfied with this policy, which complemented their disciplinary policy.[93]

The challenge of provisioning for the poor: "International aid" or "national solidarity?"

One of the government's main tasks, according to article 5 of its regulations, was to "prevent famine among the indigenous population."[94] Indeed, the population still had vivid memories of the "horrible famine" of the beginning of the Guangxu Emperor's era, which hit northern China hard in the years 1876–79. In addition, in 1900–1901, the region was confronted with another great famine in neighboring Shaanxi, described in some sources as being as severe as the one in the late 1870s. After the capture of Tianjin and the massacre, famine threatened. As a result, the Provisional Government adopted a new frugal policy. Foreigners had previously refrained from providing international aid to the victims of the spectacular famine of 1876–79, arguing that "the traditional imperial state practice of distributing non-repayable relief" was uneconomic and that the main priority was to establish free trade and promote modern techniques.[95] On the other hand, the Provisional Government sought to ensure the subsistence of the inhabitants of Tianjin in the context of a worrying drought.

The government presented itself as a benevolent power, benefactor, and nurturer of the inhabitants of the jurisdiction. The day after the city was taken, it encouraged the return of merchants, who were the only ones capable of supplying the city. The government requisitioned all the foodstuffs available in the city and the surrounding area. The rice stores discovered by the Allied forces during their march on Beijing were handed over to the Provisional Government to "serve as food for the city's population." The rice stocks of German and British troops, as well as the reserves of the China Merchants Steam Navigation Company in Tongku, were also handed over to the government. A few months later Japanese Colonel Akiyama offered the Provisional Government 2,400 bags of rice.[96]

At the beginning of August 1900 the government set the price of grain to make it accessible to most of the population. To do this it established an "office for the control and sale of rice" within the Treasury Department headed by the German Fritz Sommer. Sommer had to forecast the quantity of rice and cereals (sorghum, millet, and the like) needed each winter for the government agents and its charities. In September 1901 the government purchased four thousand bags of rice for distribution to the poor during the winter of 1901–2. The council entrusted the office with the task of responding to natural disasters. The office also took charge of recovering the grain reserves from recalcitrant officers, such as Colonel Wint, commander of the American troops, who refused to give the rice from the store he occupied in Tongku, although this stock had been given to the Provisional Government by Captain Weniger of the German detachment. The Americans delayed the transfer as long as possible in order to be able to use these rice reserves (2,385 bags) that General Chaffee, the new commander-in-chief, decided to hand over to the government at the beginning of October 1900. At the same time, the council did not hesitate to sell part of the seized rice to feed its budget: five thousand bags of rice at $3.50 each were sold at the end of August 1900.[97]

A system of rice distribution was operative before the Allied occupation. Since the 1870s the native elites had organized themselves through a network of charitable societies. Indeed, the Guangxu famine was probably the first form of "national" Chinese philanthropy to emerge from Shanghai. It was built against the old model of the mobilization of local elites who exclusively assisted the inhabitants of their city or subprefecture. These "specialists in charitable mobilization," merchants and Buddhist monks, replaced the Qing administration in the northern provinces, which had previously dealt with this issue. As early as October 1900, the "new professionals of philanthropy," as Pierre-Etienne Will called them, based in Shanghai since the 1870s, intervened in Tianjin where they sent the *Sirène*, a steamer flying the Chinese flag with a large cargo of rice and clothing collected by the charitable societies of the "Paris of the East."[98]

The social influence of Chinese charitable associations aroused the suspicion of foreign authorities. Thus, the head of the Health Service condemned the improper use of the Red Cross logo by a "so-called Chinese Red Cross Society." The Chinese secretary tried to defend the interests of the local associations by requesting the right to inscribe on their flag the words "Authorized by the Provisional Government of Tientsin." But Dr. Depasse, head of the health service, strongly opposed any official authorization granted to the charitable societies and recommended that they use a "blue cross" to distinguish themselves from the Geneva cross. While taking Depasse's advice into consideration, the council prohibited the use of a cross, regardless of its color, while authorizing these associations to continue their philanthropic activities. In this period of uncertainty about individual, professional, and institutional identities, the government tried to control the use of symbols of power—and for good reason, since local Chinese elites also were attempting to take back control of charitable works in general as well as rice distribution. The local charitable societies solicited the intervention of a close collaborator, the Reverend A. King, who officially defended before the council their proposal to have the Chinese charitable associations distribute the Provisional Government's rice to the needy population. The council refused this proposal because it wished to reserve the rice for its asylums and poorhouses and "not to have it distributed in public." A month later, Tianjin's philanthropic community, grouped in the Chinese Charitable Association and again with the support of Reverend King, returned to the council with a request for rice for the city's poor. The council replied that the government was fighting against "misery by giving employment to poor people able to work," but refused to delegate the distribution to private actors. Instead, it agreed to offer rice directly to poor people unable to work and housed in asylums of indigenous Chinese.

Thus, the government, from the beginning of 1901, gave its support to the charitable associations of the city. Through Reverend King, the Chinese secretary graciously sent them a thousand bags and gave an allowance of two bags of rice per day to Yu Li Tang, an institution for the paralytic and blind.[99]

The Japanese Colonel Harada encouraged the council to become more involved in charity work and to increase cooperation with Chinese charitable associations. To do this, the Chinese secretary worked with the notables from whom he obtained a "certified statement" of the number of poor people in each district of the walled city. In early December 1901 Colonel Harada convinced the government to adopt a plan to distribute relief through the notables. In each district, the *shendong* were personally responsible for the rice entrusted to them by the government. The government thus managed, as best it could, to formally keep control of food distribution while relying on local elites (notables, charitable associations), who rightly saw this as a way of regaining their central position in urban society.[100]

The Qing administration also played an important role once again. The treasurer of Zhili Province, for example, claimed to be defending the Chinese people by asking Field Marshal von Waldersee to abolish the Provisional Government's customs duties on rice entering Tianjin. However, the council never introduced a grain tax, and the price of rice remained relatively low in 1901, so that some import-export houses lost money. In early 1902 magistrates from neighboring Chinese districts within the Provisional Government's jurisdiction offered money to be distributed as "alms" in the Tongku district. The council accepted this generous gift on condition that the district chief distribute it himself. The following month, international police apprehended several Chinese charity workers distributing relief supplies without authorization. *Daotai* Chang, acting on behalf of the Chinese authorities, asked the council for clarification of these arrests. The government returned the recovered money to the agents of the philanthropic institutions and the Chinese secretary issued a proclamation: "Any charitable society wishing to distribute clothing, money, food, etc., to the poor, should apply to the chief of police to obtain permission to do so." They were required first to obtain a permit from the chief of police, who verified how they collected their funds. To regain control of the distribution of relief, the council entrusted the operation to the commanding officers of police sections in the city, who were given responsibility for distributing cooked rice to avoid any trafficking or stashing of aid money.[101]

In sum, the Provisional Government did not introduce social protection in China. It tried to replace Chinese charitable institutions and, failing that, to control local mechanisms. Paradoxically, the "Western" philanthropic tradition in Tianjin followed in the footsteps of Confucianism: it promoted the creation of a kind of "religious welfare state" in China that provided for redistribution to the most vulnerable.[102] The government's charitable intentions were not to be confused with those of the Chinese government. In addition, the government's charitable intentions were qualified by its constant concern with privileging its own poor and demands for work in exchange. Thus, during the floods at the end of the summer of 1901, the government distributed $5,000 worth of rice "only to those who had worked to protect the dikes and to the old and infirm."[103] The welfare policy provided the government with an abundance of free labor. This should not, however, conceal the extreme violence exercised by Allied soldiers toward a part of the population. As a French soldier testified: "Certain orders are maintained inexorably against the natives; they starve, try to steal food from our stores, and the sentries are ordered to shoot the loiterers."[104]

Did the Provisional Government establish the first form of "modern" justice in China and for the Chinese? An overly quick reading of this episode, considering the discourse of the Allied powers, might suggest it did. But as the work of Jérôme Bourgon has shown, this would ignore the fact that China was undoubtedly the first state to establish legal principles for offenses and penalties (the judge could only punish offenses previously defined by the law by imposing the designated penalty) and the rule of law, which allows the punishment of a particular offense to be decided according to the interpretation of a fixed general rule. Thus, a certain idea and ancient practice of justice had long obtained among the population of Zhili Province before the Allies founded a new judicial system in this auspicious setting.

On the other hand, Tianjin seems to be one of the first places where a "modern" police force was invented in China. A privileged instrument of appropriation and control of the territory, through a network of posts and a patrol system, it was composed of equal numbers of foreign and Chinese police officers. It continued the war, by the same means, against all forms of local contestation, while at the same time endeavoring to contain the violence and disorder the Allied soldiers created. The police had the impossible task of bringing order to this simmering urban world where countless intermediaries permanently blurred the borders and subverted the new international public order: Chinese counterfeiters, French deserters living like Chinese, Japanese private agents at the service of the villagers, American brigands, Korean traffickers, and so many others.

Figure 4.1 Indian soldiers from the Madras Pioneers demolishing a wall in Tianjin in 1900. "European, American, and Japanese Troops Engaged in Putting Down Boxer Rebellion, 1900," National Archives, CO 1069/423, "China 3."

CHAPTER IV

Regional Planning

Foreign Appropriations and Local Contestations

It seems impossible to describe the condition of the city. The shelling has not spared a single house! The city had a million people before the war with gigantic houses, many of them built in the European style, and is now nothing but a pile of rubble. In the houses where we are staying (the former medical school), you can see traces of bullets and machine-gun fire everywhere. The station is completely destroyed; half of it is burned; demolished locomotives, wagons, and torn up rails form a desolate picture. Add to that the hundreds of corpses we see floating in the Peï-Ho, swollen like barrels! And all this is nothing compared to the appalling truth.

LÉON SILBERMAN, AUGUST 26, 1900

The city of Tientsin has completely changed its appearance since last August. It was then only a heap of rubble, and now all the houses have been repaired or rebuilt; immense buildings have been erected; the station has been rebuilt; the boulevards and streets are well maintained. . . . The fields in the vicinity are well cultivated; the villages between Tientsin and Takou, destroyed last July, are slowly being rebuilt.

LÉON SILBERMAN, JUNE 1, 1901

I am going to Tientsin by train. Soldiers from all the nations that have troops in China ride in the same car. We try to start a conversation; we use the Chinese *sabir*, that is to say the few words of Chinese that every soldier has learned in the country, accompanied by expressive gestures and we manage to make ourselves more or less understood. Though sometimes you ask for tobacco and your interlocutor passes you the salt.

LÉON SILBERMAN, MAY 30, 1901

Destroying a large part of the walled city and its suburbs, the war also allowed the Allied powers to wipe the slate clean: the Provisional Government adopted an ambitious policy of urban development that the Chinese had proven incapable of. The Allied powers remained ignorant of Tianjin's pioneering and driving role in the transportation (railroads) and communication (post, telegraph, telephone) "revolution" in China at the end of the nineteenth century.

From the beginning of the repression of the Boxers in Zhili Province, the Provisional Government opposed this popular movement, which targeted the "modern" transport infrastructure. The latter would have increased the unemployment of Chinese workers (dockers, boatmen, carters, and so forth), swelling the ranks of the Boxers. The Provisional Government symbolized the imperialism of the foreign powers, who, at the end of the nineteenth century, acquired concessions to build and operate railways to create new spheres of influence. It used civil engineering to build infrastructures that allowed the Allies to control the flow of goods and people. The Promethean dimension of this project resulted from the integrated character of this highly interventionist government, a kind of microstate, which equipped itself with all the services necessary to design a complete program of transformation.

Tianjin was transformed into a huge construction site overseen by the Provisional Government. It mobilized a variety of actors (Allied troops, consuls, Chinese entrepreneurs, and foreign tycoons) to implement its various projects. At the same time, the administration produced new forms of knowledge—maps, cadastral records, statistics, and a census—that were essential for the design and implementation of transport and communication infrastructures.

These development practices, which provided the means for effectively appropriating the territory, gave rise to varied reactions within the local population, who oscillated between armed resistance and accommodation.

Cameral techniques and sciences in the service of regional planning

Maps and territories: Obsolete representations and virtual perspectives

One of the council's first decisions, in early August 1900, was to establish a topographical service, even though the Chinese authorities, the French and British consuls, and the Allied staffs already had their own maps of Tianjin. The council hired Noah Fields Drake as a "government surveyor" to draw "a map of the city at a scale of 8 inches (20 cm) to 1 mile (1.6 km)" for a fee of $400. The U.S. engineer immediately set himself to the task. Indeed, the council refused to issue building permits in strategic areas such as the wharf until it had a map of the city. To do this, the men of the Provisional Government's topographical service organized themselves as best they could. The Chinese secretary, Charles Tenney, lent his theodolite, an instrument for making triangulation measurements, to Drake to carry out his topographic surveys, for six weeks. He also needed to purchase equipment from the Chinese. Drake obtained maps and development projects for the French and Japanese concessions through the foreign consuls. Only two months later, he presented his map of the city to the council, proposing to the Public Works Department the layout of new roads. The cartography also served as an instrument to justify the extension of the Provisional Government's jurisdiction, which, at the end of December 1900, sent the military commands a map representing "the territory the Council wished to occupy." A debate ensued within the administration on the adequacy of the cartographic representation concerning the borders of the jurisdiction: the cartographer had omitted two portions of territory to the north and south of the *hsien* (district) of Tianjin and included part of Ching Hai, even though it was outside the government's jurisdiction. A new map was ordered that respected the political boundaries of the new jurisdiction. The district chiefs had to make maps of their districts to be submitted by the end of October 1901.

These soldiers possessed some cartographic knowledge,[1] but with such a short time and with few resources at their disposal they made mistakes. Major Ducat, for example, had to correct the line of the northern border on his map of Chunliangcheng. In this district, as in Tongku, the mapping process proved to be longer, since in March 1902, the exact boundaries were still "vague." Corporal Chenet, protected by an escort, went to the site to carry out the work of delimitation. The collective process of map production continued until the government's dissolution. The new version of the general map prepared by Corporal Chenet was sent to each district chief to add the "Chinese names of the villages and the roads not indicated."[2]

The unfinished nature of the government's cartographic work was theorized by Drake himself, who believed that the mapping of Tianjin was akin to a historical geography because of the rapid changes affecting the territory during the period: "Much will appear in the map of the native city which will have only historical interest."[3] Indeed, ramparts were being torn down, new concessions were taking shape, old concessions were being enlarged, and many streets were being built. "Many important changes will soon be made in the new concessions," he explained. The width of the streets changed constantly, with foreigners tending to increase to widen them and Chinese landowners seeking to narrow them because land was becoming scarce and valuable, especially for stores. Nature itself gave the map a provisional character: "The amount of marsh land around Tientsin varies very much with the seasons. As shown on the map the marshes are slightly too large for the dry season, but they are much too small to represent the wet season conditions." Thus, the map roughly represented the extent of marshes that remained throughout the year.

The map (figure 4.2) was not only an indispensable tool for planning, but also an instrument of economic promotion and political communication. For example, the Public Works Department printed small maps of Tianjin based on Drake's surveys for sale in "Tianjin, Shanghai and elsewhere." After March 1901 the surveyor took charge of marketing them for himself. The Provisional Government offered them to foreign consuls as a token of goodwill but also to mark the limits of its jurisdiction.

The mapping was not easily carried out. It provoked resistance from the village population, who were able to destroy the geodetic signals installed by Noah Drake and his agents. The government ordered the Chinese to "respect the geodetic signals" and police rounds were organized, particularly in the North Tientsin district. International police patrols were assigned to protect these tools as well as the topographic work of foreign powers, such as that of the German Geographical Service on the proposed route of the Tianjin–Chinkian (Zhenjiang) railroad.[4]

When the French discovered the city of Tianjin in *L'Illustration* of December 15, 1900, it was not through Drake's famous map but through another map, a piece of a Chinese map, some of which was translated into French.[5] This fragment of a map (figure 4.3), adapted by Raoul Charles Villetard de Laguérie, came from a superb pictorial map, "as the crow flies," by Feng Qihuang, who in 1899 depicted in detail the Chinese city of Tianjin, the concessions, the Grand Canal, the river, the railway, the factories, the temples, and so on. This aerial view of 21.65 inches (55 cm) wide and 43.7 inches (111 cm) long is owned today by the Library of Congress. Entitled "Complete Map of the Defense System of the Walled City of Tianjin and its Surroundings" (*Tianjin cheng xiang bao jia quan tu*), this view from the sky, which does not actually exist, represents a "virtual" perspective.[6] The author of the map located the main buildings and measured the distances

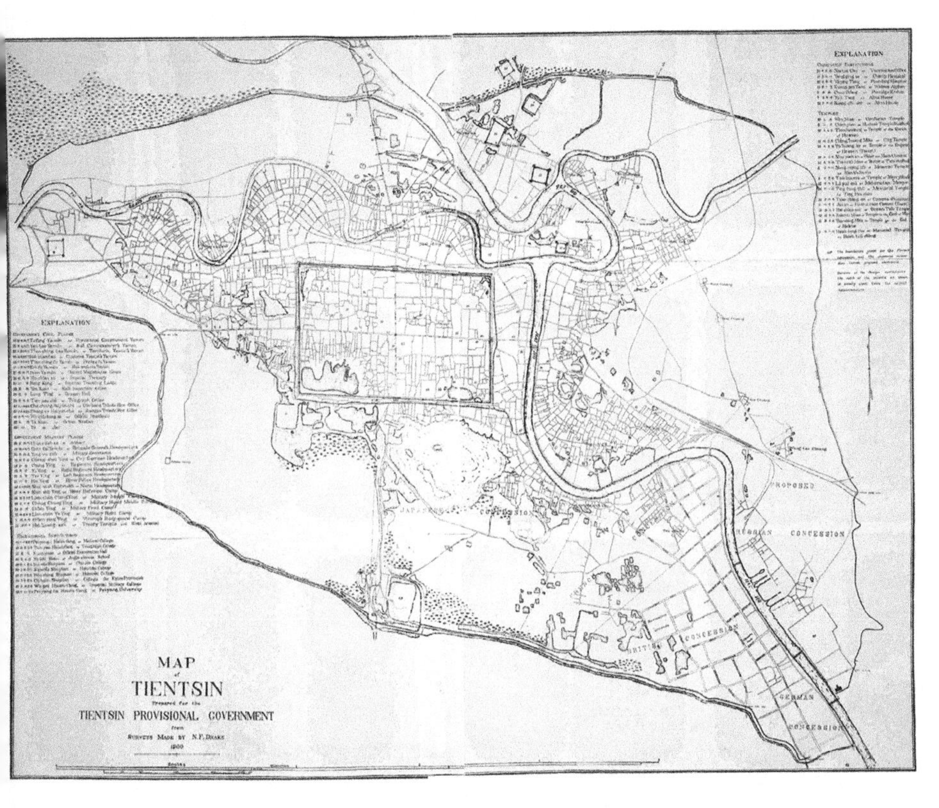

Figure 4.2 Map of Tianjin by Noah Drake, 1900.

to produce proper perspective through various projection processes. He then represented the main private and public buildings in elevation and viewpoint while accentuating their form and style.

The two contemporary maps show the importance of the unbuilt spaces—notably the two large ponds—within the city: "All Chinese cities have empty spaces within their walls; but nowhere do they occupy half the city's surface area, as in Tianjin, where they are one of its peculiar characteristics."[7] Both authors emphasize the order of the streets within the walled city, in accordance with the traditional model of the Chinese city, which roughly follows an orthogonal plan, inspired in particular by the principles of the Zhouli (Zhou dynasty, 1046–256 BCE), outlining a checkerboard. In fact, the city of Tianjin, as Noah Drake's plan clearly shows, combines the Beijing-like orthogonal imperial plan with the narrow, winding alley districts of other Chinese cities. The two plans differed

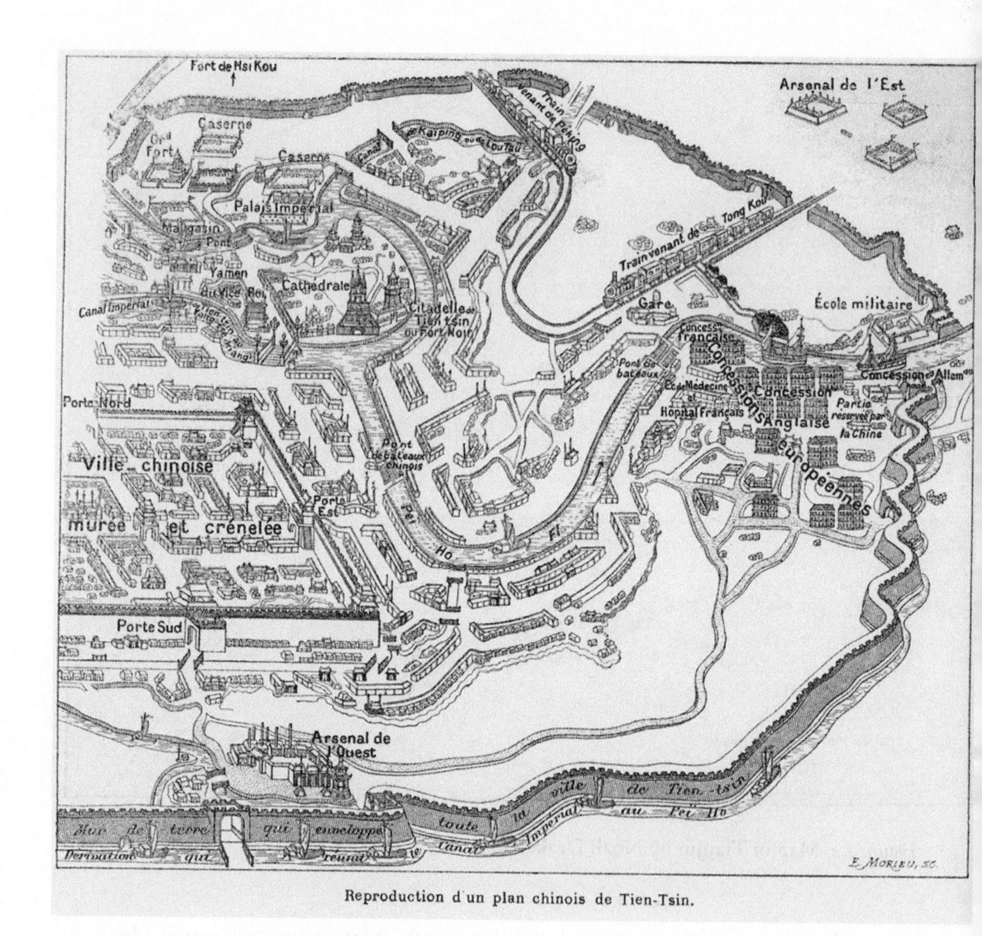

Reproduction d un plan chinois de Tien-Tsin.

Figure 4.3 Fragment of a Chinese map translated and adapted by Raoul-Charles Villetard de Laguérie. *L'Illustration*, July–December 1900.

in their centering: the Chinese map focused on the walled city, while the Provisional Government's map focused on the point of contact between the old city and the foreign concessions. Feng Qihuang greatly enlarged the native city and reduced the territory under foreign rule, while Noah Drake focused on the large area of the concessions and disregarded the location of the monument that symbolized the city: the great tower, in the center of the walled city, which majestically dominated Feng Qihuang's map. The latter disproportionately depicted the buildings symbolizing imperial power: the canal, the moat, the city walls, the earthen wall, the administration buildings, and the temples. The Chinese map shows the omnipresence of temples, distinguished by their large red gate, in the walled city and in the Chinese suburbs.

Far from revealing the superiority of Western cartography over Chinese science, these two maps offer two distinct modes of accuracy. Thus, the government map locates accurately the waterways and the route of the railroad. While the Chinese map provides important information about the relief, urban morphology (height of buildings) and economic activities (coal from Kaiping mines, factories, river navigation, and so on). Both maps fail to depict the huge salt heaps on the left bank of the Hai River, which only Herbert Hoover rendered in his July 1900 sketches. Feng Qihuang's map also provides data on the architecture of both the Chinese city and the foreign concessions, symbolized by the same two-story building replicated fifteen times.

Figure 4.4 Buildings in the foreign concessions. Detail of frontispiece. Courtesy of the Library of Congress, Geography and Map Division.

Figure 4.5 Chinese buildings in the concessions. Detail of frontispiece. Courtesy of the Library of Congress, Geography and Map Division.

Only the Chinese map and its legend show the details of each building, such as the various buildings of the Tianjin train station, built in 1888 and moved to the riverfront in 1891, indicating the place where train tickets were sold and where Chinese people stood in line, "controlled by policemen who whipped anyone who stepped out of the line."[8] Feng Qihuang clearly shows the change from two tracks to a single track from the station to the east.

Figure 4.6 Two railways to the west of the station. Detail of frontispiece. Courtesy of the Library of Congress, Geography and Map Division.

Figure 4.7 A single railway to the east. Detail of frontispiece. Courtesy of the Library of Congress, Geography and Map Division.

The map provides some information on the elevation, such as the railroad embankment that protected the tracks from flooding, and especially on the economic activities of the station whose development resulted from the transportation of coal from the Kaiping mines, opened in 1878, with an annual coal production of 700,000 tons.[9]

Figure 4.8 Elevation of the railroad. Detail of frontispiece. Courtesy of the Library of Congress, Geography and Map Division.

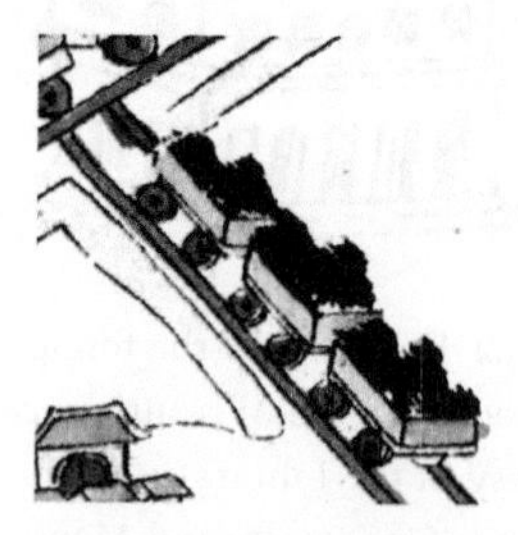

Figure 4.9 Kaiping coal stored near the station. Detail of frontispiece. Courtesy of the Library of Congress, Geography and Map Division.

Most of the coal was destined for the military arsenals in the east and west where factories and workshops manufactured gunpowder and weapons. These arsenals, like the large piles of salt, gave a visual identity to the city: "From Tientsin we first saw the high industrial chimneys of the arsenal, a sight that cheered us up after the sorry succession of ransacked and

Figure 4.10 Armament factories of the Western Arsenal and temple. Detail of frontispiece. Courtesy of the Library of Congress, Geography and Map Division.

burned villages. We felt something of Europe vibrating around us that we already missed."[10]

Like Drake's, this military map offers precious information on the city's defenses, such as the description of the walkway, the crenellated ramparts of the city, which could be ridden on horseback and held large caliber cannons, or the Jin Hua bridge, the first movable iron bridge in China, installed in 1888 in front of the offices of the viceroy of Zhili.

Figure 4.11 Walkway along the ramparts. Detail of frontispiece. Courtesy of the Library of Congress, Geography and Map Division.

Figure 4.12 Iron Bridge (1888).

The very form of the aerial and oblique shot suggests interpretations that emphasize the exceptional character of Tianjin in the Chinese urban world. The use of this omniscient perspective can be linked to a cosmic and imperial vision of Tianjin, which since the early fifteenth century meant "Gateway to the Son of Heaven (the emperor)." In the European tradition, an aerial view was also used to create a panorama: Feng presents an extraordinary agglomeration of European and Chinese elements, ships and junks, buildings and pagodas, and so on. In Tianjin, as in the United States at the end of the nineteenth century, the panoramic map could serve as a tool for the economic promotion of the city, and even for tourism, since travel guides were developed in Beijing from the middle of the nineteenth century and in Tianjin at the turn of the century.[11] Finally, the panopticism of the bird's-eye view translates a more utopian approach while at the same time precisely rendering the urban development projects in progress.

This view perfectly illustrates the dynamism of traditional Chinese cartography that continued to flourish as the imperial court sought to impose "Western" standards in the late nineteenth century. In the 1890s the Qing government attempted to standardize the cartographic practices of local and regional governments.[12] It ordered "Western" conical projection maps from provincial governments.[13] However, too few experts mastered these cartographic techniques to carry out the imperial program. Thus, in 1892 a provincial governor lamented, "In each sub-prefecture and district, the scholars familiar with the territory are rare. In addition, survey and drawing instruments are lacking. That is why, in this confused situation, it is impossible to carry out this order."[14] Some Chinese scholars remained convinced of the value of Chinese cartography, following the example of Feng Qihuang, who preferred to illustrate, or even renew, the indigenous cartographic tradition rather than abandon it in favor of "Western" science. The author of the map did not limit himself to remaining inside the walls that separated the Chinese city from its suburbs. Like numerous maps of Beijing from the same period, he continued the tradition of local monographs that inscribed cities in their regional environment.[15] Thus, in a semicolonial context, this Chinese map offered a true portrait of the city and may be interpreted both as a form of resistance to Western cultural norms and as an expression of an awareness of the foreign presence.

Land registry and the owners: Expropriation, compensation, and registration

With its new map production, the government, under section 4 of the bylaws, made it a priority to compile an inventory of real property in the jurisdiction.[16] To do this the government surveyor inventoried and described precisely all the properties in the city in a register. This land registry or cadaster, a traditional tool of police control and tax collection, enabled the Provisional Government to recover the property of the Chinese government and to proceed with the confiscation of properties belonging to the Boxers and Chinese who had fled, transforming it into "public property." It was also an indispensable tool for land use planning.

The government wished to grant lots to all the expropriated owners as part of its public works program. These lots were "marked in advance [on the cadaster] so that they may build shacks on them immediately." In some cases, like particularly coveted spaces such as the wharf, the government granted the former owners the estimated value of their house, a plot of land equal in size in another neighborhood and, in addition, 75 taels per *mou* of expropriated land. The owners of the houses in front of the river were forced to give them up within a month of the government's decision. When such an exchange was impossible or when the pressure on available land increased, the government preferred to offer the owners financial compensation: this was the case for the construction of the road from the North Gate to the Grand Canal in April 1901 for which the government offered $446 for 6.64 *mou* of land belonging to sixty-seven different owners. The Chinese secretary, more favorable to the local Chinese owners, and the chief of public works, more concerned with the government's finances, disagreed on the amount of compensation: the council decided on an "average rate" of $20 per expropriated *mou*. European missionaries were favored, as was the case with Father du Cray, a Jesuit, whose land near the German concession, was transformed into a road by the government. He was compensated at $45 per unit. Despite this preferential treatment, Father du Cray refused the sum offered and asked for the constitution of an independent jury to rule on the question. Faced with the council's refusal for "cause of public utility," the French consul played his role as protector of the Catholics and chief adversary of the Provisional Government to intervene and request that the question be settled by jury. Finally, the council complied by offering the handsome sum of $1,082.50 to Father du Cray.

The development companies working on behalf of the government invented a final form of compensation: shareholding. The German entrepreneur and former Chinese admiral Constantin von Hanneken, a pivotal figure in the social life of Tianjin and son-in-law of Gustav Detring, armed with a map of the expropriated land, offered the former Chinese owners shares in his drainage company in return. Lieutenant Colonels Arlabosse and Aoki visited the land, listed the owners and ordered that "a plan be made of each house to be demolished, with the name of the owner, the surface area, etc." One copy was kept with the Provisional Government and another given to the owners, who also received certificates—deeds of ownership—from the secretary of Chinese affairs. Thus, little by little, the land was systematically measured and incorporated into the cadaster by the agents of the public works department in exchange for a few tens of cents of taels per *mou*. The Provisional Government thus appropriated the jurisdiction's territory. For their part, almost all the Chinese owners asked for and obtained compensation. The council, anxious not to offend Chinese public opinion, was careful not to put itself in the position of the expropriating state as demonstrated when it wrote, "we will not employ the word 'confiscated.'"[17]

At first the government refused to systematically register property deeds and land transfers, since there was no clear procedure to validate property titles. In April 1901 the government's police chief proposed establishing a system of title registration to facilitate transfers and protect owners, especially foreigners, who had purchased land from the Chinese after the capture of the city. Colonel Bower strongly objected because such a procedure would require hiring many surveyors and likely cause tension with foreign consuls since almost all the applications came from Chinese owners residing in the new Austrian and Italian concessions. The council agreed with Colonel Bower. Under pressure from native landowners, the Chinese secretary returned to the issue in July, stressing the need to ensure the registration of property titles to maintain social order. Convinced, the council asked Colonel Bower to submit a draft which was adopted on August 5, 1901. The secretary of Chinese affairs, assisted by a "conductor" and an "able Chinese deputy," was officially charged with registering property titles. For this purpose, the government created the Land Registry Office as a section of the Chinese Secretariat. In return for recognizing "indigenous" property and registering it in the land registry, the government levied a 1 percent tax (a minimum of 3 taels per slack).

How did the Provisional Government solve the problem of uncertainty regarding Chinese property titles? Property transfers were to be posted on the land in question and in a frame set up for this purpose on the door of the Provisional Government's headquarters for at least one month before they were registered. This public procedure allowed for joint control by the residents of the neighborhood, who could make their claims known if necessary.[18] Before registration, the Chinese secretary needed to ascertain the validity of the property rights by examining the Chinese documents and inquiring among the neighbors. Two notables of the district were required to countersign the titles of ownership or sale since they were accountable in case the validity was questioned. The government, in continuity with the Chinese administration, registered the acts made by foreigners by working with the consul under whom he was in charge. The diplomatic corps in Beijing, which wished to retain direct control over its nationals, formally opposed this provision and forced the Provisional Government to abandon it. Foreigners had to apply to their respective consuls to register their titles but had to turn to the government's Public Works Department to obtain a building permit. The council imposed "proper building methods" on all owners. On the other hand, the government had to be extremely careful with the old and new concessionary powers. The secretary of Chinese affairs, who had maps of all foreign concessions, could not issue building permits for existing concessions and territories claimed by the Allied powers.[19]

From then on, the government kept the valid deeds in a purpose-built safe and declared all purchases and sales of real estate not registered by the Chinese secretary's office null and void. The Chinese secretary's office then had a monopoly on certifying land sales and leases. Any dispute over ownership was to be brought before the court of the Provisional Government: the party able to produce a title deed duly registered by the office was officially considered to own the land. Thus, when a certain Han claimed a piece of land in the northwestern part of the Chinese city, considered by Noah Drake to be "public property," the magistrate investigated. He found Han's rights valid against the advice of the government official and ordered the modification of the land registry by the chief of public works. The magistrate judged many usurpations of title, for example, a priest of the Ka Lo Shih temple who wished to register the title deeds of his house to Japanese merchants and was forced after the investigation of the Chinese secretary to admit that his alleged property belonged to the customs *daotai*.[20]

Through this registration process, the government sought to assert its legitimacy by defending property rights, and thus distinguishing itself from the habits and customs of the colonies. In its official discourse the government tried to be irreproachable. Any expropriation deserved compensation and any occupation necessitated remuneration. Thus, when the secretary of Chinese affairs recommended to the council that rent be paid for all buildings occupied by the government's military and civilians, the police chief responded by advocating "a small payment as compensation rather than rent." The council approved. But in reality the Chinese had to struggle to obtain this "compensation." And asserting one's rights was always easier for rich merchants and Chinese dignitaries than for the average person. So General Shih, with the help of the lawyer E. P. Allen, managed to obtain the rent of his land occupied by the German troops in Tongku. The Provisional Government paid a total of $250 per month for all the premises it occupied in the city and $27 for the buildings outside the mud wall. At the time of the handover the government took care to entrust all the detailed inventories of the properties to the Chinese government to prove its probity and its qualities of excellent management.[21]

However, any supposed novelty of the Allies' procedures must be put into perspective. On the one hand, the Provisional Government's practice of expropriation corresponded to the emperor's right to dispose, if necessary, of any private property within the empire.[22] On the other hand, the registration procedure itself already existed in the old Chinese law that remained in force at the end of the nineteenth century: "The cheoi-k'i is an act by which a new owner, having entered into a revocable or irrevocable purchase contract for a house or land, in return for a legal fee paid to the government, obtains that the local magistrate affixes his seal to the documents, hands over the diploma called the k'i-wei, and confirms the contract."[23]

The impossible census: A Japanese captain, *shendong*, and 800,000 Chinese

Maps and the land registry were the essential tools in this complex environment where ten powers were copresent and "indigenous" property had to be respected, at least officially. Regarding demographic data, the government was initially content with the vague estimates formulated by Noah Fields Drake, who considered the population of Tianjin in 1900 to be between 600,000 and 800,000, while the "European-American" population consisted of approximately 1,000 individuals.[24] The government was not satisfied with the estimates of the "European-American" population. It was not until six months later that the council first considered the proposal to conduct a population census and commissioned a report on the subject from the secretary of Chinese affairs. It took almost a year and a half to obtain the first population statistics. From February 1902, they provided figures of "population movements," marriages, and deaths for the previous month sorted by district. A few days later, labor statistics were provided, and a month and a half later, monthly crime statistics by district were established. Despite the recommendations of the council, only the Japanese Captain Satō, head of the North Tientsin district, sent his statistics to the council each month. He also submitted a table on the social conditions of the inhabitants with the "cost of living," and meteorological observations. While the other district chiefs were unable to comply with the council's specifications, the government only had the treasury's statistics on the import and export of goods at its disposal. At the beginning of March 1902 a "statistical secretary" was appointed to assist Carl Rump in the Treasury Department.[25]

Captain Satō quickly became a model civil servant for the government, which commissioned him to prepare a summary of his statistical tables to be sent to a "scientific society" and asked him to submit a draft of a general census of the jurisdiction's inhabitants. Three months later the compilation of his statistical reports was sent to the Shanghai Geographical Society. On May 5, 1902, the chief of the district of North Tientsin presented his project, the categories retained ("name, age, sex, occupation, fixed or temporary residence, married or single") and the manpower required: he discussed with Major Mockler, chief of police, to "determine how many of his men are intelligent enough to be employed in this function." The council approved the project as well as the proposals formulated the day after by Mockler, who wished to number the houses and give a name to all the streets, keeping as many of the "established names" as possible. He wished to consult the *shendong* and involve them in this project to facilitate the census operation: the notables, in charge of the "native" police sections, were to submit lists of streets, and the government agents were to paint their names on wooden plaques as well as the numbers on the houses themselves. This enterprise was the result of a coproduction between foreign officials and local notables. In each street of the jurisdiction an inhabitant became responsible for the census and signage. The statistical questionnaire drawn up by Satō was printed and distributed in all the districts as of May 12. It was so successful that the Austrian vice consul asked the council to extend the census to the Austro-Hungarian concession. The government readily agreed. When in mid-July the director of a Belgian newspaper asked the council to provide him with the latest census of Tianjin's population, the government proudly replied, "no census had been taken so far by the Chinese authorities, but the Council is currently dealing with the matter." In reality, the Qing administration had already commissioned a large census in 1842 in the aftermath of the Opium War in order to regain control of urban communities: the *Jinmen baojia tushuo*, published in 1846, counted 198,715 people in the walled city and its immediate suburbs and a total of 442,242 individuals including the population of the surrounding villages.[26] However, the Allies did not manage to carry out the census operation quickly: the government agents barely had time to number the houses and provide street names in the German and Italian sections of the Chinese city. The council, hoping to complete the census before its dissolution, ordered the work to be accelerated. But it did so in vain. The task remained unfinished.[27]

The demolition of the ramparts, or the emasculation of the city

The Provisional Government decided to demolish, "for military reasons and for the sake of hygiene,"[28] the thick brick walls of the city, whose foundations probably dated back to the beginning of the fifteenth century, when it was transformed from a small town into a large garrison to protect the new capital, Beijing. The Chinese notables petitioned against what they considered an unjust punishment and a humiliating act of vandalism.[29] The Europeans were well aware of this: "For the Chinese, a city without a wall is no longer a city worthy of the name, and all the true and sincere Tientsinois, who keep in their hearts the good and holy traditions, consider it a humiliation to live in a city deprived of this essential attribute."[30] These notables remained insensitive to a legend that then (re)surfaced: during the construction of the city walls, a fortune teller drew a large Chinese character on each large gate: *tai* (to carry), *wei* (Tianjin), *kuei* (returned to), *hai* (sea).[31] Some believed that this ancient prophecy was fulfilled in 1900 when the Allies decided to punish the Boxer supporters by razing the high walls and sending some of the bricks to Weihaiwei by the sea. The council did not entertain the indigenous claims. They witnessed firsthand during the siege the formidable usefulness of the ramparts, which resisted the Allied assaults and offered the Chinese high positions from which to fire on the foreign concessions. In addition, the Japanese, whose concession bordered the wall, considered the bases of the ramparts to be insalubrious since they were occupied by small houses, huts, and pestilent swamps. After having obtained the agreement of all Allied commanders, except for the French general, who remained silent, the council ordered the Public Works Department to demolish the walls at the end of December 1900. Destruction began with 66 feet (20 m) along the west side on December 31 to first study the wall's structure and draw up an estimate. The dismantling of the walls over the following months cost $35,000, part of which was paid for in sacks of rice, a precious commodity in these times of shortage. In addition, the contractor kept the bricks intact and gave the damaged bricks to the public works department for road construction. The space freed up allowed for the elaboration of a first urban planning project: in place of the ramparts, the council ordered the construction of a circular macadamized boulevard, quickly lined with numerous Chinese stores. The members of the council undoubtedly saw in this process of demolition initiated in Europe at the end of the eighteenth century a mark of the rise of the bourgeoisie, free trade, and freedom of enterprise.[32]

The council asked Count Alfred von Waldersee and the Allied commanders to include in a clause of the future protocol between the Allied powers and China that "this wall shall never be rebuilt."[33] Article 8 of the protocol of September 7, 1901, ordered the demolition of the Chinese forts in the Tianjin and Taku regions, as well as the demolition of military camps that "could prevent free communication between Peking and the sea."[34] The Chinese representatives asked the Allies to take care of this themselves, and the latter entrusted it to the Provisional Government. Only the arsenal in the West was preserved.[35] As early as June 20 the Allied commanders had authorized the Provisional Government to proceed with the destruction of the Chinese forts under its jurisdiction.

On September 25 the Allied troops began to dismantle the Black Fort, a symbol of Chinese firepower during the siege of the concessions, located east of the walled city. In just two years, the government services systematically destroyed the military buildings of Tianjin (the Black Fort, the Yellow Fort, the Chien Ying Fort, the Hou Ying Fort), the Siku military store, the Eastern Arsenal, the three camps of Hsin Ho, the two camps of Chunliangcheng, and about twenty forts, notably at Taku (seven forts), Peitang (six forts), and Sanhaikuan (five forts). "The legitimate defenses of the empire were sacrificed on the altar of Boxerism,"[36] judged Otto Rasmussen a few years later. The government entrusted this delicate operation to Allied troops and private contractors: the demolition of the twenty-four Chinese forts cost $177,475. It tried to finance this work by selling the materials from the destroyed forts: 500,000 bricks were sold to the German troops and 1,500,000 bricks to the British authorities at a price of $2 per 1,000 bricks. The council even considered renting the old, fortified sites to private companies, such as the location of the northwestern fort of Taku, which interested the Chinese Engineering & Mining Company, but the Italian troops occupying the fort made it known through Admiral Candiani that they refused this rental. The costly nature of these operations led the government to mobilize the prisoners, who were used as coolies in each district for public works. The government conceived this demolition program as one of its main missions: on the eve of its dissolution, at the end of July 1902, it recommended to its agents "to push this work as far as possible" and succeeded in reaching its objectives.[37]

Mastering the river: Irrigation, floods, and navigation

Tianjin is a river city. As a result, its economic fortunes and daily life are intimately linked to the Hai River, a source of prosperity (irrigation, trade) and misfortune (floods) for the residents. Chapter 1 discussed the role of the river in the Boxer movement and in the Battle of Tianjin. The foreign powers were immediately concerned with the question of its development and its canals, which led the government to extend its jurisdiction to better control them.[38] It wished to modify the course of the Yu-Ho Canal and the Hai River to gain land for construction and to increase the flow of the river. The water development program called for the canal to be deepened to 12 feet (3.6 m) to allow large ships to reach Tianjin. The government entrusted the Public Works Department with the coordination of the river's development and "repair" operations. On February 16, 1901, the council gathered all the public actors except the Chinese—including the French, German, Japanese, British, and Russian consuls, the customs commissioner, and the head of the chamber of commerce—at their headquarters to discuss "the improvement of the river and the means of dealing with the expenses it would entail." The management of the Hai River crystallized tensions between the military government and the consular corps. The consuls, under the aegis of Chaylard, met on March 13, 1901, to found a river improvement commission and invited the Provisional

Government to designate a representative within this body. Two days later, by order of the council, Albert de Linde, head of public works, was charged with beginning the operations. However, the latter refused to participate in the consular commission because he had not been consulted on its creation. The council in turn invited the consuls to appoint a representative to sit on the government commission. Marshal von Waldersee and the Allied commanders arbitrated the dispute over river jurisdiction by entrusting the Provisional Government with the task of working on the Hai River. Then, following Gustav Detring's suggestion, Waldersee reestablished the old commission responsible for supervising the work on the river in the spring of 1901. This river maintenance commission, composed of the dean of the consular corps, the customs commissioner, and chaired by Lieutenant Colonel Arlabosse, a representative of the Provisional Government, who replaced the Chinese government official, was financed to the tune of 5,000 taels per month for river maintenance. A form of emulation developed between the concessions and the government, with the latter deciding to pay a sum equal to the financing granted by all the concessions. In total, the government spent 337,500 taels on river development. The government agreed to this considerable investment to secure the commercial interests of foreigners in the port city. Article 11a of the protocol of September 7, 1901, confirmed the mission of the government and the commission, in charge of improving navigation on the Hai River. The commission also organized hydrographic works and the sounding of the Taku sandbar at the mouth of the Hai. To do so, it solicited the logistical and scientific help of all the Allied generals. They responded positively. Colonel Akiyama, commander of the Japanese troops, put a warship at the disposal of the council toward this end, and the Italians loaned him a tugboat. Without informing them, the commission finally entrusted the work on the bar to the British ship Rambler. The Japanese expressed their displeasure to the council, which asked the commission to respect the "international character" of this undertaking.[39]

For their part, the local population organized themselves through the *shendong* of the southeastern section of the Chinese city, who alerted the chief of police to the risk of flooding, particularly following the filling of ditches and the cleaning of marshes by government agents. The police chief reported this to the council and the head of public works, who decided to prevent the city from flooding by opening the Hai River diversion canals upstream of Tianjin, as the Chinese government had done previously. The

Chinese kept up the pressure on the government by publishing various articles in the "native press" presenting the possible dangers of flooding because of the Provisional Government's efforts. The council responded by issuing an official statement in the Chinese newspapers, stating that this "eventuality has been carefully examined by the government, which will do what is necessary to avoid it." But a few months later, a delegation of villagers from Ti Tou asked the Chinese secretary not to open the "floodways" near their village in order to protect their fields near the "French marsh."

One of the main issues was the control of the locks: since villagers did not hesitate to open the locks or breach the dykes to irrigate their fields, the government regularly issued proclamations forbidding the inhabitants of the Chunliangcheng and Tongku districts to open the dams and canal locks. The council's orders were disregarded by the peasants and were also criticized by the district chiefs, such as Major Ducat, head of Chunliangcheng, who pointed out that the government's prohibition made some fields, such as those in Hsiao Chan, unusable for the peasants. The council decided to organize a meeting between Major Ducat, Albert de Linde, and the "cultivators," who found a solution to maintain the ban on opening and breaking the locks while authorizing the passage of water through pipes installed through the Machang lock and the dams of Hsien Shui Ku and Hsin Cheng. This decision can be explained by the intervention, alongside Major Ducat, of the American missionary Dr. Arthur Smith and Chinese notables, who pleaded the cause of the peasants before the council for certain rice fields of Hsiao Chan, who financed charitable works in Tianjin. The council adopted a pragmatic position by inviting the chief of public works "not to strictly adhere to the instructions of the Council on this subject, but to take the measures that his experience indicated as necessary." Thus, from the beginning of July, a public works officer, Mr. Young, was dispatched to open and close the Machang lock as much as necessary to irrigate the rice fields and prevent flooding. But the following year, the district chief again considered the water supplied to the fields of Hsiao Chan insufficient. After June 1901 the district chiefs had to send daily reports by telegraph or telephone, and "several times a day, if necessary," on the level of the Hai River and the state of the dikes and dams. The effects of this prevention policy, which recommended that district chiefs identify and then list flood-prone areas during the rainy season in the vicinity of the Hai and Grand Canal, are difficult to measure, however, due to a lack of sources. Nonetheless, district chiefs did respond to villagers' petitions for government assistance in repairing the banks of the canals.[40]

From the fall of 1901, the river maintenance commission coordinated operations, particularly the various openings of locks and dams. The latter could be operated only by confirmed agents, provided with an "identification in Chinese or English." The commission fought against all the "obstructions" made to the course of the river like the numerous jetties built by the villagers. To this end, the government's river police patrolled between Tianjin and Tongku to "prevent villages from continuing this harmful practice." At the same time the commission's officials carried out dredging work, while the government's public works department was working to remove the many junks sunk during the siege of the city. The rules laid down by the commission also applied to foreign powers: the council asked the Russians, who installed buildings on stilts on the banks of their concession, to respect the statutory width of the river. And when the Chinese administration, in the person of *daotai* Chang, wished to obtain a right of inspection over certain locks like Machang, the commission insisted upon exclusive control over it.[41]

The internationalization of roads, bridges, and tramways

In addition to the development of the river, the government wished for military and commercial reasons to improve circulation within the jurisdiction, particularly between the Chinese city and the concessions. The Allies built a network of streets and roads.[42] Beginning in December 1900, they widened the wharf to sixty feet (18.2 m) and then paved it in April 1901. For the sum of $9,500, the wide boulevard that replaced the city walls was extended along the Hai River and the Grand Canal to facilitate entry and exit of the Chinese city both toward the sea and toward Beijing, as well as access to the government headquarters.[43]

The Public Works Department widened and aligned the two main arteries that intersected in the center of the city. The government agent responsible for roads was given the charge of "widening the roads wherever possible" in the city. At the same time, it was forbidden to construct buildings less than 6.5 feet (2 m) from establishments occupied by the Allies. Part of the streets were paved, like the circular boulevard and the quays, which were covered with successive layers of stone. To do so, the Public Works Department bought stone from Tongshan. The council ordered the leveling of the roads, but the steamrollers, of about ten tons, did not arrive from London in time to carry out this operation before the government was dissolved.

The latter had the "huts" near the racetrack gate destroyed, and once again the secretary of the British municipal council requested the intervention of the Provisional Government to pave the road that connected the concessions to the racetrack and plant trees alongside it. The Public Works Department assumed the task of building the "international road" at a cost of $19,400, which was intended to guarantee the neutrality of this high point of cosmopolitan sociability. Gustav Detring contributed to the construction of this new network by financing the construction of a gravel road with a sidewalk to the racetrack for pedestrians in Hai Kuang Ssu. The Allied commanders agreed to extend the council's jurisdiction to the road from the southern gate of the Chinese city to Hai Kuang Ssu in the Japanese concession and to Taku Road to allow troops to move around the city between the various occupied territories and concessions. The British municipality had no objection to the "neutrality" of Taku Road, while the French consul said that he would only ratify it if the government took charge of the "maintenance, improvement, and lighting" of this long wide street. The council categorically refused to maintain a street in the French concession but agreed to take over the management of the portion of Taku Road within the boundaries of the British and German concessions "as was done by the Chinese government."

Once again, the Provisional Government intended to explicitly follow the lead of the Qing administration, which had considered Taku Road a "strategic road," especially when it allowed the French consul, the government's primary adversary, to be bullied. When the council charged its French representative, Captain Jullian, with explaining to the French consul that the Provisional Government could not change its policy toward the French concession, the consul held firm. He would recognize the neutrality of Taku Road if, and only if, the Provisional Government took over the maintenance of the street and reimbursed all costs incurred by the municipality on that road. Following the Frenchman, the Japanese consul general agreed to make "neutral" the street from Hai Kuang Ssu to the southern gate on the condition that it be maintained by the government. Faced with these demands, the council changed its mind and suddenly became aware of the inefficiency of the choice of Taku Road as a neutral road since it "no longer communicates with the Chinese city," thus considerably complicating traffic between the center of the city and the coast. The government asked the consuls to choose together the road that could be used as an "international street." The French consul proposed a road passing in front of the new slaughterhouses, which would benefit from "unencumbered circulation"—without stopping—of carts between the concession and the Chinese city. His Japanese counterpart then proposed to make the Hai Ta Tao passage a neutral road. The British and German consuls then had to choose a street that corresponded to these proposals but were slow to find a solution. The council tried to unblock the situation by advocating the transformation of Bristow Road and its extension into a neutral street in the German concession. But the consuls were once again reluctant: the British consul general felt that a portion of the future neutral street, not incorporated into the British concession, could pose a problem when the Provisional Government was dissolved, while the French consul regretted that the financial situation of his municipality did not allow it to contribute to the project of this major international route. The German consul approved the road's direction but was opposed to the portion going from the match factory to the racetrack. The council then gave up its project.[44]

The government completed the road network with a street lighting system designed by the police chief in November 1900 as part of its law-and-order policy. He had lamps installed in the main streets of the Chinese city "at intervals of 100 paces on both sides of the street such that the lights alternated from 50 to 50 paces on each side. The government funded these measures by requiring homeowners to purchase and maintain the lights. Only the lighting along the old ramparts was paid by the government. The residents considered the system expensive and presented their objections through a petition signed by the notables; the government, inflexible, insisted on keeping this relatively efficient infrastructure for public safety and the balance of its finances. As with the lighting, the government's road projects aroused the reluctance of a part of the population. Thus, the notables of the northwestern section of the city drafted several petitions to protest the construction of a road in the district. The council pretended to consider the interests of the inhabitants by responding that "the goal of the projects of the Provisional Government are the improvement of the city and ensuring the public good, not wronging the residents." The public works department drew up a plan for a boulevard linking the northwest corner of the city to the Grand Canal. The treasurer estimated the compensation due to dispossessed property owners, and the secretary of Chinese affairs was charged with consulting with the notables and the main Chinese merchants in the neighborhood. Notables petitioned for the abandonment of the project and chose to go through the French consul to transmit their position to the council. They were entirely familiar with the consul's tenacity vis-à-vis the Provisional Government, and indeed the French diplomat seized on the new opportunity to thwart the government's plans. The council immediately ordered the Chinese secretary to identify those responsible for the petition and their connection to the French consul. The Chinese notables argued that the proposed route passed through a too densely populated area and eventually won their case, and the council agreed to their proposal to route the boulevard through the southwest corner and the Chih Yuan temple area.[45]

The crossing of the Hai River had been problematic for the Allies from the start. Indeed, the day after the city was taken, to cross it "one risked slipping into the red-ochre waters, where eight soldiers had already drowned, sometimes on steeply sloping and unstable flats and sometimes on wet junks lined up in every direction."[46] This "suggestive monument of the international agreement" connected the station to the quay de France next to the bridge. Three other boat bridges were established by the British near Barfleur Barracks, by the Russians in front of the Chinese military academy, and by the Germans south of the former U.S. concession. Tianjin, the "emperor's gateway," already had two pontoon bridges and the iron bridge above the Hai River.

Through its control of these various bridges, the government sought to control the crossing of the river as well as navigation insofar as the pontoon bridges, by definition, blocked it. In September 1900 it claimed that the boats on the German bridge belonged to it, and a few months later the Russian chief of staff ceded the "Russian bridge" to the government. At the beginning of February 1901 the council adopted a specific regulation on the bridges of Tianjin, which stipulated that they could be opened and closed only by government agents. The latter opened them systematically for the Allied ships, and "at intervals when the traffic by land will allow it" for Chinese ships. Finally, the French consul agreed that the Provisional Government would take charge of the service of the "French bridge," on condition that a French guard remain there: in practice, General Sucillon entrusted this task to his engineers, and the Provisional Government financed it.[47]

General Voyron proposed that the council pay for the construction of a metal bridge in place of the pontoon bridge guarded by the French. The military and the consuls agreed on the strategic nature of this bridge, which would link the station, the concessions, and the Chinese city. The government was ready to build this "indispensable" bridge but, "in consideration of the fact that the river itself has never belonged to the foreign concessions," it claimed ownership and control of it while willingly accepting the proposal of the French municipality to provide electricity in exchange for payment. The French consul, again and again, did not intend to let himself be dispossessed of his prerogatives over what was then called the "French bridge." He demanded that the new bridge be built by a French company, the Fives-Lille Company, a famous civil engineering firm that had built the Orsay train station and the Eiffel Tower elevators. The council invoked its policy of international tendering to reject the consul's economic patriotism. At the same time he advocated that the government services should directly take charge of the construction of the bridge's foundations. As always, the consul was not impressed by the council's recommendations, which in theory held force of law, and declared that "he was opposed to the construction of a bridge touching the French concession by anyone other than a French company." The council complained to General Voyron about the attitude of the French consul, who was preventing the construction of the international bridge: the commander-in-chief was careful not to criticize the consul, who was trying to promote national interests and observe benevolent neutrality in the matter. In July 1901 the council had to give in by accepting the conditions of the French consul and the participation of the Fives-Lille company. It deposited $10,000 each month with the Deutsch-Asiatische Bank for the new construction, which was officially named the "International Bridge" and was to "remain an international bridge in perpetuity." After the transfer of the government to the Chinese authorities, the French consul oversaw safeguarding "international interests." The latter tried to push his advantage: he reduced the share paid by the French concession to $40,000 and decided against the name "International Bridge." The council refused to change the name, arguing that the Russian consul would participate financially in the operation and policing of the future bridge. Representatives of the Fives-Lille company came to Tianjin to draw up the plans, which were presented to the council and forwarded to the Public Works Department.

In view of its forthcoming dissolution, the government provided financing for the future metal swing bridge and entrusted the bank account dedicated to this project to the French consul, who was responsible for overseeing the international work. The Provisional Government committed nearly $200,000 to its construction, which was completed in 1903.[48] Bridges could be the target of some Chinese who saw them as a symbol and a tool of foreign domination: five bridges between Tianjin and Chunliangcheng were damaged or destroyed between February and August 1901. Those responsible for this damage were sought in vain by the international police.[49]

The tramway was the subject of the last major transport infrastructure project developed under the Provisional Government, following the Boxers' destruction of a short streetcar line installed in 1899 in the suburbs of Beijing by the German company Siemens. The initiative came from a private company run by Doney and Moller, which, as soon as the new council was set up, requested authorization to build an electric tramway to link the Chinese city to the concessions. Two days later the Japanese consul reminded the council that the Qing administration had recently granted it the concession for an electric tramway and that the Provisional Government had a duty to respect this commitment. The council decided to put this thorny issue aside for several months before being reintroduced by Doney and Moller. It reaffirmed, however, that the matter was not its concern. In January 1901 foreign entrepreneurs came back once again, trying to internationalize the issue through a committee "composed of various nationalities," which was again refused by the council. The committee, which in fact represented the Electric Lighting and Traction Syndicate, headed by E. Heyl of E. Meyer & Co., had strong support from a clever government lawyer named James Bromley Eames, who also defended his interests in a private capacity, and the powerful customs commissioner Gustav Detring, who chaired the company. They managed to convince the Japanese consul to conclude, in the words of the Japanese diplomat, a "friendly arrangement" between the interests of the company and those of the Japanese concession. We do not know the terms of the agreement, but it probably involved financial compensation and an agreement on the route of the line that was to pass through the Japanese concession.

The council had no choice but to give the "syndicate" the tramway concession for the territory under the jurisdiction of the Provisional

Government. The Electric Lighting and Traction Syndicate obtained the concession in July 1901 and signed the contract in November 1901. The company had to provide compensation to dispossessed property owners, pay for half of the lighting on the streets served by the tramway, and distribute 10 percent of its profits to the government in return for assuming part of the cost of building the bridges and roads, which also needed to be open to pedestrians. Heyl then had to convince foreign concessions to receive the future tramway. The French consul seemed reluctant at first, arguing that there was a "local syndicate," that is, a French one, which already had a concession for electric lighting and traction.[50]

In the summer of 1902 this company was taken over by the International Tramway and Electric Lighting Company of Tientsin, which had been preparing the acquisition for more than a year. In March 1901 Major Baesens, a Belgian army officer and instructor of the Yuan Shikai troops, presented a project for a tramway line between the viceroy's headquarters and the German concession.[51] He convinced Consul du Chaylard by flattering his economic patriotism: Baesens undertook in his specifications to purchase half of the equipment from French manufacturers. In addition to the French consul, he obtained the tacit agreement of the Russian Consul and the support of Li Hongzhang, viceroy of Zhili, who granted him the rights to the tramway concession in the Chinese city: "On the other hand, His Excellency Li-Hung-Chang, vice-king of Pe-Tche-Li, granted me, on June 6, 1901, the tramway concession on the territory of the Chinese city. The old viceroy, out of consideration for the provisional government, postponed the signing of the contract until the time of his return to Tientsin, not wanting to sign any act relating to the prior government of Pe-Tche-Li."[52]

Despite the military occupation of Tianjin, the Chinese provincial authorities continued to be approached by foreigners, who were aware of the provisional status of the government, and Li Hongzhang established his authority by anticipating the handover and intervening in the Allies' affairs. At the same time, and concurrently with Baesens' efforts, a group of Belgian interests (Banque d'Outremer, Compagnie Internationale d'Orient, and the Empain Group) sent a team of diplomats, businessmen, and engineers (Emile Francqui, Armand Rouffart, Adolphe May, and Lambert Jadot) to Tianjin to buy the rights to the tramway. As early as 1901 they wrote several feasibility studies.[53] Thus Adolphe May estimated the number of passengers and therefore the number of engines (25) and trailers (15) needed for the future tramway based on the number of rickshaws in the city: 5,300 in the Chinese city, 2,500 in the English concession, and 2,400 in the French concession. A first-class section was even envisaged to transport the 2,000 foreigners and Chinese merchants. On June 14, 1902, the Belgian interest group formed the Compagnie de Tramways et d'Éclairage de Tientsin in Brussels, which obtained the concession one month later thanks to the purchase of the Electric Light and Traction Syndicate.[54] The council validated the transfer of rights a few days later. Numerous shopkeepers and rickshaw pushers, believing that the spatial hold of their activity and their trade itself were threatened, mobilized against this tramway project by sending a petition to the chamber of commerce.[55]

At the same time, a Japanese subject, Mr. Shimada, tried to meet the need for public transport in another way. He obtained the authorization to install a horse-drawn omnibus which ran on a fixed line at set times in the Chinese city and enjoyed tax exemption for the first three months of operation. The line was promptly opened and operated from November 16, 1901, to April 29, 1902. Two months later two other Japanese wished to establish a new transport company to link the two territories of the Japanese concession, from the north of the French concession to the south of the German concession.[56]

"War is waged by telegraph"

In China, the first telegraph installed by the Chinese linked Tianjin to Taku in 1879.[57] Under the impetus of Li Hongzhang, a telegraph school was founded in Tianjin in 1880 and a line linked Tianjin to Shanghai in 1881 and then, three years later, to Beijing. This technology played a decisive role in the Boxer Rebellion, when the Boxers placed a priority on destroying the communication infrastructure. Thus, on June 15, 1900, the telegraph wire was cut between Beijing and Tianjin, which continued to communicate with the rest of the world thanks to its line with Taku.

The Allied troops, starting in August 1900, installed their own telegraph system. The Electric Engineering & Fitting Co. obtained permission from the government, which did not have its own telegraph and telephone network and set up a new telegraph office and telephone system in the city at its own expense. For $1,200 a year, Electric Engineering provided the Provisional Government with ten telephones to ensure service for the police in the jurisdiction: the residence of the council member who supervised the police, the chief of police, the district chiefs and the police section chiefs were equipped with the precious device in May 1901. Then, new telephones were regularly installed in other government departments. The company had a monopoly on the civil construction of the government's communication infrastructure: its prices were never discussed by the council, probably because of its owner, who was none other than Constantin von Hanneken, one of the most powerful magnates in the city and an indispensable intermediary between the Qing Empire and the Allied powers.[58]

The construction of new telegraph lines met with some opposition from the local population. The German soldiers, who built the line from Tianjin to Baoding, asked for government assistance in the face of local resistance in October 1900 and again in March 1901. Sabotage against the new lines then intensified. Mr. Poulsen, head of the Electric Engineering & Fitting Co., complained regularly to the government: "The telegraph wires are being maliciously broken." The protection of the lines then officially became one of the main tasks of the Provisional Government and its district chiefs. On March 20, 1901, the council declared the neighboring villages responsible for the damage caused to the line. Over the following days the German line was destroyed three times in the districts and in the city. The council then ordered the head of the South Tientsin district to designate a person responsible in each village near the infrastructure, to arrest him, and to sentence him to death. These measures did not reduce the number of actions against the telegraph. On the contrary, the British wire was cut in the heart of the city between Temperance Hall and the southern gate of the city, just as the German lines were simultaneously cut near Siku and at the exit of the city.[59]

Faced with the destruction of telegraph lines in what became a veritable guerrilla war, the distraught council demanded that "some kind of example be set." The chief of police, noting that his measures did not lead to the apprehension of the culprits, proposed to "make the neighboring villages responsible." The idea came from the district chief of Tongku, who had been asking the council since March to hold the village chiefs, the *shendong*, responsible for the "damages." The council approved this measure, and the secretary responsible Chinese affairs issued a proclamation in the districts. The government then instituted a system of collective punishment where, as in the Chinese criminal code, responsibility was not personal: the Chinese leaders, considered jointly responsible for the criminal acts committed in their district, were sentenced for acts they had not personally committed. The foreign military was in fact convinced that the village community was at least passively responsible. In fact, the practice of collective punishment was aimed less at punishing acts of depredation than at intimidating the local population. In the minds of the council officers and district chiefs, it was a matter of preventing acts of "vandalism" by terrorizing the population. These cruel and unjust measures tended—in fact—to maintain and even strengthen the resistance movements. However, few culprits were arrested by the international police, such as a Chinese man from Tongku district, who was sentenced to fifty bamboo lashings and two years of hard labor for stealing telegraph wire.[60]

This extremely repressive strategy soon proved counterproductive. Following the cutting of the German line near Siku, Major Mockler, head of the government police, proposed to the council the arrest of notables of Hsi Yu Chuang from the neighboring village and a collective fine of $300 on the village. The council approved and doubled the amount of the fine, also demanding that the *shendong* be imprisoned until the culprits had been identified. However, this decision quickly became problematic because the strategy of indiscriminate repression did not correspond to the patient work of the foreign officers, who cooperated with the village chiefs on the ground. The next day, the head of the Siku post, French Lieutenant Venner, suggested that the council reconsider its position regarding the two Siku *shendong* arrested by the international police. Since they had "always shown a willingness to help French troops in the vicinity," the punishment seemed particularly unfair. Despite these criticisms, the government continued its repressive policy, and many Chinese notables were imprisoned following acts of damage on telegraph and telephone lines as well as on the wires of railway signals. Heavy collective fines, averaging $600, were imposed on village communities. In early 1902 Major Mockler perfected the system of collective punishment by levying a fine of 20 cents per family in villages adjacent to places where wires had been cut. A few months earlier, the district chief of South Tientsin, faced with the ineffectiveness of the fines, forced the inhabitants of the village of Tin Sekou, where a Japanese wire had been cut again, to maintain ten additional policemen until the damage ceased. The "native" policemen in charge of guarding the telegraph wires could in turn be punished for negligence or collaboration with the "vandals." The Electric Engineering & Fitting Co. sent employees to the police to conduct field investigations in the various districts. The villagers were sometimes able to defend themselves by accusing foreign troops—particularly Indian troops—of having committed the destruction. The administration of punishment became a source of rivalry between the Provisional Government and the Allied troops. Thus, in August 1901, when Japanese officers wished to impose a fine on the village of Wang Chia Chuang, near which the wire had been cut, the council solemnly declared that within its jurisdiction the Provisional Government did not allow fines to be imposed by any authority other than itself and that it was determined to punish the people concerned. Colonel Akiyama, now certain that he had won his case, replied that if the Provisional Government took "effective measures," the Japanese authorities would not intervene in the village. A few days later, the Japanese officially recognized the Provisional Government's exclusive right to punish those responsible for damage to telegraph wires within its jurisdiction. One year after the founding of the Provisional Government, its authority had finally been established.[61]

At the same time, the authorities noted an upsurge in the theft of wires and equipment, such as the five hundred yards (457.2 m) of wire stolen between the concessions and the Western Arsenal or large quantities of Japanese telephone wire from the Japanese concession. Bolts and ties were taken from the railroad. What could the Chinese do with these high-tech items that symbolized Western domination? Colonel Bower's report sheds light on the vernacular uses and reappropriation of these stolen goods by the villagers near Yangcun: "The villages in question have been heavily involved in the theft of railroad material, especially railroad ties, which they have sawed for use in doorways, etc., and building houses. . . . One house, built almost entirely of ties, was demolished."[62]

The Chinese administration of Zhili, which, under the direction of Li Hongzhang, had long been fully aware of the strategic importance of the telegraph, established its position early on. It bought the German telegraph line linking Tianjin to Baoding on behalf of the Chinese government, and Kao, the treasury agent of the viceroy of the province, obtained permission from the council to open a Chinese telegraph office in the city at the beginning of July 1901 on condition that the line be open to all foreign merchants and to the public of any nationality. A month later the Chinese telegraph administration completed the integration of the Tianjin telegraph into the Qing imperial network by connecting its main line to its new office near the northern gate of the city. The Chinese administration simply had to consult with the Public Works Department of the Provisional Government to determine the location of the poles.[63]

This obsession with telegraphy on the part of both the Chinese authorities and the Allied powers was not incompatible with the maintenance of the old means of communication used by the Chinese, such as the light signals, mentioned in June 1901 by a French commander who was concerned about "correspondence by signals, at night, south of the city of Tientsin."[64]

In 1900 Tianjin participated in the movement to standardize the administration of cities.[65] In order to repair the extensive damage caused by the war and to meet the challenge of urban growth, new techniques of "good governance" were adopted. Other tools (map, census, registration, and so forth) already existed in China but were transformed by the foreign powers. The transformation of the city of Tianjin was unparalleled in the country at that time, including in Beijing, where major works began in the summer of 1902 after the imperial court, which had taken refuge in Xi'an, returned to the capital.[66]

Contrary to the colonial model of underinvestment in urban infrastructure, the Provisional Government invested massively in land development (a total of $834,925, not counting the cost of demolishing the forts),[67] trying as much as possible to internationalize means of transport and communication to avoid tensions between the Allied powers. The city and the Chinese suburbs were quickly rebuilt, and following the Provisional Government, the concessions competed in their zeal to develop their territory:

> There are few other traces of the war. The Russians have already rebuilt the stations and have had time to paint Russian inscriptions on all the equipment. On the outskirts of Tientsin, all the villages are burned, and behind a dike there is still a huge Chinese cannon that was aimed at the French consulate. At the Tientsin train station, all the buildings were burned or bombed. . . . We are rebuilding everywhere. All the Chinese districts around the station are burned. All the rooms of the Astor House are held by General von Waldersee. . . . Except for a few burned buildings on the Bund and the Chinese part of the French concession burned by the Boxers, no trace of the bombardment can be seen on the European concessions, and everything is already repaired.[68]

The planning of the territory was imposed on the local population. At the same time, the threat against the indigenous notables explains why some, under duress, actively cooperated with the foreign authorities. Many Chinese challenged the Provisional Government's plans by destroying its facilities, sending petitions, publishing press articles, or pressuring the council through intermediaries such as the French consul. They sometimes won their case, for example by forcing the council to modify the layout of the boulevard to the west of the city, barely a year after the great massacre of the inhabitants by the Allied powers.

Figure 5.1 Cremation of Japanese soldiers killed during the storming of the Chinese City, mid-July 1900. The National Archives, CO 1069/422 [18].

CHAPTER V

A Revolution in Hygiene?

Public Health, Environmental Protection, and Population Control

Today I saw a Chinese merchant with a cache of those ingenious terracotta statuettes which are a specialty of Tientsin. Until this year, they only represented people from the Celestial Empire, of all social conditions and in all situations; but thanks to the invasion they now represent various "warriors of the West," with types and costumes reproduced with the most astonishing accuracy. Now, the meticulous modelers have given to the soldiers of certain European nations, which I prefer not to name, expressions of fierce anger, have put unsheathed sabers, truncheons, or raised whips in their hands. As for our people, wearing their country berets and very French faces with moustaches made of yellow or brown silk, they all carry Chinese babies tenderly in their arms. There are several poses, but always proceeding from the same idea; sometimes the little Chinese holds the soldier by the neck and kisses him; elsewhere the soldier amuses himself by making the baby jump and bursts out laughing; or he wraps him carefully in his winter coat. . . . Thus, in the eyes of these patient observers, while the other soldiers continue to brutalize and strike out, the soldier of our country is the one who, after the battle, makes himself the big brother of the poor enemy babies; after a few months of odd cohabitation, this is what the Chinese have discovered all by themselves, to characterize the French. It would be necessary to spread copies of these various statuettes throughout Europe and even in our country: it would be for us, by comparison, a glorious trophy brought back from this war, that would shut the mouths of a number of imbeciles [Note 3: A few days later, by order of the superior command, the accusatory statuettes were withdrawn from circulation and the molds broken. Only the French statuettes remained on sale, and they have become very rare].

—PIERRE LOTI

It is hardly necessary to explain the smell of corpses that hangs in the air. Just a short while ago, in the middle of a bank along the Peiho, near the entrance to the French concession, the body of a Chinese soldier was quietly decomposing, without a passer-by on the busy road thinking of removing and burying it. In front of the cathedral, I saw Chinese people fishing, with a bamboo skimmer, for watermelon rinds, next to huge, bloated carcasses of dogs they simply pushed aside.

—RAOUL CHARLES VILLETARD DE LAGUÉRIE

In Tientsin, where the epidemic first appeared, nearly fifteen hundred natives died daily, and although it is impossible to make even a rough estimate of the number of daily deaths in Peking, there are a thousand reasons to suppose that the proportion was not less in the capital. One detail will give an idea of the ravaging death: several cases are cited of rickshaw drivers, who started off in good health and who were found languishing at the door of the store where they had just left someone to go shopping.

—GEORGE SOULIÉ

On the last day of the T.P.G., I distributed blankets for the next winter and explained to them the difference between their past and present situations; I asked them to remember that the author of their present well-being was a cursed foreigner, a Frenchman who even now, at the moment he left them behind, was thinking of their well-being, and of their next winter in the hands of the Chinese authorities, who had been foresighted for them and who, without caring what they had been in the past, bandits or Boxers, prisoners or sworn exterminators of Europeans, had made every effort to return them to consideration as human beings, something they had lost in the eyes of their compatriots, and to create for them a comfort certainly superior to that of the majority of the workers of Tientsin.

—F. GARCIA-MESNY

A specialty of local craftsmanship, clay figurines were first used as ex-votos and educational tools to tell the story of the great operas, the daily history of unknown soldiers as well as of Chinese and then foreign heroes.[1] This technique was formalized in the middle of the nineteenth century by Zhang Mingshan, a Tianjin craftsman who made a name for himself with the striking expression of his characters, the liveliness of the colors, and the originality of the poses. The statuette, a copy of which was analyzed by Pierre Loti in the epigraph above, represented a French soldier in 1901 protecting the local population and showing concern for their welfare.

The Provisional Government's mission, according to article 2 of its regulations, was to prescribe "sanitary measures to prevent epidemics and other diseases."[2] The health service, directed by French military physicians, conceived a Promethean project at the heart of which were sanitary and hygienic concerns that reached their peak in Europe precisely at the turn of the century. Medical and public hygiene societies, founded in Great Britain (1850), Germany (1873), Japan (1875), Belgium (1876), France (1877), and Russia as well as international hygiene congresses held from 1852 onward, influenced Western and colonial municipal policies.[3] Cholera, one of the great fears of Europe, reappeared frequently from 1831 onwards and played a decisive role in the internationalization of sanitation issues and the emergence of public health policies in the second half of the nineteenth century.[4] At the same time, microbial theory and tropical medicine developed and demonstrated the causes of diseases such as cholera. Although the epidemiological theory of miasma was no longer considered relevant, it continued to permeate people's minds and gave rise to a set of good public health and sanitation practices that were maintained after the theory of miasmas was abandoned: street cleaning, odor control, drainage, and so on. From this point forward, public health specialists advocated the monitoring of individuals as potential carriers of germs just as the environment had been the main vector of miasmas.

In the Allied powers' discourse, the deficient hygiene of the Chinese legitimized a posteriori their "humanitarian intervention" and the health policy of the Provisional Government. One might challenge this assertion by pointing out that the war considerably degraded the sanitary condition of the inhabitants. From this perspective, the Allies claimed to be providing a remedy for an evil they were largely responsible for in the first place. Moreover, by the end of the nineteenth century, Li Hongzhang made Tianjin a place for the development of "modern" medicine, founding a hospital there in 1880 with J. Kenneth Mackenzie of the London Missionary Society and the first "Western" medical school in China in 1881.[5] Indeed, Ruth Rogaski has masterfully shown how hygiene and public health became a central issue of "Chinese modernity" in the second half of the nineteenth century, through the use of the concept of *weisheng* in Tianjin. But the role of French military doctors and Chinese elites in this health policy during the period 1900–1902 also requires attention,[6] for it was through the Provisional Government that the fight against diseases and the sanitation of the city were brought together as part of a global public health policy.

City sanitation and environmental protection

Forcing prisoners and the indigent to clean the streets

A range of witnesses recounted Tianjin's catastrophic sanitary situation in the aftermath of the war. James Ricalton, walking through the walled city, described the streets littered with mutilated corpses, the horror of which neither pen nor camera could capture.[7] As the temperature rose to 104° (40° C), the city reeked of garbage and rotting human flesh, greedily devoured by countless dogs. Some westerners carefully chose a few examples, attributing this insalubrity to the total lack of hygiene among the Chinese:

> The Chinese take advantage of this bloodshed of small horses and Korean and Japanese oxen. Indeed, instead of burying or burning killed horses and oxen that die of the bovine plague, they simply throw them into the water, as I have seen on the French bridge or from the wharf at the end of Admiralty Street. The Chinese, upstream, watch for the passage of the corpse, and then fish it out. They are so miserable and indifferent to all hygiene that they eat it.[8]

As early as July 17 Japanese soldiers were the first to remove bodies from the streets. Following the Japanese example, the Provisional Government decided to clean the streets and sewers and bury the corpses in large pits.[9] These collective burials, without any proper ceremony, deeply shocked the local population.[10] The public authorities developed a policy in the "health conference" held on October 12, 1900, at the government headquarters.[11] The health service began by enlisting two hundred prisoners (more than five hundred from 1901 onward) and residents of poorhouses to collect garbage on the public highway, the dumping of which was now regulated. For the task the government recruited, without remuneration, an army of coolies and sweepers in chains from among those condemned to forced labor. A Chinese man described the situation in June 1902:

> I was walking outside the south gate when I saw about thirty people being forced to work. Their braids had been cut off; their heads shaved. They wore a special uniform—half blue, half red—with the characters *weisheng* (public health) embroidered on their chests. Their legs were chained, and they carried a heavy bucket of excrement and filthy water. Behind them, pushing them along, were several armed Sikh soldiers. I looked at them for a while and realized that two people looked completely out of place: one was obviously a scholar and the other a fairly well-to-do merchant. I have no idea what they did to get there. Alas! The country is in such a precarious situation. . . .

> And after these few decades, it would seem there isn't a Chinese man who is not a coolie. What a tragedy! What suffering![12]

The garbage was removed and burned in incinerators in the city or transported outside the Chinese city to sites marked by posts. The waste from the Japanese section was dumped outside the southwest corner of the city. Two thousand tons of waste were collected during the first two months.[13] In addition, there was a cleanup operation to which the authorities had recourse depending on the sanitary situation. Thus the health service requisitioned, from time to time, some of the inhabitants to participate in cleaning the city under the watchful eye of the police. The sanitary service faught against the "bad smells" that were both a nuisance and a "danger for the health of the neighborhood." They depicted the walk along the mud wall as particularly unpleasant. The new regulations were not respected by the entire population, as shown by the regular reminders from the health service. At the start of 1902 Chinese businessmen Chi Meng Tow and Hsu Wen Fu, who understood the economic stakes that this new sector of activity could represent, offered the services of their company to clean the city. The council transmitted this contract proposal to the chief of the health service, who formally opposed it, arguing that "the offer is too advantageous to be practical." Short of arguments, Dr. René Depasse mobilized stereotypes and innuendo to prevent the Chinese from reappropriating efforts at public hygiene, which in the minds of the civil servants was necessarily a foreign science.[14]

Protecting the river and trees

As soon as the Provisional Government was founded, the council received several petitions concerning the pollution of the Hai River, "soiled by the Chinese who throw garbage into it."[15] After cleaning the streets of the city, the health department became concerned about "water pollution" in the spring of 1901. Starting on May 10, the chief of police organized patrols of "special agents" who prevented residents from dropping waste into the Hai River and the Grand Canal. A man who had disposed of his son's body in the river, north of the city, was caught in the act and sentenced to ten days in prison. In June the government opened a budget line of $3,000 to remove the garbage along the river. But its protection turned out to be a long-term job: the government solemnly recalled the same prohibitions at the beginning of June 1902, because the residents continued to dump their garbage in the Hai River despite the efforts of the river police.[16]

The emergence of environmental concerns in the eighteenth century in French and British tropical islands like Mauritius and St. Helena was a result of the colonizers' need to preserve forest resources.[17] In Tianjin the desire to protect trees came not from the Allies but from some local Chinese who asked the secretary of Chinese affairs to prohibit soldiers from cutting down trees in the cemeteries. The council used these requests to sketch an environmental policy: "The lack of greenery in the vicinity of Tientsin makes measures to protect these trees necessary." The Allied generals responded favorably to the council, and foreign soldiers were ordered to stop felling trees without permission not only in the cemeteries but throughout the jurisdiction. The government, not content with simply protecting the trees, devised a planting program: in September 1901, the Public Works Department financed the planting of 424 trees in urban areas for $509. A few months later, the international community of Tianjin, through the Tientsin Race Club, asked the government to protect the trees surrounding the racetrack. At the same time a new concern appeared in a more discreet way for safeguarding certain "reed swamps" in the district of Chunliangcheng. This request, again from the local populations, was forwarded to the district chief, but it is not known whether any action was taken.[18]

A partnership to manage potable water and wastewater?

In the aftermath of the battle, some wells had been poisoned by the Chinese fighters and water was an extremely rare commodity everywhere, apart from the British concession, which benefited from the network of the Tientsin Native City Water Works Company that supplied the concessions and the soldiers of the Provisional Government.[19] Wells were dug, and the water from the river was purified with potassium permanganate and then boiled or distilled. The marine mechanic Monnier built a water distillation machine that supplied the entire French contingent and beyond, becoming the pride of the French residents.[20] The head of the health service then wished to equip the government offices with a water distiller, but the head of public works convinced the council to be satisfied with boiling the filtered water. Dr. Depasse returned with the idea a week later. The council preferred to keep its potabilization technique, which it considered more reliable and economical. From then on, the government ordered the water sellers, and in particular the manufacturers of carbonated water in the city, to boil the water they used.[21]

In early March 1901, with the support of the Chinese secretary, three Chinese, Rui Yukun, Chen Jiyi, and Ma Yuqing, requested a franchise to build a water supply system in the city: the council agreed, provided that the Chinese company, the Tientsin Native City Water Works Company, adopted an efficient filtration system, took water from the Grand Canal upstream of Tianjin at the level of the mud wall, and did not charge in excess of twelve cents per cubic meter. The main streets of the city were to be provided with pipes and no decision was to be taken without the agreement of the council, including the size of the water pipes. The Chinese businessmen accepted the Provisional Government's conditions and joined forces with a German company to complete the deal: Arnhold, Karberg & Co, founded near Canton in 1866 by Jacob Arnhold, a German Jew, and Peter Karberg, a Danish merchant. How can the success of a Chinese company that was so easily granted a monopoly by the government be explained? The three Chinese businessmen could count on the unconditional support of the council's strongman, its secretary general Charles Denby, who was also one of the main shareholders of the Tientsin Native City Water Works Company.[22] Thus, without difficulty, the water company obtained from the government large areas in the northwestern, southeastern, and southwestern corners of the city to install water reservoirs as well as the confirmation of its monopoly on water distribution for sixty years.[23]

The council began by consulting, through the Chinese secretary, the notables of Tianjin about their ideas on the sewers. The government decided to entrust their repair and maintenance to the *shendong*, who were initially authorized to raise funds themselves, and specified that "if their work was well done and favorably appreciated, the council would compensate them for part of the expenses incurred." However, when the council learned that the notables had begun to impose a tax on property owners for sewer cleaning, it asked the Chinese secretary to remind them that only the government could levy taxes: the *shendong*, on the other hand, were empowered, on the model of the corvée, to "force the inhabitants of each district to clean the sewers in their district themselves." When the notables of the southern part of the city asked the council for $437 to pay for repairs, the government did not comply with this request. Instead, it spent $6,500 to build a sewer around the city. Some *shendong* objected to what amounted to a cleaning job, as did a prominent member of the French police section, who received a "beating" administered by an officer in response to his resistance. The police chief reserved the right to punish recalcitrant *shendong* himself. A year later a disgruntled Chinese entrepreneur was arrested by the police while urging coolies at a government construction site to desert. These forms of active resistance were severely disciplined through imprisonment and corporal punishment.[24]

What was to be done with the city's wastewater? At the end of March 1901 Albert de Linde, the head of the public works department, proposed a drainage system. The system was amended the following month by Chinese officials, who wished to direct the water to the southwest of the city. At the end of May 1901 the council adopted this proposal and signed for $5,342 with a Japanese contractor to dig a ditch, a "sewer," that would run from the southwest corner to the river along the border between the location of the Provisional Government and the Japanese concession. The Japanese consul general approved the project on condition that the owners be treated well and that the ditch be at least partially covered. The following year, several reports underlined the shortcomings of this drainage system: the wastewater could not be permanently discharged into the river. Since the installation of filters was too expensive, the public works department recommended that the sewage be discharged into a large pit to the south of the city. Constantin von Hanneken opportunistically offered the services of one of his companies, the Land Improvement Company, to drain the city and build a canal and a 100-*mou* (16.3 acre/6.6 ha) basin. The council adopted his proposal, and during the summer of 1902 Hanneken was able to build the collection canal from the southwest corner of the city to the first basin for a sum of $14,000. The Chinese landowners were monetarily compensated, but a man named Yang Lu Tang published placards accusing Constantin von Hanneken's Chinese workers of upsetting Chinese graves, thus mobilizing the local residents against the project. Hanneken had the government issue a proclamation in Chinese explaining the benevolent and beneficial nature of the development program. Following Yang, other Chinese petitioned against the drainage works and the resulting expropriation. Hanneken managed, however, to convince the complainants to send a new petition, this time in favor of his company. A few days later the British minister in Beijing received a complaint from Yang Lu Tang, through the lawyer E. P. Allen, that challenged the expropriation measures in favor of the Hanneken company. Faced with these multiple claims, the government finally granted $1,883 to the owners of the ninety-four disputed *mou* at $20 per *mou*.[25]

The government also wanted to regulate the production of human waste by prohibiting the population from urinating and defecating in public. The "civilized" powers considered the Chinese to be—literally—"troublemakers" in need of discipline. The police enforced the regulations, as in the case of a soldier who in October 1900 brutally took on an offender: "While relieving himself in a public place, a 15-year-old Chinese boy was caught by a foreign soldier. The soldier ordered the youth to pick up his feces with his hands and move them to a secluded area. The youth refused to comply; the soldier threatened him with his bayonet, and he was forced to obey. When the soldier saw the boy's disgusting hands, he just laughed and walked away."[26]

The Public Works Department built public latrines, known in Chinese as *guance* (government toilets). The government hired a Chinese contractor, Cho Lien Fu, to build 120 public latrines for $5.50 each. The latrines were then franchised to Chinese entrepreneurs, who charged for their use, sold the excrement as fertilizer, and paid the government a rent. In this way the maintenance of the latrines and the removal of waste cost the government nothing.[27] However, these "toilets" did not immediately find their public because of the relatively high cost of use: five cash coins to sit on the stool and two cash coins to urinate was beyond the means of most of the population.[28]

Governing the dead: Demolition of Chinese necropolises and the construction of public cemeteries

The government tried to reform the mortuary practices of the Chinese who, in Tianjin as in the north of China, were accustomed to burying coffins in individual mounds of earth, giving a striking relief to the plain to the west and south of the city that bristled with small cones.[29]

At first, the foreign authorities ordered the Chinese to cover the graves inside the mud wall with more soil. The government forced the families of the deceased to fill out a certificate that specified the origin of the body, the observations of the police and the doctor's report, and to go through the health service for the organization of the burial. In the spring of 1901 reports poured into the council about the stench of the coffins in the eastern part of the city. The police chief again recommended that the graves be covered with a thick layer of earth, while Lieutenant Colonel Harada persuaded the council of the need to move them beyond the railway line. The secretary for Chinese affairs then had to convince the notables that "the removal of the coffins would be for the general good and urged them to do so." For the first time the council considered creating a "general cemetery, in accordance with European practices." The government decided to build two large, closed cemeteries, reserved for the Chinese, east of the river and west of the Hai Kuang Ssu. The *shendong* were responsible for the transfer of coffins from the "family cemeteries" to the "Chinese public cemeteries." The government decided, however, to wait for cooler autumn temperatures before carrying out the transfer. On June 12, 1901, the council solemnly proclaimed the prohibition of burying bodies near the city and the concessions and the obligation for all Chinese to bury their dead in the new "public cemeteries" outside the mud wall. The municipalities of the foreign concessions then used these cemeteries created by the government.[30]

The graves were removed by the families. If they were not identified, then they were moved by a private company in charge of the drainage work or a charitable society, at the company's expense. As a result, the health service had hundreds of coffins exhumed and buried in the new "modern" cemeteries reserved for the natives, six feet (1.8 m) underground, in accordance with the British tradition, in particular to prevent dogs from opening them. These arrangements were felt to be a violent intrusion by the state—and a foreign and barbaric one at that—into the private and intimate lives of families, particularly into the sacred burial rites and the social customs of the urban community, in which the notables financed the burial of the indigent. In the eyes of the natives, this forced displacement of entire necropolises took place in parallel with the numerous desecrations of graves by Allied soldiers. In fact, during the winter of 1901–2, the region was not forested and there was a lack of coal, so the soldiers destroyed the graves to recover the wood from the coffins to heat the barracks and cook bread:

> The plain of the tombs extended to the gates of Tientsin. The bodies of the Chinese were dug up and thrown into the nearby marshes, and the coffins were burned in fireplaces. A room consumed one coffin per week. As we know, the Chinese bury their dead, not underground, but on top of it, and they cover them with a tumulus, small for the humble, and of more considerable proportions for the mandarins. The exhumation of the bodies presents no difficulty. The violation of some mandarin tombs led to the discovery of rice and money in the coffins. The cruel necessity in which we found ourselves to use the coffins for wood exasperated the natives; they overwhelmed us with insults and some dug up their dead to transfer them to safer places.[31]

This policy also transformed the suburban landscape and freed up new building space for urban development within the mud wall. In the absence of being able to fence in and clean up the Chinese necropolises, such as the "pauper's grave" to the west of the city, the government multiplied the projects for the creation of public cemeteries at the end of 1901, notably in the former military camps to the north of the city.

The Allies succeeded in imposing these new cemeteries on the Chinese but were unable to agree on a common burial policy. Thus, on October 10, 1900, General Alfred von Waldersee proposed the creation of an international cemetery for Allied soldiers before giving up in January 1901 due to disagreements between the military commanders. In August the council provided $3,500 for the establishment of a cemetery on Racecourse Road in the British concession to bury "soldiers and sailors of all nationalities." The British City Council collected the grant and did not hesitate to ask the Provisional Government for more subsidies. It did not however build anything, informing the council that it refused to bury foreign soldiers in its "old cemetery" as of January 1, 1902. Under these conditions, the government demanded the return of the $3,500. Under international pressure, the British City Council explained that it had been prevented from doing so by the floods and that it could now begin the work with the help of the government's public works department. For the latter, however, it was too late, because "the municipality, by acting as it did, forced the German military authorities to create their own cemetery, spending a large sum of money." The attempt to internationalize the cemeteries definitively failed.[32]

Treating people, preventing diseases

The sanitation work of the government and local elites was accompanied by intense medical activity in the aftermath of a bloody conflict and during a deadly epidemic.

A Franco-Japanese organization: The Government Health Service

The council appointed René Depasse, a military physician, as head of the government health service because of his close relationship to Li Hongzhang and his valuable experience as head of the Tianjin Medical School before the war. Located in a huge official building enclosed in a brick wall, on the border between the French concession and the Chinese suburbs, the school constituted, with the adjacent hospital, the main medical establishment of the city since 1880. The buildings, furnished in both European and Chinese styles, contained faculty housing, classrooms, and patient rooms. The medical school was run by Dr. Depasse and Dr. Lin, a quintessential turn-of-the-century Chinese "modern":

> What a divine figure, with an elegant and intelligent face, who speaks English like the finest sons of Albion and wears a false braid, as do his pupils. He began his studies at the University of San Francisco and did not hesitate to make this serious concession to Americanism: 'One should not have too many prejudices when traveling abroad,' and then he concluded with a smile, 'my braid is quite convenient: according to the circumstances, I take it on or off . . .' This doctor Lin is indeed so modern![33]

The braid, a prerogative of the Manchus, allowed these doctors to operate without difficulty across social and ethnic worlds. The Boxers and Chinese soldiers even spared the hospital during the siege of the concessions, proof, according to Villetard de Laguérie, of the recognition by the natives of the "great humane genius of France."[34] One might also surmise that the natives avoided bombing an institution considered to be Chinese. Another head of the government health service, Dr. Houillon, who succeeded Dr. Depasse from January 1901, also practiced in this hospital, and taught there before the war. In the aftermath of the Battle of Tianjin, the Chinese hospital actively cooperated with the government: in October 1900 it housed 180 French wounded or sick as well as patients sent by the government health service. In return, the government financed the hospital and granted it a subsidy of 10,000 taels in July 1902.[35]

Dr. Depasse was initially assisted by a Chinese associate, Soo Hao Doong. The French doctor chose to divide the city into four health districts—each headed by a "foreign health inspector"—which corresponded to the police districts. In the weeks following the battle the government transformed buildings in the city into makeshift hospitals, like the large mansion rented to the wealthy Startsef. In June 1901 the health service included a chief physician, Dr. Houillon; his deputy, Dr. Mesny, who was assigned to visit the prisons and brothels; a sanitary inspector; two Chinese physicians in charge of the free vaccination service and the government infirmary; and twelve "sanitary policemen" who supervised the cleanliness of the streets and the execution of "sanitary statutes."[36] The health department had a budget of $2,200 per month to establish women's clinics and pay the thirty or so health workers who accompanied the inspectors on their rounds. In August 1901 Dr. Houillon convinced the council to assign a Chinese physician, Dr. Lai Shin Wing, to the large prison in Tianjin. The health service employed mainly Sikh and Japanese soldiers, who had shown great efficiency during the siege of the summer of 1900: "We must admit that of all the Allied detachments around us, the Japanese detachment had the best medical provision."[37] Japanese doctors played an increasingly important role in the government health service. The Japanese command offered to the council the services of a medical officer as an assistant to the health service at its own expense. At first the council was suspicious of this generosity, and the French feared that they would lose the upper hand, but they were forced to accept the Japanese proposal and appoint Dr. Matsushima. The Japanese senior officers seemed to be both cosmopolitan and sensitive to health issues, like General Fukushima, commander of the Japanese troops, who had been stationed in Berlin in the 1890s, and Colonel Akiyama, Japan's representative in the council, who had completed part of his military studies in France and spoke the language perfectly. Inspired by Mori Ōgai, who promoted Japanese health reform (*eisei*), Japanese doctors spearheaded prevention policy in Tianjin.[38]

The health service promoted preventive medicine that sought to anticipate the spread of epidemics. The council engaged a variety of measures: it planned to transform Li Hongzhang's administrative offices into a hospital "in case of an epidemic," ordered the extermination of stray dogs, forbade the sale of dead cattle, and took preventive action against the bovine plague. The government also seemed to adopt a doctrine of temperance, which combined the prevention of distilled alcohol consumption with the introduction of high taxation. In early August 1900 the council ordered the closure of liquor stores and opium dens, which had to be licensed by the government. The police then closed several places where alcohol was consumed and where fights often occurred. At the beginning of October 1900 the government decided to prohibit the distillation of alcohol in Tianjin, but at the end of the month, it abandoned this ban and granted a license to a limited number of establishments.[39]

The government set up a special department to combat the spread of contagious diseases, which was responsible for discovering "epidemic centers," vaccinating the population, and compiling health statistics. A new "doctor of epidemics and deaths," Dr. Woo Wei You, headed the department. The police officers had to collect information from the notables about the deaths in their section. The Chinese secretary had to list all the schools and the number of schoolchildren in the city to prepare the smallpox vaccination campaign. This was not a new process in China: a vaccination office had been set up by the physician Alexander Pearson and Chinese merchants in Canton at the beginning of the nineteenth century; the practice then spread to poorhouses. The Chinese quickly accepted vaccination since they had been familiar with the process for centuries through the fight against smallpox: the voluntary inoculation of smallpox into a healthy individual to acquire immunity had been invented by the Chinese and practiced since the sixteenth century.[40] In the late nineteenth century these prophylactic treatments continued to be applied to patients. Chinese practitioners adapted vaccination to the principles of Chinese medicine, including acupuncture: native physicians pricked the left arm of boys and the right arm of girls, preferably in winter and spring. The ancient tradition of combating smallpox and the indigenization of vaccination facilitated the integration in China of a practice that, as a result, was not perceived as an instrument of foreign imperialism. However, the plan to vaccinate the city's children provoked rumors among the Chinese population, who feared that it would become mandatory. The government, through posters, reassured the inhabitants by specifying that it "offers free vaccination, for the public good, but that the population will have a choice whether to receive or refuse the benefits of this opportunity."[41]

A public pimp? Administering prostitution

As early as August 10, 1900, the government began to monitor brothels with the aim of confining them to certain areas of the city and subjecting them to sanitary controls to prevent the spread of sexually transmitted infections. At the end of the month a military brothel was established in the city for each army (French, British, American, and Japanese), while three establishments were opened outside the Chinese city for Russian troops. The military doctors of the expeditionary corps, especially the Russians, repeatedly requested the intervention of the government's medical inspectors to improve the hygienic conditions of the brothels. The health service agents isolated and treated sick prostitutes, identified infectious outbreaks, and closed certain establishments for sanitary reasons.[42] Dr. Mesny, head of the brothel service, described the diversity of his missions: "researching these houses, classifying them, registering them, monitoring them, policing them, administering justice, distributing and collecting taxes and licenses, organizing a dispensary and an adjoining hospital, regularly visiting the women, caring for those kept in hospital, searching for clandestine houses and undeclared women, and setting up a detective service to carry out these searches."[43]

How did the government finance this ambitious health policy? To obtain a license, brothels paid the government three, six, or ten dollars per month, depending on their size, and one dollar per woman per month. The fee was paid to the treasury before the chief of health would issue a license. The government increased this tax at the end of February 1902 to finance the growing health expenses that required the hiring of an additional foreign doctor, a local Chinese secretary, and another agent: four, seven, and ten dollars per month for the establishments and one, two, and three dollars per prostitute. The health department also turned the Ta Wang Miao temple into a dispensary for these women.[44]

Prostitution appears to have been a social practice relatively tolerated by the Chinese population.[45] The prostitutes in the government's "houses of tolerance" were essentially young Chinese women, who worked in appalling conditions, as evidenced by the high rate of suicide. They were joined by Japanese women whom the Japanese staff had transported with its troops as a public health measure. While they were originally reserved for their country's soldiers, French soldiers also went to see the "graceful Japanese women." At the beginning of 1902 more expensive Western prostitutes settled in Tianjin, where officers and officials of the Provisional Government frequented them: "Toward the middle of January, pretty European and American women arrived in Tientsin, with elegant dress and perfumed linen to conquer the victors of China. It cost about fifty piasters to make their acquaintance. This was too expensive for the soldier's purse. But the officers and civil servants did business with them. These ladies, after our departure, remained with the occupation corps."[46]

The council worked to stem the spread of prostitution throughout the city and concessions. For example, in February 1901 it asked the commander-in-chief of the German troops, General von Lessel, to control the dramatic increase in the number of prostitutes on Taku Road in the German concession. The northwestern district was "reserved" for prostitution to limit it in the rest of the city. Despite these efforts, brothels were established outside the reserved areas. On the other hand, the chief of police totally prohibited male prostitution in the "Hsian Kung" (sodomite) houses of the city. Before the war, male prostitution was practiced clandestinely in certain barbershops and in some theaters.[47] All establishments that remained open eight days after the ban were commandeered by the government. For their part, the brothel keepers wanted to establish a professional association to defend their interests and manage their common problems, but the government did not follow up on their request.[48]

In return for the payment of the license, the government posed as the defender of women prostitutes. According to Dr. Gérald Mesny, the health service and the dispensary were transformed into a "complaint office where they came to ask for justice, or even seek refuge from the inhumanity of their bosses."[49] The French doctor reports that the health service freed several women ripped away from their families and prevented several forced marriages. When a prostitute wished to marry without the consent of the brothel owner, the head of the health department pleaded with the magistrate on her behalf. For example, the health service defended the residents of a brothel raped by a "native of the Philippines" who was arrested and handed over to the American consul. Finally, the health service was concerned about the common practice in Tianjin of child prostitution, as reported by Dr. Matignon, who observed:

> A purely sociological curiosity led me twice to the houses of prostitution where there are small boys; first during the day, then at night, thinking that I would be less disgusted, and after each session, I came out deeply disgusted by what I had seen, which could only be described as debasement and perversion. These establishments are located in Tientsin and Europeans are admitted without difficulty, because many, I was told—something I hesitated to believe!—are regular customers of these brothels, a hundred times more vile and more ignoble than the vilest houses of our seaports. . . . The children one meets there, at least those I saw, are dirty and unkempt. When the customer arrives, they sing some fashionable refrain in a falsetto voice, perfectly unpleasant, offer you tobacco or an opium pipe, even come and sit on your lap, tell you some very rude stories and wait for you to appeal to their good will. In a house in Tientsin, out of five children, who were presented to us, two had large blisters at the corners of the mouths, that could be seen from a distance. It is possible that, by subjecting the other three to serious examination, I would have found traces of syphilis on them as well. Many of these brothels were mixed. One finds boys of ten to twelve years old and little girls, often younger, on whom the Chinese indulge in all sorts of despicable acts. Public opinion does not seem to be moved by this, and proximity to one of these establishments does not bother the neighbors, who willingly give you information about them. I remember that having left, during the day, with Mr. L . . . , a friend of mine, went to visit a "tang-ming-eul" of Tientsin, under the guidance of a Chinese officer of a European consulate. We found ourselves hesitating which way to go at a crossroads. Seeing our embarrassment, a carpenter approached us politely and said:
>
> "These noble old men are looking, no doubt, for the little boys' house? Let them take the first street on the left."
>
> In these establishments, the children are well fed, but mistreated, both by the owner and by the clients. The relationships are often painful; the little boys try to escape to the great anger of the pederasts, who bully them, hit them, and attempt to squeeze every penny from them.[50]

Child prostitution was apparently as common in Tianjin at the beginning of the century as it was in Europe, where it increased with the fear of venereal diseases.[51] At the end of the nineteenth century the city's clients paid twice as much for a child—between one and five francs—and these "little boys' establishments," which were not officially recognized, were also exempt from taxation. The Japanese colonel Harada proposed to the council that "women" under the age of thirteen should not be admitted to the brothels.[52] After having studied the question, the secretary of Chinese affairs affirmed that Chinese law did not determine a minimum age, but that it was customary to welcome young girls from the age of thirteen in brothels.[53] The council therefore intended to use these cultural considerations as a basis for adopting the minimum age of thirteen. The *shendong* of the district where the brothel was located had to vouch for the age of the young prostitutes. This reform by the council was part of the movement to promote child rights for the first time in the metropolises, with the prohibition in France of working under the age of thirteen (1881) and the law against child abuse in 1898.[54] In Great Britain the age of consent for child prostitutes was raised from thirteen to sixteen in 1885.

Preventing the plague and fighting cholera: Tianjin in a time of global pandemic

During the two years under the foreign government, a terrifying threat weighed over Tianjin. The head of the health service, in close collaboration with the customs commissioner, Gustav Detring, focused on preventing epidemics. He proposed quarantine measures and epidemiological surveillance ("sanitary visits") to combat the plague, which began in Hong Kong in 1894 and struck Bombay (1896), Calcutta (1898), Japan, the Philippines and Hawaii (1899), Sydney, San Francisco, Buenos Aires, Glasgow (1900), and Cape Town (1901). The head of the government's sanitary service and the heads of the expeditionary corps' health services consulted each other on this subject, which caused great anxiety among Chinese and foreign inhabitants. The international maritime sanitary police, planned by the government, struggled to organize itself because of the weak cooperation between the powers when the first alert occurred on June 29, 1901. The council received a note from Shanghai declaring that Port Arthur was infected with the plague. As a preventive measure, the government hired a "medical inspector" and devoted 3,000 taels to repairing the Taku asylum, which housed quarantined goods and passengers. On July 1 the council learned that Shanghai had declared a quarantine on ships coming from Port Arthur. Finally, the day after, the Russian consul in Tianjin informed the council that he had received a telegram from Port Arthur stating that there was no epidemic. For almost a week the fear of an epidemic mobilized the entire government and tested the sanitary defense of Tianjin. The government planned new quarantine facilities in Tongku if necessary. On August 26, Gustav Detring and the British municipality asked the government to take measures against the risk of plague spreading through ships from Hong Kong. The council decided to subject these ships to a medical inspection upon their arrival in Taku. In early September, all the commanders and consuls approved the quarantine rules proposed by the Provisional Government. A third serious scare occurred on November 11, 1901, with the announcement of plague in the port of Newchuang. The council immediately ordered a quarantine in Taku and then in Tongku as well as the inspection of ships and junks. The health service planned measures to clean the city in case of an epidemic and chose two asylums in the city and the suburbs where plague victims and suspected cases could be confined. The sanitary police also supervised the movement of people by road and rail. But Tianjin ultimately escaped the famous "China plague," thanks to the closing of the Newchuang port during the winter of 1901–2 while it spread to other continents.[55]

In contrast, Tianjin was hit hard by cholera. The disease, introduced on May 31, 1902, by a ship from Shanghai, killed six coolies of the Chinese Engineering & Mining Company and the Takou Tug & Lighter Company in the port of Taku. Tianjin was then affected by the sixth world cholera pandemic, which had started in Bengal in 1899, reached Southeast Asia (Burma, Singapore, Java) in 1901, affected China, the Philippines, Arabia, and Egypt in 1902 before spreading to Persia (1903), Russia (1904), the Balkans, Italy (1910), and finally New York, where a few cases were identified in 1911. The policy of prevention, conceived by the government out of fear of the plague, was applied immediately when the cholera epidemic unexpectedly broke out and, like the plague, spread by contagion. On June 1 the district chief opened the quarantine station in Taku, where a foreign doctor, a Chinese doctor, a nurse, a cook, four coolies, two police officers, and two gravediggers were immediately sent. Dr. Gérald Mesny, head of the health department, quickly went to the port to try to contain the epidemic. Every house in Taku had to be visited daily by a health worker; the sick and their relatives were transported to the quarantine station, and contaminated houses were disinfected. The council obtained from the Allied commanders additional doctors and from the foreign consuls the authorization for the government doctors to inspect, if necessary, the concessions of Tianjin. Cases of cholera were then found in Tongku, where military doctors and sixteen police officers were dispatched. Despite the sanitary measures adopted in Taku and Tongku, the epidemic spread very quickly. After June 6 Tianjin organized itself to treat the first patients and try to stop the spread of the disease. The council instructed the police to patrol the city, to visit houses, and to report all suspected cases to the health department. The health workers then evacuated the sick to the poorhouses, which were transformed into isolation centers for cholera. The officers then proceeded to incinerate the bedding and clothing of the sick. The inhabitants of the house were locked up for a quarantine period of seven days. Before that, the house was disinfected with quicklime, which was applied to the walls, floor, and furniture. Twice a day, sanitation workers also sprinkled quicklime on corpses, garbage dumps, the walls of public latrines, bridges, and public roads soiled with excrement. The immense quantity of quicklime necessary for this work of disinfection was supplied by Russian troops. Coolies were specifically assigned to handle, transport, and bury the corpses. They lived among themselves and were kept away from the other Chinese employees. However, the government was kind enough to provide them with antiseptic solutions (bichloride or mercury) to wash their hands. The council published and posted a list of precautions to be taken to avoid contamination for the entire population:

> *Tientsin, June 6, 1902, Proclamation.*
>
> The beginning of a cholera epidemic having been declared in the Chinese city, the inhabitants are advised to observe the following measures, which will prevent them from contracting the disease.
>
> - Drink only boiled water or tea.
> - Eat vegetables and fruits only after boiling them.
> - Keep bodies and especially hands in a great state of cleanliness, especially at mealtime.
> - As soon as a person is known to be ill with cholera, immediately inform the officer in command of the sector, so that he can be treated,

and the disease can be prevented from reaching relatives and neighbors. Those who know a sick person and do not declare it will be severely punished.

- It is recommended to all inhabitants to put quicklime in the private toilets and garbage inside the house. The quicklime will be given free of charge by the officers commanding the police sections, if the request is made.[56]

The government combined general hygiene advice with police measures that encouraged the inhabitants to denounce others. The chief of police wished to punish all inhabitants guilty of hiding the dead to six months of hard labor. The council moderated its ardor and decided to condemn all persons guilty of hiding cholera patients, dead or alive, to two months of hard labor "without cutting off their braids" and the cangue, where they were exposed in the streets for fifteen days. The council also tried to control the movement of the population and especially the workers. For example, it forbade contractors in charge of demolishing the forts to hire workers from Taku, Tongku, and Tianjin. During the cholera epidemic, social unrest occurred on the demolition sites of the forts, particularly that of Chang Hai Kouan, which recorded numerous worker desertions. The government, present on all fronts, compensated the contractor with $1,000 for the losses caused. A "permit" issued by the police accompanied each corpse and made it possible to trace them from the place of death to the place of burial. Similarly, lemonade and soda manufacturers were required to boil the water they used for twenty minutes or face a $500 fine and six months in jail. Government doctors wanted to prohibit the importation of melons into Tianjin that might be contaminated by sewage. Reflecting a commonplace of the nineteenth century, recorded in the *Dictionnaire des idées reçues*, Flaubert wrote a few years earlier: "Melon gives cholera. It is cured by drinking a lot of tea with rum." The council, however, preferred to guarantee free trade and simply issued a proclamation advising against the consumption of melons.[57]

Within days the poorhouses and hospitals were no longer sufficient to accommodate the sick: the government opened two large "cholera camps" to the east of the city, near the mud wall, and to the northwest of the city. Smaller "isolation stations" were set up near the train station to temporarily house sick travelers, and on the outskirts of the city, such as a small village south of the Belgian concession, on the left bank of the Hai River. The Allies also requisitioned the Ta Wang Miao to collect cholera patients. At the beginning of July, the government health service was composed of twelve foreign doctors (three French, three Japanese, three Germans, two British, and one Italian), eleven Chinese doctors "trained in the European style," fifteen sanitary inspectors, and an "army of coolies."

As George Soulié's quote at the beginning of this chapter highlights, cholera killed dozens of people every day, including the sturdiest rickshaw drivers, sometimes in a matter of hours. While Soulié exaggerated when he spoke of 1,500 victims per day, the overall figures of the *Archiv für Schiffs und Tropen-Hygiene* (1904) of 736 deaths out of 1,273 patients in the city for the entire epidemic episode seem to underestimate the epidemic's intensity.[58] Dr. Gérald Mesny probably gave a more accurate estimate when he recalled the "10,000 Chinese lives and the 50 or 60 European lives that cholera cost the Tientsin district (and I am not talking about the thousands of deaths that occurred in the rest of the province of Petchili)."[59] We have little reliable data except for the statistics of the chief of the northern Tientsin district; the exemplary government official we have already come across counted 143 patients, including 62 deaths, in the first week of the epidemic between June 6 and 13.[60] As with the census, the Japanese Captain Satō proved to be the only one to give precise figures and a list of villages affected by cholera carefully located on a map. The Japanese military played a decisive role in the fight against the epidemic in the districts but also in the Japanese concession, which was hard hit by the disease because of its proximity to the outskirts of the Chinese city. They were aware of the cholera that had struck the archipelago on several occasions from the late 1850s onward and had encouraged the emergence of a genuine public health policy. In 1899 Japan became the only country in Asia to have eradicated cholera.[61]

Home invasions as well as forced and coerced care by government agents created tensions among the population. The population employed a variety of modes of resistance: some inhabitants escaped the brutal and humiliating procedure of disinfection by burying their dead at night in their own backyards or in vacant lots; others threw the corpses into the river or fled in a junk with their dead. In the face of this resistance, Dr. Mesny encouraged wealthy Chinese merchants to establish a charitable society called the "Society of Temporary Hospitals." This association, which was Chinese in the eyes of the inhabitants even as it was controlled by the government, communicated health recommendations and regulations to the population by means of posters. Chinese charitable societies and merchant guilds provided assistance to cholera patients in these "temporary hospitals" and in three large poorhouses: the government recognized the effectiveness of this indigenous network, which it financed to the tune of 13,000 taels in early July 1902.[62] Faced with the increase in the number of patients, Dr. Mesny hired "four old-school Chinese doctors," or "old methods Chinese doctors" as he called them, specialists in traditional Chinese medicine including acupuncture, who worked in the field, as close as possible to the population, and circulated between the eleven "temporary hospitals" set up in the city and surrounding areas: "The sanitary service has been authorized to post a proclamation in the city, to the effect that Chinese doctors can treat patients with cholera, and that they will be allowed to enter the hospitals under certain conditions for this purpose."[63] On the same day the government left the "Chinese free to be treated in their own way if they preferred." George Soulié de Morant, who was to become the main apostle of acupuncture in Europe in the 1930s, testified to the effectiveness of Chinese medicine in the fight against cholera. Fluent in Chinese, he first visited Zhili Province at the age of twenty-three as a temporary secretary-interpreter for the Hankou-Beijing railroad company in 1901–2. In Tianjin and in a missionary hospital in Beijing, he observed the effects of acupuncture administered by Chinese doctors on cholera patients:

> In this hospital, I witnessed healings that plunged me into amazement mixed, of course, with disbelief. For such results, the means used were extremely straightforward. A few pricks on selected points at a depth of 3 or 4 mm with a fine copper needle without any injection of medicine. Or, in some cases, moxas made by igniting a tiny cone of mug wort leaf powder on the skin. The patient was immediately relieved. His excruciating cramps and cold disappeared. Vomiting and diarrhea no longer recurred. Enthusiastic, but suspicious, I obtained from the practitioner the loan of a needle and some patients, but not without having first carefully observed the places where to prick. To my great surprise, my patients were relieved.[64]

As a proselyte thirty years later, George Soulié may have been distorting the reality of Zhili at the beginning of the century, but his testimony is confirmed by other foreigners present in 1902, such as Monsignor Favier, who directly noted the effectiveness of acupuncture as the only way to save one of his missionaries, who "almost died."[65] And once the epidemic had passed, even the Provisional Government itself recognized the virtues of traditional Chinese medicine. In particular, it congratulated Doctors Kwan, Shao, and Wong and awarded them $100 each.[66]

After a month the epidemic slowed, and the council noted that it had "almost disappeared" from the city on July 9.[67] The coolies of Tianjin went back to work, and social life resumed its usual course. From then on the health service was considerably strengthened by the epidemic and had a permanent staff of eleven doctors (three French, one German, one Japanese, and six Chinese), two foreign sanitary inspectors, two interpreters, two chief detectives for the police in the prostitution districts, seventy sanitary policemen, and about five hundred coolies for the city's cleanliness service, not to mention the staff of the vaccination center, the hospitals, the prison, and the asylum.

What was the driving force behind this small revolution in public sanitation that transformed Tianjin at the turn of the century? Was it only the declared concern for "modernization" after the devastating war of the summer of 1900? In fact, the fierce competition between the Allies was the most powerful stimulus for the actors of these spectacular transformations, especially the military doctors in the field. Thus the French doctor at the head of the health service competed with the Japanese for control of the Chinese charitable societies:

> Freed from the visit of the women that had occupied my afternoons, I could devote my time to monitoring what were known as charities or asylums, which the Japanese, by the intermediary of the Chinese Secretariat of the Provisional Government of Tianjin, had put their hands on. At my request, I was put in charge of the supervision of all these so-called charitable institutions. I hoped to take away from the Japanese the influence they had acquired, and to improve the fate of these unfortunate people dying by hundreds on the street corners during the winter.[68]

Dr. Mesny intended to "change the opinion that [the Chinese people] had of us in the aftermath of a war that was unfortunate for everyone." In a game of multiple players, he did not hesitate to invent new sub-departments, such as those for roads and epidemics, in order to have foreign officers appointed to them, so as to keep the strategic position of the direction of the asylum for a French doctor: "I had, thus, immediately gotten rid of the Japanese doctor's application by creating a place for him, and freed up the place in the asylum for a comrade." Gérald Mesny also managed to counter the Japanese Colonel Harada, who tried to take control of the health service by graciously offering the Provisional Government twenty-eight Japanese doctors whom he had expressly brought over from Japan. At the same time, the Franco-Japanese rivalry could lead the chief physician to limit the development of his service in order not to grant his competitors management positions with administrative authority or police powers:

> We were so few French doctors in China that it was not possible for me to ask for assistants; we would have been invaded by foreigners, and I would have been obliged to give them positions as heads of departments or institutions which would have put them in the foreground in the eyes of the Chinese. This was completely contrary to our French interests and to the rule I had set for myself of assigning only secondary roles to those imposed upon me and to place them under the direction of the French to reduce any influence of their efforts.

The Japanese command was enraged, and Colonel Harada ordered Dr. Mesny to prepare a project for the construction of a large modern hospital in the city. "But as it was obvious that his only aim was to find a place for the many Japanese doctors he had brought, and to prepare the ground for the lasting medical influence of his country," the head of the department pretended to comply and dragged the matter out until the government was dissolved. The doctor was aware of the great benefits that this new establishment could have brought, but he had, in his view, to put the interests of France before "any sentiment" in the face of the "attempted invasion" of Japanese officers.[69]

If the impetus was foreign, the means of this new health policy belonged to the Chinese as well as to the Allied powers. Within the framework of a true coproduction of public health in Tianjin, the Chinese played an active role in the emergence of environmental concerns, the development of private enterprises such as the water company or the manufacture of public latrines, the maintenance of sewers, the creation of temporary hospitals by charitable societies, and in the Provisional Government's health service with the contribution of indigenous doctors, "trained in the West" or specialists in "traditional medicine." In addition, the decisive participation of a fraction of the Chinese elites allowed the new health practices to spread despite the resistance to the government's interventionism, which was intended to regulate the life of the inhabitants from birth to grave, including sexual life and scatological practices. The establishment of a new public health regime in Tianjin also marked the beginning of health transformations in other Chinese cities.[70]

Figure 6.1 Salt piles on the shores of the Hai River around 1870. Roland Belgrave Vintage Photography.

CHAPTER VI

The Salt of the City

Statebuilding and the Emergence of Civil Society

> The fin-de-siècle speculator arriving at Tientsin in search of contracts is immediately struck by the enormous stacks of salt, covered with coarse matting, along the riverbanks.
>
> —E. H. PARKER

> On the left bank of the river, from the villages in the Russian concession to the imperial canal, a high barricade rises, almost uninterrupted, which is also one of the features of Tientsin's physiognomy. It is made of bags of salt deposited there by the owners of the carousel wells and salt works of the large square between Takou and Peï-Tang. The Chinese government, which has a monopoly on sales, draws from this open-air general store according to its needs and the merchants negotiate their certificates of deposit. Protected by these bags, the Boxers shelled the French concession with their rifles and these same piles were declared a prize of war.
>
> —RAOUL CHARLES VILLETARD DE LAGUÉRIE

This is the land of salt," exclaimed Alexis Daoulas, a young officer from Brittany, upon his arrival in Tianjin.[1] Salt from the Changlu district was the main wealth and tax resource of the city, which became the main economic hub of northern China at the end of the nineteenth century.[2] On the Grand Canal, natural resources were transited from the northern regions of the empire and the production of the fertile and prosperous south toward Beijing. As a major center for the sale and taxation of salt, the city is said to have stored about 25 percent of Chinese salt.[3] Tianjin's salt fascinated foreign travelers long before the Boxer War.[4] The pyramids of bags of sodium chloride struck European travelers as they approached the city and became a symbol of its economic prosperity.[5] In the aftermath of the battle between the Allied powers and the Chinese, the possession of salt was a prerequisite for financing foreign concessions and their reconstruction in the wake of Chinese bombardment and exactions by foreign troops. It was also a decisive factor in the operation of the international military government, which intended to levy the gabelle, as well as the Chinese merchant elites, who hoped to regain their central place in urban society. In the temporary absence of the Chinese imperial state, consuls from foreign concessions, officers of the Provisional Government and Chinese merchants openly competed for the ownership of this precious commodity and clashed in the main legal controversy of the turn of the century known as the "salt mound affair." The various public (diplomats, military, administrators) and private (merchants) actors, both foreign and Chinese, called upon a series of intermediaries (compradors, lawyers, banks, *hunhunr* brigands, and so on), mobilized different legal corpuses, and employed their own resources for control of this resource. In so doing they transcended a frontier that historians have established a posteriori between public service and private interest as well as administration and civil society. By raising the question of the interactions between public policies and charitable works, this case explores the existence of a civil society in Tianjin and the margins of maneuver—or agency—of the Chinese actors (in particular, the economic elites), in the aftermath of the bloody repression of the Boxers and the sack of the city.

A legal controversy over salt ownership

Tianjin was looted by foreign troops after the battle of July 13, 1900. The salt merchants and banks that financed its trade to the tune of two million taels were left empty-handed.[6] When the American troops seized the sum of 500,000 taels from the offices of the salt commissioner in the northeast of the Chinese city, the Council of the Provisional Government demanded that the American minister return this treasure to finance its administrative services.[7] The latter replied four months later that he would forward the request to the secretary of war in Washington. As we shall see, this delaying tactic allowed the United States to keep the treasure for a few more months. Salt, and the profits it generated, obsessed the Allied powers during the two years of the Provisional Government. Upon their arrival in the city, foreign troops discovered "mountains" of salt on the riverbank south of the station, opposite the Japanese and French concessions. For the Chinese and the Allies, these piles of salt were a decisive issue: they represented a huge treasure, estimated by the foreigners at a million bags of six hundred *catties* (1 *cattie* is 21.3 ounces, or 604.53 grams) worth more than ten million francs.[8]

The salt tax was one of the main fiscal resources of the Qing dynasty.[9] In 1900 it amounted to 1.6 tael per bag of six hundred catties.[10] The gabelle was levied directly by state officials during the Han period and then leased out during the Ming and Qing periods in order to reduce costs and increase the efficiency of the levy.[11] The imperial state granted merchants the exclusive right to transport and sell salt in exchange for the guaranteed payment of the gabelle to the state. To do this, privileged merchants were individually and collectively responsible for the salt tax and maintained close connections to the city's bankers, who advanced the sums necessary for transactions and the payment of the tax.[12] Salt was indeed highly prized by the Chinese as a foodstuff; above all, in the absence of refrigeration technology, it was used to prepare sauces, pickled vegetables, salted fish, and meat: "Tientsin is a shipping center for all kinds of goods, and it is from here that preserved meat and countless boxes of salted fish of which the Chinese are so fond are shipped to the most distant provinces of the empire."[13] It is estimated that at the end of the nineteenth century, the Chinese consumed an average of 8.8 pounds (4 kg) of salt per person per year.[14] These immense piles of salt, twenty-six feet (8 m) high and sixty-six feet (20 m) long, had a strategic function and a symbolic meaning, since they were used by Chinese gunners to attack the French concession in Tianjin.[15]

On July 23, less than ten days after the Allied victory, the Russians were the first to seize part of the salt and plant their flag in it.[16] British legalists took over the other part and entrusted it to the care of the international government. But when the latter wanted to recover the salt, its agents came up against French soldiers.[17] Indeed, on July 25, 1900, at 2:00 p.m., at the order of Colonel de Pélacot, head of the French expeditionary corps, Lieutenant Baudon, a marine infantryman, and Le Conte, the acting commissioner of the colonies, took possession of 138 piles of salt (approximately 600,000 bags) under the pretext of requisitioning "goods belonging to the enemy." In doing so, Colonel de Pélacot followed the advice of the French Consul General Gustave du Chaylard, who had noted the presence of Russian flags on some of the salt heaps that very morning and ordered the head of the expeditionary corps to take possession of them. The consul proposed to the colonel to sell it on behalf of the French troops in exchange for a percentage intended to finance the reconstruction of the French concession. Pélacot was at first perplexed, considering that the salt was private property belonging to Chinese.[18] But the consul convinced him of the validity of this appropriation by insisting that these heaps were the property of the Chinese government's tax farmers. The colonel then ordered three French flags to be made and planted on three piles of salt located in front of the southern suburb of the Chinese city, in the middle of the stocks, and on the one next to those that the Russians had appropriated. A guard post was placed in front of each heap bearing a flag, and the sentries were ordered to shoot anyone trying to steal salt. Thus, several Chinese petitioners, including Wang Yung Ching, complained about the killing of three compatriots by French guards, who then threw the bodies into the river. The chief of police of the Provisional Government wrote three reports on these "murders" and sent them to the French chief of staff, who did not respond to the council's request for an explanation.[19]

As early as the second session of the council, on August 2, 1900, the Provisional Government addressed the Allied commanders-in-chief to formally claim ownership of the salt, formerly the property of the Chinese government, which it had succeeded. On this occasion, it informed the Allied commanders that the Chinese state's properties in Tianjin were governed by it according to article 4 of the Administrative Regulations for the City of Tientsin, which stipulated that the Provisional Government would take "the necessary measures to preserve the movable and immovable property belonging to the Chinese Government as well as that of private individuals, neglected by the latter." The Provisional Government was in vital need of new financial resources for its daily operations and its ambitious urban planning policy. It also declared itself responsible for the well-being, and therefore the supply, of the one million indigenous people now living under its authority. The international government, installed in the viceroy's headquarters, asserted its similarity to the Chinese imperial salt administration, which traditionally played the role of social assistance. In addition, and in accordance with its "rights and prerogatives," it intended to collect the taxes—notably the gabelle—owed to the Qing state. This eminently strategic question of salt was entrusted to the good care of the German Fritz Sommer, the treasurer's deputy, and then, in November 1900, to Hermann Emil Ballauf.[20]

General Linevich, commander of the Russian detachment in Tianjin, ignored the Provisional Government's request, and the Russians quickly decided to sell their salt. The commander of the American troops, Major

General Chaffee, had no objection to returning the salt to the international government, but he took the opportunity to criticize the young institution, which he argued might become corrupted: the sale of the salt should not be "used to pay the salaries of officers, who were already in the service of the powers." On the other hand, the French opposed the decision of the Council of the Provisional Government head-on, since General Frey, commander-in-chief of the French expeditionary corps, did not recognize its authority in this area. Faced with this refusal, the Provisional Government decided on September 25, 1900, to request the arbitration of Field Marshal Alfred von Waldersee, the supreme commander of the Allied Forces, to assert its rights over salt. He refused to accept the request. The next day, du Chaylard reiterated his refusal to give salt to the international government. The dean of the city's consular corps did not recognize the existence of the new international government and even declared its constitution illegal on September 30.[21] This declaration was made in spite of the prudence of Frey's successor, General Voyron, commander of the French troops, who asked the French consul at the beginning of October to find the "real owner of these piles of salt."[22] He also inquired as to the position of the diplomatic corps represented by the French minister in Beijing, Pichon, who recognized the existence of the Provisional Government while specifying the strict limits of its prerogatives. In the absence of a present or past state of war, including during the Boxer Rebellion, as defined by international law, the international military government could have only limited administrative powers in relation to the consuls.[23] The French delegate to the council, Lieutenant-Colonel Arlabosse, was responsible for officially defending this position.[24]

The French consul hoped to use the salt to finance the reconstruction of the French concession. He saw it as a way of compensating foreign companies "for the losses they had suffered as a result of our soldiers, who, unaware of the system of concessions in China, had believed themselves to be on conquered territory and had treated ours accordingly."[25] The French soldiers did not hesitate to apply the right of conquest within the French concession, as if operating in a colony. The council reminded the consul that "French salt" had initially been ceded to the Provisional Government by the British authorities. Gustave du Chaylard stood firm and entrusted the seized salt to a wealthy comprador from the city named Sun Zhongying.[26] The Russian military authorities entrusted the confiscated salt to the good care of the Russian-Chinese Bank, which was responsible for selling it at the best price. This was no easy task. At the beginning of July 1901, for example, junks carrying "Russian salt" were seized by the Provisional Government's troops, who did not recognize the passes issued by the Russian-Chinese Bank: the permit for each junk had to be stamped and countersigned by the Russian consul, "since the Russian-Chinese Bank could not be considered an official authority."[27] And the bank, which behaved like an autonomous colonial authority with powers of state, had to give in to the formal demands of the international government before it could continue its lucrative trade.[28] But the difficulties persisted: junks of "Russian salt," although in possession of compliant passes, were again seized by the international police a few days later.[29]

In addition to the Provisional Government's opposition, the French consul also confronted French officers, who were greedier than expected. Certainly Consul du Chaylard and General Voyron agreed on the need to legitimize the taking of salt by the right of conquest, invoking "the principle recognized by international law that all captures are considered, de jure, as belonging to the State in whose name they were acquired, and which may keep them for itself." But the diplomat and the French officer were at odds over the distribution of the gains. Thus, General Voyron asserted that the French municipality of Tianjin should recover one-fifth of the proceeds from the sale of salt, in accordance with the French decree of April 3, 1869, on "war accounting," which stipulated that one-fifth of the profits would go to the state and the rest (four-fifths) to the collectors, that is, to the army. The French consul considered this proposal insufficient for the concession and demanded a third of the proceeds from the future sale of salt because of the damage caused by the Chinese bombardment and the occupation of the French troops. The general agreed with the consul, but the minister of the navy refused to infringe upon this provision of French law.[30]

Chinese merchants' surprise victory

But this legal argument suddenly collapsed in January 1901. The French and the Russians were mistaken: the real owners of the salt made themselves known. On January 4, Chinese merchants sent a petition to the secretary general of the Provisional Government, before whom they tried to assert their rights, asking him to seize the piles of salt. And, against all expectations, the council recognized the validity of the Chinese merchants' property titles. It did so for three reasons.[31]

First, this request came at a time when the government was trying to impose tight control over the city's economy, notably with the introduction two weeks earlier of the principle of company registration. Inherited from German law and adopted in France in 1919 in the form of the trade and company register, this registration was intended to offer guarantees to the city's merchants in return. The government seized the opportunity to present itself as the protector of local trade and merchants. Second, the salt merchants, with the help of their compradors and Western associates, established on the central commercial and banking road crossing the French, British, and German concessions (rue de France, which became Victoria Road before taking the name of Kaiser Wilhelm Strasse), managed to explain to the members of the Provisional Government how the system of leasing of the gabelle and the "quasi-freedom" of the salt trade for the privileged merchants of Zhili, supervised by the imperial administration (*kuan-tu shang-pan*), functioned.[32] Here the international government had the opportunity to prove itself a worthy inheritor of the Qing Empire. Finally, the Provisional Government quickly became aware of the social power of the merchants, who had been the city's former leaders.

Indeed, strengthened by their status as tax farmers under the Qing and assembled in the Changlu (Lugang Gongsuo) guild, the salt merchants accumulated immense wealth and formed the most powerful trading community in the city. They constituted the social elite of Tianjin, along with the high officials of the imperial administration.[33] They lived in opulence and resided in the central and eastern parts of the Chinese city, a district reserved for wealthy merchants near the large market outside the eastern gate.[34] However, by the turn of the century, rich merchants, along with compradors and bankers, had also settled along the river in the French concession.[35] They gradually consolidated their power by investing in diverse areas of city life, following the weakening and relative withdrawal of the Qing state during and after the Taiping War (1850–1864), which claimed more than twenty million lives.[36] They thus had the celebrated task of welcoming the emperor when he visited Tianjin and had a pavilion built for this purpose.[37] The salt merchants were also the main patrons of the arts, organizing parades and festivals for the urban population. They subsidized public assistance through rice distribution, philanthropic works, and educational institutions with the creation of schools.

In addition, they financed and directed the city militia and firefighting. Thus, they maintained law and order, especially in times of political crisis, such as during the Taiping attack in 1853 and the foreign invasions of 1858 and 1860. At that time, the guild even acted as an interim municipal government, administering the city, organizing its defense, and negotiating directly with foreign powers.[38] To do this, the wealthy merchants mobilized the *hunhunr*, honorable brigands of humble origin, who alone could effectively enforce law and order in the city streets.[39] These brigands suppressed revolts and fought fires on behalf of the salt merchants, who had partially replaced the mandarins and were thought by some to have acquired exorbitant amounts of power. For example, the subprefect Che Chiao Kiai confided in his friend Father Leboucq in the second third of the nineteenth century:

> The salt merchants are leeches who feed off the people. Thanks to the considerable fees they pay to the central government, it can be said that their situation is, almost everywhere, independent of the local authority. They often act without informing regular authorities. They have their own guards and have powers to arrest and punish the unfortunate workers who, taking advantage of the [saltpeter] with which their field or garden is covered, make a poor-quality salt.[40]

The privileged position of this group of merchants in urban society would seem to have been exceptional in late nineteenth-century China, where the neo-Confucian social model prevailed, placing mandarins and scholars at the top, followed by farmers, craftsmen, and merchants. The dynamism and even activism of Tianjin's salt merchants contradicts Max Weber's theory of the lack of autonomy among Chinese merchants and their great dependence on the state in the absence of a public sphere. Contrary to the Chinese city theorized by Weber as an administrative center exclusively at the service of the imperial state, Tianjin was the seat of an economic power that produced an embryonic "civil society" that counterbalanced and sometimes competed with the Qing imperial administration. The example of the salt merchants of Tianjin, who at times possessed state prerogatives (police, taxation, diplomacy, and the like), demonstrates, however, the inappropriateness of establishing a stark boundary between two essentialized entities, on the one hand "civil society" and on the other hand the "state."[41] The two were in fact jointly constructed through multiple forms of cooperation and conflict, as the salt mound affair attests.

The exceptional social power of the salt merchants, combined with the urgency of restoring their economic situation, explains their activism during the siege of Tianjin and in the aftermath of the fall of the city. On June 25, 1900, they put pressure—in vain—on YuLu, the viceroy of Zhili, who sided with the Boxers, to push him to negotiate with the foreign consuls and officers for an end to the conflict.[42] At the time of the Taiping revolt and the Second Opium War, the salt merchants were trying to maintain social and political order in order to preserve their economic interests: it was a matter of both protecting the Chinese city from destruction perpetrated by the Boxers and Chinese brigands and preventing the predictable looting of the city by regular troops in the event of an Allied victory. When the council, recognizing the legitimacy of their request, invited the merchants to contact the French consul general, who had appropriated most of the salt at the time, they were not discouraged by the foreign diplomat's categorical refusal. Indeed, the owners of the 250,000 bags of salt turned to the British lawyer James Bromley Eames.[43] The choice was wise to say the least. Eames, a former professor of law at the Imperial University of Tianjin (1898–1900) and prominent Freemason, also served as "private secretary"—in fact legal advisor—to the Council of the Provisional Government of Tianjin from July 24, 1900. Paid £600 a year by the Provisional Government, he was at the same time paid by Chinese merchants to defend the convergent interests of the international organization and local elites against French interests.[44] He embodied the blurring between public and private interests that prevailed at the time. The unavoidable Eames, supported by the British civil and military authorities, also represented the interests of the young American engineer Herbert Hoover in 1900–1901 and prepared the financial organization of his mining company.[45]

The British jurist did not hesitate to refer the matter to the French minister of foreign affairs, accusing France of contravening the rules of international law that normally guaranteed the property of private individuals: "I am telegraphing you directly instead of addressing the President of the Republic. Salt is the particular property of merchants; the seizure is against all the rules of international law. . . . I am sure that an investigation by impartial people will show a great injustice. Everyone condemns this action on the part of the French commander."[46]

Following the intervention of the English barrister, the French consul was disavowed by the political leaders of the French ministry of foreign affairs, who recognized the Chinese merchants' property rights. At the end of long negotiations, the French consul general was forced to return the stolen salt in May 1901. On the strength of this legal victory obtained privately by one of its agents, the Provisional Government imposed itself as the regulating authority for such conflicts by guaranteeing the right of ownership and the salt's return to Chinese and foreign owners.[47] The council thus ordered the various powers that had appropriated piles of salt in the vicinity of Tianjin to entrust them to the good care of the district chiefs of the Provisional Government so they could return them to the city's merchants. The German troops gave up the piles they held in Tongku, while the Italians returned about twenty thousand tons stored in Taku. The Japanese troops also handed over the salt they kept in Taku and Tongku, but Lieutenant Colonel Harada hoped that in return the Provisional Government would help the Japanese "in all projects of public utility, either in the Japanese concession or outside." Viceroy Li Hongzhang was asked by the Provisional Government to draw up a list of the salt-owning merchants. The salt mound affair offered an opportunity for the Qing imperial administration to reenter the political arena. Following the merchants, Chinese officials obtained the return of the salt commissioner's treasure seized by U.S. troops: on January 24, 1902, the sum of $376,300 was paid to China.[48] In the months that followed, salt merchants continued to lobby international authorities to recover the various salt deposits. However, they were forced to comply with the procedure laid down by the Russians, who had entrusted theirs to the agents of the Russian-Chinese Bank. Thus, thanks to effective community solidarity and in particular to the collective guarantee provided by his colleagues in the Changlu district, the merchant Hua Xueqi, a member of the prestigious Hua clan, managed to borrow 34,900 taels from the Russian-Chinese Bank in order to buy back some of the salt seized by the Russian military.[49]

The salt merchants quickly regained their power. Among the Chinese, only the former "salt commissioners," members of the Changlu guild, could take part in this special trade. In July 1901 they frightened some of the local population and foreign traders again, as did S. Hattori, director of the Japanese firm Okura & Co., who asked the Provisional Government for protection against "the oppression of the Chinese salt merchants in the interior." Foreigners, including the main actors of the local trade, still had great difficulty in understanding the mixed public-private organization of the salt trade. The council wanted above all to spare the powerful merchants of Tianjin. Unlike the consuls, the Provisional Government was dependent on the great Chinese merchants from the outset and needed them to maintain order in the "indigenous" city. Thus, the day after the city's capture, the chief of police and the Chinese secretary invited the "merchants and burghers" to contribute to the organization of an "indigenous police force." The salt merchants, who were thoroughly internationalized, finally succeeded in asserting their rights by skillfully navigating various jurisdictions and deploying a diversity of foreign resources (lawyers, banks, and so on).[50]

The provisional government restores the salt tax

Once the Chinese merchants formulated their official request for restitution in January 1901, the Provisional Government ceased to claim ownership of the salt and attempted to levy the gabelle salt tax. Thus the process of reestablishing the tax began in a troubled context of confusion and usurped identities. Since the end of the nineteenth century, the system of distribution and taxation of salt seemed less and less effective owing to the rise of corruption and smuggling: the international government tried to strengthen its legitimacy by remedying these dysfunctions.

The place to begin is with the French consul, who tried to convince the Council of the Provisional Government to recognize his property rights on the salt, declaring that he was willing in return to help "collect taxes on the salt he sold." The consul also asked for the government's protection to proceed with the sale and proposed to set the tax rate at 1 tael per bag of salt of 600 catties. This request by Gustave du Chaylard was strongly supported by the French representative to the Council of the Provisional Government, Colonel Arlabosse. Having learned that salt was private property and did not belong to the Chinese government which it wanted to succeed, the council accepted the French consul's proposal out of pragmatism but fixed the amount at 1.15 tael per bag. The Frenchman reiterated his request for a reduction of the gabelle and submitted two new requests, at the risk of upsetting the council members. He wanted the Provisional Government to pay the French salt commissioner, Sun Chung Ying, who would collect the tax on behalf of the international government's treasurer. Insofar as salt from Tianjin was then subject to other taxes when sold outside the city, he recommended that only salt consumed in his jurisdiction be taxed by the government. Du Chaylard finally complained about the actions of Sun and Chang, two Provisional Government agents, who tried to collect taxes on French salt without any prior agreement. The council immediately informed the consul that the two agents were considered unauthorized usurpers, guilty of extortion. The Provisional Government's agents competed with the hunhunr, who tried to control commercial traffic on the Hai River and collect duties on the transport of goods by junks, coolies, rickshaws, peasants, as well as on salt.[51] These Chinese renegades were ideal culprits, easily instrumentalized by the mandarins and the foreign military authorities for the Boxers' crimes during the summer of 1900. In this climate of confusion, the international government reaffirmed its protective role regarding all salt merchants, foreigners, and Chinese, on condition that they pay the 1.15-tael gabelle. It categorically refused to delegate the collection of the tax to the consuls' compradors and entrusted his own treasurer with the collection of the tax. But the affair did not stop there. Gustave du Chaylard accused the treasury of the Provisional Government of inconveniencing the salt merchants, and in particular Sun Chung Ying, for whom he presented two complaints. In addition, the French consul published proclamations in the Chinese city in his name on the conditions of the salt sales. The government retorted that only it could issue proclamations in the city and that the consuls had to consult the council if they wanted to send a message to the inhabitants. The Provisional Government received complaints from the Chinese, such as a salt merchant's claim that the French consul had stolen seven thousand bags from him. At the same time, they tried to bring Gustave du Chaylard back to a more reasonable position.[52]

As relations with the French consul deteriorated and petitions from salt merchants multiplied, the Council of the Provisional Government decided to take the salt trade back into its own hands in hopes of raising valuable tax resources. On January 23, 1901, it officially authorized the sale and purchase of salt. In order to benefit from the guarantee and protection of the international government, merchants had to pay the tax (1.15 tael). In addition, salt store owners were required to pay an "ordinary license" of 20 taels per month to the government treasurer through the district chiefs, who were authorized to issue as many licenses as there were applications. Moreover, the treasurer continued to collect the $8 that the Yen-chuan, the owners of the salt and rice junks, purchased annually. A few days later, the French consul circumvented the international government's regulations by selling 510 bags of salt without paying the gabelle, claiming that the transaction had been made before the government had introduced the tax. The compradors paid by the consul and the government played cat and mouse. On February 13 du Chaylard protested a fine imposed on salt sold outside the city. The council accused the consul of taxing salt excessively. He replied that he was legitimately collecting the tax previously levied by the Chinese government. The government emphasized its benevolence in setting the amount at 1.15 tael, when the Qing administration had levied 1.60 tael. Despite its exaggerated claims of goodwill, the council unofficially reserved the right to raise the tariff. Its members presented themselves as guarantors of equity between the powers and refused to grant preferential treatment to the French consul, who was solemnly warned: "Salt, whether French or not, is subject to the same tax, and to exempt French salt would be to create a monopoly." Once again, Colonel Arlabosse tried to intercede in favor of the consul and finally expressed serious reservations about the council's decision.[53]

After this legal reminder, the Provisional Government made a concession to Gustave du Chaylard on an exceptional basis by waiving taxes on French salt sold outside its jurisdiction, provided that the salt did not return indirectly to Tianjin. The French diplomat was quick to take advantage of this privilege: the next day, he transferred 430 bags of salt to Peking by train, which were thus exempt from government taxes. The following week Gustave du Chaylard tried to push his advantage by asking the government for a permit to ship eight thousand bags of salt, free of tax, to Beijing. The council accepted under the "circumstances" but, annoyed by the French consul's opportunism, sought the advice of General Voyron, commander-in-chief of French troops. The latter vigorously defended the French consul's position that the international government could not tax "French salt" consumed outside its jurisdiction. Consequently, in accordance with government regulations, the council agreed with the French officer and wrote to Field Marshal von Waldersee and the commanding generals of the Allied troops that it would no longer require a tax on "French salt" transported out of Tianjin, but "wished to draw the attention of the commanding generals to the fact that the government's revenue was greatly diminished." The French consul then asked the council for a permit to ship seventy thousand bags of salt to Henan Province tax-free. Taking advantage of this precedent, the Russian authorities also tried to sell salt outside the city to gain maximum profit with minimum tax.

In the face of these setbacks and in constant search for new financial resources, the council decided on May 8, 1901, "to examine whether it is appropriate to propose the re-establishment of the salt monopoly" and set up an ad hoc committee composed of colonels Arlabosse and Bower as well as Major von Falkenhayn to study this crucial question. But the dream of a lucrative monopoly was quickly abandoned due to the location of the production sites outside the Provisional Government's jurisdiction, the refusal of certain generals, for whom Voyron was the spokesman, the opposition of the Qing administration, which disapproved of this intrusion into its reserved domain, and of the Chinese merchants to whom this monopoly had been delegated.[54] These circumstances led to the continuation of the option favored since January 1901, that is, taxation. From then on the government adopted a cautious position: its agents were no longer to deal with questions of salt ownership—or even mention them—but simply to collect the tax. This pragmatism was not without cynicism, since the members of the council were not concerned with respecting the principles of law and securing economic transactions: the district chief "must only collect the tax, without guaranteeing ownership, of either the seller or the buyer."[55]

The council also asked the consuls to warn foreign salt merchants of the dangers of such an enterprise as long as ownership remained so ill-defined. Indeed, salt convoys were regularly attacked outside the government's jurisdiction, and the precious product had to be transported under escort. The British consul did not hesitate to provide Sikh soldiers to accompany the convoys in the region. Foreign merchants such as the Japanese S. Hattori also faced hostility from the Chinese authorities in Zhili Province, where some prefects formally forbade the inhabitants from buying their salt. However, the Provisional Government made it a point of honor not to interfere in the province's internal affairs.

The salt merchants then mobilized to defend their interests. They intervened directly with the diplomatic corps in Peking to reduce the tax levied by the Provisional Government, while foreign merchants, through the voice of Carlowitz & Co., the most powerful German merchant in China, used petitions to try to convince a government committee on regulations for the salt trade to relax its legislation and reduce the gabelle. Since the international government did not listen to them, some foreign merchants and their compradors decided to organize the trade themselves. In Chaku, for example, the German firm Buchheister & Co. and Japanese merchants, claiming to "have the support of the Provisional Government," took the initiative to post proclamations regulating the sale of salt.

The Council of the Provisional Government then attempted to organize the salt market. Its agents had to avoid issuing too many "tax receipts" for transactions to be carried out later, since they could have unbalanced the market and allowed certain merchants to circumvent future restrictions envisaged by the government. In addition to the control of licensed merchants, the government used its district chiefs to combat salt smuggling within its jurisdiction. They hunted down arms dealers, who hid cannons and lead in salt junks, fought against competition from official salt sales recognized by the Qing administration, which broke the government monopoly, and tracked down agents of the Chinese controller, who came to collect their tax from salt merchants even in the city of Tianjin. Thus, in April 1901, the Japanese Captain Satō, head of the Tientsin-North district, denounced to the government an official salt store in the Tongku district that provided Chinese merchants with passes and permissions to transport salt: the German captain of this district was charged with punishing the store's managers. At the end of July 1901, a native agent of the "Salt Controller for the Northeast Circuit" was sought by the police, because the government treasurer found that he too was issuing "passes" and "permits" to merchants from Tianjin, who were seeking a monopoly on the sale of salt in certain villages outside the Provisional Government's jurisdiction. Chinese government officials were allowed to remain freely in Tianjin, but they were forbidden to sell permits to salt merchants, who had to go through the Provisional Government. At the same time, the foreign merchants were surprised that, in addition to the international administration's gabelle, they had to pay tax to the Chinese commissioner. Thus, junks loaded with salt from Tianjin and chartered by French and Japanese merchants were seized by Chinese magistrates because they did not have a license granted by the Chinese authorities. Questioned by the foreign merchants, the government replied that the protection it granted in return for its tax did not extend beyond its jurisdiction. The council skillfully referred foreign merchants to their respective consuls.[56]

The salt mound affair offers a kaleidoscopic view of the economic interests and political forces in Tianjin at the turn of the century. Not only does it expose the difficulty foreigners had in understanding the subtleties of Chinese society, but it also demonstrates the *agency*—the capacity for action—of the Chinese merchant elites, who managed even in the aftermath of fierce repression to succeed in a complex legal environment. Indeed, thanks to the salt trade, a form of "civil society" emerged in the nineteenth century that complemented and sometimes competed with the action of the Chinese as well as foreign administrations and armies. This episode reveals the astonishing paradox of foreign domination in Tianjin: the copresence of numerous rival powers, as well as the tensions between civil and military authorities, provided some indigenous social groups with room to maneuver and a certain autonomy vis-à-vis foreigners.

After 1902 and the return of the city to the Chinese administration, the new viceroy Yuan Shikai managed to recover and retain control of the gabelle that had been the envy of foreign powers. The new strong man of the empire rehabilitated the salt merchants and reformed administration of the precious commodity in Zhili Province and then in China during the Beiyang government experiment (1912–16).[57] He wished above all to put the fiscal system back on its feet by stimulating merchant activity and increasing the revenues of the gabelle, an important part of which was devoted to reimbursing indemnities offered to the Allied powers as compensation for the Boxer War.[58] To do so, he negotiated a new agreement with the Chinese government in 1912. He also negotiated a loan with a Japanese bank to finance the salt merchants, who had suffered losses during the Boxer occupation as well as from smuggling, seizures by foreign powers, and the establishment of the Austrian and Italian concessions, which further weakened them by forcing them to borrow large sums to move the salt heaps in 1901–2.[59] In turn, Yuan Shikai relied on salt merchants to establish his authority and fill the coffers of his administration, salt being the main source of income. At the same time, Yuan Shikai reformed the salt administration by integrating German agents before instituting a foreign inspectorate in 1913 in the new republic.

CHAPTER VII

The Urban Scramble

Dividing the City, Battling in the Streets

If this affair with the Russians were not so serious, it might be considered a farce, it is difficult to imagine anything more ridiculous than the cadenced march of a Sepoy ten steps back and forth one meter from a Cossack sentry. I think a good number of photographs of this remarkable scene will appear in European newspapers.

—EXCERPT FROM COLONEL J. M. GRIERSON'S JOURNAL, MARCH 14–20, 1901

The international understanding stopped short of making the soldiers of the various armies fraternize with each other: the English, Japanese, and Italians remained among their own. The Russians mixed much less with our troops than one might think, and our soldiers were more often grouped with Americans or Germans when they fraternized.

—RAOUL CHARLES VILLETARD DE LAGUÉRIE, 1901

The first night that I allowed myself to go for a walk in the city with a comrade, we lost our way; the night was dark, and we did not know how to escape the inextricable labyrinth of the shadowy and narrow streets. Our inexperience and bad luck led us to the Japanese section. Fortunately, I noticed it in time, because the Japanese sentries were shooting mercilessly at anyone who did not stop at their cry of "Who's there?" In our ignorance of the Japanese language, we could have been fired upon. I have never seen soldiers as service minded as the Japanese. As a precautionary measure, we raised our rifles, and if a sentry had fired at us, it might have been his last; but the best thing was to avoid a scene, so we turned back. However, we were still lost. Suddenly a patrol of Sepoys advanced. Oh no! We were in the English section where we hid in the alleyways. The patrol passed us by. We were still too fresh to attack the Sepoy patrols, but after a few days in Tientsin, the "old-timers" informed us that the Sepoy patrols had been killed by bayonets.

—JACQUES GRANDIN, 1902

Here, in Tientsin? Organization is pyramidal: exchanges between allies, squabbles, deals, and bluffs; the Germans protect all of Christianity from

Berlin while plundering the protégés of the Missions; the Russians play tricks on the English for the railroads; the Japanese push, spread, and grow. And have you seen the bazaar-like aspect of the concessions? Business doesn't seem to be going too badly, does it?

—"LETTERS FROM CHINA," *LIBERTÉ* SPECIAL ENVOY, FEBRUARY 20, 1902

All the Allied powers took advantage of the victory of July 14, 1900, to enlarge or create a new concession around the Chinese city of Tianjin. Since the middle of the nineteenth century the Qing emperors had lost control of small portions of their territory, ceded in the form of concessions, and above all in the neighboring tributary states: Annam and Tonkin became part of the French colonial empire and Burma became part of the British, while Korea came under Japanese domination. The Treaty of Shimonoseki, which put an end to the Sino-Japanese war in 1895, authorized the transfer of Taiwan. This was the first time that a significant part of the territory was granted to a foreign power. The possibility of partitioning coastal China into spheres of influence began to emerge: Great Britain in the Yangtze Valley, Russia in the Northeast, Japan in Fujian, France in the southern provinces, and Germany in Shandong.[1]

This "carving up" of the country at the turn of the century took the form of an urban scramble in Tianjin, in which the Provisional Government played a decisive role as the international guarantor of the smooth running of interimperial competition. The city witnessed the confrontation of two camps: the British, Germans, Japanese, and Americans faced the Russians, French, and Belgians.[2] On the one hand, the United States followed the British leadership's "open door" policy. On October 16, 1900, the British officially allied themselves with the Germans and gradually drew closer to the Japanese until the signing of the treaty on January 30, 1902 (the first Anglo-Japanese alliance). On the other hand, the secret military convention of 1892 linked France and Russia whose alliance was ratified by the joint declaration of March 16, 1902, on the situation in China. In Moscow in 1896, Li Hongzhang for the Chinese government and Alexey Lobanov for the Russians signed a secret alliance treaty against Japan, which entrusted the Russians with the control of the future railway line in northern Manchuria. Opposition between the two sides was exacerbated in October 1900 with the military occupation of northeastern Manchuria by Russia without consulting the other powers.[3]

The exceptional geopolitical situation of Tianjin in 1900 obliges the researcher to study diplomatic relations and social interactions simultaneously. Does a "bottom-up" approach, that is, an analysis of solidarities and dissensions between soldiers, provide perspective on the shifting alliances? Tianjin offers a unique case of the copresence in such a small space of ten powers, including China, each with its own army, to which must be added foreign nationals represented by some twenty consuls. This concentration of civilians and soldiers produced innumerable jurisdictional disputes over men and territorial sovereignty, which were settled by judicial means, diplomatic negotiations, or military confrontations. The confrontations did not cease after the capture of Tianjin; an internal war with dozens of victims was brewing and pitting some of the Allies against each other daily in the streets of the city.

Strategies of appropriation and partition of the territory

The Allied powers took advantage of the collapse of the Chinese authorities to extend their concessions and establish new ones. They adopted various strategies for appropriating territory (right of conquest, negotiations, development, and so on) which illustrated the permanent tensions between de facto occupation and justification by law and the payment of rents. The concessions thus had an ambiguous status: they were territories leased by foreign powers that nevertheless exercised all sovereignty.

Left bank: Creation of the Russian, Belgian, Austro-Hungarian, and Italian concessions

Russia launched the scramble, followed by the Belgians, then the Germans, French, Austrians, and Japanese. On November 6, 1900, the Russians officially announced, in a circular addressed to all the Allies, the occupation of the left bank of the Hai River opposite the British concession. Lieutenant General Linevich declared that his troops had appropriated the territory of about a thousand acres (405 ha) between the railway station and the oil warehouses of Meyer & Co. as of June 23, by virtue of the "right of conquest, having seized it with arms in hand and at the cost of Russian bloodshed in order to prevent the Chinese from firing on the concessions again."[4] As the Russian authorities pointed out, this seizure preceded the formation of the Provisional Government: the territory "was taken by right of war, for military purposes and is under the complete jurisdiction of the military authorities."[5] The officers planted Russian flags, and bulletins were posted on boards throughout the new concession, which was now patrolled by Cossacks. The Russians recognized and guaranteed the rights of foreign owners whose property titles had been registered before June 17, 1900, the date hostilities began.[6] The Chinese had only a few days to present theirs to the Russian consulate before their land was considered public property. The Provisional Government took charge of posting forty copies of this proclamation in the "indigenous" city, addressed to Chinese property owners.[7] This de facto appropriation did not sit well with all the foreign powers. The U.S. minister in Beijing, Edwin H. Conger, vigorously opposed what he saw as a Russian power grab: "This territory, including a major railway station and other facilities essential to international cooperation, should not be controlled by any one power."[8] The British demonstrated their disapproval in a more subtle and symbolic way by placing question marks in front of the words "Russian concession" on the concession maps of the British General Staff Intelligence Service until early 1901. This inevitably provoked the ire of General Vogak, who demanded their removal, since the concession had "been definitively established by an agreement between the Chinese and Russian governments."[9]

The day after the Russian declaration on November 7, 1900, the Belgian consul informed his counterparts that Belgium now occupied a territory of 238 acres (96 ha) south of the new Russian concession and opposite the German concession.[10] The Belgian concession extended from the E. Meyer & Co. oil depot for about two-thirds of a mile (1 km) along the river.[11] It was bounded to the east by the railroad. The Belgian flag was planted, and markers delimited the new possession. Like the Russians, the Belgian authorities recognized the rights of foreign owners registered before the concession was founded.[12] But unlike the Russians, the Belgians could not invoke the "right of conquest," despite the efforts of Leopold II, who in the early summer of 1900 wanted Belgian troops to join the international expeditionary force.[13] He created the "Belgian Legion of Volunteers in China" and recruited 633 soldiers at the Beverloo camp. The king was responding to the destruction of the Beijing legation and attempting to guarantee the safety of Belgian companies and its 294 nationals (missionaries, engineers, merchants) residing in China. Fearing the imperial ambitions of Leopold II, Germany and Austria-Hungary opposed Belgium's intervention. On August 24, 1900, the dissolution of the Belgian Legion of Volunteers in China marked a new failure for Leopold II, who in 1860, when he was duke of Brabant, had advocated before the Senate to send a contingent alongside Napoleon III's troops and the conclusion of a treaty that would have made it possible to obtain a territorial concession. Such a concession would have provided the foundation for Belgium's commercial expansion in China.[14] In the absence of a Belgian military presence in November 1900, the proclamation aroused little reaction. And for good reason. In the months that followed, the consul took care to specify that it was a "projected concession." In March 1901 the Belgian consul, lacking sufficient financial and human resources, requested the help of the Provisional Government to maintain law and order in the new concession, where the international police patrolled.[15] In fact, the "projected concession" was concretized through the convention signed on February 6, 1902, by virtue of which China ceded to Belgium a perpetual lease on the territory. However, Belgium never developed this territory and quickly forgot that it had a concession in China, so much so that in 1908 the Ministry of Foreign Affairs commissioned a report from Jules Davignon on the advisability of establishing a Belgian concession in Tianjin.[16] The Belgians, omnipresent in all the concessions through their companies (Compagnie Internationale de Tramways et d'Eléctrique de Tientsin in 1903, Société Franco-Belge de Tientsin in 1907, transformed into Crédit Foncier d'Extrême-Orient in 1910), whose activities transcended the concessions' borders, did not need a formal presence in Tianjin.[17] This economic dynamism, out of step with the lack of development of the Belgian concession, explains the decision to retrocede the concession to China on August 31, 1929.[18]

On November 28, 1900, the Austrian minister in Peking, fully embracing the collective logic of the scramble, informed the Allies that, to "protect [its] commercial and maritime interests," Austria was establishing a consulate in Tianjin and a territory of more than 148 acres (60 ha) occupied, "as a concession,"[19] in the east of the "indigenous" city, on the left bank of the Hai River.

It was indeed a question of "preserving equal rights among all the powers." In April 1901, Captain Sambuchi and the Belgian consul requested the help of the Provisional Government's police force to guarantee public security until the Austrians were numerous enough to take over. The Provisional Government preferred not to intervene in this territory, which was in fact occupied by the German troops responsible for policing it. In November, the German authorities recognized the theoretical rights of Austria-Hungary, while pointing out the prior occupation of the territory and the need for them to develop it as they wished. Faced with German reluctance, the Austrian consul officially requested the help of the Provisional Government to organize the new concession. The council agreed to accompany the Consul and convinced Austria-Hungary to maintain the German barracks and hospital as well as the international police station on its territory. Austria-Hungary also had to guarantee the neutrality and freedom of movement of the Dongfu bridge and the road leading to it from the station, the maintenance of which was the responsibility of the Provisional Government. On August 4, 1902, the Provisional Government officially ceded control of the concession, which came under the direct administration of the Austrian Consul. The latter obtained arms from the Provisional Government, which sold him seventy complete military outfits, thirty rifles with bayonets, and 1,500 cartridges. Unlike the other concessions, which were swampy and unhealthy, the Austrian territory, located on the outskirts of the Chinese city, was already densely populated before 1900. The foreign presence and the development projects gave rise to numerous conflicts with the local Chinese population from 1902 onward.[20]

Three days after the Austrian proclamation, on December 1, 1900, the Italian minister in Beijing notified foreign diplomats of the establishment of a concession of approximately 116 acres (47 ha) north of the territory occupied by the Russians and south of the Austro-Hungarian concession, invoking the principle of equity between foreign powers.[21] Italy, with the acquisition of their concession, took revenge for its repeated failures in China since the treaty of 1866, notably the unsuccessful attempt in the autumn of 1899 to obtain recognition of the San Mun Bay naval base and the Zhejiang area of influence. However, as with the Belgian and Austrian concessions, it was a "projected Italian concession," with all the legal ambiguities implied by the term. Lieutenant Valli, commander of the Italian troops in Tianjin, chose the only territory still available, "the best that was left."[22] The Italian consul, Cesare Poma, a historian and specialist of Manchuria, considered it a populous Chinese district (between 14,000 and 17,000 Chinese resided in the area) with a vast cemetery and swamps, and therefore particularly unsuitable for the development of a concession.[23] Italian soldiers settled in the territory near the railway station on January 21, 1901, but the Italian diplomats requested the assistance of the Provisional

Government to guarantee their control and to police the concession.[24] The council installed a detachment of German policemen in response.[25] At the end of August 1901 the Italian consul asked for direct control over the concession. As guarantor of international legality, the council did not wish to hand over the administration of the territory to Italy before the Chinese authorities had officially granted it a concession. This was done on September 7, 1901, following a final protocol of the Boxers, which offered Italy 5.91 percent of the indemnities and extraterritorial rights in the Beijing legations district, providing as well for the creation of an Italian concession in Tianjin. Two and a half months later, the Provisional Government transferred powers of state, including fiscal and police powers, to the Italians on the first day of the tenth moon (November 11, 1901).[26] At the end of 1901, the Society for the Development of the Italian Concession in Tianjin, administered by the engineer Rizzardi and composed of Italian engineers and technicians (A. Riva, R. de Albertis, E. Sabbioni, and E. Ghisi), was charged with the planning of the territory, the destruction of graves, the sale and "colonization" of land, and the construction of roads, drinking water, and gas pipes.[27] The imprecision of the legal definition of the concession posed practical difficulties for Italian diplomats when it came to distributing land: the Italian state had the territory in perpetuity without sovereignty—and therefore ownership—since it had to pay an annual fee to the Chinese administration. On June 7, 1902, a Sino-Italian convention was signed by the Italian minister in Beijing Giovanni Gallina and Tang Shaoyi, director of Chinese maritime customs, to "promote the development of Italian trade in northern China and in particular in the Zhili province."[28] By virtue of article 8, the Chinese could purchase land and reside in the Italian concession. In article 9, the Italian government agreed to consult with the local population for the removal of the coffins and negotiate with Chinese merchants on the salt heaps (article 4).[29] The Italians did not, however, respect all their commitments, especially the compensation of the salt merchants.[30] The concession developed slowly. On February 8, 1902, on the initiative of Cesare Poma, the first issue of the *Bollettino Italiano/Italian Settlement Gazette* appeared consisting of a single sheet of paper written in English and Chinese with official texts and practical information. As early as 1901, the Italians specialized in importing alcohol (wine, vermouth, Fernet-Branca, and the like) and food products (pasta and olive oil) to the European community and then to wealthy Chinese.[31] According to Poma, in March 1902 there were sixteen Italian residents in the concession: two hairdressers; six workers in the trattorias, including the famous Cantina Italiana; a mechanic; a miner; a public works contractor; three artists (a singer, a musician, and a painter); and two businessmen, including the representative of the Italian Trading Company, the only Italian company in Tianjin, whose head office was in Shanghai.[32] Italians were more numerous in the other concessions, where they often ran bars, restaurants, and hairdressing salons. Indeed, in 1900 "all the wigmakers you meet on the Chinese coast inevitably come from Lombardy or Piedmont."[33]

Italy, Austria-Hungary, Belgium, and Russia were all "latecomers" to colonization and their diplomats systematically invoked the most-favored-nation clause enacted by the "unequal treaties" imposed on China in the second half of the nineteenth century to obtain the same advantages as the colonial powers of the right bank.[34]

Right bank: Westward expansion of the existing French, Japanese, British, and German concessions

The French also wished to benefit from the Chinese military defeat by imposing a territorial extension of their concession towards the southwest. In fact, this became the main concern of the French authorities in Tianjin during the first half of the twentieth century. On November 20, 1900, Gustave du Chaylard, consul general of France and president of the city council, announced by consular order the extension of the French concession westward to the mud wall bordering the Hai Kouang Tze canal. All owners were required to verify and register their property titles acquired before June 17, 1900. The "extra-concession" included the land of Ma Kia K'eou between Paris Street, Taku Road, and the Quai de France, as well as the area west of the French concession between Taku Road, the British extra-concession, and the mud wall.[35] This territorial extension quadrupled the surface area of the French concession, from 69 to 292 acres (28–118 ha). The "extra-concession" had its own administrative and legal system entirely in the French consul's hands. Thus, all real estate and land transactions were to be authorized in advance by the consulate, which exercised strict control over the zone's development and allowed French interests to establish themselves on a long-term basis while preventing a Chinese real estate offensive, including through front men. Despite promises of compensation, this French annexation immediately aroused strong protests among

Chinese property owners, who mobilized to make their voices heard among Zhili mandarins and at the Imperial Court through Chinese newspapers. Faced with this opposition, the French did not invoke the right of conquest. They referred to the first request for extension that they had made in 1895 to guarantee the security of their concession and to develop the urban territory:

> At that time, in Ma Kia K'eou, that is the immediate vicinity of our old settlement, there were brothels frequented by criminals from the city and the concessions. When the Chinese police chased them, they came to us and vice versa. The records show this. We want to acquire this corner of the neighborhood to transform it into a kind of boulevard and secure our concession. Talks were held with E. Wang Ouen Tchao. He accepted our request in principle in 1898 just as he had accepted the request to extend the English concession.[36] This case was not the same, however. The English had wanted to annex a Chinese neighborhood where the foreigners' native employees lived and administer it according to their methods. We wanted to acquire a neighborhood of streets in order to demolish the houses and materially and morally ventilate our concession. But the inhabitants resisted. We said to the Viceroy, "Make a deal with them and we will compensate them," and the Viceroy replied, "Make your arrangements directly." This was the only point on which a slight dispute arose, and it was later settled when the Boxer troubles broke out.[37]

At the beginning of the hostilities, as we have seen, the Consul du Chaylard decided to set fire to the area between the French concession and Taku Road. According to his account, the goal was to prevent any offensive coming from this side of the concession, to exert control over the inhabitants of this Chinese district, and to clear the land claimed by France since 1895.[38] Nevertheless, the day after the siege, the Chinese government refused to recognize the French annexation, claiming, quite rightly, that the land belonged to local Chinese owners. After the capture of Beijing, Gustave du Chaylard drew up a plan for the expansion of the concession including the layout of new streets and the extension of old ones. The consul intended to finance this expansionist policy of major works with the salt confiscated the day after the capture of the city: "The realization of these various improvements can only be obtained with time and the necessary resources that I hope will be provided by the sale of the salt piles."[39] He decided unilaterally on this annexation and aroused the astonishment of Minister Delcassé: "The agencies announce that you have carried out the enlargement of the French concession. Is this true?"[40] In 1902, Consul Henri Leduc devised an ingenious scheme to obtain tacit recognition from the representatives of the Chinese authorities passing through Tianjin: in addition to each year's payment to the imperial government of a thousand cash coins for each acre of the French concession, the diplomat added further payments corresponding to the number of acres in the "extra-concession." The subprefect of Tianjin, who was either quick to react or ensure his own interest, delivered receipt of payment to the Consul. And the French authorities proceeded in this way every year to rely on the documents which, in China, served as a title deed. However, the "extra-concession" was not officially integrated into the concession until 1912. On the strength of this initial legal victory, Henri Leduc decided to abandon the policy of force pursued in 1900. On June 28, 1902, he formulated a new request to extend the concession to the Lao Si Kai area, located beyond the Haï Kouang Tze canal. This "alluvial plain, uncultivated, and almost uninhabited," was owned by the Chinese and the Catholic missions and was the only space still available.[41] The consul and his colleagues were concerned about the expansion of the neighboring concessions, while the venerable French establishment was only fifth in size behind Russia (three times larger but less well situated), Great Britain (twice as large), Germany, and Japan. The French request seemed so extravagant that Tang Shaoyi, the head of Chinese customs in Tientsin, did not deign to reply.[42] From then on, the French consulate tried to establish the legal basis for the occupation of the "extension" of Lao Si Kai, invoking the absence of a reply from the Chinese authorities to the request made in 1902 and arguing that the administration's silence was tantamount to tacit agreement. However, the French diplomats took care not to offend the Chinese. Thus, the consulate decided to progressively purchase land privately. It tried to impose a de facto occupation, which was then ratified by law: the brutal annexation of November 1900 was thus followed by a policy of conciliation which gave rise to interminable negotiations concerning compensation of Chinese owners. This lasted until the middle of the 1910s. However, the Chinese authorities refused to recognize these claims,[43] and French leaders in Paris failed to understand the specific political and administrative status of the concessions, such as Minister of Finance Maurice Rouvier, who in 1903 referred to "our colony of Tientsin."[44]

Following the French diplomat, the Japanese consul in turn proclaimed on December 28, 1900, the extension of the Japanese concession obtained on August 29, 1898, thanks to the agreement signed by the Chinese government and Nagamasa Tei, the Japanese consul, under the terms of the first protocol of the Sino-Japanese War.[45] This little-known episode has been ignored by scholars of the Japanese presence in China, who have tended to focus on the interwar period.[46] And yet, the period 1900–1903 marks the true foundation of the Japanese concession. The Japanese did not settle in their concession before the Boxer War. It does not appear on maps until the summer of 1900. Until then there were many Japanese workers in Tianjin—representatives of the Yokohama Specie Bank as well as cotton and wood traders—but they preferred to reside in the British and French concessions. The Japanese consulate, with its efficient consular police, was in the British concession.[47] In November 1900, the Japanese extended their concession 324 acres (131 ha) to the southeast of the Chinese city, which it now bordered, on the pretext of cleaning up this indigenously inhabited suburb filled with Boxers. They then took possession of a territory along the Hai River, south of the German concession, whose strategic position would allow them to control the foreign concessions and to have a port for commercial and military navigation.[48] The Japanese and French consuls agreed on the boundary between the two concessions and at the same time carried out clearing and alignment work.[49] Because of the proximity of the city and the density of the native population, the Japanese paid the Chinese government the highest royalty for their territory north of the French concession. The Japanese found a way to appear to be the benevolent power par excellence by offering market price, a show of respect to Chinese authorities. However, after the siege, they struggled to develop their concession. They were unable to realize the project of linking their two concessions by a tramway line and were forced to entrust the Provisional Government with the task of collecting taxes and maintaining public order. The international government contributed half of the funding ($12,672 out of $25,344) for the international road that connected the southern gate of the indigenous city to the French concession, crossing the Japanese concession. On August 10, 1902, on the eve of the dissolution of the Provisional Government, the Japanese consul general regained police powers in his concession and thanked the council for the care it had taken to protect and develop the Japanese territory: "I have the honor to inform you that I have received instructions from Baron Romura, Minister of Foreign Affairs, to show your Council the high appreciation of the Japanese government for your offices, which have greatly contributed to the maintenance of good order and the material improvement of the Japanese concession at Tientsin, during the time you have, at our request, had temporary charge of the jurisdiction in this concession."[50] In 1902, the Ministry of Foreign Affairs in Tokyo made a strong commitment to the operation of the concession by drawing up an urban development plan that was to explicitly compete with the other Allied powers. On February 12, 1902, the Japanese government entrusted part of the concession to the care of a large private company, the Tokyo & Investment Building Co. which was to construct buildings, "not necessarily elegant and imposing, but sufficiently decent and worthy of comparison with those of other concessions."[51] The company was to encourage Japanese residents of Tianjin before 1900 to settle in the concession by offering them land at cost. It also undertook to sell real estate to Japanese nationals at 10 percent below market price. The Tokyo & Investment Building Co. began work in May 1903 and completed it in May 1908: without counting the thousands of Chinese, 1,452 Japanese resided in 385 houses in the Japanese concession. West of Fukushima Street, the Ministry of Foreign Affairs did not intervene and invited Chinese merchants and entrepreneurs to settle to spur economic activity. Consul Ijuin attracted them by exempting them from business taxes. Chinese companies quickly built residences, cabarets, and theaters in this area, especially on Asahi Street, which became one of the main entertainment districts of the city. By 1900 the Japanese concession was also famous for its brothels and opium dens. In April 1900 Consul General Ijuin ceded back to China the territory southeast of the German concession, retaining the right to reclaim it if necessary.[52]

The German consul general in Tianjin, Alfred Zimmermann, announced on April 18, 1901, "with the consent of the Chinese authorities," the extension of the German concession to the west and southwest of Taku Road, ratified by the Sino-German treaty signed on July 20, 1901. Obtained on October 30, 1895, as a reward for Germany's intervention against the cession of the Liaodong Peninsula to Japan, the concession originally embodied the special cooperative relationship between the two countries. However, the German government made no investment in the 371-acre (150 ha) concession, entrusting its development to a German commercial bank, the Deutsch-Asiatische Bank, which became the de facto head of the concession. The German consul asked the Provisional Government to maintain order in the extension of the German concession and the international police ensured that the Chinese did not build houses without authorization. The concession began to develop slowly after the capture of the city with the construction of the first roads and buildings. Within a few years it became a highly sought-after residential area for foreigners and wealthy Chinese, who had the right to buy real estate and land there. Finally, the victory of the Allies offered the British the opportunity to double the size of their possession in Tianjin. After the territorial expansion ("extra-concession") of 1897 (255 ac/103 ha), they obtained in 1901 an "extra-mural extension" (588 ac/238 ha), to the west of the mud wall. In 1897 the Chinese government defended its interests as well as those of the indigenous residents by forbidding the British to expropriate the Chinese, who resided in the "extra-concession" except in the case of building streets at market price. Thus, this area had a more favorable status for the local Chinese owners, who had an "advisory voice" in discussions concerning the area's development. Finally, the Chinese government could arrest Chinese there without any possible objection by the British.[53]

The expansionist policy of Great Britain, France, Japan, and Germany, which attempted to extend their concessions westward, was explained by the desire of their representatives on the ground to prevent encirclement by neighboring concessions. Blocked to the east by the river, the Allied powers pursued a race toward the hinterland.[54]

The failure of the American project: An "international" or "private" concession

The grab game in which the Allied powers were engaged in Tianjin was vigorously denounced by Secretary of State John M. Hay and Edwin H. Conger, the U.S. minister in Beijing. According to them, this partition of the Chinese suburbs of the city violated the great principles displayed by the Allies, who claimed that through this "humanitarian intervention" they were defending the general interest and not obtaining new colonial possessions. He asked his counterparts that "all action in relation to securing new or extending old concessions should be deferred until order is restored, the Chinese Government reestablished, and the rights and interests of all can be considered."[55] As early as November 16, 1900, John Hay emphasized the danger that the creation of the Russian concession posed to international harmony in Tianjin and China. Therefore, he asked Conger to coordinate the discussions between the Allied powers and to consider founding an "international concession" that would incorporate the former American concession.[56]

However, the "open door" policy defended by Washington came up against the scramble of the Allies to share the last vacant territories in the agglomeration. The United States was unable to prevent or slow down this distribution through the "international concession" project, and it intended to take part in its own way, not without some contradiction. It had indeed become an Asian power since 1898 with the conquest of the Philippines, even as it challenged the traditional colonial model.[57] Consul James W. Ragsdale, convinced of the need for the United States to control its own territory, worked to reactivate the old concession ceded to the Chinese.[58] In Beijing, Conger seemed skeptical about the financial cost of such an undertaking, but came around to the political decision.[59] The commander-in-chief of the American troops, General Adna Chaffee, and the American members of the Provisional Government (notably Charles Denby and Colonel Foote) advocated for the creation of a permanent garrison and the restoration of the concession.[60] On February 24, 1901, the consul was asked to notify his counterparts that the United States would not allow the occupation of their former concession by another power. The very next day, American troops took possession of it again.[61] At the same time, in accordance with the 1896 agreement, James Ragsdale officially requested the Chinese administration return the territory, in the name of defending the economic interests of his country threatened by the monopolistic practices of the Allies.[62]

Seeking the best way to secure U.S. interests at the lowest cost, diplomats from the legation and consulate negotiated with their British counterparts to include the "former U.S. concession" in the British concession, which, in return, offered U.S. representation on the city council, access to the Bund, billets for U.S. soldiers, and assurances that equal commercial rights would be respected.[63] The Chinese authorities objected that the territory was already occupied by two large Chinese companies, the China Merchants Steam Navigation Company and the Chinese Engineering & Mining Company, which had come under British ownership.

They proposed that the United States move to another area between the German concession and the Japanese lands at the southeast end of the city.[64] Located in a flood zone and surrounded by foreign concessions, the territory abandoned by the Japanese did not suit Ragsdale, who declined the offer because the development costs were too high and there were no prospects for territorial expansion. But Ragsdale did not abandon his idea of recreating a concession. Relying on the active American community scattered throughout the British and French concessions and the Chinese city, he advocated founding a new concession within the Chinese city. This location corresponded perfectly to the economic, missionary, and strategic interests of the American nationals, who declared in a petition they were ready to finance its development.[65] This petition had been launched by J. H. "Tientsin" Brown, who mobilized American missionaries and businessmen in January 1902 to put pressure on American authorities and the Chinese administration.[66] According to the consul, the Chinese administration favored the project, but it was ultimately refused by the State Department, which considered that in addition to its excessive cost the reconstitution of this "white elephant" would violate the "open door" policy.[67] Alvey A. Adee, acting secretary of state, and William W. Rockhill, the State Department's specialist on Chinese affairs, favored the creation of an "international concession" or the integration of the "former American concession" into the British concession. In March 1902 Consul Ragsdale and the American businessmen had to give up their dream of a national concession and resume negotiations with Ernest Satow on the integration of the former American concession into the British concession. The British minister confirmed the guarantees offered to the American citizens and the American army on March 23, 1902. The Chinese authorities officially transferred jurisdiction over the territory of the former concession to the British authorities on October 23, 1902.

The old concession had not been developed by the United States between the 1860s and the early twentieth century. In 1902, the eighty-five U.S. citizens registered at the consulate did not live in the "old American concession," and the four major U.S. firms were located in the Chinese city (Walter B. Tuttle & Co. and N. Townsend & Co.), the French concession (R. H. Maclay and Company, specialists in the import-export of fruits and furs), and the British concession (American Trading Company).[68] The former concession was a lawless zone, a no man's land where brigands, former Boxers and traffickers could find refuge from Chinese justice as well as from foreign jurisdictions. A naturalized American citizen of Russian origin, Brown embodied this underground economy (brothels, casinos, etc.) and the culture of the slums of the former American concession in Tianjin. He began humbly as a saloon keeper and supplier of all sorts of more or less illegal products to the American troops, then invested in real estate and brothels, to the point of opening the Alhambra "house of amusement"[69] in Shanghai in 1903. To escape justice, he masterfully used the extraterritoriality and legal blockages of Tianjin by claiming a different nationality depending on the jurisdiction he was in.

The ambiguity of the U.S. relationship to territorial appropriation was clear in Tianjin in 1900–1902. At the beginning of the twentieth century, the United States prospered in Tianjin but still left their seat on the British municipal council vacant from 1902, the ultimate proof of their disinterest in the formal presence of their country in the city. Washington diplomats unreservedly condemned traditional colonization while allowing their nationals to personally acquire numerous plots of land and buildings around the Chinese city within the Provisional Government's jurisdiction. And when the British and French consuls reported to the council and condemned in unison such "speculation," which amounted to individual scrambling, the U.S. consul modestly declared that "he could not endorse the proposals of the British Consul General, concerning land purchased by foreigners outside the concessions."[70] At the turn of the century, U.S. diplomatic and military interventionism in Tianjin served to ensure the "informal" presence of U.S. nationals and businesses.

Internecine warfare: The geopolitics of daily interactions

The day after the city's capture, observers described a climate of cordial understanding between the various allied troops: "camaraderie is excellent and we do each other favors," wrote Corporal Léon Silbermann on August 26, 1900.[71] But tensions between the various nationalities soon became apparent. The French soldiers were aggressive toward the Provisional Government's representatives and did not hesitate to confiscate the flags issued by the council on Chinese ships. The Russian and German soldiers blocked the passage of the river police from their pontoon bridge. The Chinese government police were mistreated by foreign soldiers, who almost systematically hindered their duties. German soldiers attacked "indigenous" officers in Hsi Lou Chuang. Russian soldiers frequently attacked the Chinese police. And the French were not to be outdone in this category, as demonstrated by a group of soldiers on holiday in the city, who attacked a representative of the authorities:

> Once, at the café-concert, we had the wild idea to push the singers, who were standing on stage. We didn't hesitate. The singers' legs were suddenly in the air as they pirouetted onto the crowd of spectators. General panic reigned as it was assumed we were provoking a massacre. The Chinese ran toward the narrow doors where they fought for escape. The uproar attracted an indigenous policeman; informed of the facts, he accused us. We responded with a rifle butt to the head and went elsewhere.[72]

The only kind or even respectful soldiers to the native agents seemed to be the Americans. The latter complained about German and French soldiers, who fired rifles near their headquarters without warning. German soldiers attacked Japanese patrols. A brawl occurred between Italian sailors and the Japanese guard at Hsin Fu Chiao, and so on.[73]

And even when the different contingents maintained cordial relations, deadly confrontations could still occur. For example, on October 2, 1900, a vanguard company of the First Zouave Battalion on its way to Chanhaikwan stopped in front of what appeared to be abandoned forts. Suddenly a Russian flag was raised on one of the forts and a barrage of bullets fired on the French, who immediately returned fire. After ten minutes, the officers obtained a cease-fire. This mistake cost the lives of two soldiers and nine wounded on the French side, and one man dead and three wounded in the Russian ranks. The Russian general apologized and visited the French wounded in the military hospital of the station and promised them a decoration. Because of the alliance between the two nations and their friendly relations. On the other hand, this affair brought about a new questioning of the Zouaves' uniform, inspired by traditional Algerian dress. Unknown to foreign troops, it consisted of a bedaïa, a dark blue cloth jacket, and a fez, a red felt cap. General Voyron repeatedly and unsuccessfully asked the minister of the navy to avoid these colors, which in China corresponded to the blue uniform of the Chinese regulars and the red headdress of the Boxers.[74]

In this endless list of international brawls, two conflicts stand out that regularly opposed the French and the British as well as the British and the Russians.

The Anglo-Russian battle of the trenches around the station: "Farce," "spectacle," or international conflict?

The concessions of Tianjin were distributed through conflict. The traditional Anglo-Russian imperial rivalry, expressed through "grand strategy" in the second half of the nineteenth century, was exacerbated after the Allied victory by the Russian occupation of Manchuria. This new expansionism irritated and worried both the Japanese and the British. The railroad and the railway station were one of the main strategic issues for the Allies, with Great Britain and Russia at the forefront. The day after the battle, Russian soldiers interrupted the construction of a telegraph line by a British officer and his men on the left bank of the Hai River "under the pretext that the land belongs to the Russians."[75] The commander of the British troops in Tianjin told the Russians that the land was under the control of the Provisional Government and placed himself under the protection of the council to complete the line's construction. The strategy of internationalizing the territory adopted by the British seemed to work. While Colonel Woronow asserted that Admiral Alexeyev had ordered Russian flags to be placed on the territory in question, the Provisional Government stated its prerogatives: any territory not belonging to the former concessions was in principle under its jurisdiction. The council thus claimed to "avoid any regrettable friction between the Allied Powers."[76] But, despite the government's declaration, the Russian flags and guards remained in place. A few days later, the British companies Butterfield & Swire and Forbes & Co. declared themselves owners of the disputed land and, angry over the Russian occupation of the left bank of the Hai River, had the Russian flags and "boards" removed from the riverbank on October 15, 1900. The Russians insisted they were defending the general interest of the Allied powers and claimed that this strategic space could not be the "exclusive possession" of a few British subjects. To establish Russian ownership along the river, Lieutenant General Linevich, commander-in-chief of the Russian Expeditionary Force, invoked the recent shift in the course of the Hai River and the appearance of a new territory from silt:

> This claim seems to me to be all the more excessive in that at the time of the acquisition of the land by Messrs. Forbes & Co. the river was almost wetting the wall of their compound and that it is only in the course of the last few years that a new strip of land has been formed, thanks to the silt, which, you will agree, could not have been foreseen nor stipulated in the original deed of purchase. It follows from the above that the presence of the Russian flags on the shore cannot in any way interfere with the property rights of Messrs. Forbes & Co. and Butterfield & Swire.[77]

Great Britain, dean of the imperial nations in Tianjin and manager of the Peking-Tianjin-Shanhaikwan imperial railroad directed by Claude Kinder since the agreement concluded on February 21, 1901, opposed Russia, which controlled the railway from Yangcun to Shanhaikwan from October 1900 to February 1901 and occupied militarily the territory around the station of Tianjin during the siege of the Boxers.[78] The train station was a site for soldiers of different nationalities: "All the platforms were invaded by armies that rubbed up against each other fighting for territory. Disembarking in front of the station, in the middle of the ruins of the burned Chinese village, we kept a sharp eye on our packages as they were ogled by the Cossacks. Around the station, Greek, Italian, and Russian cabarets were set up. The most varied and heterogeneous uniforms, all of them repulsively dirty, paraded by."[79]

On the ground, the soldiers confronted one another while the staffs fought for control of the strategic line between Beijing and the sea, which allowed them to control the capital. Between the rails and the waters of the Hai River, the Russians occupied a large village whose territory was reduced to develop warehouses: "The village must be reduced in order to build rail sidings that are indispensable for the railway. Hence the conflict of last February between the English, who administrated the railroad and were eager to enlarge the station, and the Russians, who were to be expropriated and did not want to consent."[80]

There were four rail sidings (see figure 7.1) upstream of the French bridge—one for the Italians, one for the French, and two for the Russians—which were in constant use by these four nations to unload military equipment and supplies into their warehouses. The other Allies had to manage as best they could, unloading from the station itself. Great Britain spoke for the "trackless" nations and proposed the construction of four new rail

Figure 7.1 British plan for the layout of the tracks at Tianjin station (March 1901), showing existing railroads, railway lines proposed by the British, and the boundaries of the Russian concession.

sidings between the railway line and the river on land that would escape the Russian concession.[81] Indeed, the British claim that the future tracks would be built on land owned by the Railway Company they administered, even though the title deeds were burned at the station during the Boxer War. The Russians, on the other hand, planted their flag on the same land, claiming it as part of their concession.

The British considered the Russian concession "imaginary" because it had never been officially granted to them.[82] On the morning of March 15, when the men of the First Madras Pioneers led by Captain Kinder were about to resume work on siding A, about 328 feet (100 m) from the river, they found themselves face to face with a guard of Cossacks, who had orders to use any means necessary to prevent them from continuing their work. The situation was explosive. But this initial confrontation did not lead to armed conflict. The Russian soldiers dug a trench and settled in while forty-six feet (14 m) away, the British took position near a heap of garbage.[83] All day long, the Chita Cossack sentries and the Indian "Sepoys" faced off at little more than a meter at the end of the track under construction (see figure 7.2). Neither party wanted to start hostilities or abandon their positions. A British colonel accurately described the scene: "The situation soon became ridiculous for the crowd of spectators, who had come to see the spectacle, many of them armed with kodaks."[84] "If this affair with the Russians were not so serious, it might be considered a farce, nothing more ridiculous can be imagined than the cadenced march of a Sepoy ten steps back and forth one meter from a Cossack sentry. I think a good number of photographs of this remarkable scene will appear in European newspapers."[85]

The spectacular dimension of this scene was exacerbated by its austerity and by the recognizable uniforms of these "indigenous" soldiers from two immense empires, coming respectively from southeastern Siberia and southeastern British India. This scramble was staged by troops like an operetta, immortalized by dozens of photographers and hundreds of spectators, who had become accustomed to the violent confrontation between Chinese and foreigners during the siege of the concessions and then the

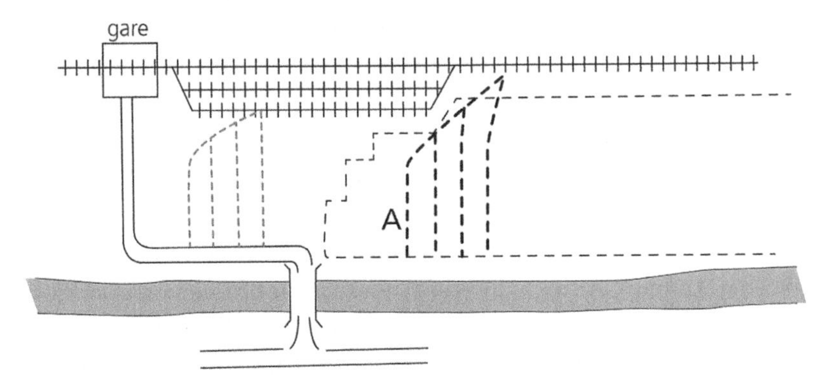

Figure 7.2 Confrontation between Chita Cossacks and Indian soldiers of the First Madras Pioneers on a rail siding in Tianjin, March 16, 1900. Australian War Memorial, Sydney.

beheadings of the so-called Boxers. In retrospect, the senior British officers believed that the only real threat that might aggravate this tense situation was the inebriation of the Cossack commander, who did not hesitate to advance near the Anglo-Russian "front" line, totally drunk and brandishing a sword. His men remained calm and disciplined, avoiding an armed confrontation. At the end of the day, General Campbell managed to convince General Vogak to relieve the Cossack commander. They agreed to take no action during the night. Meanwhile, the Russians and the British counted their forces and prepared for the possibility of battle. The Russians had 450 infantrymen and 100 Cossacks, and the British believed that a coup de force by Vogak was impossible without additional reinforcements, but they were ready to intervene and carefully observed the troop movements of their ally.

The situation remained unchanged on the next day, Saturday, March 16. The Russians declared that the British construction project interfered with the route of the future road that was to cross their concession. The matter was raised in the House of Commons by Lord George Hamilton, who urged the British parliamentarians to trust the men once again in the field, known for their caution and efficiency.[86] Generals Campbell and Vogak agreed not to increase the size of their guard in order to prevent any escalation and to maintain the status quo. On Sunday, March 17, Anglo-Russian tensions were exacerbated by a "riot" of French soldiers against the British. At the same time, the military situation seemed to stabilize on the "front" where the number of guards on both sides was reduced to twenty-seven. Russia, declared that the rights of its territorial concession were superior to those of the British railway concession and took economic retaliatory measures by closing the branch of the London Chartered Bank in Port Arthur, where Russia proclaimed a monopoly for the Russian-Chinese Bank.[87] On Tuesday, March 19, the British general staff decided to send one hundred men from the Hong Kong Regiment, four hundred men from the Royal Welsh Fusiliers, sixty Australian soldiers from the New South Wales Contingent based in Beijing, and one hundred marines stationed in Taku to Tianjin.[88] At the same time, Russian troops moved from Port Arthur to Tianjin, and eight hundred Russian soldiers left Odessa for Port Arthur.[89] The Russian foreign minister, Count Lamsdorf, and the British prime minister, Lord Salisbury, accepted the arbitration of Count von Waldersee, who met with General Campbell and General Vogak in

Tianjin on March 19, but was unable to settle the dispute between the two empires: the former wished to maintain its sentries until a solution was found, while the latter declared that the honor of the Russian flag had been violated and that an apology was required before any discussions on property rights could begin.[90] Both generals refused Waldersee's proposal to interpose "neutral guards" between the two sides. "There are complications on all sides," wrote a French corporal stationed in Tianjin on March 20, 1901, in his diary.[91] The same day, ninety marines replaced the "hot-blooded" Sikhs on the "front": the command hoped that the "cool mindedness" of the Marines would prevent an incident.[92] The next day, thanks to the intermediation of General von Schwarzhoff, the meeting at the Allied headquarters in Beijing between General Barrow and Colonel Grierson on the one hand, and General Vogak on the other finally led to an agreement. Barrow stated that "the insult to the Russian flag was not voluntary on the part of the British authorities and that the removal of the Russian boundary markers, alleged by the Russians, had not been carried out on the orders of the British military authorities."[93] The work will not continue until property rights are recognized by both parties or a compromise is reached. To avoid "risk of accident," the disputed territory was to be evacuated first by British and then Russian troops, according to a carefully established protocol. The two powers were also to remove the flags planted on the territory since the outbreak of the "incident." There remained the dispute concerning a flag planted further back near a Russian tent. But this was a secondary issue, as Grierson noted: "No one can say with certainty that this flag was not planted there before, and as the others have been removed, I think that, in the interests of the Allies, we can afford to leave this one in place."[94]

Before being forgotten, this incident had become something of an event because of its media coverage and its counterfactual dimension. According to most observers, it could have degenerated into a real war because of the play of alliances. Thus, on March 16, at 1:48 p.m., a journalist stated, "The Chinese are enjoying the spectacle of Russian and British troops drawn in hostile array with the possibility of bloodshed at any minute."[95] A New Zealand newspaper said that "the situation is very critical, and an indiscrete step might lead to a great war, in which more than two of the great Powers would be involved," while an Australian newspaper said that "The Tientsin dispute between Russia and Britain has narrowly escaped ending in war."[96] In fact, the outbreak of a military conflict was unlikely, since the military were primarily interested in preserving the status quo through a show of force and testing the resolve of their rivals.

After the withdrawal of troops on both sides, armed conflict was avoided, but the legal dispute remained for another two years until Gustav Detring, commissioned by the various parties to find a solution, proposed a settlement to the dispute between Great Britain and Russia over the construction of the railway siding on April 27, 1903.[97] The arbitration of Detring, the most important owner and true leader of the British concession, was unsurprisingly favorable to Great Britain. At the same time, in order to preserve the honor of both parties, that is, to "save face," as Detring had learned to do when he worked alongside Li Hongzhang, he conceded that some Russian claims were well-founded.[98] The portion of the territory had indeed been acquired by the British railroad company before the Boxer War, but its development could not be carried out without the agreement of the Russians, who controlled that part of the left bank of the Hai River.[99]

International clashes and imperial solidarity: French, British, Indians, and Germans in the streets of Tianjin

To avoid essentializing international relations and fixing them in a binary relationship of hostility or cooperation, one may also understand them "from below" through daily social interactions. The latter are particularly numerous in Tianjin due to the copresence of the various allied contingents. There is no doubt that on the city streets relations were tumultuous between the French and the British, or to be more precise and less essentialist, between Parisians and Alsatians on the one hand, and Welsh and Punjabis on the other. The old tensions between the "hereditary" enemies of the "Second Hundred Years War" between the French and the British in the eighteenth century, had been revived by the Fashoda Incident in the nineteenth century and then once again in Tianjin.[100] In mid-June 1900, a first incident pitted French marine infantrymen against British railroad inspectors over the disputed ownership of a locomotive. The US consul managed to calm the situation.[101] The press, however, aggravated the dispute, as in the case of the "the fiendish *Pekin and Tientsin Times*," which offered the British "the weekly joy of a gentle scolding of France."[102] From the day after the capture of Tianjin to the handover of the city to the Chinese authorities, the French soldiers considered themselves in open conflict with the Chinese authorities: "We had the worst relations with the English garrison; we were almost in a state of war with them," wrote one French soldier.[103] The "hatred against the British" continued relentlessly. As new soldiers arrived, they continued the old quarrels of their comrades already stationed in Tianjin. The French soldiers made it a habit not to salute the British officers whom they abhorred and the Japanese officers whom they despised. Every Sunday, when the pubs were closed in the French concession, they went to those in the British concession to provoke the tommies. At 8:30 p.m. every night in the French concession they organized a retreat with a brass band that welcomed many foreign soldiers, especially Germans and Russians. These demonstrations were an opportunity to scold the British by singing the "Parisian refrains": "V'là les Engliches, oh! Yes!"[104] Stories of fights between soldiers from both countries in drinking establishments were legion, so much so that from November 1900 onward British officers advised their soldiers not to go to the French concession when off duty.[105] French soldiers took every opportunity to express their Anglophobia. In January 1901 a detachment of British soldiers from the international police apprehended a French soldier. A French guard, in direct disobedience of the Provisional Government, freed him by force.[106] On March 11, 1901, the French police arrested two coolies and their cargo belonging to the British firm Wilson & Co. on Taku Road on the grounds that they did not have a "license," that is, authorization to enter the French concession. The British rightly saw this as an attempt at extortion.[107]

But it was during the second half of March 1901, at the time of the Anglo-Russian confrontation near the railway station, that international hatreds rose to new heights in the city and British soldiers were directly attacked by French soldiers: "A veritable battle broke out in Tientsin between the English, French, and Germans."[108] On Sunday, March 17, women and children were insulted by a group of six or eight Frenchmen who crossed the British concession, pushing and insulting bystanders.[109] Soldiers from the Royal Horse Artillery were called in to restore order. General Campbell then asked General Voyron to forbid French soldiers from entering the British concession, except for those on duty.[110] The French commander was reported to have exclaimed, "But what will my men say?"[111] This proclamation provoked a "riot" of French soldiers, who escaped the control of their officers and invaded the streets of the French concession, shouting slogans hostile to the British and singing the praises of other nations, especially the Boers. British officers and soldiers passing through the concession were booed and in some cases physically assaulted. The French officers were unable to control their men, and only the police dispatched by General Voyron managed to calm down their compatriots. French police were placed in front of the British concession to prevent the entry of French soldiers, while the Australian soldiers of the naval brigade were posted in front of the French concession to prevent the Sikhs from entering.[112] Only a few French soldiers managed to enter before being quickly overpowered. On March 18, 1901, their excitement had subsided slightly. One could still hear booing of British soldiers and insults to Indian soldiers systematically labeled "coolies." On the same day, Major Mockler, a British officer working for the Provisional Government, was assaulted by French soldiers in the French concession.[113]

Colonel Grierson recounted in detail the "riot" of March 1901, in which French soldiers revived the recent memory of the humiliation at Fashoda and evoked the contemporary resistance of Afrikaners to British rule. Adopting a counterfactual analysis, he wondered whether the bloodbath had been narrowly avoided thanks to the French senior officers' spirit of responsibility and their ability to control their "enslaved" men:

> I do not attach any serious importance to the riot. . . . The main culprits were the two French line infantry battalions formed by the 61st and 98th regiments, made up mainly of Parisian volunteers who had already completed their military service. As one may imagine, these men were not exactly the elite. They had distinguished themselves throughout the campaign by a marked tendency to rob, rape, and commit other crimes. Their officers were afraid of them, and the non-commissioned officers had no power over them. If General Voyron had not sent police reinforcements to Tianjin that evening, the British concession would have been subjected to riot and disorder, if not a bloodbath, last Sunday. Fortunately, this was avoided and the only British subjects, who had cause to complain of indignities or ill-treatment were those compelled by their professional activity or duty to go to the French concession. I was among the latter. That morning I went down to Tongku to visit the Taku forts with Major Blane and on my return, I found myself in the midst of a party. The French soldiers were dancing, hooting, and hollering, their most common cry was "Down with the English!," "Long live the Boers!" and,

strangely enough, "Fashoda!" It was unpleasant to pass through such a crowd, but, short of insolence, we were not the object of violence until we entered the British concession. At that point a stone was thrown at us by a crowd of men held back by the gendarmes, which struck the car. I regret to report that many German soldiers fraternized with the French. I saw them myself arm in arm and heard the words "Verdammte Engländer" [damned Englishmen] used freely. For several days they were heard shouting "coolie!" at the indigenous soldiers and in general their behavior was hostile and obnoxious.[114]

General Bailloud ordered the withdrawal of the Parisian regiment involved in the "riot."[115] In the days that followed, resentment between the French and Germans on one side and the British on the other continued to grow and began to spread to Beijing, where several cases of German soldiers insulting Indian soldiers were reported. On March 21 a British officer refused to be arrested by the German guard following an argument with a French officer and was killed in the street. On Sunday, March 30, another was again violently attacked by French soldiers.

July 14, 1901, offered a moment of international harmony during which France celebrated the taking of Tianjin and the storming of the Bastille. But it was also the occasion of a new incident between the French and the British. The French troops paraded on the Quai de France at 8:00 a.m. The French municipality spent about eighty thousand francs to decorate the concession with flags and set up a banquet and refreshment stands where Japanese beer was distributed free of charge. In the afternoon the French and the other Allies gathered around the attractions: theatrical performances, dance shows, boxing matches, and so forth. A bullfight was even organized with two drunken men disguised with ox skins:

During the games, a serious incident almost occurred; the English general had the audacity to come to our concession, half lying down in a carriage drawn by six horses; he was escorted by 20 Sepoys on horseback, sabers in hand. He would have been better off to go to the Transvaal to see if we were there. We shouted: "To the water! To the water!" He turned pale and quickly returned to the English concession where he should have stayed in the first place. If he had stayed any longer with us, he would not have escaped unscathed despite his 20 Sepoys.[116]

Bloody brawls continued until the government was dissolved. On a Sunday in early January 1902, following a fight in the British concession in which two Frenchmen and a German lost their lives, French soldiers carried out a veritable vendetta against the British, described with exaggeration by a French soldier: "Every night after this attack, Englishmen and Sepoys disappeared into the marshes of the plain of the tombs. The English authorities were obliged to order their soldiers to go out in armed groups. This order brought an end to it and the concession remained ours."[117] The French criticized the pride of the English, "which is truly stupid and excites everyone to the utmost," while the British officers stigmatized the inexperience of the noncommissioned officers, their Parisian origins, and the indiscipline of the rowdy troops.[118] They emphasized the brevity of military service, which was insufficient for training good soldiers. At the same time, the British command praised the good will of the French senior officers, who did everything possible to control the "riotous Parisian volunteers."[119]

Though they were allies of the British, the Germans participated in these manifestations of violent Anglophobia alongside the French. The Belgian Jules Jadot was struck by the friendly ties that united the former enemies of 1870: "The French and the Germans fraternize continually here!" This was particularly visible during the military parades.[120] On Sunday, March 17, 1901, many German soldiers joined the French in the British concession, where they brutally beat the trumpeter of the Royal Horse Artillery. On March 18 the British officers complained about the behavior of the German soldiers in a private meeting with Lieutenant Colonel Gundell, the commander of the German Expeditionary Force in Tianjin, who promised to take action to stop this unacceptable behavior. On March 30 Colonel Grierson tried to convince German General von Schwarzhoff of the need to discipline his soldiers, but Schwarzhoff accused the British of having started the hostilities in Tongku when the British troops called the Germans "coolies" immediately upon arrival.

Schwarzhoff regretted British relentlessness toward the German soldiers, who were regularly accused of looting in Tianjin. Faced with the reproaches of the German general, the British colonel underlined the difference between their military cultures:

> From our old experience (more than 250 years) of wars in Eastern countries, we have come to the conclusion based on our convictions that the best way to wage war with small armed forces in such vast

theaters of operations is to conciliate the indigenous population, finance our operations ourselves, and bring with us all the necessary equipment, etc.; whereas the Germans have adopted the system of financing the war through the war itself, requisitioning supplies, clothing, and means of transportation on site. This system, especially in a country that Europeans consider a place to amass wealth, soon degenerates into looting. So it is not surprising that British officers, who seek the consent of the inhabitants in their system of warfare should object to such practices and report on foreigners who ruin their efforts.[121]

The brawls continued despite attempts to work together. On May 6, 1901, two German soldiers insulted a Bengal lancer, calling him a "coolie" and beating him before being arrested and sentenced to three days in the brig. The sentence was proclaimed during a military parade to warn the soldiers that this type of outrage would henceforth be punished even more severely.[122] At the same time, German soldiers fired on a British merchant ship and wounded two British men. German incivility—"unseemly conduct" and "arrogance"—also seemed to increase on trains to and from Tianjin, where foreign troops were concentrated and mixed in the same cars.[123] A report by the railway inspectorate estimated that eighteen of the twenty-five cases of railway disorder during April and May 1901 were caused by German troops.[124]

The German and French military harbored a particular hatred for Indian soldiers in the British army, whom they called "coolies" and considered particularly cruel and violent "mercenaries."[125] Grierson was surprised by this accusation, which he felt was unfounded, since "the word 'coolie' was well known to British soldiers, who had served in India and was never used as a dishonorable nickname."[126] Schwarzhoff considered the word to be entirely Chinese and discovered by foreign soldiers in Tianjin. The difference in perception of this imperial lexicon—"coolie" comes from the Tamil word *kuli*, meaning worker—is in fact the result of the pejorative use of this term by the Germans and the French applied to Indian soldiers. While passing through the Tianjin region, Pierre Loti perfectly expressed the French stereotypes of these soldiers: "In China, England has been represented above all by hordes of Indians, and everyone knows, alas! what kind of work its troops are presently doing elsewhere."[127] While their physique and appearance impressed the French, they still mocked them: "These

Indian soldiers are enormous, tall as the day is long and made taller still by the infinite turban which rolls up above their head like a series of towers on top of their bronze faces . . . and the idea has emerged that these tremendous soldiers, who stroll with a straight slowness are more for show than for action."[128] On the other side, the Indian soldiers openly despised foreign troops deemed—with the exception of the Japanese—dirty, undisciplined, and ill-dressed."[129]

Thus one of the distractions of the French troops was to mock and attack the Indian soldiers during nights out in the Chinese city, which was in principle forbidden to foreign soldiers since September 1900.[130] With their rifles, the soldiers jumped over the wall of their barracks and went preferably to the part of the city assigned to their nation, certain of benefiting from the indulgence of their compatriots. During these expeditions, Jacques Grandin and his comrades made a specialty of attacking the Sepoys, in this case the Sikhs, who so fascinated the French:

> Suddenly a patrol of Sepoys advanced. Oh no! We were in the English section where we hid in the alleyways. The patrol passed us by. We were still too fresh to attack the Sepoy patrols, but after a few days in Tientsin, the "old-timers" informed us that the Sepoy patrols had been killed by bayonets. . . . The Sepoys were, along with the Chinese, our victims. They are handsome men, tall, well bearded, with fine features and supple bodies, but as weak in muscle as the Chinese themselves. When a Sepoy was tripped, he would cover two lengths of ground, and be unable to get up; when we stumbled on one in a Chinese house, we threw them into the street by the shoulder. Fortunately for them they never resisted.[131]

When Jacques Grandin wanted to acquire some shoes, he and his comrades naturally decided to ambush an Indian soldier and did not hesitate to shoot him coldly to steal his boots: "Suddenly, the tall figure of a Sepoy swung into view at the entrance to the field. The Hindu walked slowly, his arms swaying gently to the rhythm of his step, he went quietly without suspecting any danger. He stopped within my sites, I shouldered my gun, aimed at the tip of his feet. The man stopped abruptly, as if some kind of idiot and raised his arms toward the sky. Then he fell backwards like a mass."[132] The small band of French troops left the Sikh lying on the ground wounded and unconscious and then realized that the shoes were too big for Grandin's feet.

These fights had an ethnic dimension as witnessed by the Indian night watchman of the British firm Jardine, Matheson & Co. On his return from a mission to Tongku, he was violently attacked by French soldiers on the evening of March 18, 1901, even though he was not in uniform as he passed through the French concession.[133] Generally Indian soldiers were known for their discipline and did not respond to French and German provocations. However, the newspapers reported the anecdote of an Indian officer who, on March 21, 1901, spat on a French sergeant because of his bad behavior.[134] Two more cases made the headlines in December 1901. Sikhs were sent to find an Indian soldier who killed two of his comrades. In the meantime, the Indian was killed by German soldiers, who also shot at the Sikhs sent to arrest the Indian soldier. A gunfight ensued causing three deaths on each side.[135] The same month, a soldier of the Fourth Punjabi Regiment entered a German police station and killed an inspector with a rifle.[136]

Numerous testimonies evoke the violence perpetrated by Indian soldiers toward the Chinese population. During her visit to Tianjin in 1901, a Swiss woman, Cäcilie von Rodt, was impressed by the Sikhs' brutality as their "blows fell like hail on the backs of the poor Chinese coolies, who were used to being beaten."[137] The Chinese elites experienced the humiliation of being subjected to the domination of these swarthy individuals, who were themselves indigenous peoples from the British Empire. From the point of view of the Chinese, as well as of the foreign powers, this was seen as a form of Indian "subimperialism" in China between 1900 and 1902.[138]

Confronted with the difficulty of the Indians' behavior in this Chinese context, both Colonel Grierson and the Indian officers regretted the small number of British-born soldiers in China:

> Although our Indian troops are undoubtedly fighting better than those of the foreign powers here, and although they have a high contempt for the better part of these foreign troops, and although the foreign officers praise their conduct on the battlefield, they do not know how to behave, and they do not possess the prestige of a white face. The events of November 14, when Indian troops were violently attacked and looted by Germans, would have been impossible with troops of British origin.[139]

The omnipresence of Indian soldiers, who made up most British troops in China (15,433 Indians, including 2,554 at Tianjin, and 2,062 British, including 577 at Tianjin, in March 1901), posed a problem for the British general staff. They constituted an indispensable force for Britain to maintain its status as a great Asian power. But this dependence on Indian contingents also revealed its weakness in relation to the two other regional powers, Russia and Japan.

The innumerable brawls did not degenerate into a widespread conflict thanks to the senior officers. The petty hatreds, as observers perfectly understood, were not instrumentalized, but rather channeled by the authorities and managed as law-and-order issues, and not international problems.[140] Moreover, these rivalries did not exactly correspond to the game of alliances between the Allied powers, since the German soldiers attacked the British, while the diplomats and generals of both countries supported the same Chinese faction against the French and Russians.

Streets, houses, and men: Territories of law and conflicts of jurisdiction

Between the Chinese authorities, the numerous concessions, and the Provisional Government, jurisdictional conflicts were a daily occurrence at several levels. The actors controlled, or at least thought they controlled, the different jurisdictions and tried to play them off. This was the case with the Beaume affair, which troubled the French concession during the summer of 1902. On July 20 two police officers from the French municipality, Simon Susini and François Vallée, were on their daily patrol along Taku Road. They came across two French soldiers playing billiards with a civilian in a café named the Hotel Kaiserhof. The two police officers instructed the soldiers to come with them in accordance with the orders given by their superiors:

> The two soldiers immediately sought to obey our request but the civilian, Monsieur Beaume, a French subject and a butcher living on the rue de France, pushed them into the room on the opposite side of the exit door and prevented them from coming despite all their good will. He insisted [pointing at us]: "They have no right to come here. They don't belong here." He then showed us the door and said:

> "You don't belong here. This is a gambling hall." The two soldiers, who finally escaped this drunk individual came toward us, but while we were talking to them Monsieur Beaume yelled at us disrespectfully and incited them to continue the game and deny our responsibilities: "Do not listen to these people, they are nothing here. They only have rights in the French concession." Then turning to us, he repeatedly cried out insults: "It is not the soldiers you should be afraid of but me. Know that I am French and that you are talking to a Frenchman and tomorrow I will take care of you. Give me your name Brigadier. You are not only the one who will file a report. I will too! And tomorrow I warn you that you will be sentenced to eight days in prison."[141]

The young and robust Beaume was twenty-six years old and summoned to appear on July 29, 1902, before the consular court, presided over by the French consul, Henri Leduc, and two judges: a merchant by the name of Mr. Redelsperger and an employee of the Chinese Imperial Customs, Mr. Guernier. The accused recognized having pronounced the words written in the report but attempted to prove his good faith: he claimed that the gendarmes did not have the right to intervene in a private house located outside the French concession. In fact, Jean Beaume asserted that he and the soldiers were in a room adjoining the Hotel Kaiserhof, which he rented and that had a private entrance: "under these conditions, this was his home." In fact, the hotel, despite its name, was located on the British portion of Taku Road. Moreover, to prevent fights between French and German soldiers and British soldiers since the beginning of June 1901, General Voyron had forbidden French soldiers to use this street or to cross the British concession in general.[142] This was precisely the reason for the arrest of the two soldiers by Sergeant Susini, thirty-two years old, and Gendarme Vallée, twenty-seven years old. The court condemned Beaume to a twenty-five-franc fine for contempt and charged him with paying all costs.

Jurisdiction changed from concession to concession, from street to street, and from house to house. Thus, the foreign owner endowed his entire house with consular protection: the international police could not arrest any Chinese individual in the "house of a German subject" wherever it was in the city without the permission of the German consul. This rule also applied to ships flying foreign flags. The agents of the Provisional Government or the policemen of the concessions could not enter the missions without the permission of the "occupying foreigners." These spaces constituted, within each concession, legal enclaves whose status could change rapidly, like the Italian house lent to bersaglieri by the German army in the Austrian concession.[143]

Why did the Allied powers establish this military government? Why did they maintain it after the fall of Beijing in mid-August 1900? It was undoubtedly to protect transportation and communication lines to the capital and to maintain pressure on the Chinese government to obtain a significant indemnity. But other motives also became clear in November 1900, when the Allied powers openly affirmed their plans to extend existing concessions and create new ones. The government was the international guarantor of the scramble. Although the foundations of concessions or "extra-concessions" were each the result of a distinct national initiative, they all adopted the same legal form. In addition, the government allowed the Allies to take possession of new territories in the absence of sufficient military means: in this respect, it was an international colonial enterprise. Tianjin represented one of the privileged places of rapprochement between Great Britain and Japan. The former, weakened at the same time in southern Africa, understood at the end of June 1900 that it needed the Japanese army to fight against the Boxers and to counteract Russian expansionism. The British and Japanese commands experimented in Tianjin in 1902 with cooperation between intelligence agents, coordinated by Major Alfred Wingate.[144]

The streets of Tianjin constituted an echo chamber for the game of alliances between the Powers. On the other hand, between 1900 and 1902 the policy of the imperial court was fully in line with the rivalry between the British and Russian camps. With the defeat of the Boxers, the Manchu Zaiyi and Gangyi factions which had been favorable to the Boxers between 1898 and 1900, ceded power to the two great "pro-Western" factions: the Ronglu party led by Yuan Shikai and the Qing prince group led by Li Hongzhang. It was in this context that the Allies intervened directly in the internal conflicts of the Imperial Court for the first time.[145] The Russians and their French allies maintained excellent relations with Li Hongzhang and his disciple Zhou Fu, whom they wished to see appointed viceroy of Zhili following his master.[146] The British and their Japanese partners chose to support Yuan Shikai to succeed Li Hongzhang and he became head of the province in December 1901.[147] With this appointment, the Empress

Dowager was rewarding the man who had offered her 200,000 taels during her exile in Xi'an in 1900–1901. Above all, she was trying to regain control by tempering Russian ambitions into Manchuria and fueling interimperial rivalries in China. In the field of foreign policy, as with the competing factions of the court, Cixi's legitimacy was fragile, and she was only able to maintain power through shifting alliances according to the political context.

The Chinese political elites were aware of the Allied powers' difficulties in northern China and in Tianjin in particular. The rise in tensions at the end of 1900 made it necessary to accelerate negotiations with the Chinese government to prepare for the withdrawal of troops.[148]

Figure 8.1 Commemorative medal of the Tianjin Provisional Government, 1902.

CHAPTER VIII

A Government for Posterity?

Retrocession of the City and Administrative Continuities

Since the Allied powers have always maintained that they were not at war with China, the Provisional Government must be regarded as having acted for the Chinese Government, and the Chinese Government must recognize the validity of its acts, as if they had been done in the name of the Chinese Imperial authorities themselves. If the validity of these acts were now allowed to be challenged in any detail, it would be an insult to the founders of the Government, would bely the whole theory of its existence, and open the door to endless disorder and confusion.

—DECLARATION BY THE COUNCIL OF THE PROVISIONAL GOVERNMENT

The Chinese are not rancorous by nature and thus disremembered our coups; they accompanied us to the city and overwhelmed us with best wishes. They are definitely a good people, we promised to see them again one day; having said that, they were perhaps happy to be rid of us.

—JACQUES GRANDIN, 1902

Viceroy Yuan showed how much could be accomplished, even in China, through the massive introduction of modern methods and conveniences for the improvement of people's living conditions in such a short time. It is thanks to Yuan, who had the courage and wisdom to carry out the projects conceived by a foreign military government, that Tianjin owes its reputation as the most progressive and enlightened city in China.

—LETTER FROM J. RAGSDALE TO W. W. ROCKHILL, JUNE 4, 1907

The members of the government, some of whom had been contemplating its dissolution since its first months of operation, were obsessed with the legacy that this political and administrative experience would leave behind in China. As a result, they sought to ensure the collective memory of their work, which they considered to be part of an ongoing project of transformation.

Once the negotiations were completed and the territorial gains secured, the Provisional Government could handover responsibilities to Yuan Shikai, the new strongman of the Chinese Empire, and the Allied powers could withdraw to their foreign concessions. The Allies set as the main condition for the handover recognition and continuation of their administrative work by the Chinese authorities.

The new viceroy had no difficulty following in the footsteps of a foreign military government that claimed to act on behalf of the Chinese imperial authorities. He hired foreign experts and pursued police and health reforms that reinforced Tianjin's role as the Middle Kingdom's laboratory for administrative experiments.

Perpetuating the memory of the Provisional Government: Trophies, medals, and archives

The armed forces collected military memorabilia and relics such as trophies. The government produced souvenirs like medals to celebrate its work and prepared the conservation of the archives to ensure this experience, which they considered extraordinary, would be documented and remembered.

During the two years following the capture of the city, the Provisional Government military as well as civilians besieged in the concessions during the summer of 1900 were obsessed with recovering military "relics" to preserve the "memory" of this event. At the same time, the ruins in the districts entirely devastated by the bombardments and fires disappeared in a few months. Imperial flags of the Chinese as well as the Boxers were scarce, so foreigners collected Chinese and "Western" weapons (bayonets, rifles, guns, ammunition, and so forth). The demand increased so fast that in November 1900 the Provisional Government decided to regulate this traffic in "old" weapons, which was largely clandestine. Every week, the council had to rule on numerous requests for "trophies." The officers used them to decorate the numerous garrisons in the jurisdictions as well as for their personal collections. The government usually granted permission to remove weapons from the Chinese arsenals. Some trophies were also displayed in public spaces to signify the passing of time, like the old meridian cannons transformed into solar clocks, as was done in Europe. The old Krupp guns acquired by the Chinese army were much sought after. Thus, in January 1902, when British artillery officer Captain Woods asked the government to lend him the Krupp cannon in order to make it sound every day at noon, the council preferred to keep it in the "indigenous city." Finally, British perseverance won out at the end of July 1902, when the government, on the eve of its dissolution, agreed to give the Krupp cannon to the British concession. Each nation and even each regiment sought to obtain its military memorabilia. Thus, the Russians recovered a Russian cannon of 1836 from the city's Chinese arsenal, which testified to the ancient diplomatic and commercial relations between the two empires. Civilians also wanted to keep a souvenir of the siege of the city, like Herbert Hoover, who obtained permission to take "three old rifles" from the arsenal at the end of January 1901. Others, like the Australian Captain Keegh asked for "samples of Chinese weapons" and adopted the strategy of a veritable collector. This passion for weapons was such that by the end of March 1901 the government could no longer satisfy the requests for trophies. The arsenal in the Chinese city was empty. The government then advised officers and soldiers to exchange these relics among themselves, which in turn created a trophy market. All the soldiers seemed to leave with their "war souvenirs," as Jacques Grandin wrote when leaving Tianjin: "We quickly packed our bags, wrapped our little Buddhas and our little bronzes, souvenirs of the war, and left."[1] Alexis Daoulas brought back the famous terracotta figurines and a piece of shrapnel, acquired on July 3, 1900, during the siege of the concessions, illustrating the complexity and specificity of this war in China: "An 80 mm projectile, that was still hot, set fire to a pile of paperwork that had fallen into disarray near a library. I had the fire put out immediately and took the piece of steel with me as a souvenir. This projectile is proof to me of how up to date Chinese ammunition is. It is a segmented shell base, a special projectile that we have been making ourselves in France for only a short time."[2]

The trophies traveled and participated in the construction of the collective memory and the personal success of certain veterans. Thus, after ten years in China and the benefit of his experience of the siege of the concessions, Rev. Charles F. Grammon, representative of the American Bible Society in Tianjin, returned to the United States for a series of lectures at the beginning of 1901. Touring major American universities, he systematically illustrated his point with an "exhibition of a great variety of Boxer relics" such as weapons, placards, and flags. During his stay at Harvard University, an exhibition was organized at the Bible House in Boston.[3] These objects had an important impact on the long-term construction of family imaginaries, as Marc Boulet testifies: "China has marked me too, since childhood, when I was jumping on my great-grandfather Louis Boulet's lap. He had fought in China during the Boxer War of 1900. He had brought back some objects that decorated a wall in the dining room of our family home. . . . Trophies that he had probably stolen."[4]

The Provisional Government kept a living trophy: the "two goddesses of the Boxers," leaders of the rebellion, and especially the Red Lanterns, imprisoned in the Provisional Government's headquarters. The day after the capture of the city, the foreign military had pulled them out of the river with their mother as they tried to escape on a junk. The Allies recognized the importance of what they considered the "fetishes," who had protected and inspired the Boxers.[5] On October 14, 1900, the chief of the international police accompanied a group of foreign officers—three Frenchmen, including Pierre Loti, two Englishmen, and a Russian—to visit the two "goddesses" cloistered in an outbuilding of the viceroy of Zhili's headquarters:

> In the middle of a lamentable disorder, in a half-darkened room where the evening sun was blocked, twilight was setting in on two poor girls, two sisters, who resembled each other sitting with their heads down, or rather collapsed, in poses of supreme consternation. One was on a chair and the other on the edge of the ebony bed that they must have shared to sleep. They wore humble black dresses. Here and there bright silks and tunics embroidered with large flowers and golden chimeras were tossed about the floor as if abandoned. They had worn these to go to the front of the armies, among the whistling bullets, on the days of battle; they were the attires of warriors and goddesses. . . . For they played the role of a Joan of Arc—if it is not a blasphemy to pronounce such a pure name in reference to them. They provided a symbolism, posted in the pagodas riddled with shells to protect the altars and inspired those, who walked into fire with cries to lead the soldiers. They were the goddesses of these incomprehensible Boxers, atrocious and admirable at the same time, great hysterics of the Chinese fatherland, who stirred the hatred and terror of the foreigner, who one day fled fearfully without fighting, and the next day, as if possessed, threw themselves with knives to meet death under the rain of bullets against troops ten times more numerous. As captives, the goddesses became the property—and even curious trinkets, one might say—of the seven allied nations. They were not

mistreated. They were only locked up, lest they commit suicide, which had become their obsession. What was their fate in the future? We had already grown tired of seeing them and we did not know what to do.[6]

Transformed into a "curious ornament" by the Allies, the two young girls' dignity and courage forced respect and aroused the compassion of Pierre Loti, who considered this visit to be "one of the most tragic memories of the whole campaign."[7] Having come to the headquarters "to be amused by a curious spectacle," he left in silence with a heavy heart and the unpleasant feeling that the winners did not deserve this trophy. At the beginning of January 1901, the council feared that the imprisonment of the Boxers' goddesses would cause trouble in the city and considered releasing the two young "so-called Boxer" girls. The chief of police proposed to "deport" them to an orphanage in the Catholic mission of the Fathers of the Church of St. Joseph in Shanghai, where they were sent in mid-April 1901. The Provisional Government continued to provide for their needs. When in June 1901 Father du Cray, in charge of the mission, wondered what would happen to the girls, the council reminded them that they should never return to Tianjin but that they belonged exclusively to the government. In March 1902 it asked the Catholic mission to prepare the release of the two girls to the Chinese authorities at the same time as the dissolution of the Provisional Government. The missionaries solemnly handed them over to the representatives of the Chinese government in Shanghai on August 15, 1902.[8]

Short on trophies and having run out of Chinese weapons, the government decided to produce its own official souvenirs to commemorate the exceptional experience even while it was still under way. Thus, at the beginning of July 1902, Colonel Harada proposed to award different commemorative medals to those who served the Provisional Government based on precise criteria. The gold medal was awarded to all current and former members of the council, heads of government departments and district chiefs, while the silver medal was awarded to all foreign civil and military officials of the Provisional Government. Finally, some particularly deserving Chinese government employees were awarded a bronze medal. The proposal was approved by the council, which offered only a bronze medal to minor foreign officials earning less than $125. In early August, 6,100 yen ($2,500) deposited by the government at the Yokohama Specie Bank in Tianjin, enabled the order of 26 gold, 101 silver, and 167 bronze medals.

Designed by J. Chevet and made by the Japanese jeweler Tenshodo, the 52-mm-diameter medallions depicted the flags of Germany, the United States, France, the United Kingdom, Italy, Japan, and Russia, tied together by a band inscribed with the pacific motto of the Provisional Government, *Pax labor.* The obverse carried the Chinese inscription indicating the Provisional Government of Tianjin surrounded by a crown of oak and laurel. These three hundred medals were not a reward of individual merit but rather were designed to celebrate a collective experience while clearly marking the difference between foreigners and natives.

Beyond preserving individual memories, the council also hoped to maintain collective memory and inscribe this political and administrative experience in the great history of the spread of civilization. To this end, as early as April 1902, it protected the archives of the Provisional Government by having the minutes of the council copied in French and then translated into English and Chinese to make its work known to the greatest number of people in China and abroad, and in particular to the members of the consular and diplomatic corps as well as to the commanders and the Chinese authorities. The French text was to prevail in case of dispute. More than two thousand pages were translated in a few weeks by three Chinese interpreters, and fifty copies of these translations were printed. But the Chinese version was only a compilation of the most important decisions, expurgated of what the Chinese secretary considered to be potentially embarrassing for the Chinese authorities. Finally, at the end of July 1902, the council ordered the end of the Chinese translations and the destruction of previous ones "in order to prevent an incorrect Chinese translation from being accepted as correct." Many foreigners were fascinated by this "extraordinary" history in the making, which they wanted to hold on to before it faded away. In June 1902, for example, W. H. Smith, an official in the Justice and Treasury Departments, requested permission from the council to consult the archives to "write a history of the Tientsin Provisional Government." The council granted him permission, while explaining that "an official history of the government was in preparation." The latter never saw the light of day. The Allies asked the head of the consular corps in Tianjin, the British consul general, to host the archives of the Provisional Government after the handover of the city. However, the British diplomat only had a "small room" in the consulate in which the archives could be stored but hardly communicated to the public. The consulate also housed the archives of each district, which were solemnly transferred into the custody of a noncommissioned officer at noon on August 15, 1902. The district chiefs had carried out such a drastic classification and selection that all the archives of the life of a district for two years fit entirely into "a small white box."[9] In the minds of the Allies, the archives were to survive the government's withdrawal. The staff of the head of the Provisional Government's secretariat remained on for six months, more than three months after the dissolution, to complete the classification of the archives, at the expense of the Allies but for the edification of the Chinese authorities. Indeed, it was a question not only of perpetuating the memory of the Provisional Government but also of preserving the interests of the Allied powers and their nationals in Tianjin. Since the minutes of the council had force of law, one of the conditions for the handing over of the city to the Chinese authorities was that "each person, who considers that they have an interest in these minutes, should be able consult them through the mediation of their Consul and the rights which may be claimed must be recognized by Chinese authorities if they are proven valid by the minutes of the Council." Freedom of access to administrative documents appeared at an early stage for practical reasons.[10]

The dissolution of the Provisional Government and the retrocession of the city to the Chinese authorities

The military government was officially "Provisional," and the Allies already began considering the question of handover by the end of 1900. In April 1901 Field Marshal von Waldersee told the council that he wanted the Provisional Government to remain in place until the end of the Allied occupation of the region. To the contrary, the American representative William Rockhill stated that it was preferable to hand over the city to the Chinese authorities as soon as possible. The French, British, and Russian diplomats approved this position in principle, which did not commit the Allied powers to setting a timetable for withdrawal. Only the German minister in Beijing refused to comment on the issue, preferring to prolong the exercise of the Provisional Government as long as possible. On May 28, 1901, the diplomatic corps finally agreed to express its wish that the "evacuation of the native city of Tientsin and the transfer by the (International) Provisional Government to the Chinese authorities of the authority with which it had been entrusted by the commanders of the troops in

North China during the period of disorganization resulting from the occupation of Tientsin, should be brought to a close as soon as possible."[11]

Following the signing of the peace protocol on September 7, 1901, the Allied troops evacuated Beijing and the Imperial Court returned to the capital on January 7, 1902.[12] All eyes turned to Tianjin, but the withdrawal of the forces of the eight-nation alliance still did not occur, exacerbating Chinese suspicions about the foreigners' good faith and the true nature of their intentions.[13] In Tianjin until early 1902, the Allies sought to buy time to advance their work, complete the "pacification" of the region, and secure their territorial gains through new concessions and "extra-concessions."

Tired of these delaying tactics and strengthened by the reestablishment of imperial power in Beijing, Yuan Shikai tried to obtain the gradual withdrawal of foreign troops from Zhili Province. At the beginning of January 1902, he approached the American secretary of state, John Hay, so that Tianjin "might be returned to the Chinese authorities, and the new viceroy might fully exercise his powers."[14] The Chinese government requested the support of the United States since, like the Japanese, the day after the city was taken, their diplomats had distinguished themselves from the other Allies in opposing the destruction of Zhili forts (although the United States ultimately shifted its position following the change of mind of the Japanese representative).[15] The head of U.S. diplomacy replied that his country, which had always advocated the rapid evacuation of the city, would consult with the other powers to set a date for the dissolution of the Provisional Government.[16] The U.S. ambassadors in London, Paris, Berlin, Rome, and Tokyo were given the task of obtaining the official position of each nation on this subject. Washington considered it unnecessary to consult Russia, which had been marginalized by its unilateral decisions in Manchuria.

Lansdowne, the British foreign secretary, argued for a rapid dissolution of the military government. He considered that its continuation would not only be useless but would also interfere in a harmful way with Chinese authority in Zhili Province and work against the "final protocol of the Boxers."[17] His position was in line with the general policy of withdrawing British troops from China, which was being reduced from six thousand to two thousand men (not counting legation guards). The head of British diplomacy proposed May 1 as the date for the handover to find an intermediary solution between April 1, proposed by the Chinese authorities, and June 1, initially proposed by the Germans. Théophile Delcassé, the French minister of foreign affairs, declared himself in favor of handing over Tianjin to the Chinese authorities on the sole condition that the latter complete the work started by the Provisional Government.[18] On February 21, Giulio Prinetti, the Italian minister of foreign affairs, announced that Italy approved the "principle" of a rapid handover and hoped that the Allied powers would act jointly to achieve it.[19] Japanese diplomacy also declared support for a rapid abolition of the international government, but only if it did not call into question the foreign military presence that maintained freedom of communication and circulation between Beijing and the sea.[20] In Germany, Baron von Richthofen was more reserved, formally endorsing the American proposal while hoping that the handover would not take place before "the end of the building along the Beiho, which is essential for the security of the foreign legations in Peking."[21] The government's continued existence was also justified by the support of foreigners and Chinese merchants for its actions. When Andrew White, the U.S. ambassador in Berlin, reminded him that the viceroy should take charge of continuing the work, Richthofen retorted that Germany would gladly withdraw its troops as soon as it obtained financial guarantees concerning the completion of the work along the river.[22] To prove their goodwill, the Germans said they were ready to set a date, for example in the middle of 1902, to dissolve the Provisional Government. Their hope was to obtain a few months' reprieve.

At the same time, in Tianjin, the Japanese tried to accelerate the process of restitution, which became a matter of concern for foreigners from March 1902. On March 17 Colonel Akiyama, commander of the Japanese troops, proposed to the Council of the Provisional Government that they begin discussing the conditions for handing over the administration of the city to Chinese authorities. The council refused the proposal and left the decision to the Council of Allied Generals, which alone could decide when the government would be dissolved. However, after learning of the discussions taking place in the chancelleries and staffs in February–March, the members of the council changed their attitude and began to consider the prospect of dissolution. They planned to pay two months' wages to Chinese employees after the government was dissolved, except for "outside" agents working in the police or tax administration (*likin*). At the end of March the Allied commanders, through the British General Creagh, officially asked to prepare a report on the administrative conditions of the handover. The council proceeded as usual by soliciting contributions from all the department and district heads, who had to draw up a report on the transfer within a week.[23]

Foreign companies were also concerned with guaranteeing their interests. For example, the managing directors of the Electric Traction & Lighting Co. anticipated the withdrawal of the Allies by obtaining from the council that the concession granted to them be maintained by the Chinese authorities. Likewise, the owner of the Electric Engineering & Fitting Co, Constantin von Hanneken, obtained from the council the inclusion of his telephone network in the government's legacy to be preserved by the Chinese government. "As a conduit to progress," these telephones should remain for "the public good." As a general principle, the council worked to get the Chinese authorities to accept the continued validity of contracts with foreign companies that had worked for the Provisional Government. Thus the Allies demanded that the Chinese authorities recognize the various tramway, electric lighting, and water distribution concessions.[24]

Government officials laid down other conditions essential to withdrawal and made some suggestions. First, it was essential in the eyes of the Allies that the authority of the council's decisions be unquestioned by the Chinese government, which needed to fully recognize its acts and guarantee their full "force and effect" if they did not contravene Chinese customs. To do so, the Chinese government was asked to officially continue the work of the Provisional Government, which had already claimed in August 1900 to be taking over on behalf of the Chinese authorities: "The continuity of the government is not broken. All previous acts are valid as if they had been done in the name of the Chinese imperial authorities themselves." The Provisional Government justified this administrative continuity by the alleged absence of a state of war between the Allied powers and China in 1900. Thus the council planned to provide the list of sentences to the Chinese authorities, who were to apply them. The prisoners from the districts were to be transferred to the main prison of the city, accompanied by a notice "indicating the length of the sentence they had to undergo, the date of the beginning of the sentence and the offence committed." The Chinese authorities were responsible for protecting the Chinese employees of the Provisional Government who were to suffer no repercussions for their services to the Allies. Likewise, the *shendong* and the villages that collaborated with them were to be defended by the new administration. The council also recommended that the Chinese government not abolish the river police, which it considered useful. The government asked the Chinese administration to maintain the network of public toilets, roads, and sewers and suggested that work in this area be continued. It needed to agree not to oppose the construction of a steel swing bridge and to prohibit residents from erecting buildings or tents on the streets laid out by the public works department. On the other hand, the work of destroying the forts was to be completed by the Allied troops maintained in Zhili Province by virtue of article 9 of the protocol of September 7, 1901. The horses, weapons, and police equipment were to be delivered to the Chinese authorities as well as all the movable and immovable property belonging to the departments and districts. Only the archives and seals of the council and the district and department heads were to remain in the possession of the Allies. The council asked Viceroy Yuan Shikai to be present at the ceremony of the government handover. Finally, the Allied commanders demanded that Chinese military troops be banned from an 18.6-mile (30 km) radius around the city, where only Chinese police officers could be tolerated. The United States once again intervened in June to condemn this condition as not only "humiliating" for the Chinese but also ineffective, since this measure, which was not applied in Beijing, could not protect foreigners from the risk of aggression beyond the protection zone.[25] Inspired by Edwin Conger, Secretary of State Hay succeeded in changing the Allies' position, reducing the ban to about six miles (10 km).[26]

On July 18, 1902, the Qing Prince declared that the Chinese government accepted the twenty-eight conditions and the two recommendations of the Allies concerning the surrender of the city of Tianjin. The date for the handover was set for the following month.[27] Contrary to the argument made by historian Otto Rasmussen, we have found no trace of mobilization on the part of Chinese elites in favor of the continuation of the Provisional Government. Certainly some merchants sent the council a few letters of thanks for the work accomplished, but no petition requesting the continuation of the government appears in the minutes. It is possible that Rasmussen, silent about his sources, invented these testimonies to better exalt the work of a Provisional Government that he venerated as "an example of what a prudent administration can accomplish for a Chinese city using modern methods."[28]

At the beginning of August, articles in the Chinese press explained to the local Chinese population that claims, requests, and invoices were to be sent to the council by August 10. Gifts were presented to the council, such as the three red umbrellas donated by the city's three orphanages and widow asylums and a plaque purchased by the village of Yang Liu Ching. This allowed the government to present itself once again as a protective institution for the local population. It provided for a two-week transition period in early August for the new Chinese officers to familiarize themselves with the affairs of each department and district with the foreign officers in charge. By asking the viceroy to send one of his senior officials to each district and department head, the government attempted to impose its administrative structure on the Chinese authorities. A general consultation meeting was held on August 4 between representatives of the government and all the district and department heads. For several weeks, Tang Shaoyi, an experienced diplomat and loyal adviser to Yuan Shikai, had been coordinating the preparations for the transfer on his behalf. The new senior Chinese officials assigned to Tianjin—Tang Shaoyi, Salt Commissioner Yang Tsang-lien, Prefect Lin, *daotai* Chang Lien-fen, Magistrate Chang, Police Chief Tsao Chiao-hsiang, and Wang Chin-nien (William Quincey)—were received at 8:30 a.m. by members of the government, who submitted their proposals for the handover and obtained their consent. The council took care of protocol and sent the viceroy an invitation written in French and signed by all its members to lunch on August 15. The Chinese dignitaries invited the members of the council to a dinner at the administrative headquarters on behalf of Yuan Shikai the evening before the transfer of power. For the first time in two years, Chinese officials were allowed to move freely within the jurisdiction if they did not interfere with the administration of the city before August 15. As of August 12, the Chinese police of Yuan Shikai were authorized to take up quarters in the city and in the districts in groups of no more than one hundred men and were forbidden to walk the streets with their weapons until 1:00 p.m. The Provisional Government intended to maintain its authority over the inhabitants of the jurisdiction until the last moment. Public proclamations on the handover of the city were not posted in the city and published in the Chinese newspapers until the morning of August 14. The council took the opportunity to thank its local Chinese employees in the press, in Chinese. The day before the dissolution of the Provisional Government, the council submitted to Yuan Shikai, through the *daotai* Tang Shaoyi, a draft in English and Chinese of the minutes of the last meeting on August 15. Thus the handover ceremony was a true coproduction between the Allies and the Chinese authorities.[29]

The ceremony lasted all day on August 15. At 11:00 a.m. at the Tianjin railway station, the members of the council stood in the presence of the viceroy's 2,600 police officers, who had arrived in Tianjin the day before. They welcomed Yuan Shikai and his four hundred guards as well as several dozen high-ranking officials. The viceroy first visited the Allied generals at General Lefèvre's house in the French concession. There he also met with Major General von Rohrscheidt (Germany), Major General Creagh (Great Britain), General Akiyama (Japan), and Lieutenant Colonel Ameglio (Italy), in addition to the French senior officer. He was then invited to an official reception at noon at the Provisional Government's headquarters, on which a banner was hung with the Chinese inscription "Friendship forever." During this meeting with the heads of the various departments, Yuan Shikai officially received powers over the jurisdiction. The members of the council solemnly handed over to the viceroy a copy of the minutes, the list of court sentences, the works in progress, the contracts between the government and private companies, the state of the finances, the sums committed, and the sums still needed to complete the public works begun since the summer of 1900. The government treasurer gave Yuan Shikai's officials a check for the available tax revenues and another check to finance the works in progress. In two years, the Provisional Government collected more than 2.7 million taels and spent a little less than 2.6 million: the Chinese government thus disposed of 185,024 taels left by the Allies.[30] The minutes of this last meeting were signed in eight copies by the viceroy and the members of the council. At 1:00 p.m., Yuan Shikai and the high-ranking officials were invited to lunch by the council in the headquarters, which no longer belonged to the Provisional Government. At the same time, the Chinese government police officially took control of the city streets. Finally, at 7:30 p.m., the members of the council were invited by Yuan Shikai to dine in the palace of the viceroy of Zhili before leaving the city with the international police, who had gathered near the "iron bridge" to reach the foreign concessions.

Some observers criticized the harshness of the conditions imposed by the Allies: "The conditions under which Tientsin has been retaken are humiliating for China. They reveal a real distrust of the Chinese authorities. They contain clauses which display so clearly that the Chinese government is under trusteeship held by the foreigners that one fears there will be a revolt of national dignity, which remains very strong among the Yellows, as the events of 1900 clearly demonstrated."[31]

Nonetheless, this episode revealed the adaptability of Yuan Shikai and his advisors, who finally managed, as soon as the handover ceremony took place, to circumvent the ban on stationing Chinese soldiers in Tianjin. Thus, the Allied officers surrounding Yuan Shikai were stunned when they saw a battalion of Chinese commanded by Superintendent Zhao Bingjun approach their offices. The agreement between the Allied powers and the Chinese government seemed broken. But when the foreign officers questioned Yuan Shikai, he invited them to take a closer look at his men: "They are not soldiers, but policemen," the viceroy was quoted as saying.[32]

Tianjin, a laboratory for Chinese modernization? Retaining foreign experts and continuities in public policy

According to the U.S. consul in Tianjin, James W. Ragsdale, Yuan Shikai had "the courage and wisdom to carry out the plans conceived by a foreign military government."[33] A pragmatic and conservative statesman, he was considered "pro-Western" and adopted most of the policies of the Provisional Government and even accelerating them in some areas. He mainly followed in the footsteps of his former mentor, and later his main rival, Li Hongzhang, who had transformed Tianjin into a laboratory for Chinese modernization prior to the foreign military government. Yuan Shikai did not hesitate to differentiate himself from Li. For example, in February 1901 he denounced the attitude of the Allies, who "went too far in demolishing the city wall."[34] Yuan Shikai welcomed the new paved boulevards that he wished to keep in accordance with the Allies' proposed plans.[35]

In February 1903 the Belgian Jules Jadot took note of Yuan Shikai's dynamism in the summer of 1902, which led him to pursue reforms in all areas:

> This idea of Chinese progress under Chinese management, with Europeans as employees, is manifest in all the Viceroy's actions. He is a supporter of all European innovations, roads, and streets paved by steam rollers, electric lighting, tramways, canals, bridges, railroads, and mines. He wants to do everything himself with as little foreign capital

as possible, employing European agents under Chinese management. When he has to resort to foreign companies to obtain foreign capital, he reduces their shares to a minimum by bringing them under the Chinese. Furthermore, he demands clauses providing for a fast buy-out, figuring that in a few years he will be in a position to manage all the business. He has plans for everything, even the most delicate issues, such as the introduction of the gold standard in China.[36]

In the realm of health policy, Yuan Shikai followed the Provisional Government. He adopted the street-cleaning duty imposed on the poor in the poorhouses and founded a municipal health office that coordinated administrative initiatives with merchants and philanthropic societies. He kept the system of free latrines, which he entrusted to contractors. The republics that followed adopted this system as well.[37] He signed a new three-year contract with the contractor Li Yuen Cheng for the construction and maintenance of the city's public toilets, as provided for in the handover agreement. The new administration quickly built fifty latrines and seventy-five garbage collection centers. The viceroy also established an epidemic prevention office and a provincial ship and port inspection corps. At the end of 1902 he reestablished the Medical School created by Li Hongzhang with French doctors. The school was founded on a Japanese model and recruited Japanese instructors led by Hiraga Seijirō, who taught *eisei* (Japanese public health) to generations of Chinese military doctors, who also learned to speak perfect Japanese.[38]

In the area of security, Yuan Shikai apparently aimed to break with the old *baojia* system, considered "ineffective against bandits, and [which] often disturbed public order."[39] He founded China's first "modern" police force after an initial setback. When the 1,300 Chinese police officers of the Provisional Government left office at 1:00 p.m. on August 15, Yuan Shikai's 3,000 men, trained at the Baoding Police Academy, quickly encountered problems. They proved unable to adapt to the new terrain and the new forms of daily interaction brought about by the police patrol system introduced by the Provisional Government. The Provisional Government's Chinese policemen were therefore recalled by Yuan Shikai on August 18, 1902. Eight police stations maintained public order throughout the city and the Chinese suburbs. Yuan Shikai pursued the Provisional Government's repressive policy against banditry, which he believed was rampant in the city: thirty-two brigands were beheaded between August 19 and

November 4, 1902.[40] On August 31 the new government proclaimed that behaving in a disorderly manner or wearing braids and clothes with large sleeves was to be punished by arrest and without mercy. Gambling was banned on September 2. Despite the new law enforcement agencies, the old *baojia* system continued to function as part of the new police administration. Thus, after the city was returned to Chinese authorities, Tianjin's magistrate, Zhang Tao, decided to place the officers of the eighteen Bao under the jurisdiction of the new police department: these officers of the Xiang-Jia office continued to conduct their own investigations alongside the police. Cases of corruption and police blunders seemed to continue as before.[41] Yuan Shikai drew up a list of 125 offences (kidnapping, contempt, obstruction of traffic, cheating, disturbance of public order, destruction of public property, and indecent exposure, among others), which constituted the first "public security penal code" in China. As with the police, Yuan kept the fire department of about one hundred firefighters created by the Provisional Government while he renewed his confidence in the traditional Chinese associations (*shuihui*), which were often the first to arrive at a fire. The use of these associations proved to be indispensable for some major fires, such as the one in Gongbei on January 9, 1903.[42]

The viceroy reorganized the judicial system by abolishing the district magistrates' private guards, recruiting their secretaries by examination, and creating two types of prison for criminals and outcasts, based on the new principle of reeducation through work. Following the Allies, Yuan Shikai fought against certain monopolies: those of the two large dockworkers' guilds, controlled by criminal networks, were banned.[43] Tianjin was also home to the first "modern" courts—that is, courts independent of the administrative powers—within the Chinese Empire. It is worth noting that there were also continuities with the old Chinese judicial practices under Yuan Shikai's government. Indeed, many Chinese officials remained in office and did not reject the new judicial system. Just as the basic courts often continued to judge as before.[44] Finally, the independence of the judiciary was relative due to continued administrative oversight.

Yuan Shikai founded a bank and a mint in 1904 to combat the currency crisis triggered by the foreign invasion and the sudden disappearance of silver and bronze coins, which were taken out of the city, buried, or looted by the Boxers and the Allies.[45] One of the main promoters of Chinese industrialization and financial advisor to the viceroy, Zhou Xuexi, founded in 1905 the Tianjin Guan Yinhao, the first Chinese deposit bank that welcomed individual accounts from as little as 1 yuan and also fulfilled the functions of a state bank.[46] In May 1903 Yuan created a new chamber of commerce in order to facilitate the resolution of conflicts and to protect Chinese entrepreneurs from abuse by crooks and the police. This foundation, relying mainly on Chinese merchants from other regions (notably Guangdong, Zhejiang, Jiangsu, Anhui, and Henan) was a failure. The following year Tianjin's salt merchants founded a new chamber of commerce that brought Chinese traders from outside Zhili Province under its control.[47] It can be hypothesized that the company registration system introduced by the Provisional Government inspired the introduction of compulsory business registration from 1904 onward.

The viceroy established a Department of Public Works in September 1902 to continue the dredging of the river and canals, the construction and repair of bridges and roads, the registration of properties, and street lighting. Yuan Shikai completed the work of numbering and signaling streets, which had been started by the Allies in February 1901. After February 1903 he developed new districts, especially in the Hebei area north of the city. The new administration opened the city's first major post office on October 15, 1902.[48] However, Yuan Shikai renegotiated the contracts that had been imposed on him. As for the operation of tramways and electric lighting, he considered the fifty-year concession period to be excessive and the terms for the Chinese to buy back the network (twenty years after the inauguration) to be restrictive.[49] The viceroy, anticipating the placement of the Tramway Company under Chinese control, brought it under his patronage and insisted that the adjective "international" be removed. During the transitional period following the dissolution of the Provisional Government, diplomats and entrepreneurs worked hard to secure their interests with the Chinese authorities. The Belgian consul, Henri Ketels, obtained their compassion, in particular the protection of the customs *daotai* Tang Shaoyi, by voluntarily losing at a poker game: "Mr. Ketels continued to help us as much as he could, in particular by playing poker with Tong and Tsai, who took 1,400 dollars from him last month. This is generous, even for a Belgian Consul, and on various occasions the wife of the Consul appealed to my conscience and that of the Tramway Company. I have undertaken to apply for a special credit for consular proceedings under the heading of . . . gambling."[50] After the Chinese authorities ratified the contract on April 26, 1904, Tang Shaoyi was awarded the Croix de l'Officier de l'Ordre de Léopold. The Belgian company was granted a fifty-year monopoly on construction and operation within a 1.9-mole (3 km) radius from the central tower of the Chinese city. The ticket price was set at five Mexican cents. The concessionary company paid the Chinese authorities a royalty of 3.5 percent of the gross revenue, agreed to celebrate the birthdays of the emperor and empress dowager by installing hundreds of lamps in the city, and to provide electricity at half price to Chinese charities and government departments. The Chinese municipality had to wait twenty years before buying the network. A local board composed of Chinese and foreign notables managed the relationship between the tramway and the population. At the time of its inauguration in 1906, it was the first real electric urban tramway network in China.[51] The company planned to expand from the Chinese city where the main network, factory, and streetcar depot were located toward the concessions after 1906.

Tianjin finally became a place of political experimentation, promotion, and even democratization of local government. In 1905–6 residents organized a highly effective boycott of U.S. products to protest the Chinese Exclusion Act, introduced in 1882 and confirmed in 1902, which prohibited Chinese immigration. Chinese political organizations developed rapidly in the city from 1902 onward. In 1907 Yuan Shikai organized the first local elections in China to determine the thirty members of the Tianjin Council. The council met for the first time on August 18, 1907, and appointed the directors of the city's administrative services.[52] Thousands of more affluent inhabitants voted on July 4, and about two thousand people crowded around to watch the ballot count. Thus Tianjin undoubtedly played a role in the 1911 revolution as a hub of constitutional reform.

These numerous reforms were conceived and implemented by a group of Chinese and foreign experts around Yuan Shikai. The latter was surrounded by native advisors experienced in the techniques of power developed overseas in the United States, Europe, and Japan. The viceroy entrusted the task of negotiating with the Allies to one of his closest friends, Tang Shaoyi, born in 1862 into a Guangdong family descending from Tang Tingshu, the great industrial entrepreneur, who allowed him to be among the 120 people sent to the United States as part of the first Chinese educational mission beginning in 1874. He first lived in Springfield, Massachusetts, where he was enrolled in elementary school, then continued his studies at Hartford High School in Connecticut before attending Columbia University in New York for a year to study liberal arts. Speaking perfect English, Tang Shaoyi emerged from this experience with a network of anglicized Chinese friends and a Western nickname, "Ajax," exclusively used by the educational mission's alumni.[53] His professional career depended entirely on his friend Yuan, whom he assisted as a diplomat in Korea in the 1880s and 1890s before becoming head of the foreign affairs office of Shandong Province in 1900, and then first president of the Imperial University of Shandong in 1901. Appointed *daotai* of customs in Tianjin by Yuan Shikai, he cosigned the treaties establishing foreign concessions in 1901–2 and negotiated the conditions of the handover of the Chinese city. Maritime customs were traditionally entrusted to the care of an elder of the Chinese educational mission (Wu Zhongxian, Lin Peiquan, Tang Shaoyi, and Zhou Changling). Tang also became a key intermediary in the Chinese Empire's relations with the Allied powers. In 1903 he became president of the University of Tianjin before being sent to India in 1904 to negotiate with Great Britain on issues concerning Tibet. In 1906 he signed the "Convention Between Great Britain and China Respecting Tibet," which integrated Tibet into China.[54] In 1906–7 he was appointed vice president of the foreign affairs office in Beijing and tried to recover the customs, mining, and railway rights monopolized by the Allies. He then served as governor of Fengtian Province (Liaoning), where he tried to fight the growing influence of the Japanese. He became the first prime minister of the republic presided over by Yuan Shikai in March 1912. After three months he was disappointed by Yuan Shikai's authoritarianism. As a result, he resigned and joined Sun Yat-sen's government in Guangzhou. His son-in-law, Vi Kyuin Wellington Koo, was sent to represent the Republic of China at the Paris Peace Conference of 1919.[55] Assassinated by the Kuomintang in Shanghai in 1938, Tang Shaoyi had become the perfect embodiment of the English-speaking elite that surrounded the viceroy, along with another emblematic figure, William W. Quincey.

Solicited by Tang Shaoyi and Yuan Shikai, Quincey took charge of the Tianjin police.[56] Born in the early 1850s and taken in by Charles Gordon in a village destroyed during the Taiping Rebellion, this orphan followed the famous British officer to Great Britain in 1864, where he received an English education for five years, partly in a military academy.[57] "Chinese" Gordon gave his young protégé the name "Wong of Kunshan" (Prince of Kunshan), which was quickly changed to Quincey during his stay in Europe. Baptized around 1869, he adopted the first name William, while Wong was shortened to the initial "W."[58] In Tianjin he sometimes used his Chinese family name, Wang Chin-nien.[59] The obituaries praised his ability to learn many dialects and to disguise himself as a peddler, worker, or pirate. Such qualities made him an excellent investigator, intelligence specialist, and power broker. Quincey joined the Hong Kong police force in 1870. He was promoted to detective-inspector in 1884 before joining the Shanghai police force in 1899. In early April 1902 Quincey and his fifty Indian policemen were asked by Yuan Shikai to train his new police force in Baoding, the capital of Zhili. After April 8 he devoted himself to developing the police department, which rose to three thousand militarily trained men. In May the Baoding Police Academy was founded. Then the Tianjin Police Academy was established in September 1902. Yuan appointed his lieutenant Zhao Bingjun as the head of this police force. Quincey then served the new viceroy of Shandong, Zhou Fu, previously lieutenant governor of Yuan Shikai, and founded the police academy of Jinan (Tsinanfu) in May 1903. Finally, from 1910 to 1922, Quincey was superintendent of the Shanghai-Nanjing railway police.

Alongside his close Chinese collaborators, the viceroy of Zhili surrounded himself above all with foreign advisers and experts he recruited directly among the former cadres of the Provisional Government. "Fortunately, Yuan Shi Kai is an intelligent man, and he took advantage of the solid foundations established by the Provisional Government, its police force and the maintenance of the roads and boulevards, which leave little to be desired. . . . The viceroy retained some subordinate members of the old administration, but the Japanese element soon overwhelmed them."[60] Thus, even before the dissolution of the Provisional Government, the Chinese secretary, Charles Tenney, was the first to leave his post in mid-May 1902 to return to his position as president of Peiyang University.[61] At the end of the year in Berlin he negotiated the purchase of the former property of the Imperial University by the Germans, who integrated it into their concession. The compensation he obtained made it possible to build new university buildings in Siku, north of the Chinese city. Tenney served as director of educational affairs in the viceroyalty administration for nearly four years. In 1906, as xenophobic tensions increased, he left the presidency of the university to become director of the Chinese University Mission to the United States, located at Harvard University in Massachusetts until 1908.[62] There he was accompanied by some thirty students from Tianjin University, including Chao T'ien-lin, who later became president of Peiyang University; Liu Jui-heng, future minister of health; and Chung

Shih-ming, future minister of finance in Zhang Zuolin's military government in Beijing. From 1908 to 1920 Charles Tenney pursued a diplomatic career as Chinese secretary at the U.S. legation in Beijing, then became consul in Nanjing (1912) before returning to Beijing as an advisor and then chargé d'affaires. Another pillar of the Provisional Government, former secretary general Charles Denby, became Yuan Shikai's main diplomatic adviser until 1905.[63] He then served as chief of staff at the State Department in Washington until 1907 before becoming consul general in Shanghai (1907–9) and Vienna (1909–14). Denby was appointed vice president of the Hupp Motor Car Company in Detroit (1915–17), then special envoy of the State Department to Japan and China in 1918.[64] The viceroy hired Carl Rump, treasurer of the Provisional Government, as head of Chinese customs in Tianjin. At the same time he continued to lead the city's financial networks as a founding member of the Bankers Association of China.[65] In 1908 the former German banker was appointed auditor of the northern section of the Tianjin-Pukow railroad and in 1912 advisor to the Chinese Ministry of Finance.[66] The government public works engineer, Noah Drake, served as a consulting geologist for the American China Development Company (1902–1904) before returning to his position as professor of geology and mining sciences at the Imperial Peiyang University until 1911. At the same time he was president of the Tientsin Land and Investment Company Ltd. (1904–11). In 1911 Drake returned to the United States, where he taught his specialty as an associate professor at Stanford University for one year before becoming a professor of geology and mining sciences at the University of Arkansas (1912–20). Dr. Gérald Mesny, former head of the Provisional Government's health service, became scientific director of the Imperial School of Medicine in Tianjin and took an active part in the fight against plague epidemics (1903–5), then against typhus (1904) and cholera (1907). He died in Manchuria in 1911 of pulmonary plague. In 1902–3 Yuan Shikai's administration welcomed other less illustrious foreigners who had not passed through the Provisional Government: a former British officer who worked as a judge of the Tientsin High Court; a German citizen and former mechanic in the Chinese navy who became the director of the Tianjin road system; and an Englishman who became a road engineer after having been the captain of the port of Qinhuangdao.[67] British experts were concentrated in the communication services of Zhili (railroads, telegraphs). However, the Westerners quickly gave way to the increasing number of Japanese advisors to the viceroy from 1903 onward: "There are many Japanese in his entourage who seem to hold key places within Yuan's small court."[68] Japanese officers quickly became omnipresent in the health office and the police department. This Japanization of the cadres did not take place suddenly. On the contrary, it was the result of patient cooperation between the Japanese military and local elites beginning in the summer of 1900. Thus, Yan Xiu, a salt merchant turned teacher, maintained friendly, intellectual, and political relations with the Japanese: "Yan and his Japanese guests drank tea, discussed education and modernization, and exchanged calligraphy as a token of the strength of their friendship. Yan Xiu embarked on his first visit to Japan in the fall of 1902."[69]

Not all the foreign officials of the Provisional Government entered the Chinese administration. The Allies kept a certain number in their service. Thus, Colonel Foote was hired as a military attaché at the British legation in Beijing (1902–5). Raised to the rank of colonel in 1910, he commanded the glorious Poona Horse (1908–12) before retiring. Albert de Linde, Director of the public works department, remained in the area until 1904 as engineer of the international regulation commission of the Hai River before moving to London. Lieutenant Tenner, assistant to the district chief of Tongku, joined the new municipal council of the German concession and became its secretary while at the same time presiding over the Tageblatt Company for northern China. Some, like Benjamin Wegner Nørregaard, went elsewhere. The Norwegian became a war correspondent for the *Daily Mail* during the Russo-Japanese War (1904–5) and the Balkan War (1912–13) and worked for the Norwegian Ministry of Foreign Affairs as a press advisor in Paris and Berlin (1909–11).

What about the ordinary soldiers in the service of the Allied powers? Most of them returned home, a few stayed on and carried out various commercial and military activities, but, according to Jacques Grandin, the vast majority felt they had lived through an exceptional experience, similar to the most extraordinary colonial campaigns:

> We are looking forward to disembarking. We are happy to return to France, but our happiness is not without some ambivalence. We feel that we are leaving behind a time of youth and abundance, and, in France, we are going to return to our bitter struggle for daily bread. In France, we will once again be proletarians. While over there, we have been victorious and demanding soldiers. Some comrades have

> obtained permission to be honorably discharged and remain in China, either as employees of large construction companies or as clerks in export houses. They have signed five-year contracts with a monthly salary of 500 francs. They may have made the right decision.[70]

Some soldiers seemed transfigured by their experience, such as the Italian soldier Benvenuti, who was initially contemptuous of the Chinese but returned a few months later convinced that Westerners had much to learn from them: "The Chinese are considered barbarians because we would prefer them to be so. And yet, in many areas they surpass us to such an extent that they could be our masters."[71]

The continuities Yuan Shikai pursued with the Provisional Government should not be interpreted as a betrayal but rather as a means of maintaining order and stability, a fundamental principle of Chinese political philosophy, which guarantees universal harmony.[72] If the new viceroy did not hesitate to mix "foreign" institutions (a police force, fire department, and so on) with vernacular forms of social regulation (*baojia*, firefighting associations, and the like) it was because he was supporting an evolution that had begun with the Provisional Government. Social control of the population was shifting from nongovernmental organizations (merchant guilds, *shendong*, charitable societies, and so forth) to public authorities. This reform policy originated before the Provisional Government under Li Hongzhang's viceroyalty, in which foreign experts participated in three successive governments between the end of the nineteenth and the beginning of the twentieth century. In 1902, however, Yuan Shikai marked a change of alliances in favor of Great Britain and Japan, which quickly provided the bulk of the foreign experts in the new Tianjin administration and welcomed more and more Chinese students:

> There are many Japanese who serve as instructors in Yuan-Chi-Kai's army. Every year their influence grows on the Chinese; a thousand celestial students take turns in the Japanese universities. There they understand and appreciate Western methods which hardly impressed them in the West, but now strike them in a nation close to their own that has been strengthened by their adoption. They return with a brand of patriotism almost unknown to old China. Japanese influence is exerted with increasing force over the Middle Kingdom. The

> Japanese are actively pursuing their dream of being the initiators, directors, and saviors of the yellow world, and a Sino-Japanese alliance to drive the Russians out of Manchuria would be the beginning of its realization.[73]

So modern and at the same time so close, Japan came to occupy a special place among the powers present in China.

CONCLUSION

"Straddling East and West at the Turn of the Century"

A Contribution to the History of Modernity in 1900

On New Year's Eve 1900, the young reformist intellectual and leading theorist of the "new history" Liang Qichao was on a ship in the Pacific bound for the United States. That night he wrote a poem to illustrate his experience straddling East and West at the turn of the century.[1] Three years earlier he had written an article about the Gregorian calendar, which fascinated him: "Westerners begin their historical chronology with Jesus Christ and have called the years from 1800 to 1900 the nineteenth century."[2] His teacher Kang Youwei criticized this Western division of time, which omits the great non-European sages and thinkers who lived before and after Christ. In 1895 he and his disciples adopted a new chronology that began 2,373 years earlier with the birth of Confucius.[3]

Liang Qichao showed a certain pragmatism. The symbol of a round date as well as foreign intervention, war, and destruction, and the destabilization of the imperial power all offered small and large opportunities to modernize China. Thus, a portion of the Chinese reformist elites shared a culture of "1900 modernity," marked, according to Christophe Charle, by a taste for anticipation, science fiction, and scientific utopias: "As many of the contemporaries of 1900 changed centuries, they believed they were entering a new era that needed to realize the still unfulfilled dreams of the nineteenth century."[4] The history of modernity is a history of possible futures as much as a study of the processes of modernization.

This modernization, in the eyes of Liang Qichao, the reformists of the Hundred Days, and the Tianjin notables, presented a cosmopolitan face that carried the stamp of Japan. In September 1898 Liang Qichao, after the failure of the reform policy, naturally took refuge in the Japanese consulate in Tianjin before going into exile in Tokyo, where he was joined by Kang Youwei in November 1898. They then adhered to the Japanese pan-Asian project whose imperial ambitions seemed less threatening than those of Russia. Russian expansionism, the rise of Japanese power, and the growth of the United States on the other side of the Pacific challenged European hegemony and exacerbated interimperial rivalries.

The rivalries were concentrated in Tianjin, where the Japanese made a name for themselves in almost every area. They played a decisive role during the Boxer War by winning the Battle of Tianjin on July 13 and 14, 1900, after having won a war against China in 1895. They shined by their courage and solidarity in battle. After the capture of the city the Japanese seemed to distinguish themselves from the other Allies by protecting civilians from massacres and by sometimes showing consideration for Chinese culture and arts. Omnipresent in the city, they represented almost half of the twenty thousand soldiers of the expeditionary force sent to Tianjin, where a thousand Japanese soldiers remained to maintain order. They then played a leading role in the rapid metamorphosis of the city, embodying in the eyes of the Chinese an alternative to the modernity of the Western powers. They proved enterprising and reformist, like Captain Satō, a model officer, who transformed his district of North Tientsin into a veritable laboratory for the Provisional Government's policies (cartography, statistics, health, and so forth). The Japanese also distinguished themselves by the efficiency of their health service and promoted the development of the Provisional Government's social services, notably the distribution of rice to the poor. They further demanded a ban on prostitution of children under the age of thirteen, which was common in the city's brothels. Throughout these two years the Allied powers were struck by the "politeness" and "refinement" of the Japanese military, and the Sikhs praised their "cleanliness" compared to the dirtiness of European and Russian soldiers. Japan thus embodied in the eyes of the rest of the world a reforming and civilizing power par excellence.

The Japanese were noted for their proximity to the Chinese, at once "foreign colonizers and familiar cousins."[5] They facilitated the indigenization of "Western" modernity in China. Japanese officers and Chinese notables frequented each other assiduously, exchanged views on reforms, and identified with one another. For example, the Japanese did not hesitate to organize sumo wrestling demonstrations to introduce their Chinese hosts to the pleasures of their culture.[6] This strategic position of intermediaries was reflected in the city's new geography, since the Japanese concession was located precisely between the Chinese city and the other foreign concessions. The concession grew rapidly, from 77 Japanese in 1899 to 1,210 in 1901. The Japanese were also the first to advocate, along with the United States, the retrocession of the city to Chinese authorities. After the dissolution of the Provisional Government, the new viceroy of Zhili, Yuan Shikai, made Japan his main ally and recruited mainly Japanese experts and advisers, who continued the reforms introduced in the fields of education, health, and police. On the mainland, the Japanese were aware of their new status as *primus inter pares* in China, symbolized by the heroic capture of Tianjin. The echoes of their achievements resounded throughout the archipelago, as Jean-Jacques Matignon, a doctor at the French legation during the siege of the Boxers, testified in an innocuous description of the streets of Nagasaki in the wake of the war: "A charlatan improvises a demonstration to sell his razors; a clown blows his horn; a ventriloquist imitates a cat's meow; a kind of magic lantern popularizes the recent war against China: depicting Japanese troops as they storm the forts of Tientsin. All the while, European troops watch them from afar in amazement."[7]

This 1900 moment was characterized by the rapid rise of the Japanese in Tianjin, where globalization was taking an imperial turn. This sometimes-contradictory movement induced different forms of social interaction in just a few months. Tianjin, the capital of the Boxers, suffered the horrors of the first world war of the twentieth century or the last "crusade" of the nineteenth century. The city was destroyed, and the population partially massacred in the context of a war that officially did not take place and which, nonetheless, continued within the jurisdiction of Tianjin for many months after the capture of Beijing. While the carnage continued and the new government carried out a bloody repression, the Allied officers elaborated an unprecedented program of urban reconstruction and social transformation. The city was then a place of cultural ferment and experimentation, symbolized by the profusion of sports practices (soccer/football, table tennis, British cricket, American basketball, Japanese sumo, and Chinese martial arts), which made it the sports capital of the Middle

Kingdom, a symbol of the process of cultural globalization four years after the games of the first new Olympic games in Athens. In 1902 Tianjin, hit by the sixth cholera pandemic, illustrated the globalization of infectious diseases. War, colonization, disease, and sport were the privileged vectors of a globalization that was indissociably violent and enriching as well as a modernization that was as destructive as it was transformative, oppressive, and protective.

In 1900 Tianjin was at once an active force and a product of globalization, transformed into a global microcosm that was staged and displayed in all its spectacular glory (military confrontations, colorful parades of troops, architectural styles, and so on). This unique atmosphere at the beginning of the century was described by John Hersey, who lived there as a child:

> What a weird city I grew up in! For three or four Chinese coppers, I could ride in a rickshaw from my home, in England, to Italy, Germany, Japan, or Belgium. I walked to France for violin lessons. I had to cross the river to get to Russia, and often did, because the Russians had a beautiful wooded park with a lake in it. I hold in my nostrils to this day the strange odor of tadpoles captured in Russian waters and taken back to England.[8]

The city of Tianjin, as witnessed by the famous American journalist ("copper coin," "rickshaw," "violin") naturally invites us to write a material history of globalization, of Asian and Western objects that promoted or reveal interactions between Chinese and foreigners such as maps, flags, terracotta statuettes, coins, medals, cadasters, business cards, and rickshaws. These objects circulated far beyond Tianjin across the world, among them the relics of the Boxers in the United States, the seal of the Provisional Government in London, machine parts in Germany, and saddles from India for mounted police.[9]

Tianjin took the form of a pluralist society where national groups and legal affiliations were intertwined. The boundary between state and civil society, public and private, but also between Chinese and foreigners was blurred and constantly shifting. Indeed, the same intermediaries, such as businessmen Gustav Detring, Constantin von Hanneken, and Herbert Hoover, served the interests of the international government, a foreign company, and the Chinese imperial administration at the same time. The history of Tianjin was hardly written in "yellow and white." During the war, Boxers and Chinese regulars often clashed. In addition, Chinese from Weihaiwei fought alongside the British, while some European experts defended the Chinese city against Allied assaults. Most of the Allies were Asian troops (Japanese, Mongols, Vietnamese, and Indians). This diversity reflects the ethnic cleavages that divided each imperial society ("Annamites"/French, Sikhs/British, Mongolians/Russians, Han/Manchus).[10] After the Allies took the city, multiple cultural intermediaries blurred the line between Chinese and foreigners. European deserters with real braids settled in Zhili villages, while "modern" Chinese with fake braids officiated at the Tianjin Medical School. Cosmopolitan experts (Tenney, Depasse) served both the Chinese administration and foreign authorities. The latter quickly proved to be dependent on the Chinese, as evidenced by the Provisional Government's police force, which was largely composed of Chinese and whose finances were managed by a Chinese bank.

The Powers agreed to found what seemed to be the first international government. This regime of military occupation closely resembled a *coimperium*, a community of states exercising "exclusive territorial jurisdiction" in a territory belonging to a third power.[11] Tianjin was nonetheless the scene of tensions between the major "partner-competitors," who opposed each other within the Council of the Provisional Government and the consular corps and on some occasions violently clashed in the city streets. The Allied camp had its own set of alliances within it, and the Provisional Government posed as the guarantor of international peace. This relative stability of the balance of power allowed for the rise of a true "collective imperialism" that, after 1902, asserted its bipolar tendency between Russia and Japan and rapidly evolved toward military confrontation.

The international military government, like all states, was two-sided: domination was not opposed to integration but rather they reinforced each other mutually.[12] It sought to accelerate the transformations of the Chinese city, which had been ravaged three times in just five years (1895, June 1900, and July 1900). Similar cases of urban reconstruction are rare before 1945: London after the Great Fire of 1666, Lisbon after the earthquake of 1755, Chicago after the fire of 1871, or San Francisco after the earthquake of 1906. In Tianjin the new government did everything possible. To prevent a new insurrection and rationalize urban space, it ordered the destruction of the city walls and the houses that leaned against them, replacing them with a wide circular boulevard. At the same time, to fight against the risks of epidemics resulting from decomposing corpses, the government built sanitary infrastructures (public toilets) and set up a new drainage system and drinking water supply. An imposing river police force led by the Italians was charged with hunting down the "pirates" operating on the river. The policy of public works initiated by the Provisional Government in all areas (roads, telegraph, tramway, bridges, public lighting, river development, quays) in turn motivated the consuls and European businessmen in the foreign concessions. The government tried to regulate the private and intimate life of the inhabitants, from cradle to grave, including sexual and sanitary practices. Ultimately, the experience of the international administration of Tianjin laid the foundations for the Allied powers' evolution toward a colonial reformism—"development" and "ethical" government of the colonies—which advanced from the beginning of the twentieth century with the Dutch policy in Java and then the League of Nations mandates.

With more than 2.5 million taels spent by the Provisional Government, Tianjin did not fit the traditional colonial model of underinvestment in public infrastructure.[13] The Chinese city and the foreign concessions were transformed into laboratories of urban modernity. At a time when universal exhibitions multiplied across Europe, the concessions seemed to function as permanent exhibitions where the colonial powers put themselves on display as both benevolent and civilizing forces. Thus, in a single city at the beginning of the twentieth century a visitor could admire Chinese pagodas, Bavarian farmhouses, a majestic Japanese torii, a Gothic castle (Gordon Hall), a Tuscan villa, a church in the style of the Artois region (Notre-Dame-des-Victoires), Salzburg Baroque-style buildings, and a Sikh temple.

The government also largely continued the work of the Chinese administration by recruiting foreign experts, who had previously served Li Hongzhang and reappropriating Chinese practices and symbols. After 1902 Yuan Shikai drew on his international experience to reform the city. The continuities seem at least as strong as the rupture of the Boxer War was violent. Nonetheless, the conflict and the establishment of the Provisional Government transformed this "open port" into a colonial city, the provincial metropolis became a global city. The short but extremely intense colonial moment was decisive in the history of this great Chinese city. It is easy to see why the experience of international military government has been elided by Chinese and Western historiography, since it reveals both the colonial origins of international governance and the ambiguous links between imperialism and modernity. In the years 1900–1902 the government was careful never to appear colonial, but everything betrays, in the sources and lexicon used, its colonial nature: the walled city was systematically referred to as a "native city," the Chinese were called "natives," and so on. From the historian's perspective, however, the brevity of the experience and the small size of the territory concerned prevent us from essentializing the "colonized" Chinese on one side and "colonizing" foreigners on the other. The experience of Tianjin further resists a traditional Marxist interpretation based exclusively on the study of the univocal exploitation of the Chinese by foreigners. Nor does it fit neatly within a "revisionist" approach focusing solely on the "modernization" imported by foreigners and on its "positive" contributions.[14]

At the end of this investigation one has a better sense of the government's mission and function, since it remained in place not only after the fall of Beijing but also after the return of the Qing to the capital. It was not only a question of suppressing the Boxers, securing Zhili province, and preparing for the "liberation" of the concessions. The government allowed the Allies to maintain their pressure on the Imperial Court through September 1901 with negotiations on the compensation of 450 million silver taels, that is, 1 tael per Chinese.[15] The Provisional Government also acted in the name of posterity. Its administrative, technical, and legal work illustrated the Powers' greatness, legitimized international intervention, and guaranteed the foreign economic and political interests in Tianjin. After November 1900 the international military government became the instrument of collective imperialism, facilitating the territorial expansion of each power and maintaining peace by guaranteeing a form of equity between small and large colonial states. By the end of 1902 the total area of foreign concessions represented eight times the area of the Chinese city. In Tianjin the Powers thus did the opposite of what they claimed in the eyes of the rest of the world: disinterested humanitarian intervention resulted in the foundation of a colonial (micro)state. As the concessions multiplied, the colonization of China proved impossible because of the sheer size of the Middle Kingdom, the size of the Chinese population, and the fierce competition between the Powers. The Boxer War also taught the Allies that they had to deal with the Chinese and exert their influence through the Imperial Court. The Provisional Government thus participated in safeguarding the Chinese state and the imperial power of the Qing. It was explicitly part of an imperial continuity and claimed to act on behalf of the Chinese government. Indeed, the Powers feared the collapse of the Qing administration and the chaos that would ruin foreign economic interests in China. They had a vested interest in maintaining a sovereign but weak China that was nevertheless able to pay compensation and repay the loans taken out for this purpose.

The analysis of relations between Chinese and foreigners in Tianjin sheds light on the complex history of social interactions in an imperial context. One cannot help but notice the diversity of forms of resistance and protest strategies adopted by the indigenous population: the activism of the Red Lanterns offered a form of alternative modernity that broke with Confucian patriarchy. There was also armed struggle between the Boxers and the Chinese regulars, guerrilla warfare and marauding bands of "brigands," destruction of telegraph and telephone wires, damage to railways and landfill material, obstruction of the Hai River, opening of breaches in the dikes and locks, robberies and extortion, contestation through placards and rumors, usurpation of identity and function, forgery and use of false administrative documents and counterfeit money, refusal to use the public latrines or the "modern" cemeteries, the list goes on. These multiple forms of "infrapolitical" resistance clearly indicate the lack of consent of a significant part of the indigenous population.[16] The Chinese also challenged foreign domination through legal channels that were tolerated or even organized by the Provisional Government: the Imperial Court's refusal of a number of foreign requests, such as the order to execute General Dong Fuxiang, the diplomatic negotiations initiated by the Chinese government to regain a foothold in the city, petitions to the council, requests to the consuls, campaigns in the press, refusal to be vaccinated, or even sports competitions. Thus, a famous and no doubt partly legendary sporting confrontation between a Chinese and a foreigner ended in Chinese victory because the foreigner did not show. The hero of this symbolic revenge on foreign powers was the future great reformer of Chinese martial arts, Huo Yuanjia, who inspired the Hong Kong film *Fist of Fury* (1972) and its lead actor, Bruce Lee. Belonging to a family of bodyguards mastering the secret techniques of Mizongquan ("lost track skill"), he officiated in Tianjin from 1896 on, defending the interests of a local merchant named Nong Jingsun against the brigands of the city. In 1901 he took up the challenge of a Russian champion, who claimed to be the strongest man in the world and had insulted the Chinese people through the press. The Russian, upon learning of Huo's impressive reputation, gave up the fight and admitted to being a mere actor and even acceded to making a public apology to the Chinese in a Tianjin newspaper.[17] A few months after a crushing defeat on the battlefield, Huo Yuanjia demonstrated that China was hardly the "sick man" of Asia.

From the day after the capture of the city, Chinese merchant guilds returned to the forefront of public affairs and constituted a form of "civil society" that through notable philanthropic works competed with or replaced the action of the international military government.[18] The Provisional Government took special care to keep the *shendong*, who remained an indispensable relay of its authority and channeled its claims through a traditional system of petitions. Some of these urban elites became bicultural, achieving "a balance between modernity and Chinese identity, living with the times while remaining themselves."[19] They were not only an essential part of the "colonial state" of 1900–1902: they also captured a form of modernity. Thus, in Tianjin the Chinese coproduced public health policy by bringing out new environmental concerns, by creating private companies to distribute water or manufacture public latrines, by maintaining the sewers, by founding hospitals, and by associating "traditional medicine" with Western therapeutics in the fight against cholera. This decisive participation of a fraction of the Chinese notables appears to have been a sine qua non condition for the appropriation of the new sanitary practices among a growing number of inhabitants. This elite did not emerge weakened from the two years of foreign government. On the contrary, it took advantage of the failure of the Boxers, who directly attacked its interests,[20] to break with tradition and assert itself politically by obtaining the organization of the first local elections in China in Tianjin in 1907. This rise in power of the notables was part of a process of political and military "decentralization" with the empowerment of increasingly powerful viceroys, such as the governors of Zhili Province. For the first time these urban Chinese elites seem to have been closer to foreigners than to the rest of the population, who continued to live in a "traditional" structure. They were the main Asian actors in this "modernity of 1900" and the processes of "imperial globalization," alongside the Japanese and Indian military.

These Chinese elites in Tianjin and Shanghai have long been considered insignificant in the face of China's vastness, like "a modern fringe . . . stitched along the hem of the ancient garment."[21] Indeed, Tianjin is not China. And the work of the Provisional Government increased the gap between this city and the rest of the Middle Kingdom, except for the other large "open ports." These locations were perceived as failures or defeats that Chinese imperial policy managed to ward off in the interior of the country, preserved from the harmful influence of the West.[22] These urban enclaves were the price to pay for maintaining political, cultural, and economic control over the empire. The concessionary cities, and especially Tianjin in 1900–1902, thus reveal the strength and intensity of the impact of imperial globalization, but also its narrow geographical scope. Despite the privileges obtained through the "unequal" treaties and the creation of numerous concessions, foreigners never really managed to penetrate Chinese markets: "Curiously, the system of open ports was rather an obstacle to the commercial penetration of Europeans and Americans in China."[23] Although foreign economic activities, such as finance and transport were dynamic, trade in the Middle Kingdom remained the preserve of Chinese merchants. In fact, in Tianjin foreign entrepreneurs and traders were perfectly connected to their counterparts in other Asian "open ports" but had little or no relationship with the Chinese interior. They played a "marginal role" in the economic development of the Qing Empire, which was largely self-sufficient. The foreigners of Tianjin lived as if weightless above a China about which they knew almost nothing, as Jean-Jacques Matignon, a doctor at the French legation in Beijing, wrote: "The opinion of the residents of open ports or large centers, like Peking or Tientsin, is of little value. In general, these Europeans know nothing about China. They rarely leave their 'concessions' and only see Chinese people who have been used to foreigners for generations. The ignorance of diplomats in Chinese matters has always amazed me."[24] Similarly, the existence of real spheres of influence of the Powers should be put into perspective: Chinese officials, having mastered international law, often managed to limit foreign interventions outside the "open ports."[25] Tianjin thus represented an enclave, but also a possible path to modernization, from which statesmen, notably Li Hongzhang and Yuan Shikai, were able to draw inspiration in implementing new public policies. From this point of view it embodied a possible future of the world, as sketched by Zola in 1898: "Following the civilization around the Atlantic, which had become a center bordered by master cities, another civilization would be born, centered on the Pacific with other capitals, which could not be foreseen, whose seeds lay dormant on unknown shores. And then another, always another, renewed again and again!"[26]

APPENDIX

Archives Around the Globe: A Note on Sources

The history of Tianjin in 1900, and specifically of the international military government, may be told thanks to the archival documents, in particular the minutes of the Council's meetings, which are available at the Widener Library of Harvard University, managed by Joe Bourneuf. Many documents are also available in the Service Historique de la Défense (Vincennes, France) in subseries 11 H, which contains several precious boxes on the European expeditionary corps in China and Tianjin. These unpublished archives have been systematically examined to reconstruct the Provisional Government's day-to-day activities. The study of these "colonial" archives confirms the valuable complementarity of sources and points of view adopted by sinologists and specialists of imperial history.

The same is true for the archives of the foreign concessions. They contain a wealth of material for both diplomatic history and the social history of the city's neighborhoods. I similarly consulted the various consular, commercial, and political correspondences of the French consulate in Tianjin at the end of the nineteenth and beginning of the twentieth centuries in the Archives of the Ministry of Foreign Affairs (subseries 148 CPCOM and P 19229-31 in La Courneuve, France, and the dossiers of the Consulate General in Nantes, France). They too contain a rich collection of plans, maps, and tracings of Tianjin. The Foreign Office collection held at the National Archives in Kew Gardens on the British Consulate in Tianjin (series FO 674), the posts in China (FO 228–233 / FO 925), and the War Office documents concerning the Boxer War (WO 32 and 102) provided essential information. The insights of the India Office Records at the British Library, with its rich archives of the China Expedition (collection 402), were extremely useful. Thanks to Nicolas Vaicbourdt, I was able to consult the National Archives and Records Administration in Washington, in particular series RG 84 of the archives of the diplomatic posts of the State Department, which includes the cartons and registers of the Tianjin consulate, as well as series RG 395 on the American China Relief Expedition. In Belgium, at the invitation of the Université Libre de Bruxelles and Valérie Piette, I had the opportunity to search the archives of the Tientsin Tramways and Lighting Company (V2) in the Archives Générales du Royaume (Brussels). I also obtained diplomatic documents from the Archivio Centrale dello Stato (Rome, Italy), the Bundesarchiv (Berlin, Germany), and the Österreichisches Staatsarchiv (Vienna, Austria), thanks to Mathieu Gotteland. Unfortunately, despite several attempts, I was unable to locate the archives of the Japanese and Russian concessions at the Japanese Ministry of Foreign Affairs (Tokyo) and the National Archives in Moscow.

Finally, I was able to consult the municipal archives of Tianjin, which contain foreign-language documents. Though I was able to communicate with an official of the Tianjin Communist Party and Zhou Licheng, director of the research department of the city archives, these conversations did not allow me to acquire further information; the "Chinese" archives of the concessions had not yet been organized and translated and consequently were not available to researchers. Fortunately, duplicates of most of these foreign-language documents exist in the various centers mentioned earlier. Finally, I studied the diaries and memoirs of the Chinese campaign, which are abundant and rich, mainly in French and English, published at the beginning of the century, and which undoubtedly represent a highpoint for (1901–1902) publications in English, French, German, and Italian concerning Tianjin for the entire contemporary period.[1]

Translator's Note

Throughout this book, the proceedings of the Provisional Government have been translated from the French version of the archives. The notes have therefore kept the references for the French version of the archives throughout, including PVGPT, *Procès verbaux gouvernement provisoire de Tianjin*. For Chinese proper names and places, in some cases the initial Chinese characters were not provided in the original non-Chinese sources. In these cases, the translator has attempted as consistently as possible to provide Pinyin transliterations. The translator thanks the anonymous reviewers as well as Jeff Wasserstrom and Tze-ki Hon for their comments on the translation, and Jacob Bromberg for his help in the final stages of manuscript preparation.

Notes

ARCHIVE ABBREVIATIONS

BL	British Library (London, UK)
CADN	Centre d'Archives Diplomatiques de Nantes (Nantes, France)
MAE	Archives du Ministère des Affaires Étrangères (Paris, France)
NA	*National Archives* (London, UK)
PVGPT	Procès-verbaux du Gouvernement Provisoire de Tianjin, Harvard Widener Library (Cambridge, Massachusetts, USA)
SHD	Archives du Service Historique de la Défense (Vincennes, France)

Introduction

1. Herbert Hoover, *The Memoirs of Herbert Hoover*, vol. 1, *The Years of Adventure, 1874–1920* (New York: Macmillan, 1952).
2. John K. Fairbank, ed., *The Cambridge History of China: Late Ch'ing 1800–1911*, vol. 1 (Cambridge, MA: Cambridge University Press, 1978).
3. Li Zhaojie and Li James, "Traditional Chinese World Order," *Chinese Journal of International Law* 22, no. 1 (2002): 20–58.
4. Odd Arne Westad, *Restless Empire: China and the World Since 1750* (New York: Basic Books, 2012).
5. Li Hongtu, "De 'Sous-le-Ciel' (*tianxia*) à l' 'Outre-océan' (*yang*): Évolution de la représentation du monde extérieur chez les Chinois," *Monde(s)* 3 (2013):

91–112; Lydia H. Liu, *The Clash of Empires: The Invention of China in Modern World Making* (Cambridge, MA: Harvard University Press, 2004); David C. Kang, "Hierarchy in Asian International Relations, 1300–1900," *Asian Security* (January 2005): 53–79; Shogo Suzuki, *Civilization and Empire: China and Japan's Encounter with European International Society* (New York: Routledge, 2009).

6. Yuan Fang, "Influences of British Architecture in China: Shanghai and Tientsin 1843–1943" (PhD diss., University of Edinburgh, 1995).
7. François Gipouloux, *La Méditerranée asiatique: Villes portuaires et réseaux marchands en Chine, au Japon et en Asie du Sud-Est, xvie–xxie siècle* (Paris: CNRS Éditions, 2009), 173.
8. Robert Bickers, *The Scramble for China: Foreign Devils in the Qing Empire, 1832–1914* (London: Penguin Books, 2012).
9. Luo Shuwei, ed., *Jindai Tianjin chengshi shi/Tianjin's Modern Urban History* (Beijing: Chinese Academy of Social Sciences Press, 1993), 21–113.
10. Man Bun Kwan, *The Salt Merchants of Tianjin: State-Making and Civil Society in Late Imperial China* (Honolulu: University of Hawaii Press, 2001).
11. Yuan, "Influences of British Architecture," 40.
12. Man Bun Kwan, *The Salt Merchants of Tianjin*, 7.
13. Lewis Bernstein, "A History of Tientsin in the Early Modern Times, 1800–1910" (PhD diss., University of Kansas, 1988), 32.
14. Charles Chenevix Trench, *The Road to Khartoum: A Life of General Charles Gordon* (New York: Dorset Press, 1988).
15. Kaoliang is a variety of sorghum.
16. John Innocent, cited in Otto Durham Rasmussen, *Tientsin: An Illustrated Outline History* (Tientsin: The Tientsin Press, 1925), 38.
17. The *sapèque* was the French term for a Chinese cash coin. The *tael* was a unit equivalent to 1.3 ounces of silver. Together they were the principal monetary units: ten cash coins (*sapèques* in French or *qian* in Chinese) was the equivalent of one *tael* in silver (*liang*). There were 170 different taels in China at the turn of the century. This translation will use "cash coin" for the French *sapèque*. The *mou* is a Chinese unit of measure that is approximately equivalent to 7,150 square feet (665 m^2). See Chan Chung Sing, *Les concessions en Chine* (Paris: PUF, 1925), 73.
18. Raoul Charles Villetard de Laguérie, "Tien-Tsin après la défaite des Boxeurs ('voyage exécuté en 1900')," *Le tour du monde, nouveau journal des voyages* 7, no. 41 (October 12, 1901): 486.
19. In Tianjin it was John Innocent, Methodist minister; Doctor Blodget, missionary from the American Board Mission; J. Mongan, the British vice consul; Captain J. Henderson of the Lindsay & Co. enterprise; J. A. T. Meadows of Meadows & Co.; E. Waller of Phillips & Moor; H. C. Maclean of Jardine,

Matheson & Co.; T. Platt; Mr. Stamford; Mr. Richard C. Grant; C. Mellor; and Mr. Stamman. George T. Candlin, *John Innocent: A Story of Mission Work in North China* (London: United Methodist Publishing House, 1909).

20. Villetard de Laguérie, "Tien-Tsin après la défaite," 487.
21. Yan Yan, "Le protectorat religieux de la France en Chine (1840–1912)" (PhD diss., University Paris 1 Panthéon-Sorbonne, 2011); Ernest P. Young, *China's Catholic Church and the French Religious Protectorate* (Oxford: Oxford University Press, 2013).
22. John K. Fairbank, "Patterns Behind the Tientsin Massacre," *Harvard Journal of Asiatic Studies* 20, nos. 3–4 (December 1957).
23. Otto D. Rasmussen, *The Growth of Tientsin* (Tientsin: The Tientsin Press, 1924); Otto D. Rasmussen, *Tientsin: An Illustrated Outline History* (Tientsin: The Tientsin Press, 1925).
24. Gustav Detring owned 5,689 of the 6,018 *mou* of the concession at the end of the nineteenth century. *Lishunde dafandian* (The Astor Hotel) (Tianjin: Jinguo zhongdian wenwu baohu danwei, 1993), 47.
25. "Chine: Tientsin et Pékin," *Revue française de l'étranger et des colonies et Exploration, Gazette géographique* 25 (1900): 519–20.
26. See the historiographical note. Recent historical surveys, which are very helpful on other issues, do not even mention the city, among them Jacques Weber and François de Sesmaisons, eds., *La France en Chine (1843–1943)* (Paris: L'Harmattan, 2013), and Bickers, *The Scramble for China*.
27. Zhang Chang and Liu Yue, "International Concessions and the Modernization of Tianjin," in *Harbin to Hanoi: The Colonial Built Environment in Asia, 1840 to 1940*, ed. Laura Victoir and Victor Zatsepine (Hong Kong: Hong Kong University Press, 2013), 92.
28. Bernstein, "A History of Tientsin," 31.
29. Endymion Wilkinson, *Chinese History: A New Manual* (Cambridge, MA: Harvard University Press, 2013), 259.
30. Dong Wang, *China's Unequal Treaties: Narrating National History* (Lanham, MD: Lexington Books, 2005), 10; Christopher Ford, *The Mind of Empire: China's History and Modern Foreign Relations* (Lexington: University Press of Kentucky, 2010), 142.
31. The Grand Hotel of Beijing was inaugurated in 1900 and the Palace Hotel (the current building to the south of the Peace Hotel) in Shanghai in 1906.
32. Dana Arnold, "Construire la modernité urbaine: La concession britannique à Tianjin, 1860–201," *Outre-Mers: Revue d'histoire* 382–383 (June 2014): 89.
33. The administration of Chinese customs was founded in 1861 in Tianjin and entrusted to the British under Robert Har, who hired Gustav Detring to represent him in Tianjin. Henri Cordier, "Les douanes impériales maritimes chinoises," *T'oung Pa* 7, no. 4 (1906): 222–40.

34. Message from Robert Hart to his agent in London, James Duncan Campbell (in 1881), cited in John K. Fairbank, Martha Henderson Coolidge, and Richard J. Smith, *H. B. Morse, Customs Commissioner and Historian of China* (Lexington: University Press of Kentucky, 1995), 38n4.
35. Thierry Sanjuan, ed., *Les grands hôtels en Asie: Modernité, dynamiques urbaines et sociabilité* (Paris: Publications de la Sorbonne, 2003), 81.
36. Frank Dikötter, *Exotic Commodities: Modern Objects and Everyday Life in China* (New York: Columbia University Press, 2013), 148.
37. Chen Cai, "Introduction," in *A Pictorial Record of the Qing Dynasty: Business Documents* (Singapore: China Renmin University Press, 2009), xiii.
38. Yongming Zhou, *Historicizing Online Politics: Telegraphy, the Internet, and Political Participation in China* (Stanford, CA: Stanford University Press, 2006), 33–34.
39. Merle Curti and John Stalker, "'The Flowery Flag Devils': The American Image in China 1840–1900," *Proceedings of the American Philosophical Society* 96, no. 6 (December 1952): 667.
40. Previously numerous short lines were built and then rapidly abandoned in Beijing and Shanghai in the 1860s and 1870s.
41. Albert-August Fauvel, "Le chemin de fer de Peking à Nieou-Tchouang," *Annales de géographie* 9, no. 46 (1900): 374.
42. Li Hongzhang cited in Liu Heung Shing, *China Revolution: The Road to 1911* (Hong Kong: Hong Kong University, 2001), 241.
43. Stanley Spector, *Li Hung Chang and the Huai Army: A Study in Nineteenth-Century Chinese Regionalism* (Seattle: University of Washington Press, 1974), 163.
44. Edward J. M. Rhoads, *Stepping Forth Into the World: The Chinese Educational Mission to the United States, 1872–1881* (Hong Kong: Hong Kong University Press, 2011), 198.
45. Peter Howarth, *China's Rising Sea Power: The PLA Navy's Submarine Challenge* (London: Routledge, 2006), 119.
46. Edward A. McCord, *The Power of the Gun: The Emergence of Modern Chinese Warlordism* (Berkeley: University of California Press, 1993), 32.
47. Anita M. O'Brien, "Military Academies in China, 1885–1915," in *Perspectives on a Changing China*, ed. Joshua A. Fogel and William T. Rowe (Boulder, CO: Westview Press, 1979), 157–58.
48. Rhoads, *Stepping Forth*, 199.
49. Judy Polumbaum, "From Evangelism to Entertainment: The YMCA, the NBA, and the Evolution of Chinese Basketball," *Modern Chinese Literature and Culture* 14, no. 1 (2002): 178–230.
50. Allen Guttmann, *Sports: The First Five Millennia* (Amherst: University of Massachusetts Press, 2007), 206.

51. Li Rong-Zhi and Xiao Huan-yu, "Introduction of Table Tennis into Modern China and Its Development," *Journal of Chengdu Sport University* 5 (2012): 1–6.
52. Postcard from Mr. Chosson sent from Tianjin to his family living in Brussels, January 22, 1902.
53. James Ricalton, *China Through the Stereoscope* (New York: Underwood & Underwood, 1901), 247.
54. Roy Bin Wong, *China Transformed: Historical Change and the Limits of European Experience* (Ithaca, NY: Cornell University Press, 1997), 154.
55. Jules Verne, *Claudius Bombarnac* (Paris: Hetzel, 1892), 249.
56. Pierre Singaravélou, "Les stratégies d'internationalisation de la question coloniale et la construction transnationale d'une science de la colonisation à la fin du xixe siècle," *Monde(s)* 1 (2012): 135–57.
57. Christophe Charle, *Paris fin de siècle: Culture et politique* (Paris: Seuil, 1998); Philip Mansel, *Constantinople: City of the World's Desire 1453–1924* (New York: St. Martin's Press, 1998); Jonathan Schneer, *London 1900: The Imperial Metropolis* (New Haven, CT: Yale University Press, 2001); Michael Haag, *Alexandria: City of Memory* (New Haven, CT: Yale University Press, 2004); Mark Mazower, *Salonica, City of Ghosts: Christians, Muslims and Jews 1430–1950* (London: Harper, 2005); Christophe Charle, ed., *Le temps des capitales culturelles xviiie–xxe siècles* (Seyssel: Champ Vallon, 2009); Vincent Lemire, *Jérusalem 1900: La ville sainte à l'âge des possibles* (Paris: Armand Colin, 2013); Christophe Charle, *Paris 1900: La capitale des capitales?* (Paris: Petit-Palais, 2014).
58. Pierre-Yves Saunier and Shane Ewen, eds., *Another Global City: Historical Explorations Into the Transnational Municipal Moment 1850–2000* (New York: Palgrave Macmillan, 2008).
59. Richard White, *The Middle Ground: Indians, Empires, and Republics in the Great Lakes Region, 1650–1815* (Cambridge: Cambridge University Press, 1991).
60. Stephen R. Mackinnon, *Power and Politics in Late Imperial China: Yuan Shih-k'ai in Beijing and Tianjin, 1901–1908* (Berkeley: California University Press, 1980); Robert Bickers and R. G. Tiedemann, eds., *The Boxers, China, and the World* (Lanham, MD: Rowman & Littlefield, 2007); Thomas G. Hotte, *The China Question: Great Power Rivalry and British Isolation, 1894–1905* (Oxford: Oxford University Press, 2007); Bickers, *The Scramble for China*, 2012; Westad, *Restless Empire*, 2012.
61. Richard Drayton, "Masked Condominia: Pan-European Collaboration in the History of Imperialism, c. 1500 to the present," *Global History Review* 5 (2012): 308–31; James R. Fichter, *So Great a Proffit: How the East Indies Transformed Anglo-American Capitalism* (Cambridge, MA: Harvard University Press, 2010).
62. Gipouloux, *La Méditerranée asiatique*.

1. "Pandemonium"

1. Xiang Lanxin, *The Origins of the Boxer War: A Multinational Study* (London: Routledge, 2003), 156.
2. Bruce A. Elleman, *Modern Chinese Warfare, 1795–1989* (London: Routledge, 2001), 128.
3. Even when historians have not entirely ignored the siege of Tianjin, they have made errors on its chronology. For example, the historian Jerome Ch'en, who has provided rigorous analysis elsewhere, places the fall of the walled city on August 5, 1900, when it took place on July 14. Jerome Ch'en, *Yuan Shih-k'a* (Stanford, CA: Stanford University Press, 1972), 69.
4. Joseph Esherick, *The Origins of the Boxer Uprising* (Berkeley: University of California Press, 1987), 231.
5. Alexis Daoulas, *Le siège de Tien-Tsin (15 juin–15 juillet 1900)* (Paris: Berger-Levrault, 1903), 146.
6. Honglin Ma, "Lin Hei'er," in *Biographical Dictionary of Chinese Women: The Qing period, 1644–1911*, ed. Lily Xiao Hong Lee, A. D. Stefanowska, Sue Wiles, and Clara Wing-chung Ho, 131–33 (London: M. E. Sharpe, 1998).
7. Some sources have suggested that she had been a prostitute. See Jonathan Spence, *The Search for Modern China* (New York: W. W. Norton, 1991), 333.
8. Daoulas, *Le siège de Tien-Tsin*, 59.
9. Esherick, *The Origins of the Boxer Uprising*, 298.
10. Kazuko Ono, *Chinese Women in a Century of Revolution, 1850–1950* (Stanford, CA: Stanford University Press, 1989), 48.
11. The *daotai* is a high-level civil servant under the authority of the provincial viceroy. Arnold Henry Savage-Landor, *China and the Allies* (London: William Heinemann, 1901), 2:143.
12. This Boxer Manifesto was distributed in the London Missionary of Tianjin on March 30, 1900. See James Hudson Roberts, *A Flight for Life* (Boston: Pilgrim Press, 1903), cited in William Alexander Parsons Martin, *The Awakening of China* (New York: Doubleday, Page & Company, 1910), 175.
13. Daoulas, *Le siège de Tien-Tsin*, 63.
14. Lee Khoon Choy, *Pioneers of Modern China: Understanding the Inscrutable Chinese* (Singapore: World Scientific, 2005), 372.
15. Xiang, *Origins of the Boxer War*, 276.
16. Mark Elvin, "Mandarins and Millenarians: Reflections on the Boxer Uprising of 1899–1900," lecture, School of Oriental and African Studies, June 6, 1979, 118.
17. Chien Po-tsan et al., eds., *I ho t'uan* (The Boxers) (Shanghai: Shen-chou kuo-kuang she, 1951), 11 and 18.

18. Elvin, "Mandarins and Millenarians," 124.
19. Guillaume G. H. Dunstheimer, "Religion et magie dans le mouvement des Boxeurs d'après les textes chinois," *T'oung Pao* 47, books 3–5 (1959).
20. Po-tsan, *I ho t'uan*, 153, cited in Elvin, "Mandarins and Millenarians," 123.
21. Tang Diansan, "Anecdotes durant les troubles Boxeurs à Tianjin," in *Yi He Tuan*, ed. Bozan Jian (Shanghai: Shenzhou guogang she, 1961), 2:68; Po-tsan, *I ho t'uan*, 12.
22. Bruce A. Elleman, *Modern Chinese Warfare, 1795–1989* (London: Routledge, 2001), 126–27.
23. Esherick, *The Origins of the Boxer Uprising*, 301.
24. "Un mois à Tianjin," in Bozan, *Yi He Tuan*, 2:142–43.
25. Xiang, *Origins of the Boxer War*, 278.
26. Paul A. Cohen, *History in Three Keys: The Boxers as Event, Experience, and Myth* (New York: Columbia University Press, 1997).
27. Otto D. Rasmussen, *Tientsin: An Illustrated Outline History* (Tientsin: The Tientsin Press, 1925). For example, in the important work of the sinologist Delphine Spicq, *L'avènement de l'eau courante à Tianjin (1900–1949)* (Saarbrücken: Éditions Universitaires Européennes, 2012) the attacks on June 15, 16, and 17 are attributed to the Boxers (5). This analysis of the siege by the author is surprising: "The conquest of the city was long because the Chinese fought ferociously" (7).
28. Savage-Landor, *China and the Allies*, 138; "Notes et impressions de Tien-Tsin (2 août 1900)," *Le Temps*, September 27, 1900.
29. Daoulas, *Le siège de Tien-Tsin*, 143, 26.
30. Lynn E. Bodin and Chris Warner, *The Boxer Rebellion* (Oxford: Osprey Publishing, 1979), 13; "Tells of Tientsin Siege. H. C. Hoover Engineer Describes Boxer Attacks," *The Sun*, November 19, 1900, 3.
31. "The Fighting at Tientsin. Experiences of Two Railway Engineers," *Straits Times* (Singapore), August 4, 1900, 3.
32. "Journal du siege de Tientsin," *La revue de Paris*, January 15, 1902, 224.
33. Daoulas, *Le siège de Tien-Tsin*, 36–37.
34. "Hoover's Work in Tientsin Siege Recalled at Gridiron Club Dinner," *The Reading Eagle*, April 25, 1930; Charles Cabry Dix, *The World's Navies in the Boxer Rebellion (China 1900)* (London: Digby, Long & Co., 1905), 47.
35. Bern Dibner, "Hoover and Agricola," *Technology and Culture* 13, no. 3 (July 1972): 421.
36. William E. Leuchtenburg, *Herbert Hoover: The 31st President, 1929–1933* (New York: Macmillan, 2009), 13.
37. Larry Clinton Thompson, *William Scott Ament and the Boxer Rebellion: Heroism, Hubris and the "Ideal Missionary"* (Jefferson, NC: McFarland, 2009), 137–38.

38. Charles Tenney, "Experiences in China," 1919-1925b, MS-794-005, Papers of Charles Daniel Tenney, Dartmouth College Library, Hanover, New Hampshire, 9.
39. Charles F. Grammon, "The Siege of Tien-Tsin: Vivid Description of the Horrible Experiences of the Missionaries," *Boston Evening Transcript*, February 1, 1901.
40. Letter from Y. F. Hg, Chinese resident to his wife, 8:40 p.m., June 15, 1900, cited in Savage-Landor, *China and the Allies*, 142.
41. For the United States, Britain, and Japan, the common language was generally French. The foreign officers often called upon the French military to serve as interpreters. General Dorward at the War Office, July 19, 1900, PRO ADM 116/114, cited in David Silbey, *The Boxer Rebellion and The Great Game in China* (New York: Hill and Wang, 2012), 138. See Daoulas, *Le siège de Tien-Tsin*, 41.
42. Daoulas, *Le siège de Tien-Tsin*, 77.
43. Daoulas, *Le siège de Tien-Tsin*, 84.
44. Z. Charles Beals, *China and the Boxers* (New York: M. E. Munson, 1901), 40; *News of the World*, July 15, 1900.
45. Spicq, *L'avènement de l'eau courante*, 5.
46. "The Fighting at Tientsin," *The Advertiser* (Adelaide, Australia), Monday, July 30, 1900, 5.
47. Dix, *The World's Navies*, 55.
48. Liang Yiqun, "Lin Hei'er: 'Hongdengzhao' dashijie," in *Gujin zhuming funü renwu* (Shijiazhuang: Hebei renmin chubanshe, 1986), 1:360–64; Liao Yizhong, "Lin Hei'er," in *Qingdai renwu zhuangao* (Beijing: Zhonghua shuju, 1987), 3:98–101.
49. "Scenes of Horror in Tien Tsin," *Reading Eagle* (Pennsylvania), July 23, 1900.
50. Marcel Monnier, *Le drame chinois: Juillet–août 1900* (Paris: Félix Alcan, 1900), 10.
51. Daoulas, *Le siège de Tien-Tsin*, 123.
52. Elleman, *Modern Chinese Warfare*, 128.
53. "Journal du siege de Tientsin," 230.
54. Xiang, *The Origins of the Boxer War* 2003.
55. Daoulas, *Le siège de Tien-Tsin*, 148.
56. "The Fighting at Tientsin," *The Advertiser*, 5.
57. James Ricalton, *China Through the Stereoscope* (New York: Underwood & Underwood, 1901), 203; Charles F. Grammon, "The Siege of Tien-Tsin: Foreigners' Desperate Plight Described by Charles F. Grammon," *New York Times*, August 2, 1900.
58. Dix, *The World's Navies*, 66.

59. Charles-Baltazar de Pélacot, *Expédition de Chine de 1900 jusqu'à l'arrivée du général Voyron* (Paris: H. Lavauzelle, 1903), 35–36.
60. "Journal du siege de Tientsin," 234.
61. Vernon Kellogg, *Herbert Hoover: The Man and His Work* (New York: D. Appleton and Company, 1920), 96–97; Hoover, *The Memoirs of Herbert Hoover* (New York: Macmillan, 1952).
62. A shamisen is a Japanese lute. Jean Ruffi de Pontevès, *Souvenirs de la colonne Seymour* (Paris: Librairie Plon, 1903), 281.
63. Daoulas, *Le siège de Tien-Tsin*, 240.
64. Daoulas, *Le siège de Tien-Tsin*, 236, 254.
65. "Journal du siege de Tientsin," 241–42.
66. Silbey, *The Boxer Rebellion*, 148.
67. Seymour to the Ministry of the Navy, July 12, 1900, PRO ADM 116/114, cited in Silbey, *The Boxer Rebellion*, 149.
68. Quentin Deluermoz and Pierre Singaravélou, *Pour une histoire des possibles: Analyses contrefactuelles et futurs non advenus* (Paris: Seuil, 2016), 239–47.
69. "The Tien Tsin Siege: Chinese Gaining Ground," *The Age*, July 14, 1900.
70. Daoulas, *Le siège de Tien-Tsin*, 233–34.
71. Daoulas, *Le siège de Tien-Tsin*, 254–55.
72. This is contrary to Silbey: "None of the Japanese spoke English" (*The Boxer Rebellion*, 138). Daoulas, *Le siège de Tien-Tsin*, 254.
73. "Tells of the Tientsin Siege," 3.
74. "Journal du siege de Tientsin," 245.
75. Ricalton, *China Through the Stereoscope*, 191.
76. "Journal du siège de Tientsin," 251.
77. Arthur A. S. Barnes, *On Active Service with the Chinese Regiment* (London: Grant Richards, 1902), 78.
78. Ricalton, *China Through the Stereoscope*, 219.
79. Lewis Bernstein, "Tianjin (Tientsin), China, Battle and Siege," in *The War of 1898 and U.S. Interventions*, ed. Benjamin R. Beede (New York: Routledge, 1994), 542.
80. Ricalton, *China Through the Stereoscope*, 220.
81. Frederick Brown, *From Tientsin to Peking with the Allied Forces* (London: C. H. Kelly, 1902), 38.
82. G. Cotenson, "De l'art militaire des Chinois, d'après leurs classiques," *La nouvelle revue* (August 1900).
83. Sun Tzu, *L'art de la guerre* (Grenoble: Éditions Philosophie, 2008), 7.36.
84. Esherick, *The Origins of the Boxer Uprising*, 309.
85. Silbey, *The Boxer Rebellion*, 157.
86. "Tells of Tientsin Siege," 3.

87. "Scenes of Horror in Tien Tsin."
88. The Chinese figures are from "Scenes of Horror in Tien Tsin"; the figures for the Allied soldiers are in "The Fighting at Tientsin," *Star* (New Zealand), 12 mahuru (September) 1900, 4.
89. "It would seem that there was general desertion." Georges Weulersse, *Chine ancienne et nouvelle: Impressions et réflexions* (Paris: Armand Colin, 1902), 340.
90. "Chine," *Le Temps*, July 21, 1900.
91. Barnes, *On Active Service*, 84, cited in Silbey, *The Boxer Rebellion*, 146.
92. "The Fighting at Tientsin," *Star*, 4.
93. "The Fighting at Tientsin," *Star*, 4.
94. Daoulas, *Le siège de Tien-Tsin*, 142.
95. Silbey, *The Boxer Rebellion*, 157.
96. Dix, *The World's Navies*, 177; "Cruautés chinoises," *L'express du Midi*, August 26, 1900.
97. Ruth Rogaski, *Hygienic Modernity: Meanings of Health and Disease in Treaty-Port China* (Berkeley: University of California Press, 2004), 171.
98. John F. Bass, "The Sack of Tien-Tsin Was a Scene of Shame: Soldiers of Christian Powers Vied with the Scum and Riff-Raff of the Chinese in Looting the Prostrate City," *Daily Mail and Empire*, September 10, 1900.
99. "Russians Charged with Atrocities," *Bathurst Free Press and Mining Journal*, July 21, 1900.
100. "Looting of Tien Tsin: Colonel Coolidge Writes of the Thieving Propensities of the French Troops," *Los Angeles Herald*, September 4, 1900.
101. "Tells of Tientsin Siege," 3.
102. Bass, "Sack of Tien-Tsin."
103. Jacques Semelin, "Analyser le massacre: Réflexions comparatives," *Questions de recherches* 7 (September 2002): 42.
104. Wilhelm II, speech at Bremerhaven to the troops leaving for China on June 27, 1900, *Nordwestdeutsche Zeitung*, July 28, 1900.
105. Bass, "Sack of Tien-Tsin."
106. "Journal du siege de Tientsin," 255–56.
107. "There is no doubt that the only part of this war that will draw the interest of the Chinese in the future will be the destruction and pillaging of Tientsin," wrote Savage-Landor. *China and the Allies*, 191.
108. "The Tientsin Siege," *Hawke's Bay Herald*, June 25, 1900, 3.
109. Special correspondent in Shanghai, *Daily Mail*, July 3, 1900; "Bad News from Pekin," *Boston Evening Transcript*, July 6, 1900, 1.
110. Robert B. Edgerton, *Warriors of the Rising Sun: A History of the Japanese Military* (New York: W. W. Norton, 1997), 86.

111. "Massacred by the Boxers: 1,500 Foreigners Killed at Tien Tsin. Report Is Doubted," *The Evening Hour*, June 22, 1900, 1.
112. Georges Weulersse, "Au Petchili et sur les frontières de Mandchourie," *Le tour du monde, nouveau journal des voyages* 7 (1901): 36.
113. "Notes et impressions de Tien-Tsin (August 2, 1900)"; report by the French consul Henri Leduc, 1902, CADN, 691 PO / 1, "Tientsin consulat," 291.
114. Some articles gave the figure of twenty thousand Chinese dead. See "Looting of Tien Tsin: Colonel Coolidge Writes."
115. "The Looting of Tien-Tsin," *Colonist*, October 18, 1900, 2.
116. "Journal du siège de Tientsin," 255–56.
117. James Hevia, "Loot's Fate: The Economics of Plunder and the Moral Life of Objects," *History and Anthropology* 6, no. 4 (1994): 319-345.
118. Savage-Landor, *China and the Allies*, 190.
119. Bass, "Sack of Tien-Tsin."
120. Savage-Landor, *China and the Allies*, 194.
121. Savage-Landor, *China and the Allies*, 202.
122. Savage-Landor, *China and the Allies*, 207.
123. Daoulas, *Le siège de Tien-Tsin*, 123–24.
124. Savage-Landor, *China and the Allies*, 197–99.
125. Bass, "Sack of Tien-Tsin."
126. "The Looting of Tien-Tsin: Spoils to the Victors. Some Big Hauls," *Daily Telegraph*, October 31, 1900, 5.
127. Jane E. Elliott, *Some Did It for Civilisation, Some Did It for Their Country* (Hong Kong: The Chinese University Press, 2002), 395. The Provisional Government then organized at the end of 1900 and beginning of 1901 auctions of confiscated objects (clothing, jewelry, and so forth) in order to increase the government's resources. PVGPT, January 16, 1901, 92.
128. "Smuggled Loot from Tien Tsin Captured from Naval Officers," *Los Angeles Herald*, September 21, 1900.
129. Bass, "Sack of Tien-Tsin."
130. "The Looting of Tien-Tsin: Spoils to the Victors," 5.
131. "The Looting of Tien-Tsin," *Colonist*, 2.
132. Édouard Charton, "Journal d'un officier du corps expéditionnaire de Chine," *Le tour du monde* (January 1902), 68.
133. "Notes et impressions de Tien-Tsin (August 2, 1900)."
134. "Scenes of Horror in Tien Tsin."
135. Savage-Landor, *China and the Allies*, 214.
136. Telegram from Gustave de Chaylard, Tianjin, July 17, 1900, received in Tche Fou, July 20, 1900, MAE, 148 CPCOM 101, "July 1900 China."
137. Bernstein, "Tianjin (Tientsin), China, Battle and Siege," 542.

138. Elliott, *Some Did It for Civilization*, 532.
139. Q. Deluermoz and P. Singaravélou, *A Past of Possibilities: A History of What Could Have Been*, trans. Stephen W. Sawyer (New Haven, CT: Yale University Press, 2021).
140. "Tells of Tientsin Siege," 3.
141. Pierre Loti, "Les deux déesses des Boxeurs," Sunday, October 14, 1901.
142. Dibner, "Hoover and Agricola,"421.
143. Hervé Drévillon, *Batailles: Scènes de guerre de la table ronde aux tranchées* (Paris: Seuil, 2007), 16.
144. First day of the symposium "New Campaign History," December 8, 2011, École Militaire, Paris.
145. Loti, "Les deux déesses des Boxeurs."
146. A *godown* was a British Indian depot.
147. Raoul Charles Villetard de Laguérie, "Tien-Tsin après la défaite des Boxeurs (Voyage exécuté en 1900)," *Le tour du monde: Nouveau journal des voyages* 7, no. 41 (October 12, 1901): 490–92.

2. The Invention of an International Government

1. David Silbey, *The Boxer Rebellion and the Great Game in China* (New York: Hill and Wang, 2012), 143.
2. Jean-François Brun, "Intervention armée en Chine: L'expédition internationale de 1900–1901," *Revue historique des armées* 258 (2010): 13.
3. Otto D. Rasmussen, *Tientsin: An Illustrated Outline History* (Tientsin: The Tientsin Press, 1925). Since then, only a short article by Lexis Bernstein has taken interest in the subject. Lewis Bernstein, "After the Fall: Tianjin Under Foreign Occupation, 1900–1902," in *The Boxers, China, and the World*, ed. Robert Bickers and R. G. Tiedemann (Lanham, MD: Rowman & Littlefield, 2007).
4. PVGPT, March 28, 1902, 485; January 9, 1902, 421; Conseil du gouvernement provisoire, *Règlements du gouvernement provisoire du district de Tientsin*, Harvard Widener Library, 1; Rasmussen, *Tientsin*, 221.
5. Bertrand Badie, *L'État importé: L'occidentalisation de l'ordre politique* (Paris: Fayard, 1992); Michel Cahen, "Africando: Bilan 1988–2009 et projets 2010–2018," (Thesis, École des Hautes Études en Sciences Sociales, 2010), 1:110.
6. Karl Wittfogel, *Oriental Despotism: A Comparative Study of Total Power* (New Haven, CT: Yale University Press, 1957), 307.
7. Telegram from Gustave du Chaylard, Tianjin, July 17, 1900, MAE, 148 CPCOM 1010 "Juillet 1900, Chine." The consul proposed in the same

message to promote his Russian superior officer, Constantin Vogak, to the rank of Commander of the Legion of Honor.

8. Letter from the French ambassador to Saint Petersburg to Minister of Foreign Affairs Delcassé, July 20, 1900, MAE, 148 CPCOM 101 "Juillet 1900, Chine."
9. Raoul Charles Villetard de Laguérie, "Tien-Tsin après la défaite des Boxeurs (Voyage exécuté en 1900)," *Le tour du monde: Nouveau journal des voyages* 7, no. 41 (October 12, 1901): 492.
10. Telegram from Gustave du Chaylard, Tianjin, July 18, 1900, to Minister of Foreign Affairs Delcassé, MAE, 148 CPCOM 1010 "Juillet 1900, Chine."
11. The word *yamen*, which we have translated as headquarters, has been used in French since the seventeenth century and in English since the eighteenth century. PVGPT, July 30, 1900, 3.
12. Wu Hung, "Tiananmen Square: A Political History of Monuments," *Representations* 35 (Summer 1991): 91.
13. Each office in the *yamen* occupied by a foreign civil servant was also used as lodging. This was another means of establishing a continuity with the Chinese authorities. In the headquarters of the Provisional Government, the civil servants worked from 10:00 a.m. to 4:00 p.m. every day except Sunday. PVGPT, February 22, 1901, 132; August 30, 1901, 305; PVGPT, August 14, 1901, 12.
14. A cangue (*mu jia*) was an instrument of corporal punishment and public humiliation. It was a heavy square worn around a prisoner's neck with writing on it that indicated the name, address, and crime of the individual.
15. Loti, "Les deux déesses des Boxeurs," Sunday, October 14, 1901.
16. PVGPT, September 17, 1900, 34; September 01, 1900, 23; February 8, 1901, 117.
17. PVGPT, January 10, 1901, 85; January 11, 1901, 89; the government substituted the "foreign calendar" for the Chinese calendar at the end of January 1901 (January 26, 1901, 101); February 8, 1901, 113; February 25, 1901, 135.
18. PVGPT, June 24, 1901, 245; June 26. 1901, 247; September 2. 1901, 308.
19. Rasmussen, *Tientsin*, 224; Ruth Rogaski, *Hygienic Modernity: Meanings of Health and Disease in Treaty-Port China* (Berkeley: University of California Press, 2004), 172.
20. PVGPT, August 4, 1900, 5.
21. PVGPT, August 21, 1900, 16.
22. Council of the Provisional Government, *Règlement du gouvernement provisoire*, 1.
23. Alexis Daoulas, *Le siège de Tien-Tsin (15 juin–15 juillet 1900)* (Paris: Berger-Levrault, 1903), 51.

24. Letter from General Voyron to the Council of the Provisional Government, October 3, 1900, PVGPT, October 5, 1900, 43; October 11, 1900, 48.
25. PVGPT, January 26, 1901, 102; February 1, 1901, 106; Rasmussen, *Tientsin*, 224–25; letter from Lessel to the Government Council, October 11, 1900, PVGPT, October 13, 1900; PVGPT, October 29, 1900, SHD, 11H39, 3; November 09, 1900, SHD, 11H39, 10.
26. PVGPT, November 24, 1900, SHD, 11H39, 25; letter from General Voyron to the Council of the Provisional Government, PVGPT, December 5, 1900, 60; December 10, 1900, 63; January 22, 1901, 95; January 14, 1901, 90; March 6, 1901, 144; April 9, 1901, 174; April 15, 1901, 182; letter from Commander Casanuova to General Sucillon, January 13, 1902, 422; January 20, 1902, 427; minutes from the Commanders Conference (February 5, 1902), February 17, 1902, 449.
27. PVGPT, September 29, 1900, 41; October 8, 1900, 46; Rasmussen, *Tientsin*, 224; PVGPT, May 4, 1901, 204; April 29, 1901, 199; June 11, 1902, 546.
28. According to the official rate, a pound sterling corresponded to roughly ten Mexican dollars (PVGPT, November 5, 1900, SHD, 11H39, 7) and twenty-five French francs (PVGPT, January 14, 1901, 90).
29. Council of the Provisional Government, *Règlements du gouvernement provisoire*, 2; PVGPT, November 20, 1900; September 11, 1900, 31; September 25, 1900, 39; October 17, 1900, 52; October 29, 1900, SHD, 11H39, 4; November 5, 1900, SHD, 11H39, 6; November 13, 1900, SHD, 11H39, 12; April 19, 1901, 190; January 7, 1901, 83; April 17, 1901, 185; June 7, 1901, 231; June 19, 1901, 242; August 19, 1901, 296; August 30, 1901, 305; October 9, 1901, 341.
30. Ch'ü T'ung-tsu, *Local Government in China under the Ch'ing* (Stanford, CA: Stanford University Press, 1969).
31. Chung Yam Po, *Westerners in Li Hongzhang's Mufu: With References to Gustav Detring and Hosea Ballou Morse* (Hong Kong: Hong Kong Baptist University, 2010).
32. "An American in China," *New York Times*, August 24, 1902; Michael H. Hunt, *The Making of a Special Relationship: The United States and China to 1914* (New York: Columbia University Press, 1983).
33. Archie R. Crouch, ed., *Christianity in China: A Scholar's Guide to Resources in the Libraries and Archives of the United States* (Armonk, NY: M. E. Sharpe, 1989), 222.
34. Daoulas, *Le siège de Tien-Tsin*, 44; *La liberté des colonies*, January 13, 1901, 1.
35. *San Francisco Call*, June 23, 1900, 1; George Gipps, *The Fighting in North China* (Shanghai: Kelly and Walsh, 1901), 11.
36. "Carl Rump," *The Sun*, June 19, 1913, 9; Georg Baur, *China um 1900: Aufzeichnungen eines Krupp-Direktors* (Cologne: Böhlau Köln, 2005), 666; *The London Gazette*, September 13, 1887; Gordon Casserly, *The Land of the Boxers or China Under the Allies* (London: Longmans, 1903), 18.

37. Vera Schmidt, *Aufgabe und Einfluss der europäischen Berater in China: Gustav Detring (1842–1913) im Dienste Li Hung-changs* (Wiesbaden: Otto Harrassowitz Verlag, 1984); Ricardo K. S. Mak, "Western Advisers and Late Qing Chinese Military Modernization: A Case Study of Constantin von Hanneken (1854–1925)," *Journal of Northeast Asian History* 2, no. 10 (2014): 47–70; Regine Thiriez, *Barbarian Lens: Western Photographers of the Qianlong Emperor's European Palaces* (Amsterdam: Gordon and Breach, 1998), 90–91.
38. Tongku (Captain Wollseiffen, German); Chunliangcheng (Major Ducat, British); Tientsin-Nord (Captain Satō, Japanese); Tientsin-Sud (Captain Farrère, French); (PVGPT, February 8, 1901, 116; May 3, 1901, 204; May 4, 1901, 206; June 5, 1901, 230).
39. Rasmussen, *Tientsin*, 223; PVGPT, February 8, 1901, 115; April 15, 1901, 212; February 8, 1901, 118; February 8, 1901, 116; December 20, 1901, 409.
40. Bradly W. Reed, *Talons and Teeth: County Clerks and Runners in the Qing Dynasty* (Stanford, CA: Stanford University Press, 2000).
41. PVGPT, July 10, 1901, 259; April 25, 1902, 502.
42. Jacques Grandin, "Mes exploits pendant la guerre de Chine de 1901 (Journal d'un volontaire)," *La revue des revues* 41 (1–15 May 1902): 397–98.
43. PVGPT, May 31, 1901, 224.
44. Mark A. Allee, *Law and Local Society in Late Imperial China: Northern Taiwan in the Nineteenth Century* (Stanford, CA: Stanford University Press, 1994).
45. PVGPT, June 23, 1902, 559; July 7, 1902, 574; April 5, 1901, 172.
46. PVGPT, November 2, 1900, SHD, 11H39, 6; PVGPT, June 1, 1901, 243; March 22, 1901, 159; April 11, 1901, 178; November 1, 1901, 362.
47. PVGPT, December 28, 1900, 76; February 8, 1901, 117.
48. PVGPT, September 16, 1901, 319; April 9, 1902, 492; May 14, 1902, 519; April 15, 1901, 182; December 16, 1901, 405; December 18, 1901, 407.
49. PVGPT, December 31, 1900, 77; January 2, 1901, 78; March 20, 1901, 157; May 4, 1901, 206; May 17, 1901, 214; May 22, 1901, 217; March 21, 1902, 473.
50. PVGPT, March 6, 1901, 150; March 20, 1901, 156–57; March 29, 1901, 164; November 11, 1901, 373; February 21, 1902, 452.
51. PVGPT, August 11, 1902, 619; December 30, 1901, 415; May 27, 1901, 223; July 25, 1902, 592; August 13, 1902, 624.
52. Luke S. Roberts, "The Petition Box in Eighteenth-Century Tosa," *Journal of Japanese Studies* 20, no. 2 (Summer 1994): 456.
53. Fang Qiang, "A Hot Potato: The Chinese Complaint Systems from Early Times to the Present" (PhD diss., SUNY Buffalo, 2006).
54. Ho-fung Hung, *Protest with Chinese Characteristics: Demonstrations, Riots and Petitions in the Mid-Qing Dynasty* (New York: Columbia University Press, 2011).

55. Fang Qiang, "Hot Potatoes: Chinese Complaint Systems from Early Times to the Late Qing (1898)," *Journal of Asian Studies* 68, no. 4 (November 2009): 1112.
56. Léon Vandermeersch, "L'institution chinoise de remontrance," *Études chinoises* 13, nos. 1–2 (Spring–Fall 1994): 31–45.
57. Excerpt from the *Classic of Filial Piety* (*Xiaojing*), published at the beginning of the Han, cited in Vandermeersch, "L'institution chinoise," 39.
58. Viren Murthy, "The Democratic Potential of Confucian Minben Thought," *Asian Philosophy: An International Journal of the Philosophical Traditions of the East* 10, no. 1 (2000): 33–47.
59. Zhongli Zhang, *The Chinese Gentry: Studies on Their Role in Nineteenth-Century Chinese Society* (Seattle: University of Washington Press, 1955).
60. Joseph Esherick and Mary Backus Rankin, eds., *Chinese Local Elites and Patterns of Dominance* (Berkeley: University of California Press, 1990), 118.
61. Philip Huang and Kathryn Bernhardt, eds., *Research from Archival Case Records: Law, Society and Culture in China* (Leiden: Brill, 2014), 472.
62. Mary Backus Rankin, *Elite Activism and Political Transformation in China: Zhejiang Province 1865–1911* (Stanford, CA: Stanford University Press, 1986): 17–21; Mary Backus Rankin, "Local Elites and Community Affairs in the Late Imperial Period," *Études chinoises* 9, no. 2 (Fall 1990): 13–60.
63. PVGPT, February 8, 1901, 117; May 25, 1902, 503; May 2, 1902, 509; May 5, 1902, 510; May 9, 1902, 514.
64. PVGPT, June 30, 1902, 567; July 2, 1902, 567; July 23, 1902, 589; August 13, 1902, 624; August 6, 1902, 613; August 4, 2002, 607.
65. PVGPT, February 8, 1901, 119; December 20, 1900, 71; February 8, 1901, 117; July 5, 1901, 255; December 9, 1901, 399.
66. PVGPT, March 1, 1901, 141; October 30, 1901, 361; August 6, 1900, 7; September 4, 1901, 308; September 25, 1901, 327; October 9, 1901, 340; February 8, 1901, 117.
67. PVGPT, April 5, 1901, 172; proposal for a resolution sent to the Council of the Provisional Government of the district of Tientsin by Colonel Foote, April 5, 1901 (April 11, 1901), 177; June 13, 1902, 547.
68. Pierre Singaravélou, "Dix empires dans un mouchoir de poche: Le territoire de Tianjin à l'épreuve du phénomène concessionnaire (années 1860–1920)," in *Territoires impériaux: Une histoire spatiale du fait colonial*, ed. Hélène Blais, Florence Deprest, and Pierre Singaravélou (Paris: Publications de la Sorbonne, 2011).
69. Departure letter from the Lieutenant Colonel Arlabosse to the members of the Council, Tianjin, January 22, 1902, PVGPT, January 15, 1902, 426–27.

70. If the difference was not decided in this way, then it had to be decided by the governments of the various Allied powers. PVGPT, December 20, 1900, 71; December 24, 1900, 73.
71. PVGPT, June 26, 1901, 281.
72. Chen Bofeng, "Excessive Litigation, *Xinfang* and Legal Traditions of New China," *Peking University Law Journal (zhongwai faxue)* 16, no. 2 (2004): 230; Isabelle Thireau and Hua Linshan, "The Moral Universe of Aggrieved Chinese Workers: Workers' Appeals to Arbitration Committees and Letters and Visits Offices," *China Journal* 50 (July 2003): 83–103.

3. "Bringing Order to Chaos"

The title of this chapter is taken from the "Thank You" message sent to the Provisional Government by the merchants and bankers of Tianjin, PVGPT, August 11, 1902, 620.

1. As early as September 1900, under the impulse of Li Hongzhang, the Chinese government ordered imperial troops to pursue the Boxers in the region of Beijing before pulling back to the limits of Zhili Province, to the north of the Great Wall.
2. Max Weber, *Religions of China: Confucianism and Taoism* (Glencoe, IL: Free Press, 1951), 148–49.
3. Jérôme Bourgon, "'Sauver la vie': De la fraude judiciaire en Chine à la fin de l'empire," *Actes de la recherche en sciences sociales* 133 (June 2000): 32.
4. Teemu Ruskola, "Law Without Law, or Is Chinese Law an Oxymoron?," *William & Mary Bill of Rights Journal* 11, no. 2 (2002–3): 655–69.
5. Jérôme Bourgon, "La coutume et le droit en Chine à la fin de l'Empire," *Annales: Histoire, sciences sociales* 54, no. 5 (1999): 1073–1107.
6. Pär Kristoffer Cassel, *Grounds of Judgment: Extraterritoriality and Imperial Power in Nineteenth-Century China and Japan* (Oxford: Oxford University Press, 2012).
7. Chen Li, "Legal Specialists and Judicial Administration in Late Imperial China, 1651–1911," *Late Imperial China* 33, no. 1 (June 2012): 1–54
8. Derk Bodde and Clarence Morris, *Law in Imperial China: Exemplified by 190 Ch'ing Dynasty Cases (With Historical, Social, and Juridical Commentaries)* (Cambridge, MA: Harvard University Press, 1967); Frank Dikötter, *Crime, Punishment and the Prison in Modern China* (New York: Columbia University Press, 1992).
9. Philip Huang, *Civil Justice in China: Representation and Practice in the Qing (Law, Society, and Culture in China)* (Stanford, CA: Stanford University Press, 1996).

10. Li Zhaojie and Li James, "Traditional Chinese World Order," *Chinese Journal of International Law* 1 (2002): 40.
11. Michael Dutton, *Policing and Punishment in China: From Patriarchy to "The People"* (Cambridge: Cambridge University Press, 1992).
12. Kwan Man Bun, "Order in Chaos: Tianjin's Hunhunr and Urban Identity in Modern China," *Journal of Urban History* 27, no. 1 (November 2000): 75.
13. Hsiao Kung-Ch'üan, *Rural China: Imperial Control in the Nineteenth Century* (Seattle: University of Washington Press, 1960); Philip Kuhn, *Rebellion and Its Enemies in Late Imperial China* (Cambridge, MA: Harvard University Press, 1970).
14. Frank Y. C. Yee, "Police in Modern China," (PhD diss., University of California, Berkeley, 1942).
15. Kam C. Wong, *Police Reform in China* (Boca Raton, FL: CRC Press, 2011), 266.
16. Stephen R. MacKinnon, "Police Reform in Late Ch'ing Chihli," *Late Imperial China* 3, no. 4 (December 1975): 82; Frederic Wakeman Jr., "Models of Historical Change: The Chinese State and Society, 1839–1989," in *Perspectives on Modern China: Four Anniversaries*, ed. Kenneth Lieberthal (Armonk, NY: M. E. Sharpe, 1991), 78; Kam C. Wong, *Chinese Policing: History and Reform* (New York: Peter Lang, 2009), 31.
17. Council of the Provisional Government, *Règlements du gouvernement provisoire du district de Tientsin*, Harvard Widener Library, 1.
18. PVGPT, March 28, 1902, 485.
19. PVGPT, August 15, 1900, 12; November 13, 1901, 376; February 8, 1901, 119.
20. PVGPT, August 16, 1900, 13; September 5, 1900, 26; May 26, 1901, 196; July 29, 1901, 274; September 2, 1901, 307; translation of a letter to Huang-chien-huen, former *daotai* of customs in Tianjin, addressed to the Council of the Provisional Government, October 17, 1900, 51–52; letter from General Mei to the Council of the Provisional Government August 2, 1901, 279; account by the magistrate of Ching hsien, January 4, 1901, 81; February 22, 1901, 132; March 25, 1901, 160; Da Gong Bao (Ta Kung Pao), August 24, 1902, cited in Chen Ke, "Nongovernmental Organizations and the Urban Control and Management System in Tianjin at the End of the 19th Century," *Social Sciences in China* 11, no. 4 (1990): 69.
21. Proclamation to the population of Tianjin, PVGPT, July 30, 1900, 4; November 22, 1900, SHD, 11H39, 21; July 4, 1901, 81; January 10, 1901, 87; June 30, 1902, 567; July 7, 1902, 573; petition from the magistrate of Chang Li to the Council, September 18, 1901, 322.
22. Jacques Grandin, "Mes exploits pendant la guerre de Chine de 1901 (Journal d'un volontaire)," *La revue des revues* 61 (May 1–15, 1902): 410–11.

23. PVGPT, July 30, 1900, 4; August 28, 1900, 20; August 2, 1900, 3; December 17, 1900, 69; request of Reverend Arthur H. Smith, resident in Pao Chia Chuang, November 19, 1900, SHD, 11H39, 16; August 2, 1900, 3; the accusations of pillaging before July 18, 1900, against Chinese property owners could be pursued and judged until March 31, 1901 (February 22, 1901, 132); August 8, 1900, 8; August 28, 1900, 20.
24. Grandin, "Mes exploits," 277–78.
25. Grandin, "Mes exploits," 402.
26. Grandin, "Mes exploits," 407, 410.
27. PVGPT, October 22, 1900, 54; February 25, 1901, 137; September 11, 1901, 316; June 26, 1901, 247; July 30, 1902, 597.
28. Grandin, "Mes exploits," 411–12.
29. "Marauding Bands," *Los Angeles Herald*, March 15, 1901.
30. PVGPT, February 1, 1901, 107; February 4, 1901, 109; February 8, 1901, 114.
31. Émile Edmond Legrand-Girarde, "Le génie en Chine (1900–1901)," *Revue du génie militaire* (January 1902): 115.
32. PVGPT, April 17, 1901, 186; May 3. 1901, 203; Villetard de Laguérie, "Tien-Tsin après la défaite," 492; August 28, 1900, 19; account of the attack on the customs house near Tongku, March 28, 1901 (April 17, 1901), 185; May 3, 1901, 202.
33. PVGPT, April 4, 1902, 488; July 11, 1902, 577; report to the head of the district of Tientsin-Sud, May 23, 1902, 525, 528.
34. We do not know what happened to him (letter from the Council of the Provisional Government to the British Consul), November 7, 1900, NA, FO 674 / 80; PVGPT, November 7, 1900, SHD, 11H39, 9.
35. PVGPT, October 23, 1901, 355; October 28, 1901, 358; November 13, 1901, 376; letter from the French Consul Leduc to the Minister of Foreign Affairs, July 7, 1903, CADN, 691 PO / 1 Tientsin consulat, 291.
36. PVGPT, August 23, 1901, 300; August 21, 1901, 297; September 4, 1901, 310; April 7, 1902, 490; May 28, 1902, 530; July 16, 1901, 272; August 12, 1901, 287; August 19, 1901, 296.
37. PVGPT, August 1, 1901, 251; s.d., around August 10, 1901, 258; rapport no. 349 by the secretary of Chinese affairs, June 25, 1902, 560.
38. Petition from the notables of Wang Chia Kou, PVGPT, November 20, 1900, SHD, 11H39, 18; December 7, 1900, 63; December 12, 1900, 64.
39. PVGPT, February 8, 1901, 117.
40. PVGPT, August 29, 1900, 21; October 13, 1900, 48; November 20, 1900, SHD, 11H39, 18; letter to General Mei translated by the Chinese secretary, November 24, 1900, SHD, 11H39, 24.
41. PVGPT, August 28, 1900, 20; August 30, 1900, 21–22; March 18, 1901, 154; April 26, 1901, 195; March 25, 1901, 160.

42. PVGPT, September 4, 1901, 310; January 14, 1901, 90; December 24, 1900, 73; rapport du colonel Bower, April 13, 1901, 179; February 28, 1902, 458; May 4, 1901, 206; letter from the magistrate of Shun Tien Fu in response to the request of the Council concerning the protection of merchants from Sheng Fang (February 14, 1902, 448).
43. PVGPT, August 21, 1900, 15; August 27, 1900, 18; November 28, 1900, 56.
44. Quentin Deluermoz and Jérémie Foa, eds., *Usurpations de fonction et appropriations du pouvoir en situation de crise (xixe–xxe siècle)* (proceedings of a workshop on January 16, 2010, Centre d'histoire du XIXe siècle, 2012), 9.
45. PVGPT, November 7, 1900, SHD, 11H39, 8; letter from General Mei, November 16, 1900, SHD, 11H39, 14; petition from the notables of Wang chia kou, November 20, 1900, SHD, 11H39, 18; November 22, 1900, SHD, 11H39, 23; December 28, 1900, 76.
46. PVGPT, May 9, 1901, 176; May 13, 1901, 179; letter from *daotai* Chang to the Provisional Government Council, December 13, 1901, 403; May 1, 1901, 201; May 4, 1901, 206; June 14, 1901, 237; June 18, 1902, 554; September 21, 1901, 326; July 18, 1902, 585.
47. PVGPT, December 20, 1900, 71; December 28, 1900, 76; letter from the British Consul General to the Provisional Government Council, April 16, 1901, PVGPT, April 17, 1901, 185; April 19, 1901, 189. Counterfeit dollars continued to circulate, as evidenced by the arrest of Lin San and Lin Shun Ho, two merchants who attempted to smuggle fake dollars into the city (December 27, 1901, 413).
48. PVGPT, December 5, 1900, 61; February 13, 1901, 125; February 27, 1901, 138; March 6, 1901, 147; April 15, 1901, 182; letter from the French consul to the Provisional Government Council, April 17, 1901, PVGPT, April 22, 1901, 190; April 22, 1901, 190; letter from Marshal von Waldersee to the French Minister in Peking, PVGPT, May 3, 1901, 203; May 4, 1901, 204.
49. PVGPT, December 3, 1900, 59; report by the head of the North Tientsin district, April 10, 1901, PVGPT, April 11, 1901, 179. A gang of counterfeiters was also arrested in South Tientsin District in December 1901 (December 4, 1901, 394) and two counterfeiters in the North Tientsin district (July 30, 1902, 597) and Chinese notables from Cheng Li Chuang village in North Tientsin district, involved in counterfeit money trafficking (March 24, 1902, 476); April 13, 1901, 181; report from Captain Carrère, PVGPT, April 17, 1901, 186; May 4, 1901, 205; March 14, 1902, March 21, 1902, 473–74; May 14, 1902, 518. At the same time, the government banned money changers from the city's streets (April 14, 1902, 496).
50. Report from Charles Tenney, PVGPT, April 25, 1902, 503–4; PVGPT, July 12, 1901, 260; letter from "indigenous banks" to the Council of the Provisional Government, PVGPT, September 6, 1901, 312. The increase in

the value of the dollar in 1902 posed a problem for the government treasurer, who complained that it was difficult to obtain "large numbers" of dollars (July 18, 1902, 584); September 9, 1901, 314; September 18, 1901, 322; February 3, 1902, 440; March 7, 1902, 464; report from the Treasurer to the Provisional Government, PVGPT, March 29, 1902, 482; May 18, 1902, 497.

51. PVGPT, December 28, 1900, 76; January 14, 1901, 91; May 8, 1901, 208; May 20, 1901, 217; May 24, 1901, 221; March 14, 1902, 467; May 14, 1902, 518; December 18, 1901, 407; February 19, 1902, 452; translation of the letter from *daotai* Chang, PVGPT, June 16, 1902, 552.
52. Boris Gobille, "Usurpation de fonction et appropriation du pouvoir selon différents types de situations de crise: Éléments de discussion," in Deluermoz and Foa, *Usurpations de fonction*, 75.
53. François Thierry, "Fausses dates et vraies monnaies: Rites, information, propagande et histoire dans la numismatique chinoise," *Extrême-Orient, Extrême-Occident* 32 (2010): 41–60. In China, money itself cannot be fake or genuine: the issuer is legitimate or not, and what Westerners call fake money, *si zhu* ("private money"), is opposed to *guan zhu* ("official money").
54. Emmanuel Poisson, "Faux, falsification, pouvoir et société," *Extrême-Orient, Extrême-Occident* 32 (2010): 5–6.
55. PVGPT, 06/02/1901, 111.
56. "The Fighting at Tientsin," *Star*, 4; Régis Voyron, *Rapport sur l'expédition de Chine, 1900–1901* (Paris: Henri Charles-Lavauzelle, 1904), 41; Raoul Charles Villetard de Laguérie, "Tien-Tsin après la défaite des Boxeurs (Voyage exécuté en 1900)," *Le tour du monde: Nouveau journal des voyages* 7, no. 41 (October 12, 1901): 492; PVGPT, November 22, 1900, SHD, 11H39, 22.
57. PVGPT, August 31, 1900, 22; July 30, 1900, 4; September 8, 1900, 27; report of Major von Falkenhayn, PVGPT, November 20, 1901, 382; April 17, 1901, 185. Chinese people, who disrupted traffic, engaged in unseemly behavior in public, or violated public hygiene in the streets of the city could be sentenced to up to twenty-five lashings. Traffic regulations in Tientsin, PVGPT, April 3, 1901, 171; April 22, 1901, 191; August 16, 1901, 293; April 19, 1901, 188; January 6, 1902, 422; September 4, 1900, 24; August 9, 1901, 285; report of the Treasurer, PVGPT, March 20, 1901, 157; PVGPT, March 6, 1901, 149; July 8, 1901, 257; July 29, 1901, 275; report of chef of North Tientsin, April 30, 1902, 507.
58. PVGPT, July 30, 1900, 3; August 8, 1900, 8; January 7, 1901, 84; January 10, 1901, 86; report from head of the district of Chunliangcheng, PVGPT, April 1, 1901, 168; August 9, 1900, 9; August 10, 1900, 10; September 10, 1900, 28; reports from Colonel Woronow and Captain Petroff, PVGPT, January 4, 1901, 80; January 10, 1901, 85; January 14, 1901, 91; reduction of

Japanese police corps effective March 1, PVGPT, February 20, 1901, 130; May 13, 1901, 210.

59. A junk is distinguished by its compartmentalized hull and its sails stretched by bamboo slats. PVGPT, October 10, 1900, 47; October 29, 1900, SHD, 11H39, 3; November 9, 1900, SHD, 11H39, 11; June 17, 1901, 239.
60. Otto D. Rasmussen, *Tientsin: An Illustrated Outline History* (Tientsin: The Tientsin Press, 1925), 228.
61. This fourth post was created in December 1901 (PVGPT, December 13, 1901, 403); regulation of "river police," PVGPT, August 12, 1901, 289; February 28, 1902, 460; February 28, 1902, 460; December 9, 1901, 399; February 8, 1901, 116.
62. PVGPT, August 9, 1900, 9; August 10, 1900, 10; August 12, 1900, 12; February 8, 1901, 117; August 30, 1900, 21; February 8, 1901, 117. The bureau chiefs regularly requested Mausers, but with no success (March 6, 1901, 149).
63. PVGPT, February 8, 1901, 118.
64. Report of the chief of police, PVGPT, April 18, 1902, 497; March 21, 1902, 474; April 28, 1902, 505.
65. PVGPT, July 16, 1901, 272; health service report on "special agent" Sho Chok Hing, PVGPT, October 7, 1901, 339; July 29, 1901, 277; Ke, "Nongovernmental Organizations," 66; PVGPT, February 3, 1902, 440.
66. Report by the police chief, PVGPT, April 18, 1902, 497; March 21, 1902, 474; April 28, 1902, 505.
67. PVGPT, January 2, 1901, 79; November 7, 1900, SHD, 11H39, 8; November 19, 1900, SHD, 11H39, 16; report from the Chinese secretary, PVGPT, August 9, 1901, 285; April 3, 1901, 171. For example, the police chief employed a "secret agent," who was closely monitored by his superiors, at a salary of $60 per month (PVGPT, October 2, 1901, 334).
68. Conseil du gouvernement provisoire, *Règlements du gouvernement provisoire*, 2; PVGPT, October 9, 1901, 341; October 18, 1901, 350; December 2, 1901, 392.
69. PVGPT, July 5, 1901, 256; October 11, 1901, 343; report by Major Ducat, PVGPT, May 4, 1901, 205; April 15, 1901, 182; April 17, 1901, 186.
70. PVGPT, July 5, 1901, 256; October 11, 1901, 343; report by Major Ducat, PVGPT, May 4, 1901, 205; April 15, 1901, 182; April 17, 1901, 186.
71. PVGPT, November 7, 1900, SHD, 11H39, 9; November 19, 1900, SHD, 11H39, 16; PVGPT, August 30, 1901, 305; October 9, 1901, August 21, 1901, 298; August 30, 1901, 305 (the chief of Chunliangcheng built a "large permanent prison" there at a cost of $1,000); February 8, 1901, 119; March 6, 1901, 150.
72. Pierre-Étienne Will, "Science et sublimation de l'État," *Actes de la recherche en sciences sociales* 133 (June 2000): 20.
73. General Chaffee, quoted by George Lynch, *The War of Civilizations* (London: Longmans, 1901), 84.

74. PVGPT, July 28, 1902, 594; December 18, 1901, 407; Timothy Brook, Jérôme Bourgon, and Gregory Blue, *Death by a Thousand Cuts* (Cambridge, MA: Harvard University Press, 2008); PVGPT, August 29, 1900, 20; report by G. Lealand Frantzmann, deputy to the Head of the Secretariat, PVGPT, August 17, 1901, 265.
75. Thiriez, *Barbarian Lens*.
76. PVGPT, September 2, 1901, 307; September 21, 1901, 324; December 7, 1900, 62; December 14, 1900, 66.
77. Proclamation of the Council of the Provisional Government, PVGPT, May 10, 1901, 209; January 15, 1902, 427; April 15, 1901, 183; June 28, 1901, 248; June 28, 1901, 249; August 19, 1901, 294; December 27, 1901, 413; June 26, 1901, 281; June 2, 1901, 247; affairs "Wu San et Chang Fu" January 25, " Li Te Fu " of January 31, and "Chang Tao et Lin Lao" of January 27, PVGPT, February 3, 1902, 442; March 27, 1901, 162.
78. PVGPT, July 22, 1901, 268; report of the head of judicial service, PVGPT, February 3, 1902, 441; PVGPT, September 4, 1901, 309 (the investigation carried out by Major von Falkenhayn does not seem to have been successful); report of the Chief of Police and decision of the Provisional Government Council, PVGPT, August 2, 1901, 279; PVGPT, May 26, 1902, 528.
79. Report by the Chief of Police, PVGPT, January 26, 1901, 101; September 25, 1901, 329.
80. PVGPT, February 12, 1902, 447; January 22, 1902, 431; February 4, 1902, 438; report of the head of the district of Chunliangcheng, PVGPT, December 27, 1901, 413; February 7, 1902,444; December 2, 1901, 390; December 4, 1901, 393; report of the head of the district of Tongku, August 6, 1902,613.
81. Rapport of the Chief of Police, PVGPT, June 1, 1901,243; July 29, 1901, 277.
82. PVGPT, January 6, 1902, 420–21; report of the Head of the Judicial Service, PVGPT, June 2, 1902, 533; June 4, 1902, 537; April 21, 1902, 499; affaire "Li San," district of South Tianjin, PVGPT, April 28, 1902, 505; report of the Head of the District of South Tianjin, PVGPT, May 23, 1902, 525; report of the Head of the Judicial Service, PVGPT, June 13, 1902, 548; July 21, 1902, 588; rapport of the magistrate, PVGPT, February 3, 1902, 441; June 30, 1902, 567; Letter from Butterfield & Swire, PVGPT, June 4, 1902, 536.
83. PVGPT, November 27, 1901, 386. PVGPT, 319th session, July 23, 1902, p. 589; report of the magistrate, PVGPT, 310th session, June 30, 1902, 566.
84. PVGPT, October 14, 1901, 345; November 4, 1901, 369–70; November 27, 1901, 386; report of the Head of River Police, PVGPT, July 18, 1901, 266; August 19, 1901, 295; May 2, 1902, 508; report of the Head of the North Tianjin district, PVGPT, May 31, 1901, 225; June 7, 1901, 232; June 17, 1901, 239; December 16, 1901, 406; rapport no. 223 of the Chief of Police,

August 7, 1901, 284; report of the Chief of Police on agent no. 392, PVGPT, December 23, 1901, 411; February 14, 1902, 449; June 2, 1902, 533; October 16, 1901, 347.

85. PVGPT, August 7, 1901, 284; report of Major Ducat, PVGPT, September 21, 1901, 325; December 20, 1901, 409; report of the Head of the North Tianjin District, May 26, 1902, 528; May 28, 1902, 530; August 6, 1902, 612.
86. PVGPT, August 7, 1901, 284; report of Major Ducat, PVGPT, September 21, 1901, 325; December 20, 1901, 409; report of the Head of the North Tianjin District, May 26, 1902, 528; May 28, 1902, 530; August 6, 1902, 612.
87. Grandin, "Mes exploits," 397.
88. PVGPT, March 20, 1901, 156; April 11, 1901, 178; April 19, 1901, 188; May 31, 1901, 224; June 7, 1901, 230.
89. PVGPT, October 14, 1901, 346.
90. "Since the troubles of 1900, material life has improved considerably and as a consequence the indigenous salaries have undergone an increase of 50 to 60%," letter from the French Consul Henri Leduc to the Minister of Foreign Affairs, January 7, 1904, CADN, 691 PO / 1 "Tientsin consulat," 291.
91. PVGPT, August 21, 1900, 15; report from the engineer of the River Commission, PVGPT, December 18, 1901, 406; December 23, 1901, 411.
92. PVGPT, August 22, 1900, 17; August 30, 1900, 22; September 18, 1901, 322; report of the Chinese secretary, PVGPT, October 2, 1901, 334; October 16, 1901, 348; October 25, 1901, 357; February 7, 1902, 445.
93. PVGPT, January 20, 1902, 428; January 22, 1902, 431; report to the Chinese secretary, PVGPT, February 3, 1902, 441; February 12, 1902, 447; February 4, 1902, 439; February 17, 1902, 450; report to the head of the Health Service, PVGPT, February 10, 1902, 446; March 24, 1902, 475; March 26, 1902, 478; February 14, 1902, 448; May 28, 1902, 529.
94. Conseil du gouvernement provisoire, *Règlements du gouvernement provisoire*, 1.
95. Pierre-Étienne Will, "Ingénieurs, philanthropes et seigneurs de la guerre dans la Chine républicaine, 1911–1935," Annuaire du Collège de France (2007–2008), 706–7; see also the role of Tianjin in the struggle against the famine of 1744–45. Pierre-Étienne Will, *Bureaucratie et famine en Chine au xviiie siècle* (Paris: Éditions de l'EHESS-Mouton, 1980).
96. Hosea B. Morse, *The International Relations of the Chinese Empire* (New York: Longmans, 1918), 3:295; PVGPT, August 4, 1900, 6; September 19, 1900, 36; PVGPT, November 2, 1900, SHD, 11H39, 5.
97. PVGPT, August 6, 1900, 7; August 10, 1900, 10; September 4, 1901, 311; report of the Chinese secretary, PVGPT, September 11, 1901, 317; report of the Treasurer, PVGPT, August 13, 1900, 11; October 4, 1900, 42; August 29, 1900, 20.

98. Pierre-Étienne Will, "Ingénieurs, philanthropes et seigneurs de la guerre dans la Chine républicaine, 1911–1935," *Annuaire du Collège de France, 2007–2008*, 705–6; report of the Chinese secretary, PVGPT, October 24, 1900, 55.
99. Report of the head of the Health Service, PVGPT, November 16, 1900, SHD, 11H39, 14; report of the Chinese secretary, November 20, 1900, SHD, 11H39, 18; Report of the head of the Health Service, November 24, 1900, 24; November 19, 1900, SHD, 11H39, 16; petition of the Chinese Charitable Association, December 20, 1900, 70; report of the Chinese secretary, February 13, 1901, 126; report of the Chinese secretary, April 17, 1901, 187.
100. PVGPT, November 8, 1901, 372; report of Colonel Harada, December 6, 1901, 397; December 11, 1901, 401; December 18, 1901, 408; December 23, 1901, 411.
101. PVGPT, March 25, 1901, 159; report of the head of the Tongku district, January 3, 1902, 417; report of Chief of Police, February 4, 1902, 438; report of Chief of Police, February 5, 1902, 440; February 7, 1902, 444; February 5, 1902, 440; report of Chinese secretary, February 7, 1902, 444.
102. Mariya Tait Slys, *Exporting Legality: The Rise and Fall of Extraterritorial Jurisdiction in the Ottoman Empire and China* (Geneva: eCahiers de l'Institut, The Graduate Institute, February 2014); Zhaojie and James, "Traditional Chinese World Order," 37; Lillian M. Li and Alison Dray-Novey, "Guarding Beijing's Food Security in the Qing Dynasty: State, Market, and Police Source," *Journal of Asian Studies* 58, no. 4 (November 1999): 992–1032.
103. Report of Major Ducat, PVGPT, September 11, 1901, 316.
104. Grandin, "Mes exploits," 407.

4. Regional Planning

1. Philippe Boulanger, "Les espaces coloniaux dans la géographie militaire française (1871–1939)," in *L'empire des géographes: Géographie, exploration et colonisation (xixe–xxe s.)*, ed. Pierre Singaravélou (Paris: Belin, 2008), 135–46.
2. PVGPT, August 10, 1900, 10; September 6, 1900, 26; March 13, 1901, 149; March 18, 1901,154; August 30, 1900, 21; October 10, 1900, 46; December 26, 1900, 74; February 8, 1901, 114; October 21, 1901, 352; April 9, 1901, 175; March 19, 1902, 471; April 30, 1902, 507.
3. Noah Fields Drake, *Map and Short Description of Tientsin* (Tianjin: n.p., 1900), 9–10.
4. PVGPT, January 14, 1901, 91; July 5, 1901, 255; March 18, 1901, 154; March 18, 1901, 155.

5. Raoul Charles Villetard de Laguérie, "En Chine: La physionomie de Tien-Tsin," *L'Illustration*, December 15, 1900, 382.
6. Jean-Marc Besse, "Catoptique: Vue à vol d'oiseau et construction géométrique" (communication for the workshop "La Vue aérienne: savoirs et pratiques de l'espace," CNRS-British Academy, Paris, June 9, 2007). This is unless Feng Qihuang was able to observe the city from the sky, because Tianjin was the first city in China over which a hydrogen balloon flew, made in 1887 by mathematician Hua Hengfang, a professor at the city's military academy.
7. Villetard de Laguérie, "En Chine," 483.
8. Ruth Rogaski, *Hygienic Modernity: Meanings of Health and Disease in Treaty-Port China* (Berkeley: University of California Press, 2004), 184.
9. A.-A. Fauvel, "Le chemin de fer de Peking à Nieou-Tchouang," *Annales de géographie* 9, no. 46 (1900): 374.
10. E. J. M. Rhoads, *Stepping Forth Into the World: The Chinese Educational Mission to the United States, 1872–1881* (Hong Kong: Hong Kong University Press, 2011), 198; Jacques Grandin, "Mes exploits pendant la guerre de Chine de 1901 (Journal d'un volontaire)," *La revue des revues* 61 (May 1–15, 1902): 274.
11. Susan Naquin, *Peking: Temples and City Life, 1400–1900* (Berkeley: University of California Press, 2000).
12. Cordell D. K. Yee, "Traditional Chinese Cartography and the Myth of Westernization," in *The History of Cartography*, vol. 2, book 2: *Cartography in the Traditional East and Southeast Asian Societies*, ed. J. B. Harley and David Woodward (Chicago: University of Chicago Press, 1994), 195.
13. The ellipsoid is projected onto a cone tangent to an ellipse or to two ellipses. The cone is then unrolled to obtain the map.
14. Zhang Zhidong, *Zhang Wenxiang gong quanii* (Complete Works of the Honorable Zhang Wenxiang, 1928) (Taipei: Wenhai Chubanshe, 1970), 31.
15. Li Xiaocong, *A Descriptive Catalogue of Pre-1900 Chinese Maps Seen in Europe* (Beijing: International Culture Publishing Corporation, 1996).
16. Conseil du gouvernement provisoire, *Règlements du gouvernement provisoire du district de Tientsin*, Harvard Widener Library, 1.
17. PVGPT, October 26, 1900, SHD, 11H39, 2; March 20, 1901, 156; December 10, 1900,64; November 22, 1900, SHD, 11H39, 23; January 4, 1901, 80; November 22, 1900, SHD, 11H39, 22; April 29, 1901, 198; July 30, 1902, 598; July 30, 1902, 598; August 4, 1902, 609; August 8, 1902, 615; August 11, 1902, 622; July 21, 1902, 585; January 7, 1901, 85; February 25, 1901, 135; December 2, 1901, 392; January 28, 1901, 104; June 7, 1901, 331.
18. The British administration adhered to this registration procedure and requested the government's assistance in registering Chinese land outside the concession. PVGPT, August 28, 1901, 303.

19. PVGPT, December 28, 1900, 76; April 15, 1901, 183; July 29, 1901, 277; December 27, 1901, 412; August 5, 1901, 282; January 20, 1902, 429; November 11, 1901, 373; December 2, 1901, 391; December 2, 1901, 391; December 27, 1901, 412; January 3, 1902, 416; January 15, 1902, 426; May 17, 1901, 215.
20. PVGPT, December 2, 1901, 392; January 27, 1902, 435; July 21, 1902, 588.
21. PVGPT, March 25, 1901, 160; the annual rent was 5 percent of the approximate value of the land, estimated at 2,400 taels, which is to say 120 taels per year. PVGPT, July 16, 1902, 580; July 23, 1902, 590; May 13, 1901, 180; August 8, 1902, 618.
22. Bin Li, "La protection de la propriété en Chine: Transformation du droit interne et influence du droit international" (PhD diss., University Paris 1 Panthéon-Sorbonne, 2009), 8.
23. Pierre Hoang, *Notions juridiques sur la propriété en Chine* (Shanghai: Imprimerie de la Mission Catholique, 1897), 22.
24. Drake, *Map and Short Description.*
25. PVGPT, February 4, 1901, 109; February 7, 1902, 444; February 12, 1902, 447; March 21, 1902, 474; March 12, 1902, 466; March 7, 1902, 464.
26. Lewis Bernstein, "A History of Tientsin in Early Modern Times, 1800–1910" (PhD diss., University of Kansas, 1988); Rogaski, *Hygienic Modernity*, 54.
27. PVGPT, April 23, 1902, 501; July 28, 1902, 595; May 5, 1902, 510. The chief of police proposed as early as April 1901 to give names to the city streets, April 9, 1901, 176; May 7, 1902, 512; May 12, 1902, 516; May 21, 1902, 521; June 4, 1902, 536; July 16, 1902, 582; July 21, 1902, 588; August 4, 1902, 608.
28. PVGPT, November 26, 1900, SHD, 11H39, 27.
29. Otto D. Rasmussen, *Tientsin: An Illustrated Outline History* (Tientsin: The Tientsin Press, 1925), 227.
30. "La ville actuelle de Tien-Tsin et l'oeuvre du gouvernement militaire provisoire," *À travers le monde* 1904, 366.
31. Miss G. M. Rees, *Tientsin Early History* (Tientsin: The Tientsin Press, n.d.): 3–4.
32. Jean-Luc Pinol and François Walter, *La ville contemporaine jusqu'à la seconde guerre mondiale* (Paris: Seuil, 2003), 24. See also Xavier Huetz de Lemps, " 'À bas les murailles!' Le débat sur le dérasement des fortifications dans les villes espagnoles (xixe–début xxe siècle)," in *Les passions d'un historien: Mélanges en l'honneur de Jean-Pierre Poussou*, ed. Reynald Abad, Jean-Pierre Bardet, Jean-François Dunyach, and François-Joseph Ruggiu (Paris: Presses de l'Université de Paris-Sorbonne, 2010), 1105–14; PVGPT, December 20, 1900, 71; December 28, 1900, 75; April 29, 1901, 199.
33. PVGPT, November 26, 1900, SHD, 11H39, 27.

34. Jonathan Spence, *The Search for Modern China* (New York: W. W. Norton, 1991).
35. J. M. Grierson, colonel, vice-adjudant général, au sous-secrétaire d'État à la guerre, doc. secret no. 41, Beijing, April 6, 1901, NA, WO 32/6148.
36. Rasmussen, *Tientsin*, 227.
37. PVGPT, November 27, 1901, 387; July 22, 1901, 268; November 27, 1901, 387; July 29, 1901, 275; August 7, 1901, 283; October 9, 1901, 340; November 11, 1901, 373; October 16, 1901, 348; October 11, 1901, 342; October 25, 1901, 356; April 25, 1902, 502; July 25, 1902, 591.
38. The international administration of a river was not a new phenomenon, since the first international organization, the Central Commission for the Navigation of the Rhine, was founded in 1815.
39. PVGPT, January 22, 1901, 96; February 1, 1901, 107; February 18, 1901, 130; February 11, 1901, 123; February 16, 1901, 129; March 15, 1901, 152; March 18, 1901, 153; March 25, 1901, 159; May 3, 1901, 202; May 10, 1901, 208; June 12, 1901, 336; April 9, 1901, 174; May 22, 1901, 219; July 7, 1902, 489; June 30, 1902, 564–65; April 18, 1902, 497; May 23, 1902, 523; June 13, 1902, 546; June 30, 1902, 565; July 7, 1902, 572; Rasmussen, *Tientsin*, 228;
40. PVGPT, April, 15, 1901, 183; April 19, 1901, 189; April 22, 1901, 191; April 29, 1901, 198; May 3, 1901, 203; around July 10, 1901, 259; June 6, 1902, 540; June 26, 1901, 282; July 30, 1902, 598; August 30, 1901, 306.
41. PVGPT, May 16, 1902, 519; PVGPT, May 7, 1902, 489; July 28, 1902, 593; April 24, 1901, 193; August 1, 1902, 599; August 4, 1902, 609; June 6, 1902, 539.
42. Luca Gabbiani, "À la recherche du lustre d'antan: La réhabilitation de la voirie de Pékin pendant la première décennie du xxe siècle," *Études chinoises* 23 (2004): 181–271.
43. Rasmussen, *Tientsin*, 226; PVGPT, April 17, 1901, 186; August 21, 1901, 298; December 7, 1900, 63; November 22, 1901, 383; August 7, 1901, 283; August 12, 1901, 287; September 4, 1901, 308.
44. PVGPT, April 15, 1901, 212; May 24, 1901, 220; May 27, 1901, 223; September 4, 1901, 311; September 6, 1901, 312; November 29, 1901, 388; December 6, 1901, 395–96; January 20, 1902, 428; letter from Theodore Delcassé, Minister of Foreign Affairs to Mr. Pichon, Minister of the French Republic to Peking, December 1, 1900, MAE, P 19231, Politique étrangère, "Concession de Tien-Tsin"; PVGPT, February 21, 1902, 453; March 7, 1902, 464; March 7, 1902, 464; March 10, 1902, 465; March 21, 1902, 474; March 26, 1902, 476; around March 28, 1902, 479; April 14, 1902, 495; April 18, 1902, 497; May 2, 1902, 508; June 23, 1902, 559; June 25, 1902, 560; June 11, 1902, 546.

45. PVGPT, November 22, 1900, SHD, 11H39, 22; August 23, 1901, 300; May 5, 1902, 510; February 24, 1902, 455; March 14, 1902, 468; around March 28, 1902, 479–80.
46. Raoul Charles Villetard de Laguérie, "Tien-Tsin après la défaite des Boxeurs (Voyage exécuté en 1900)," *Le tour du monde: Nouveau journal des voyages* 7, no. 41 (October 12, 1901): 488.
47. PVGPT, September 26, 1900, 39; January 23, 1901, 98; February 4, 1901, 108; December 13, 1901, 402; December 18, 1901, 408.
48. Rasmussen, *Tientsin*, 226.
49. PVGPT, June 12, 1901, 234; June 1, 1901, 243; June 24, 1901, 244; June 26, 1901, 246; July 1, 1901, 251; July 12, 1901, 261; July 17, 1901, 262; April 23, 1902, 501; August 11, 1902, 623; August 19, 1901, 296.
50. PVGPT, August 6, 1900, 7; August 8, 1900, 7; November 30, 1900, 57; December 3, 1900, 58; January 2, 1901, 79; May 27, 1901, 221; May 31, 1901, 225; June 12, 1901, 234; July 12, 1901, 262; around November 2, 1901, 364–67; June 19, 1901, 240; July 1, 1901, 253; June 19, 1901, 240.
51. Letter from Gustave du Chaylard to Théodore Delcassé, Minister of Foreign Affairs Affaires, June 13, 1902, MAE, P 19231, Politique étrangère, "Concession de Tien Tsin."
52. Registered letter of the commander Baesens (Belgian army) to Théodore Delcassé, Minister of Foreign Affairs, May 28, 1902, MAE, P 19231, Politique étrangère, "Concession de Tien Tsin."
53. Roland Dussart-Desart, *Les tramways de Tientsin: Un réseau sous six drapeaux* (Brussels: Tramania, 2017).
54. PVGPT, July 25, 1902, 591; July 28, 1902, 593.
55. Kwan Man Bun, *The Salt Merchants of Tianjin: State-Making and Civil Society in Late Imperial China* (Honolulu: University of Hawaii Press, 2001), 113.
56. PVGPT, August 30, 1901, 305; September 4, 1901, 308; September 4, 1901, 309; November 18, 1901, 379; April 30, 1902, 506; June 25, 1902, 561; July 2, 1902, 569.
57. The statement "war is waged by telegraph" is from Jules Claretie in 1883 in his appended commentary to the edition of Jules Verne, *Les tribulations d'un chinois en Chine* (Paris: Arvensa Éditions, [1883] 2014), 191. On the first telegraph in China, see Erik Baark, *Lightning Wires: The Telegraph and China's Technological Modernization, 1860–1890* (Westport, CT: Greenwood Press, 1997).
58. PVGPT, around March 28, 1902, 479; February 13, 1901, 126; February 15, 1901, 128; February 22, 1901, 131; May 22, 1901, 218; May 24, 1901, 221; September 2, 1901, 306; December 18, 1901, 407; August 8, 1902, 613.
59. PVGPT, October 15, 1900, 50; March 18, 1901, 153; March 6, 1901, 147; March 20, 1901, 156; March 27, 1901, 161; March 27, 1901, 162; March 25, 1901, 159; March 29, 1901, 164; April 1, 1901, 166.

60. PVGPT, April 9, 1901, 174; April 17, 1901, 184; April 17, 1901, 186; July 18, 1901, 265; August 19, 1901, 294; September 21, 1901, 323; April 1, 1901, 167; April 3, 1901, 170; January 20, 1902, 429.
61. PVGPT, April 11, 1901, 178; April 13, 1901, 180; April 15, 1901, 183; May 13, 1901, 211; May 20, 1901, 216; January 28, 1902, 437; April 22, 1901, 192; July 16, 1901, 271; March 24, 1902, 475; August 19, 1901, 295; March 10, 1902, 465; September 9, 1901, 314–15; September 27, 1901, 331; March 24, 1902, 475; report from the Japanese Captain Satō on May 14, PVGPT, May 17, 1901, 214; August 2, 1901, 279; "26 juin" (in fact August 6, 1901), 280; August 21, 1901, 297.
62. Rapport from Colonel Bower, PVGPT, May 17, 1901, 214.
63. PVGPT, April 9, 1901, 174; January 22, 1902, 431; July 16, 1902, 581; July 3, 1901, 255; August 2, 1901, 278.
64. PVGPT, June 6, 1902, 538.
65. Pierre-Yves Saunier and Shane Ewen, eds., *Another Global City: Historical Explorations Into the Transnational Municipal Moment 1850–2000* (New York: Palgrave Macmillan, 2008).
66. Gabbiani, "À la recherche du lustre d'antan," 181–271.
67. PVGPT, June 24, 1901, 245; October 2, 1901, 335; January 11, 1901, 89; April 22, 1901, 191; August 21, 1901, 298; October 16, 1901, 348.
68. Letter from Jules Jadot to his wife, Tianjin, September 24, 1900, transcribed in Ginette Kurgan-Van Hentenryk, *Jean Jadot: Artisan de l'expansion belge en Chine* (Brussels: Académie Royale des Sciences d'Outre-mer, 1965).

5. A Revolution in Hygiene?

1. Alexis Daoulas, *Le siège de Tien-Tsin (15 juin–15 juillet 1900)* (Paris: Berger-Levrault, 1903), 87; Brian Power *The Ford of Heaven: A Cosmopolitan Childhood in Tientsin* (Oxford: Signal Books, 2005), 52.
2. Conseil du gouvernement provisoire, *Règlements du gouvernement provisoire du district de Tientsin*, Harvard Widener Library,1.
3. Patrice Bourdelais, ed., *Les hygiénistes: Enjeux, modèles et pratiques, xviiie–xxe siècles* (Paris: Belin, 2001); Jean-Luc Pinol and François Walter, *La ville contemporaine jusqu'à la seconde guerre mondiale* (Paris: Seuil, 2003), 173–74.
4. Patrice Bourdelais and Jean-Yves Raulot, *Une peur bleue: Histoire du choléra en France 1832–1854* (Paris: Payot, 1987); Philippe Chemouilli, "Le choléra et la naissance de la santé publique dans le Japon de Meiji. 1. Modernité, choléra et pensée hygiénique," *Médecine sciences* 20, no. 1 (January 2004): 109–14; Valeska Huber, "The Unification of the Globe by Disease? The

International Sanitary Conference on Cholera, 1851–1894," *Historical Journal* 49, no. 2 (June 2006): 454–74; Thibault Weitzel, *Le fléau invisible: La dernière épidémie de choléra en France* (Paris: Vendémiaire, 2011); Céline Paillette, "Épidémies, santé et ordre mondial: Le rôle des organisations sanitaires internationales, 1903–1923," *Monde(s): Histoire, Espaces, Relations* 2, no. 2 (November 2012).

5. Edward J. M. Rhoads, *Stepping Forth Into the World: The Chinese Educational Mission to the United States, 1872–1881* (Hong Kong: Hong Kong University Press, 2011), 199.
6. In her excellent book, Ruth Rogaski nonetheless focuses primarily on the Japanese and thus underestimates the importance of French military doctors (Depasse, Houillon, Mesny, etc.) and Chinese elites in developing a global approach to health policy during the period 1900–1902. Ruth Rogaski, *Hygienic Modernity: Meanings of Health and Disease in Treaty-Port China* (Berkeley: University of California Press, 2004).
7. James Ricalton, *China Through the Stereoscope* (New York: Underwood & Underwood, 1901), 234.
8. Raoul Charles Villetard de Laguérie, "En Chine: La physionomie de Tien-Tsin," *L'illustration*, December 15, 1900, 382.
9. Bass, "The Sack of Tien-Tsin was a Scene of Shame."
10. Rogaski, *Hygienic Modernity*, 174.
11. PVGPT, October 24, 1900, SHD, 11H39; December 20, 1900, 71.
12. Zhu Renxun, *Wenjian lu*, entry GX 28/5/19 (June 24, 1902), cited in Rogaski, *Hygienic Modernity*, 175.
13. Lewis Bernstein, "A History of Tientsin in Early Modern Times, 1800–1910" (PhD diss., University of Kansas, 1988).
14. PVGPT, November 7, 1900, SHD, 11H39, 8; June 14, 1901, 238; April 5, 1901, 173; April 22, 1901, 190; April 24, 1901, 193; April 26, 1901, 195; letter from the chief of staff of the German troops to the Council of the Provisional Government, July 3, 1901, 253; May 1, 1901, 201; December 16, 1901, 405; January 6, 1902, 423; January 20, 1902, 428.
15. Letter from Dr. Weinbaum, divisional physician of the Russian Expeditionary Corps, to the Provisional Government Council, October 5, 1900, PVGPT, October 22, 1900, 53.
16. PVGPT, March 4, 1901, 143; May 10, 1901, 209; September 2, 1901, 307; September 11, 1901,316; June 7, 1901, 231; June 5, 1901, 229; June 19, 1901, 241; June 6, 1902, 539.
17. Richard Grove, *Green Imperialism: Colonial Expansion, Tropical Island Edens and the Origins of Environmentalism, 1600–1860* (Cambridge: Cambridge University Press, 1995).

18. PVGPT, April 24, 1901, 194; April 29, 1901, 197; May 1, 1901, 200; September 16, 1901, 320; letter from the Tientsin Race Club to the Council of the Provisional Government, June 30, 1902, 565; October 11, 1901, 343.
19. Jacques Grandin, "Mes exploits pendant la guerre de Chine de 1901 (Journal d'un volontaire)," *La revue des revues* 61 (May 1–15, 1902): 275; Delphine Spicq, *L'avènement de l'eau courante à Tianjin (1900–1949)* (Saarbrücken: Éditions Universitaires Européennes, 2012), 7.
20. Villetard de Laguérie, "En Chine," 382.
21. PVGPT, 16/11/00 (p. 14), 19/11/00 (p. 16), 24/11/00 (p. 25), SHD, 11H39; report from the Doctor Morgenroth, to the Chief of Staff of the German troops, 12/07/1901, 260.
22. Spicq, *L'avènement de l'eau courante*, 52.
23. PVGPT, March 6, 1901, 144, 150; March 15, 1901, 152; September 21, 1901, 325; January 15, 1902, 424.
24. PVGPT, April 3, 1901, 171; April 13, 1901, 181; April 17, 1901, 187; April 15, 1901, 182; May 27, 1901, 223; August 12, 1901, 288; June 19, 1901, 241; August 21, 1901, 298; rapport from Colonel Arlabosse, April 24, 1901, 194; May 5, 1902, 510.
25. PVGPT, March 29, 1901, 164; April 22, 1901, 191; May 27, 1901, 223; July 8, 1901, 258; letter from the Consul General of Japan to the Provisional Government Council, May 9, 1902, 512; rapport from Captain Jullian presented to the Council of the Provisional Government, March 7, 1902, 464; April 7, 1902, 489; April 14, 1902, 495; May 2, 1902, 509; June 25, 1902, 561; June 30, 1902, 566; July 16, 1902, 583; July 21, 1902, 585–87; June 11, 1902, 545; June 13, 1902, 548; June 16, 1902, 552; letter from Colonel O'Sullivan to the Council of the Provisional Government, August 6, 1902, 610; August 8, 1902, 613.
26. Warwick Anderson, "Excremental Colonialism: Public Health and the Poetics of Pollution," *Critical Inquiry* 21, no. 3 (Spring 1995): 640–69.
27. PVGPT, April 26, 1901, 196; April 17, 1901, 186.
28. Zhu Renxun, *Wenjian lu*, entries GX 28/4/24 (May 10, 1902) et GX 28/5/22 (June 27, 1902), cited in Rogaski, *Hygienic Modernity*, 177n36; PVGPT, May 23, 1902, 525.
29. Rogaski, *Hygienic Modernity*, 174.
30. PVGPT, April 1, 1901, 168; February 25, 1901, 134–35; May 17, 1901, 215; May 22, 1901, 218; May 24, 1901, 221; May 27, 1901, 223; June 12, 1901, 233–35; June 3, 1901, 227; May 26, 1902, 526.
31. Grandin, "Mes exploits," 403.
32. PVGPT, October 14, 1901, 346; October 23, 1901, 355; November 22, 1901, 383; November 27, 1901, 386; January 23, 1901, 97; August 16, 1901, 293; September 25, 1901, 327; August 26, 1901, 301; November 22, 1901, 383; November 27, 1901, 387.

33. Daoulas, *Le siège de Tien-Tsin*, 54.
34. Villetard de Laguérie, "En Chine," 382.
35. PVGPT, January 10, 1901, 86; June 5, 1901, 229; July 30, 1902, 597.
36. "Notes sur mon rôle pendant le Gouvernement provisoire du District de Tientsin (1901–1902)," May 10, 1903, family archives of F. Garcia-Mesny.
37. Daoulas, *Le siège de Tien-Tsin*, 251.
38. PVGPT, November 13, 1900, SHD, 11H39, 12; August 18, 1900, 14; August 4, 1900, 5; August 4, 1900, 5; October 14, 1901, 346; August 21, 1901, 298; February 17, 1902, 450; February 24, 1902, 457. Alongside the Japanese doctors, it is also necessary to add private actors like the Japanese individual who asked at the beginning of July 1902 for authorization to establish a "private hospital" in Tianjin (July 9, 1902, 574).
39. PVGPT, April 17, 1900, 185; July 30, 1900, 4; September 26, 1900, 39; October 5, 1900, 44; August 8, 1900, 8; August 11, 1900, 11; August 23, 1900, 17; December 17, 1900, 69; March 6, 1901, 149; April 28, 1902, 505; October 4, 1900, 43; October 29, 1900, SHD, 11H39, 3. Distilleries needed to acquire a license of 50 taels per month, and liquor stores for Chinese people were taxed 25 taels per month.
40. Angela Ki Che Leung, "'Variolation' and Vaccination in Late Imperial China, ca. 1570–1911," in *History of Vaccine Development*, ed. Stanley A. Plotkin (New York: Springer, 2011), 5.
41. PVGPT, April 15, 1901, 182; May 14, 1902, 518; rapport from the head of the health service, March 17, 1902, 470; April 7, 1902, 490; April 9, 1902, 491.
42. PVGPT, August 10, 1900, 11; August 27, 1900, 18; October 22, 1900, 53; October 29, 1900, SHD, Vincennes, 11H39, 3; December 3, 1900, 58; December 10, 1900, 64; December 17, 1900, 68; April 1, 1901, 166.
43. Garcia-Mesny, "Notes sur mon rôle."
44. PVGPT, June 5, 1901, 229; August 7, 1901, 284; report from the head of the health service, February 24, 1902, 456; February 24, 1902, 457.
45. Christian Henriot, *Belles de Shanghai: Prostitution et sexualité en Chine aux xix*[e]*–xx*[e] *siècles* (Paris: CNRS Éditions, 1997).
46. Grandin, "Mes exploits," 406–7.
47. Jean-Jacques Matignon, *La Chine hermétique: Superstitions, crime et misère* (Paris: Geuthner, 1898), 317.
48. Letter to the Council from General von Lessel, February 6, 1901, 112; October 2, 1901, 334; October 7, 1901, 339; rapport to the head of the health service around the March 28, 1902, 481; June 12, 1901, 336; February 10, 1902, 446.
49. Garcia-Mesny, "Notes sur mon rôle."
50. Matignon, *La Chine hermétique*, 314–16.

51. Christine Machiels and Éric Pierre, "La prostitution des mineur(e)s au xxe siècle," *Revue d'histoire de l'enfance "irrégulière"* 10 (2008): 7–12.
52. PVGPT, October 2, 1901, 336; rapport from the Chinese secretary, October 23, 1901, 355.
53. Jacques Houdaille and Louis Henry, "Célibat et âge au mariage aux xviiie et xixe siècles en France: II. Âge au premier mariage," *Population* 34, no. 2 (March–April 1979): 413.
54. Jean-Jacques Yvorel, ed., "Cent ans de répressions des violences à enfants," *Revue d'histoire de l'enfance " irrégulière"* 2 (1999): 9–11.
55. Rapport from the head of the health service to the Council of the Provisional Government, June 12, 1901, 235; rapport from commander Casanuova to the Council of the Provisional Government, June 29, 1901, 249; July 1, 1901, 250; rapport from the Russian Consul to Tianjin, July 3, 1901, 253; rapport from Captain Wollseiffen, July 29, 1901, 273; rapport from the head of the health service, July 29, 1901, 277; rapport from Gustav Detring, August 26, 1901, 301; August 30, 1901, 304; September 2, 1901, 306; September 4, 1901, 308; September 9, 1901, 313; September 11, 1901, 316; November 11, 1901, 375; November 13, 1901, 375; November 15, 1901, 377; November 18, 1901, 380; November 29, 1901, 289; December 6, 1901, 397; December 11, 1901, 400.
56. Rapport of the head of the health service, PVGPT, June 2, 1902, 534; rapport of the head of the health service, June 2, 1902, 534; June 2, 1902, 532; June 4, 1902, 537; June 6, 1902, 539–41; instructions of June 6 to the commanding officers of the sectors, June 6, 1902, 540–41; August 21, 1900, 15.
57. PVGPT, June 13, 1902, 547–49; July 9, 1902, 543; July 30, 1902, 603; July 2, 1902, 568; rapport of the Chinese secretary, July 18, 1902, 585.
58. J. Tsuzuki, "Bericht über meine epidemiologischen Beobachtungen und Forschungen während der Choleraepidemie in Nordchina im Jahre 1902 und über die im Verlaufe derselben von mir durchgefürhten prophylaktischen Massregeln mit besonderer Berücksightigung der Choleraschutzimpfung," *Archiv für Schiffs und Tropen-Hygiene* 8 (1904): 74.
59. Garcia-Mesny, "Notes sur mon rôle."
60. Rapport of Captain Satō, PVGPT, June 18, 1902, 554; rapport of the head of Tientsin-Nord, June 30, 1902, 567; June 13, 1902, and June 16, 1902, 549.
61. Chemouilli, "Le choléra et la naissance de la santé publique" (January)," 109–14, and Chemouilli, "Le choléra et la naissance de la santé publique dans le Japon de Meiji. 2. Forces et faiblesses d'une politique de santé publique," *Médecine sciences* 20, no. 2 (February 2004): 236–40.
62. PVGPT, June 20, 1902, 557; July 9, 1902, 576.
63. Garcia-Mesny, "Notes sur mon rôle"; rapport of the head of the health service, PVGPT, June 18, 1902, 554.

64. George Soulié de Morant, *L'acupuncture chinoise: Doctrine, diagnostic thérapeutique* (Paris: Mercure de France, 1934), 33; cited in Johan Nguyen, *La Réception de l'acupuncture en France: Une biographie revisitée de George Soulié de Morant* (Paris: L'Harmattan, 2012), 27.
65. Pierre-Marie-Alphonse Favier, *Péking, histoire et description* (Paris: Desclée de Brouwer, 1902), 351.
66. PVGPT, August 8, 1902, 616.
67. PVGPT, August 9, 1902, 576. The epidemic seemed to arrive in the capital at the end of the month: "General Lefèvre has indicated that a death from cholera has taken place in the international hospital of Peking the 27th of this month." PVGPT, August 30, 1902, 596.
68. Garcia-Mesny, "Notes sur mon rôle."
69. Garcia-Mesny, "Notes sur mon rôle."
70. Luca Gabbiani, "Les origines de la santé publique à Pékin, 1901–1911: Influences et conséquences," in *Les hygiénistes: Enjeux, modèles et pratiques, xviii*[e]*–xx*[e] *siècles*, ed. Patrice Bourdelais (Paris: Belin, 2001), 373–92.

6. The Salt of the City

1. Alexis Daoulas, *Le siège de Tien-Tsin(15 juin–15 juillet 1900)* (Paris: Berger-Levrault, 1903), 25.
2. The extraction and sale of salt was a state monopoly administered by a department called the Changlu Salt Fields, on the shores of the Bohai Sea southeast of Tianjin. The Changlu Salt District was one of the eleven districts of the empire. E. T. Williams, "Taxation in China," *Quarterly Journal of Economics* 26, no. 3 (May 1912): 502.
3. Lewis Bernstein, "A History of Tientsin in the Early Modern Times, 1800–1910" (PhD diss., University of Kansas, 1988), 39. There are also salt piles in Tong-Ku and Beitang. See Charles Condamy, "Histoire du gouvernement provisoire de Tien-Tsin (1900–1902)," *Revue des troupes coloniales* 2 (July–December 1905): 38. See also Onésime Reclus and Élisée Reclus, *L'empire du milieu, le climat, le sol, les races, la richesse de la Chine* (Paris: Hachette, 1902), 172–73.
4. More broadly, we must mention the ancient fascination of foreigners for Chinese salt and their occasional involvement in the administration of the gabelle, such as Marco Polo, who was an active member in the region of the mouth of the Yangzi. René Grousset, *Histoire de la Chine* (Paris: Fayard, 1942), chap. 27.

5. Johann-Christian Hüttner, *Voyage à la Chine* (Paris: Pillot Jeune, 1803), 26; George Léonard Staunton and Jean-Henri Castéra, *Voyage dans l'intérieur de la Chine* (Paris: Ferdinand Buisson, 1798), 220; E. H. Parker, "The Chinese Salt Trade: An Opening for British Enterprise," *Economic Journal* 9, no. 33 (March 1899): 117.
6. Kwan Man Bun, *The Salt Merchants of Tianjin: State-Making and Civil Society in Late Imperial China* (Honolulu: University of Hawaii Press, 2001), 138.
7. Hosea B. Morse, *International Relations of the Chinese Empire* (New York: Longmans, 1918), 3:367; PVGPT, September 19, 1900, 36; PVGPT, January 18, 1901, 4.
8. Henri Frey, *Français et alliés au Pé-Tchi-Li, campagne de Chine de 1900* (Paris: Hachette, 1904); Noah Fields Drake, *Map and Short Description of Tientsin* (Tianjin: n.p., 1900), 2.
9. Jean-Claude Hocquet, "Production du sel et changement technique en Chine," *Annales: Économies, sociétés, civilisations* 46, no. 5 (1991): 1021.
10. Condamy, "Histoire du gouvernement provisoire," 38–39.
11. The Middle Kingdom was largely built on salt. The Chinese seem to have been pioneers in the extraction of salt with the *shai* technique (evaporation of sea water using solar energy), as well as its fiscal management with the first forms of taxation. The establishment of a state monopoly on salt made it possible, during the Han dynasty (202 BCE–9 CE, 25–220 CE), to finance the development of the central administration, the army, and imperial expansion. With the freezing of the land tax after 1712 the Qing focused on the exploitation of the salt tax. See Samuel A. M. Adshead, "Un cycle bureaucratique: L'administration du sel en Orient et en Occident," *Annales: Économies, sociétés, civilisations* 38, no. 2 (1983): 222 and 230.
12. Bun, *Salt Merchants of Tianjin*, 8.
13. Daoulas, *Le siège de Tien-Tsin*, 178.
14. The French of the same period consumed 8.8 kilos per year. Adshead, "Un cycle bureaucratique," 223 and 227.
15. Charles-Baltazar de Pélacot, *Expédition de Chine de 1900 jusqu'à l'arrivée du général Voyron* (Paris: H. Lavauzelle, 1903), 123.
16. MAE, series A, Chine 636, carton 27, dossier 13, copy of the minutes of the taking of the salt piles, "Mainmise par les troupes françaises des approvisionnements de sel appartenant au gouvernement chinois."
17. Condamy, "Histoire du gouvernement provisoire," 39.
18. Pélacot, *Expédition de Chine*, 130.
19. PVGPT, November 20, 1900, 18.
20. PVGPT, August 2, 1900, 4; PVGPT, *Règlement d'administration pour la ville de Tientsin*, 1; November 9, 1900, 10.

21. Letter number 39 from September 30, 1900, from the commanding general of the first French brigade to General Vogak, commander of the expeditionary forces, cited in Condamy, "Histoire du gouvernement provisoire," 256.
22. Letter from General Voyron to the Comte du Chaylard, October 3, 1900, MAE, 148 CPCOM 101.
23. Letter from M. Pichon, French minister in Peking to General Voyron, March 30, 1901, MAE, 148 CPCOM 101.
24. Condamy, "Histoire du gouvernement provisoire," 258.
25. Letter from the Consul Comte du Chaylard to General Voyron, October 5, 1900, MAE, 148 CPCOM 101.
26. Born in Ju Kow, Jiangsu, in 1863 to a very rich family of merchants in Nanjing, Sun Chung Ying was trained at the Torpedo and Naval College. Beginning in 1886 he worked as an interpreter for the company Jardine, Matheson & Co. In 1888 he became a comprador and then a shareholder of H. Mandl & Co, a government partner. See C. Y. Sun *Who's Who in China: Biographies of Chinese Leaders* (Shanghai: 1932), 210. This important merchant from Tianjin, who became president of the Tientsin City Waterworks offered his protection to orphans, the underprivileged, and the sick. During the cholera epidemic of 1901, Sun financed the construction of ten medical centers with fifty beds each. See Arnold Wright, ed., *Twentieth Century Impressions of Hongkong, Shanghai, and Other Treaty Ports of China* (London: Lloyds Greater Britain Publishing Company, 1908), 752–53.
27. PVGPT, July 5, 1901, 256.
28. Rosemary Quested, *The Russo-Chinese Bank: A Multinational Financial Base of Tsarism in China* (Birmingham: Birmingham University Press, 1977); Kazuhiko Yago, "The Russo-Chinese Bank (1896–1910): An International Bank in Russia and Asia," in *The Origins of International Banking in Asia: The Nineteenth and Twentieth Centuries*, ed. Shizuya Nishimura, Toshio Suzuki, and Ranald C. Michie (Oxford: Oxford University Press, 2012); Hugues Tertrais, "Une révolution sous influence: La république chinoise face au consortium bancaire," in "Le premier moment révolutionnaire," special issue, *Matériaux pour l'histoire de notre temps* 109–110 (2013): 25–31.
29. PVGPT, July 17, 1901, 263.
30. Letter from the Comte du Chaylard to General Voyron, October 5, 1900; Letter from General Voyron to the French Consul General, October 27, 1900; Letter from General Consul Chaylard to General Voyron, October 30, 1900; Letter from General Voyron to the French Consul General, November 5, 1900; Letter from the Minister of the Navy to the Minister of Foreign Affairs, January 15, 1901 (MAE, 148 CPCOM 101).
31. PVGPT, January 4, 1901, 82; PVGPT, December 20, 1900, 70.

32. There were different administrative systems in the different districts of the empire. Adshead, "Un cycle bureaucratique," 224.
33. In the late nineteenth century ambitious young men flocked to Tianjin, hoping to serve in the imperial administration or work in the lucrative salt trade. Linda Grove argues that the salt and grain trade was the main source of immigration to Tianjin. Thus the "old" dialect of the city is closer to that of the remote province of Anhui than to that of the surrounding rural areas. Linda Grove, "International Trade and the Creation of Domestic Marketing Networks in North China, 1860–1930," in *Commercial Networks in Modern Asia*, ed. Linda Grove and Shinya Sugiyama (London: Routledge, 2013), 97.
34. Liu Haiyan, *Kongjian yu shehui: Jindai Tianjin cheng shi yanbian/Space and Society: Changes in Modern Tianjin* (Tianjin: Tianjin Academy of Social Sciences Press, 2003).
35. The Boxer War accelerated this process, and the wealthy Chinese moved more and more into the French and Italian concessions.
36. Bun, *Salt Merchants of Tianjin*.
37. Brett Sheehan, *Trust in Troubled Times: Money, Banks, and State-Society Relations in Republican Tianjin* (Cambridge, MA: Harvard University Press, 2003), 46.
38. Sheehan, *Trust in Troubled Times*, 64.
39. Bun, "Order in Chaos," 75.
40. Associations de la Chine, *Lettres du Père Prosper Leboucq publiées par un de ses amis* (Paris: F. Wattelier et Cie, 1880), 293.
41. Yves Chevrier, "La question de la société civile, la Chine et le chat du Cheshire," *Études chinoises* 14, no. 2 (Fall 1995): 165.
42. Albert-François-Ildefonse d'Anthouard, *La Chine contre l'étranger: Les Boxeurs* (Paris: Plon, 1902), 68–69.
43. Condamy, "Histoire du gouvernement provisoire," 38.
44. PVGPT, September 11, 1900, 31. James Bromley Eames's effectiveness in both public and private affairs led to his reappointment as government councilor until 1902.
45. James B. Eames, *The English in China: Being an Account of the Intercourse and Relations Between England and China from the Year 1600 to the Year 1843 and a Summary of Later Developments* (London: Sir I. Pitman and Sons, 1909).
46. Telegram from Mr. James Bromley Eames (Paris-Tientsin 257 230 11, 1h.35s V. Malte) to the Minister of Foreign Affairs, cites in the telegram of the Minister of Foreign Affairs to the French Minister in Peking on March 21, 1901, MAE, series A, Chine 6363, carton 27, dossier 13.
47. For example, Japanese merchants solicited the government's help to recover salt seized by Russian authorities. PVGPT, September 11, 1901, 316.

48. Morse, *International Relations of the Chinese Empire*, 367.
49. Bun, *Salt Merchants of Tianjin*, 139.
50. PVGPT, May 22, 1901, 217; May 24, 1901, 218; July 1, 1901, 251; October 9, 1901, 341; July 12, 1901, 261; August 10, 1900, 10.
51. Salt was usually transported by large and beautiful junks on canals and rivers, which was twenty to forty times cheaper in the middle of the nineteenth century than transport by land. See Adshead, "Un cycle bureaucratique," 222.
52. PVGPT, January 10, 1901, 87; January 14, 1901, 90; January 18, 1901, 94; January 22, 1901, 96; January 23, 1901, 98.
53. PVGPT, March 29, 1901, 165; August 27, 1900, 19; January 30, 1901, 105; February 13, 1901, 125; July 29, 1901, 274; February 15, 1901, 127.
54. Condamy, "Histoire du gouvernement provisoire," 39.
55. PVGPT, Februry 16, 1901, 129; February 22, 1901, 131; March 4, 1901, 142; May 13, 1901, 211.
56. PVGPT, May 24, 1901, 221; July 24, 1901, 272; April 15, 1901, 213; July 22, 1901, 269; July 18, 1901, 267.
57. Ralph Thaxton, *Salt of the Earth: The Political Origins of Peasant Protest and Communist Revolution in China* (Berkeley: University of California Press, 1997), 65.
58. Sheehan, *Trust in Troubled Times*, 52.
59. Bun, *Salt Merchants of Tianjin*, 138.

7. The Urban Scramble

1. Robert Bickers, *The Scramble for China: Foreign Devils in the Qing Empire, 1832–1914* (London: Penguin Books, 2012).
2. Alfred Whitney Griswold, *The Far Eastern Policy of the United States* (New York: Harcourt, Brace & Company, 1938); Andrew Malezemoff, *Russian Far Eastern Policy, 1881–1904* (Berkeley: University of California Press, 1958), 174; Lung Chang, *La Chine à l'aube du xxe siècle* (Paris: Nouvelles Éditions Latines, 1962), 273–303; George W. Monger, "The End of Isolation: Britain, Germany and Japan, 1900–1902," *Transactions of the Royal Historical Society* 13 (1963): 103–21; L. K. Young, *British Policy in China, 1895–1902* (Oxford: Clarendon Press, 1970).
3. Michel Vié, "La Mandchourie et la 'Question d'Extrême-Orient,' 1880–1910," *Cipango, cahiers d'études japonaises* 18 (June 2011): 19–78.
4. Circular from Lieutenant General Linevich, Commander-in-Chief of the Russian Expeditionary Force, November 6, 1900, NA, FO 674 / 80.
5. PVGPT, November 7, 1900, SHD, 11H39, 9.

6. Letter addressed by the Russian Consul in Tien-Tsin to Comte du Chaylard, Consul General of France, November 15, 1900, MAE, P 19231, "Concession de Tien Tsin 1861 à 1897."
7. PVGPT, February 25, 1901, 136.
8. Letter from E. Conger to M. de Giers, November 14, 1900, *Foreign Relations of the United States*, 1901, 45, cited in Hosea B. Morse, *The International Relations of the Chinese Empire* (New York: Longmans, 1918), 324.
9. PVGPT, January 24, 1901, 432.
10. Morse, *International Relations of the Chinese Empire*, 326.
11. Letter from Chevalier de Melotte, Belgian consul, to members of the consular corps, 7 November 1900, NA, FO 674 / 80.
12. Letter from the Consul of Belgium in Tien-Tsin to Comte du Chaylard, Consul General of France, November 17, 1900, diplomatic archives of La Courneuve, P 19231, "Concession de Tien Tsin 1861 à 1897."
13. Albert Duchesne, "Les aspects diplomatiques du projet d'expédition belge en Chine en 1900," *Revue belge de philologie et d'histoire* 32, no. 1 (1954): 77–96.
14. Prime Minister Charles Rogier opposed the project, arguing that the construction of the Antwerp fortifications should have priority. J. Garsou, "Léopold Ier, le duc de Brabant et la Chine, 1859–1860," *Archives diplomatiques et consulaires* (November 1937): 482–87.
15. Letter from the Belgian Consul to the Provisional Government Council, March 21, 1901, PVGPT, March 25, 1901, 160.
16. Agenda of Jules Jadot, April 3, 1908, Papiers Jadot, cited in Kurgan-Van Hentenryk, *Jean Jadot*.
17. Agenda of Jules Jadot, April 3, 1908, Papiers Jadot, cited in Ginette Kurgan-Van Hentenryk, *Jean Jadot: Artisan de l'expansion belge en Chine* (Brussels: Académie Royale des Sciences d'Outre-mer, 1965).
18. The concession was retroceded to China on January 15, 1931.
19. Georg Lehner and Monika Lehner, *Österreich-Ungarn und der "Boxeraufstand" in China* (Innsbruck: StudienVerlag, 2002).
20. Letter from Captain Sambuchi to the Council of the Provisional Government, PVGPT, April 1, 1901, 166; letter from the Minister of Austria-Hungary in Peking, October 28, 1901, PVGPT, November 8, 1901, 372; letter from the Consul of Austria-Hungary, PVGPT, April 11, 1902, 493; April 14, 1902, 494; July 28, 1902, 593; July 30, 1902, 604.
21. Roberto Bertinelli, "La concessione italiana di Tientsin," *Nuova Antologia* 212 (1907): 726–33; Maurizio Marinelli, "An Italian 'Neighbourhood' in Tianjin: Little Italy or Colonial Space?," in *Twentieth-Century Colonialism and China: Localities, the Everyday and the World*, ed. Bryna Goodman and David S. G. Goodman (London: Routledge, 2012), 92–107.

22. Mario Valli, *Gli avvenimenti in Cina nel 1900* (Milan: Urico Hoepli, 1905), 647–48.
23. Vincenzo Fileti, *La concessione italiana di Tien-tsin* (Genoa: Barabino e Graeve, 1921), 15; Letter from Poma to the Minister of Foreign Affairs, August 26, 1901, Archivio Storico dello Stato Maggiore dell'Esercito (ASME), b. 426, folder "402."
24. Arnaldo Cicchiti-Suriani, "La concessione italiana di Tient Tsin (1901–1951)," *Rassegna italiana di politica e cultura* 31 (October 1951): 563.
25. Letter from the Consular agent of Italy to the Council of the Provisional Government, PVGPT, March 27, 1901, 162; August 26, 1901, 300.
26. PVGPT, November 15, 1901, 377; letter from the Italian Minister in Peking, PVGPT, November 25, 1901, 384.
27. Archivio Storico dello Stato Maggiore dell'Esercito, b. 426, dossier "1902," "Schema dell'Atto di convenzione tra il R. Governo e la Società italiana," "Pro-memoria" citato, cited in Bertinelli, "La concessione italiana di Tientsin," 223–24.
28. Archivio Storico dello Stato Maggiore dell'Esercito, folder 9, leaflet 13.
29. Bertinelli, "La concessione italiana di Tientsin," 219.
30. Maurizio Marinelli, "Projecting *Italianità* on the Chinese Space: The Construction of the 'Aristocratic Concession' in Tianjin (1901–1947)," in *Italy's Encounters with Modern China: Imperial Dreams, Strategic Ambitions*, Basingstoke, ed. Maurizio Marinelli and Giovanni Andornino (New York: Palgrave Macmillan, 2014), 10.
31. Marinelli, "Projecting *Italianità* on the Chinese Space," 10.
32. Report from Cesare Poma, General Consul of Italy in Tientsin, "Cina: Sul commercio di Tientsine," *Bollettino del Ministero degli Affari esteri* (March 1902): 109–30.
33. Alexis Daoulas, *Le siège de Tien-Tsin (15 juin–15 juillet 1900)* (Paris: Berger-Levrault, 1903), 220.
34. This provision guaranteed third countries the trade benefits of most favored nation.
35. Copy of an "Express" published by the French Consul General in Tianjin, November 20, 1900, MAE, P 19231.
36. The first extension of the British concession dates from 1897.
37. Report of January 6, 1911, written by the French consul in Tianjin and addressed to the minister of the French Republic in Peking, "Tientsin, Consulate," 34, CADN.
38. Telegram from Consul du Chaylard to Foreign Minister Delcassé, 29 November 1900, MAE, P 19231.
39. Letter from the Consul General to the Minister of Foreign Affairs, 26 November 1900, DEA, P 19231.

40. Telegraphic dispatch from Delcassé, Minister of Foreign Affairs, to the French Consul General, November 28, 1900, MAE, P 19231.
41. "Les incidents de Tientsin," note from the Consul General of France, January 23, 1917, MAE, E Asie (1918–1940), 344.
42. "Affaires de Tientsin (octobre 1916–janvier 1917)," note from the French legation in Peking, May 1917, MAE, E Asie (1918–1940), 345.
43. Letter from the Minister of France in Peking to the Minister of Foreign Affairs, September 3, 1906, MAE, P 19231.
44. Letter from Maurice Rouvier, Minister of Finance, to the Minister of Foreign Affairs, April 5, 1903, MAE, P 19231.
45. T. O. Matzmura, "History of the Development of the Japanese Concession, Tientsin," *North China Stat*, Anniversary Magazine, August 12, 1920, 10, CADN, 691 PO / 1 / 44.
46. Marjorie Dryburgh, "Japan in Tianjin: Settlers, State and the Tensions of Empire before 1937," *Japanese Studies* 27, no. 1 (May 2007): 19–34.
47. "Affaires de Tientsin (October 1916–January 1917)," note from the French legation in Peking, May 1917, MAE, E Asie (1918–1940), 345.
48. Raoul Charles Villetard de Laguérie, "Tien-Tsin après la défaite des Boxeurs (Voyage exécuté en 1900)," *Le tour du monde: Nouveau journal des voyages* 7, no. 41 (October 12, 1901): 489; Matzmura, "History of the Development of the Japanese Concession."
49. Letter from the Consul General to the Minister of Foreign Affairs, November 26, 1900, MAE, P 19231.
50. Letter from H. Ijuin, Consul General of Japan, to the Council of the Provisional Government, August 9, 1902, PVGPT, August 11, 1902.
51. Specifications drawn up by the Japanese Ministry of Foreign Affairs, cited in Matzmura, "History of the Development of the Japanese Concession," 10.
52. PVGPT, December 3, 1900, 58; rapport from Lieutenant Colonel Harada, PVGPT, June 14, 1901, 237; September 2, 1901, 306; September 6, 1901, 312; August 6, 1902, 610; letter from H. Ijuin, Consul General of Japan to the Council of the Provisional Government, August 9, 1902, PVGPT, August 11, 1902, 620.
53. PVGPT, April 19, 1901, 188; May 13, 1901, 211; June 19, 1901, 240; letter from M. Delcassé, Minister of Foreign Affairs to Mr. Pichon, Minister of the French Republic to Peking, MAE, P 19231.
54. "From the point of view of size and geographical situation, the French concession of Tientsin was clearly in an inferior position compared to the other foreign concessions. As early as 1902, a claim had been formulated by the French authorities, which recognized the danger of our concession being surrounded in the future." "Affaires de Tientsin (octobre 1916–janvier 1917),"

note from the French Legation in Peking, May 1917, MAE, E Asie (1918–1940), 345.

55. I would like to thank Nicolas Vaicbourdt for his invaluable help with this section. Tai En Sai, *Treaty Ports in China: A Study in Diplomacy* (New York: Columbia University, 1918), 124.
56. Letter from E. Conger to J. Hay, November 14, 1900; letter from J. Hay to E. Conger, November 16, 1900, Foreign Relations of the United States, 1901, 39; letter from E. Satow to Consul Campbell, March 6, 1901, NA, FO 674 / 9.
57. Nicolas Vaicbourdt, "De la 'me too policy' aux ambitions contradictoires: La brève histoire de la concession américaine de Tianjin, 1860–1902," *Outre-Mers: Revue d'histoire* 382–383 (June 2014): 27–46.
58. Letter from J. W. Ragsdale to Colonel Foote, February 15, 1901, Foreign Relations of the United States, 1901, 50.
59. Letter from E. Conger to J. Hay, December 31, 1900, Foreign Relations of the United States, 1901, 40.
60. Letter from General Chaffee to E. Conger, February 21, 1901, Diplomatic Couriers, Roll 111, No. 551.
61. Letter from E. Conger to J. Hay, February 26, 1901, enclosure 3, cited in Vaicbourdt, "De la 'me too policy' aux ambitions contradictoires."
62. Letter from E. Conger to J. Hay, September 9, 1901, Foreign Relations of the United States, 1901, 54.
63. Letter from Mr. Squiers to M. Hay, July 25, 1901, *Foreign Relations of the United States*, 1901, 52–54.
64. Letter from E. Conger to the Secretary of State, October 11, 1901, Diplomatic Couriers, Roll 115, No. 769, Enclosure 1, cited in Vaicbourdt, "De la 'me too policy' aux ambitions contradictoires."
65. Letter from E. Conger to Secretary of State, January 21, 1902, Diplomatic Couriers, Roll 116, No. 889, Enclosure 6.
66. Eileen P. Scully, *Bargaining with the State from Afar: American Citizenship in Treaty Port China, 1844–1942* (New York: Columbia University Press, 2013), 103.
67. This is how, since the 1880s, the British referred to colonial possessions considered costly and useless; letter from W. W. Rockhill to A. A. Adee, November 20, 1091, Diplomatic Couriers, Roll 116, No. 769, cited in Vaicbourdt, "De la 'me too policy' aux ambitions contradictoires."
68. Letter from E. Conger to M. Ragsdale, March 27, 1902, Diplomatic Couriers, Roll 116, No. 1399 and attached documents, cited in Vaicbourdt, "De la 'me too policy' aux ambitions contradictoires."
69. Scully, *Bargaining with the State*, 101.
70. Letter from the British Consul General to the Provisional Government Council, PVGPT, December 17, 1900, 68; letter from the French Consul General

to the Provisional Government Council, January 7, 1901, 85; letter from the United States Consul to the Provisional Government Council, PVGPT, January 10, 1901, 86

71. Léon Silbermann, *Journal de marche d'un soldat colonial en Chine* (Paris: Henri Charles-Lavauzelle, 1908), 9.
72. Jacques Grandin, "Mes exploits pendant la guerre de Chine de 1901 (Journal d'un volontaire)," *La revue des revues* 61 (May 1–15, 1902): 402.
73. PVGPT, September 5, 1900, 26; rapport from the Chief of the River Police, PVGPT, August 18, 1901, 266; August 2, 1901, 278; rapport from Captain Wakasone, Chief of the Japanese Police, April 24, 1901, 193; rapport from Major V. Glasenap, July 18, 1901, 265; August 23, 1901, 299; September 9, 1901, 314; rapport from Colonel Moale, September 12, 1900, 32; rapport from Lieutenant von Bosse, January 14, 1901, 91; rapport from Major von Falkenhayn, September 25, 1901, 328–329.
74. Letter from General Voyron to the Minister of the Marine, October 17, 1900, SHD, Vincennes, 11H45.
75. Letter from the commander of British troops in Tianjin to the Provisional Government Council, PVGPT, October 4, 1900, 42.
76. PVGPT, October 5, 1900, 43.
77. Letter from Lieutenant General Linevich, Commander-in-Chief of the Russian Expeditionary Force, to Mr. Campbell, British Consul General, 24 November 1900, NA, FO 674 / 80.
78. German engineers were working on repairing the section between Yangcun and Beijing. Édouard de Laboulaye, *Les chemins de fer en Chine* (Paris: Émile Larose, 1911), 82–83; letter from Jules Jadot to the Société d'étude des chemins de fer en Chine, Tianjin, February 1, 1903, transcribed in Kurgan-Van Hentenryk, *Jean Jadot*, 120.
79. Letter from Jules Jadot to his wife, Tianjin, September 24, 1900, transcribed in Kurgan-Van Hentenryk, *Jean Jadot*, 110–11.
80. Villetard de Laguérie, "Tien-Tsin après la défaite," 483.
81. Diary of the British representative on the Marshal's staff, Friday, March 15, March 14 to March 20, 1901, NA, WO 32 / 6148.
82. From the Diary of Colonel J. M. Grierson, Deputy Adjutant General, March 14–20, 1901, addressed to the Under Secretary of War, Secret Doc. No. 37, Peking, March 21, 1901, NA, WO 106 6266.
83. "The Tientsin Siding Difficulty," *Wanganui Chronicle* (New Zealand), March 22, 1901, 3
84. Diary of the British representative on the Marshal's staff.
85. Grierson, Secret Doc. No. 37.
86. "French Rowdyism," *Otago Witness* (New Zealand), March 20, 1901, 24.

87. "An Anglo-Russian Fracas," *The North Western Advocate and the Emu Bay Times*, March 15, 1901.
88. Grierson, Secret Doc. No. 37.
89. "The Tientsin Siding Difficulty," *Sydney Morning Herald*, March 22, 1901, 3; "Precautions at Tientsin, Disorderly French Soldiers," *The Inquirer and Commercial News* (Perth), March 29, 1901.
90. "The Anglo-Russian Trouble at Tientsin," *The Register* (Adelaide), March 26, 1901; Diary of the British Representative on the Marshal's Staff, Friday, March 15–March 14 to March 20, 1901, NA, WO 32 / 6148, 6.
91. Léon Silbermann, *Journal de marche d'un soldat colonial en Chine* (Paris: H. Charles-Lavauzelle, 1908), 96.
92. "Tientsin Siding Difficulty."
93. Statement of General Barrow, Beijing, March 21, 1901, 3, Secret Doc. No. 37, Beijing March 21, 1901, NA, WO 106 6266.
94. Excerpt from the Diary of Colonel J. M. Grierson, Deputy Adjutant General, March 14–20, 1901, to the Undersecretary of War, Secret Doc. No. 40, Peking April 2, 1901, NA, WO 32 / 6148.
95. "Most Serious Is Situation at Tientsin," *San Francisco Call*, March 17, 1901.
96. "The Position in China," *The Colonist* (New Zealand), March 15, 1901, 2; *The Inquirer and Commercial News* (Perth), March 22, 1901, 8.
97. "Tientsin Railway Siding: The Anglo-Russian Dispute," *Bendigo Advertiser* (Australia), April 29, 1903, 2.
98. "Tientsin Railway Siding: The Anglo-Russian Dispute," 2.
99. "Tientsin Railway Siding Dispute," *The Brisbane Courier* (Australia), July 4, 1903, 5; John R. Seeley, *L'expansion de l'Angleterre* (Paris: Armand Colin, [1884] 1901), 30.
100. Fabrice Serodes, *Anglophobie et politique: De Fachoda à Mers el-Kébir* (Paris: L'Harmattan, 2010).
101. Telegram from the Tianjin consulate to the Ministry of Foreign Affairs, June 14, 1900, political and commercial correspondence, in the folder "Incident Franco-Incident. Affaire d'un train pris de force par les fantassins français," file "Sociétés secrètes—Troubles du Tchéli," new series 1897–1914, MAE, series A, China 636, political department, box 27.
102. Villetard de Laguérie, "Tien-Tsin après la défaite," 492.
103. Grandin, "Mes exploits," 403.
104. Grandin, "Mes exploits," 404.
105. Diary of the British Representative on the Marshal's Staff, 5.
106. Rapport from the Chief of Police, PVGPT, January 4, 1901, 81.
107. Letter from the representative of Wilson & Co. to Consul Campbell, March 19, 1901, NA, FO 674 / 88.

108. Silbermann, *Journal de marche*, 96.
109. Diary of the British Representative on the Marshal's staff, 4–5.
110. "French Rowdyism," 24.
111. Diary of the British Representative on the Marshal's staff, 5.
112. "Trouble at Tientsin," *The Advertiser*, March 22, 1901; "Precautions at Tientsin."
113. "The Situation in China," *The Press* (Canterbury), March 19, 1901, 5.
114. Grierson, Secret Doc. No. 37.
115. "The Anglo-Russian Trouble at Tientsin."
116. Grandin, "Mes exploits," 413.
117. Grandin, "Mes exploits," 406.
118. Silbermann, *Journal de marche*, 97; Grierson, Secret Doc. No. 40.
119. J. M. Grierson, Colonel, Deputy Adjutant General, to Under Secretary of War, Secret Doc. No. 51, Peking, May 18, 1901, NA, WO 32 / 6148.
120. Letter from Jules Jadot to his wife, Tianjin, September 28, 1900, transcribed in Kurgan-Van Hentenryk, *Jean Jadot*, 112.
121. Grierson, Secret Doc. No. 40.
122. Diary of the British Representative on the Marshal's staff, 3.
123. Silbermann, *Journal de marche*, 127.
124. Diary of the British Representative on the Marshal's staff, 6.
125. Grierson, Secret Doc. No. 40.
126. Letter from Colonel J. M. Grierson, Deputy Adjutant General, to the General Officer of the Command, British Contingent, China Expeditionary Force, Secret Doc. No. 125, March 30, 1901, p. 14, NA, WO 32 / 6148.
127. Loti, "Les deux déesses des Boxeurs."
128. Daoulas, *Le siège de Tien-Tsin*, 256.
129. Grierson, Secret Doc. No. 37.
130. PVGPT, September 5, 1900, 26.
131. Grandin, "Mes exploits," 400–401.
132. Grandin, "Mes exploits," 403.
133. Letter from Jardine, Matheson & Co. representative to Consul Campbell, March 19, 1901, NA, FO 674 / 88.
134. "French Troops Make Trouble," *San Francisco Call*, March 22, 1901.
135. "Fracas at Tien-Tsin: Free Fight Between Indian and German Troops—Six Men Killed," telegram received on December 10, 1901, *The Press* (Canterbury), December 11, 1901, 8.
136. India Office Records, Aide-mémoire, M 7837, 1902, BL.
137. Cäcilie von Rodt, *Voyage d'une suissesse autour du monde* (Neuchâtel: F. Zahn, 1904), 201.
138. Thomas Metcalf, *Imperial Connections: India in the Indian Ocean Arena, 1860–1920* (Berkeley: University of California Press, 2008).

139. "Du colonel Grierson au sous-secrétaire d'État à la guerre," Diary of the British Representative on the Marshal's staff, November 20, 1900, 3, NA, WO 32 / 6148.
140. "The shooting in Tianjin will be treated as a police matter," wrote the author of the article "Tientsin Fight Duly Explained," *San Francisco Call*, June 5, 1901.
141. Statement against Mr. Beaume, July 21, 1902, CADN, 691 PO / 1, Tientsin Consulate, 319, register of acts of the civil, commercial and criminal jurisdiction, 92.
142. "The Taku Road Fracas: Action by the French General," *The Argus* (Melbourne), June 11, 1901, 5.
143. PVGPT, February 6, 1901, 111; letter from the British Consul General to the Council of the Provisional Government, August 17, 1901, 289; report from the Chief of Police, October 2, 1901, 335; report from the Chief of Police, June 13, 1902, 548; letter from the Commander of Italian Troops to the Council of the Provisional Government, June 25, 1902, 560.
144. Phillips O'Brien, *The Anglo-Japanese Alliance, 1902–1922* (London: Routledge, 2004), 92.
145. Stephen R. Mackinnon, *Power and Politics in Late Imperial China: Yuan Shih-k'ai in Beijing and Tianjin, 1901–1908* (Berkeley: California University Press, 1980), 30.
146. Boris Aleksandrovich Romanov, *Russia in Manchuria, 1892–1906* (Ann Arbor: American Council of Learned Societies, 1952), 232–50.
147. Mackinnon, *Power and Politics in Late Imperial China*, 25.
148. J. M. Grierson, Colonel, Deputy Adjutant General to the Commander in Chief, British Contingent, China Expeditionary Force, Secret Doc. No. 39, March 23, 1901, NA, WO 32 / 6148.

8. A Government for Posterity?

1. Jacques Grandin, "Mes exploits pendant la guerre de Chine de 1901 (Journal d'un volontaire)," *La revue des revues* 61 (May 1–15, 1902): 413.
2. PVGPT, November 28, 1900, SHD, 11H39, 27; November 16, 1900, SHD, 11H39, 15; November 22, 1900, SHD, 11H39, 21; December 5, 1900, 60; December 7, 1900, 62; January 4, 1901, 82; January 22, 1901, 97; January 30, 1901, 105; November 24, 1900, SHD, 11H39, 23; November 26, 1900, SHD, 11H39, 26; letter from the Council to Captain Woods, January 20, 1902, 427; letter from the Council of the Provisional Government to Colonel O'Sullivan, July 30, 1902, 597; December 20, 1900, 70; January 30, 1901, 105; February 8, 1901, 115; reply from the Council to General

Campbell, March 22, 1901, 158; Alexis Daoulas, *Le siège de Tien-Tsin (15 juin–15 juillet 1900)* (Paris: Berger-Levrault, 1903), 248.

3. "The Siege of Tien-Tsin," *Cambridge Chronicle*, February 23, 1901.
4. Marc Boulet, *Ma famille chinoise* (Paris: Seuil, 1998), 104–5.
5. "Un entretien avec M. Pierre Loti," *The Lotus Magazine* 4, no. 1 (October 1912): 31–35.
6. Pierre Loti, *Les derniers jours de Pékin* (Paris: Calmann-Lévy, 1901), ch. 2, "Dimanche, 14 octobre 1900."
7. "Un entretien avec M. Pierre Loti," 31–35.
8. PVGPT, January 7, 1901, 85; Report of the Chief of Police to the Council of the Provisional Government, PVGPT, January 10, 1901, 87; April 17, 1901, 186; PVGPT, April 19, 1901, 189; April 29, 1901, 198; June 12, 1901, 235; Letter from the Council of the Provisional Government to Father du Cray, PVGPT, March 21, 1902, 473; July 25, 1902, 591.
9. Letter from the head of the South Tianjin district to the British Consul General, August 15, 1902, NA, FO 674 / 93.
10. PVGPT, around March 28, 1902, 485; April 30, 1902, 506; July 30, 1902, 596; June 16, 1902, 550; August 2, 1902, 604; August 13, 1902, 624; August 8, 1902, 613; letter from the Council of the Provisional Government to the Diplomatic corps of Beijing, May 23, 1902, 523.
11. Tai En Sai, *Treaty Ports in China: A Study in Diplomacy* (New York: Columbia University Press, 1918), 132.
12. This return was celebrated in Tianjin by the *shendong*, who received the blessing of the Provisional Government to decorate the facades with lanterns for five days in early January. PVGPT, January 6, 1902, 420.
13. William R. Manning, "China and the Powers Since the Boxer Movement," *American Journal of International Law* 4, no. 4 (October 1910): 863.
14. Letter from Wu Ting-fang, Chinese Minister of the Chinese Legation in Washington, to Secretary of State John Hay, January 20, 1902, United States Department of State, Papers relating to the foreign relations of the United States, with the annual message of the President transmitted to Congress December 2, 1902, 184.
15. Letter from Mr. Rockhill to Mr. Hay, U.S. Secretary of State, Peking, April 17, 1901, Expedition No. 70, 137–138, Report of William W. Rockhill, Former Commissioner to China, with accompanying documents, Washington, D.C., Government Printing Office, 1901.
16. Letter from Secretary of State John Hay to Wu [Ting-fang], Chinese Minister of the Chinese Legation in Washington, January 30, 1902, United States Department of State, *Papers Relating to the Foreign Relations of the United States, with the Annual Message of the President Transmitted to Congress December 2, 1902*, 184.

17. Letter from Joseph H. Choate, U.S. Ambassador to London, to Secretary of State John Hay, February 12, 1902, in United States Department of State, *Papers Relating to the Foreign Relations of the United States*, 187.
18. Letter from Théophile Delcassé, Minister of Foreign Affairs, to Horace Porter, Minister of the United States in Paris, February 16, 1902, in United States Department of State, *Papers Relating to the Foreign Relations of the United States*, 186.
19. Letter from Giulio Prinetti, Italian Minister of Foreign Affairs, to Mr. Meyer, U.S. Ambassador to Rome, February 21, 1902, in United States Department of State, *Papers Relating to the Foreign Relations of the United States*, 189.
20. Letter from Baron Komura, Japanese Minister of Foreign Affairs, to Mr. Buck, United States Minister in Tokyo, March 6, 1902, in United States Department of State, *Papers Relating to the Foreign Relations of the United States*, 190.
21. Letter from Baron von Richthofen, German Foreign Minister, to Andrew White, U.S. Ambassador to Berlin, February 25, 1902, in United States Department of State, *Papers Relating to the Foreign Relations of the United States*, 189.
22. Letter from Andrew White, U.S. Ambassador to Berlin, to Secretary of State John Hay, February 26, 1902, in United States Department of State, *Papers Relating to the Foreign Relations of the United States*, 188.
23. Intervention of Colonel Harada before the Council of the Provisional Government, PVGPT, March 17, 1902, 468; March 24, 1902, 475; March 26, 1902, 476.
24. Letter from Representatives Meyer & Co. to the Provisional Government Council, PVGPT, March 17, 1902, 469; April 9, 1902, 491; letter from Hanneken to the Provisional Government Council, August 8, 1902, 613; reply from *daotai* Chang to the Chinese Secretary of the Provisional Government, August 13, 1902, 624; June 13, 1902, 547.
25. Letter from E. Conger to J. Hay, 11 June 1902; letter from E. Conger to J. Hay, 28 June 1902; letter from J. Hay to E. Conger, 2 July 1902; letter from E. Conger to J. Hay, 15 July 1902, in United States Department of State, *Papers Relating to the Foreign Relations of the United States*, 190–98.
26. PVGPT, around March 28, 1902, 483–86; July 30, 1902, 597–99 and 604–5; letter from the head of Chunliangcheng to the Provisional Government Council, August 6, 1902, 613; May 23, 1902, 524.
27. Letter from Prince Qing to E. Conger, July 18, 1902, in United States Department of State, *Papers Relating to the Foreign Relations of the United States*, 201; "Chine," *Journal des débats politiques et littéraires*, July 20, 1902, 2.

28. Otto D. Rasmussen, *Tientsin: An Illustrated Outline History* (Tientsin: The Tientsin Press, 1925), 226, 228.
29. PVGPT, July 30, 1902, 601; August 11, 1902, 623; around March 28, 1902, 484; July 30, 1902, 602, 605; August 4, 1902, 606; August 8, 1902, 617.
30. Hosea B. Morse, *The International Relations of the Chinese Empire* (New York: Longmans, 1918), 364.
31. PVGPT, August 8, 1902, 617; July 30, 1902, 599, 603; August 15, 1902, 626.
32. Louis Pellerin, "En Chine," *Le journal du dimanche*, July 27, 1902.
33. Letter from J. Ragsdale to W. W. Rockhill, June 4, 1907 (dispatch no. 675), Peking Legation Report to the Department of State, Record Group 84, dispatched from Tientsin, 1907, National Archives, Washington.
34. Letter from Li Hongzhang, Governor General of Zhili, to Sir E. Satow, February 17, 1901, NA, FO 674 / 91.
35. "La ville actuelle de Tien-Tsin," 366.
36. Letter from Jules Jadot to the Société d'étude des chemins de fer en Chine, Tianjin, February 1, 1903, transcribed in Kurgan-Van Hentenryk, *Jean Jadot*, 121.
37. Rogaski, *Hygienic Modernity*, 347, note 36.
38. Rogaski, *Hygienic Modernity*, , 188.
39. Yuan Shikai, *Memorial to the Throne* (1903), 636.
40. Da Gong Bao (Ta Kung Pao), cited in Chen Ke, "Nongovernmental Organizations and the Urban Control and Management System in Tianjin at the End of the 19th Century," *Social Sciences in China* 11, no. 4 (1990): 69.
41. Da Gong Bao, April 28, 1903, and May 8, 1903, cited in Ke, "Nongovernmental Organizations."
42. Da Gong Bao, January 10, 1903, cited in Ke, "Nongovernmental Organizations."
43. Da Gong Bao, September 15, 1902, cited in Ke, "Nongovernmental Organization."
44. Record of Changes and Developments in the Administration and Popular Customs of Tianjin, cited in Ke, "Nongovernmental Organizations," 72.
45. Bun, *Salt Merchants of Tianjin*, 108.
46. An equivalent bank was founded in Beijing in 1908. Brett Sheehan, *Trust in Troubled Times: Money, Banks, and State-Society Relations in Republican Tianjin* (Cambridge, MA: Harvard University Press, 2003), 124.
47. Sheehan, *Trust in Troubled Times*, 51.
48. Letter from the French consul in Tianjin, E. Saussine, to Mr. Maugras, chargé d'affaires of the French Republic in Beijing, June 14, 1921, CADN, 691 PO / 1 / 105.

49. Roland Dussart-Desart, *Les tramways de Tientsin* (Brussels: Tramania, 2017).
50. Letter from L. Jadot to É. Francqui, March 4, 1904, quoted in Dussart-Desart, *Les tramways de Tientsin*, 3.
51. A short line had been inaugurated in 1899 in the suburbs of Beijing but was quickly destroyed by the Boxers.
52. Roger R. Thompson, *China's Local Councils in the Age of Constitutional Reform, 1898–1911* (Cambridge, MA: Harvard University Press, 1995), 38.
53. Edward J. M. Rhoads, *Stepping Forth Into the World: The Chinese Educational Mission to the United States, 1872–1881* (Hong Kong: Hong Kong University Press, 2011), 68.
54. Louis T. Sigel, "The Diplomacy of Chinese Nationalism, 1900–1911," in *Myth and Reality: Social and Political Change in Modern China, 1860–1949*, ed. David Pong and Edmund Fung (Lanham, MD: University Press of America, 1985), 223–33.
55. Stephan Craft, *V. K. Wellington Koo and the Emergence of Modern China* (Lexington: University Press of Kentucky, 2004), 28.
56. Stephen R. MacKinnon, "Police Reform in Late Ch'ing Chihli," *Late Imperial China* 3, no. 4 (December 1975): 82–99.
57. "William Quincey," *The North-China Herald*, August 25, 1923, 40.
58. Interview with John Wong-Quincey, *Le temps de Genève*, October 23, 1957.
59. *The China Mail*, April 8, 1902.
60. "La ville actuelle de Tien-Tsin," 366.
61. PVGPT, May 14, 1902, 518.
62. *New York Times*, February 4, 1906, cited in Elizabeth LaCouture, "Modern Homes for Modern Families in Tianjin, China, 1860–1949" (PhD diss., Columbia University, 2010), 139.
63. Michael H. Hunt, *The Making of a Special Relationship: The United States and China to 1914* (New York: Columbia University Press, 1983).
64. "An American in China." *The New York Times*, August 24, 1902.
65. *The Brooklyn Daily Eagle*, June 19, 1913, 3.
66. "Herr Rump's Death," *Weekly Sun*, July 26, 1913, 10; Georg Baur, *China um 1900: Aufzeichnungen eines Krupp-Direktors* (Cologne: Böhlau Köln, 2005), 666.
67. Letter from Jules Jadot to the Société d'étude des chemins de fer en Chine, Tianjin, February 1, 1903, transcribed in Kurgan-Van Hentenryk, *Jean Jadot*, 122.
68. Letter from Jules Jadot, transcribed in Kurgan-Van Hentenryk, *Jean Jadot*, 123.
69. Yan Xiu, cited in Rogaski, *Hygienic Modernity*, 184.
70. Grandin, "Mes exploits," 414.

71. Giuseppe Messerotti Benvenuti, *Un italiano nella Cina dei Boxer: Lettere (1900–1901)*, ed. Nicola Lablanca (Modena: Panini, 2000), 44.
72. Derk Bodde and Clarence Morris, *Law in Imperial China: Exemplified by 190 Ch'ing Dynasty Cases (With Historical, Social, and Juridical Commentaries)* (Cambridge, MA: Harvard University Press, 1967).
73. "Chine," *Journal des débats politiques et littéraires*, November 15, 1903, 2.

Conclusion

1. Fang Zhiqin and Liu Sifen, eds., *Liang Qichao shiwen xuan* (Guangzhou: Guangdong Renmin Chubanshe, 1983), 522, cited in Jing Li, *China's America: The Chinese View the United States, 1900–2000* (Albany: SUNY Press, 2012), 11.
2. 'Lun xuexiao qi" (On Schools, 7th), *Shiwu bao*, GX23 / 4 / 21 (May 22, 1897), II, 1805, cited in Luke S. K. Kwong, "The Rise of the Linear Perspective on History and Time in Late Qing China c. 1860–1911," *Past & Present* 173 (November 2001): 180.
3. Kang Youwei, "Shili gongfa quanshu" (Substantial Truths and Universal Laws), in *Kang Youwei quanji* (The Complete Works of Kang Youwei), ed. Jiang Yihua et al. (Shanghai: Shanghai guji chubanshe, 1987), 292, cited in Kwong, "The Rise of the Linear Perspective," 181.
4. Christophe Charle, *Discordance des temps: Une brève histoire de la modernité* (Paris: Armand Colin, 2011), 326–27.
5. Ruth Rogaski, *Hygienic Modernity: Meanings of Health and Disease in Treaty-Port China* (Berkeley: University of California Press, 2004), 186.
6. Hua Xuelan, *Xinchou riji* (Shanghai: Shangwu yinshu guan, 1936), cited in Rogaski, *Hygienic Modernity*, 184.
7. Jean-Jacques Matignon, *L'Orient lointain: Chine, Corée, Mongolie, Japon* (Lyon: Adrien Storck, 1903), xviii.
8. John Hersey, "A Reporter at Large: Homecoming. 1: The House on New China Road," *New Yorker*, May 10, 1982, 54.
9. PVGPT, February 22, 1901, 132.
10. Edward J. M. Rhoads, *Manchu & Han: Ethnic Relations and Political Power in Late Qing and Early Republican China, 1861–1928* (Seattle: University of Washington Press, 2000), 10.
11. Alfred Verdross, *Fondements du droit international*, Recueil des cours, Académie de Droit International de la Haye (1927), 16:396; Hans Aufricht, "On Relative Sovereignty," *Cornell Law Review* 30, no. 2 (November 1944): 154; Finn Seyersted, *Common Law of International Organizations* (Leiden: Brill, 2008), 190.

12. Pierre Bourdieu, *Sur l'état: Cours au Collège de France (1989–1992)* (Paris: Seuil, 2012), 351–52.
13. Otto D. Rasmussen, *Tientsin: An Illustrated Outline History* (Tientsin: The Tientsin Press, 1925), 229.
14. Bernard Brizay, *La France en Chine: Du xviii*^{e} *siècle à nos jours* (Paris: Plon-Perrin, 2013).
15. The compensation amounted to 928 million with interest. The Chinese paid 668 million taels between 1901 and 1939, which was equivalent to USD61 billion in 2010.
16. James C. Scott, *Weapons of the Weak: Everyday Forms of Peasant Resistance* (New Haven, CT: Yale University Press, 1985).
17. Glen Stanway, *Fearless: The Story of Chin Woo Kung Fu* (Royston, UK: GMax Academy, 2013), 30.
18. Hao Yen-p'ing, *The Comprador in Nineteenth Century China: Bridge Between East and West* (Cambridge, MA: Harvard University Press, 1969); Shmuel N. Eisenstadt and Wolfgang Schluchter, "Introduction: Paths to Early Modernities: A Comparative View," *Daedalus* 127, no. 3 (Summer 1998): 1–18.
19. Lynn Pan, *Sons of the Yellow Emperor* (New York: Kodansha USA, 1994), 373–74.
20. Joseph Esherick, *The Origins of the Boxer Uprising* (Berkeley: University of California Press, 1987).
21. Richard Henry Tawney, *Land and Labor in China* (London: Allen and Unwin, 1932), 13.
22. Rhoads Murphey, *The Treaty Ports and China's Modernization: What Went Wrong?* (Ann Arbor: University of Michigan Press, 1970); Rhoads Murphey, "The Treaty Ports and China's Modernization," in *A Chinese City Between Two Worlds*, ed. Mark Elvin and G. William Skinner (Stanford, CA: Stanford University Press, 1974), 17–71; Rhoads Murphey, *China Meets the West: The Treaty Ports* (New York: Macmillan, 1975); Rhoads Murphey, *The Outsiders: The Western Experience in India and China* (Ann Arbor: University of Michigan Press, 1977).
23. Albert Feuerwerker, *The Chinese Economy, ca. 1870–1911* (Ann Arbor: University of Michigan Press, 1969), 58–61; François Gipouloux, *La Méditerranée asiatique: Villes portuaires et réseaux marchands en Chine, au Japon et en Asie du Sud-Est, xvi*^{e}*–xxi*^{e} *siècle* (Paris: CNRS Éditions, 2009), 176.
24. Jean-Jacques Matignon, *La Chine hermétique: Superstitions, crime et misère* (Paris: Geuthner, 1898), 274.
25. Gilbert Rozman, ed., *The Modernization of China* (New York: Free Press, 1981), 39.

26. Émile Zola, *Rome* (Paris: Bernouard, [1898] 1929), 686, cited in Charle, *Discordance des temps*, 309.

Appendix

1. Google's language app, Ngram Viewer, points to the years 1901–1902 as the peak usage of the term "Tientsin" or "Tien-Tsin" in works in its English, French, German, and Italian language databases between 1800 and 2014.

Bibliography

Primary sources

Associations de la Chine. *Lettres du Père Prosper Leboucq publiées par un de ses amis*. Paris: F. Wattelier et Cie, 1880.

Aufricht, Hans. "On Relative Sovereignty." *Cornell Law Review* 30, no. 2 (November 1944): 318–49.

Barnes, Arthur A. S. *On Active Service with the Chinese Regiment*. London: Grant Richards, 1902.

Beals, Z. Charles. *China and the Boxers*. New York: M. E. Munson, 1901.

Benvenuti, Giuseppe Messerotti. *Un italiano nella Cina dei Boxer: Lettere (1900–1901)*. Ed. Nicola Lablanca. Modena: Panini, 2000.

Bertinelli, Roberto. "La concessione italiana di Tientsin." *Nuova antologia* 212 (1907): 726–33.

Boulet, Marc. *Ma famille chinoise*. Paris: Seuil, 1998.

Brown, Frederick. *From Tientsin to Peking with the Allied Forces*. London: C. H. Kelly, 1902.

Bozan Jian, ed. *Yi He Tuan*. Shanghai: Shenzhou guogang she, 1961.

Burton, St. John. *Guide to Tientsin and Neighbourhood*. Tientsin: The China Times, 1908.

Candlin, George T. *John Innocent: A Story of Mission Work in North China*. London: United Methodist Publishing House, 1909.

Casserly, Gordon. *The Land of the Boxers or China Under the Allies*. London: Longmans, 1903.

Chan Chung Sing. *Les concessions en Chine, thèse pour le doctorat en droit*. Paris: PUF, 1925.

Charton, Édouard. *Journal d'un officier du corps expéditionnaire de Chine*. Paris: Le Tour du Monde, 1902.

"Chine: Tientsin et Pékin." *Revue française de l'étranger et des colonies et exploration: Gazette géographique* 25 (1900): 519–21.

Condamy, Charles. "Histoire du gouvernement provisoire de Tien-Tsin (1900–1902)." *Revue des troupes coloniales* (July–December 1905): 168–80.

Cordier, Henri. "Les douanes impériales maritimes chinoises." *T'oung Pao* 7, no. 4 (1906): 222–40.

Cotenson, G. "De l'art militaire des Chinois, d'après leurs classiques." *La nouvelle revue*, August 1900.

d'Anthouard, Albert-François-Ildefonse. *La Chine contre l'étranger: Les Boxeurs*. Paris: Plon, 1902.

Daoulas, Alexis. *Le siège de Tien-Tsin (15 juin–15 juillet 1900)*. Paris: Berger-Levrault, 1903.

Dix, Charles Cabry. *The World's Navies in the Boxer Rebellion (China 1900)*. London: Digby, Long & Co., 1905.

Drake, Noah Fields. *Map and Short Description of Tientsin*. Tianjin: n.p., 1900.

Eames, James B. *The English in China: Being an Account of the Intercourse and Relations Between England and China from the Year 1600 to the Year 1843 and a Summary of Later Developments*. London: Sir I. Pitman and Sons, 1909.

Fauvel, A.-A. "Le chemin de fer de Peking à Nieou-Tchouang." *Annales de géographie* 9, no. 46 (1900): 373–76.

Favier, Pierre-Marie-Alphonse. *Péking, histoire et description*. Paris: Desclée de Brouwer, 1902.

Fileti, Vincenzo. *La concessione italiana di Tien-tsin*. Genoa: Barabino e Graeve, 1921.

Frey, Henri. *Français et alliés au Pé-Tchi-Li, campagne de Chine de 1900*. Paris: Hachette, 1904.

Garsou, J. "Léopold Ier, le duc de Brabant et la Chine, 1859–1860." *Archives diplomatiques et consulaires*, November 1937, 482–87.

Gipps, George. *The Fighting in North China*. Shanghai: Kelly and Walsh, 1901.

Grandin, Jacques. "Mes exploits pendant la guerre de Chine de 1901 (Journal d'un volontaire)." *La revue des revues* 61 (May 1–15, 1902): 257–81.

Griswold, Alfred Whitney. *The Far Eastern Policy of the United States*. New York: Harcourt, Brace & Company, 1938.

Hoang, Pierre. *Notions juridiques sur la propriété en Chine*. Shanghai: Imprimerie de la Mission Catholique, 1897.

Hoover, Herbert. *The Memoirs of Herbert Hoover*, vol. 1, *The Years of Adventure, 1874–1920*. New York: Macmillan, 1952.

Laboulaye, Édouard de. *Les chemins de fer en Chine*. Paris: Émile Larose, 1911.

Laffan. "How They Looted: When Tientsin Was Taken." *West Gippsland Gazette* (Australia), November 20, 1900.

Legrand-Girarde, Émile Edmond. "Le génie en Chine (1900–1901)." *Revue du génie militaire*, January 1902, 1–277.

Loti, Pierre. *Les derniers jours de Pékin*. Paris: Calmann-Lévy, 1901.

——. "Les deux déesses des Boxeurs." Sunday, October 14, 1901.

Lynch, George. *The War of Civilizations*. London: Longmans, 1901.

Manning, William R. "China and the Powers Since the Boxer Movement." *American Journal of International Law* 4, no. 4 (October 1910): 848–902.

Martin, William Alexander Parsons. *The Awakening of China*. New York: Doubleday, Page & Company, 1910.

Matignon, Jean-Jacques. *La Chine hermétique: Superstitions, crime et misère*. Paris: Geuthner, 1898.

——. *L'Orient lointain: Chine, Corée, Mongolie, Japon*. Lyon: A. Storck, 1903.

Monnier, Marcel. *Le drame chinois: Juillet–août 1900*. Paris: F. Alcan, 1900.

Morse, Hosea B. *The International Relations of the Chinese Empire*. New York: Longmans, 1918.

Parker, E. H. "The Chinese Salt Trade: An Opening for British Enterprise." *Economic Journal* 9, no. 33 (March 1899): 116–25.

Pélacot, Charles-Baltazar de. *Expédition de Chine de 1900 jusqu'à l'arrivée du général Voyron*. Paris: H. Lavauzelle, 1903.

Rasmussen, Otto D. *The Growth of Tientsin*. Tianjin: The Tientsin Press, 1924.

——. *Tientsin: An Illustrated Outline History*. Tientsin: The Tientsin Press, 1925.

Reclus, Onésime, and Élisée Recluse. *L'empire du milieu, le climat, le sol, les races, la richesse de la Chine*. Paris: Hachette, 1902.

Rees, Miss G. M. *Tientsin Early History*. Tientsin: Tientsin Press, n.d.

Ricalton, James. *China Through the Stereoscope*. New York: Underwood & Underwood, 1901.

Roberts, James Hudson. *A Flight for Life*. Boston: Pilgrim Press, 1903.

Rodt, Cäcilie von. *Voyage d'une suissesse autour du monde*. Neuchâtel: F. Zahn, 1904.

Ruffi de Pontevès, Jean. *Souvenirs de la colonne Seymour*. Paris: Librairie Plon, 1903.

Savage-Landor, Arnold Henry. *China and the Allies*, vol. 2. London: William Heinemann, 1901.

Seeley, John R. *L'expansion de l'Angleterre*. Paris: A. Colin, 1884.

Silbermann, Léon. *Journal de marche d'un soldat colonial en Chine*. Paris: H. Charles-Lavauzelle, 1908.

Soulié de Morant, George. *L'acupuncture chinoise: Doctrine, diagnostic, thérapeutique*. Paris: Mercure de France, 1934.

Sun Tzu. *L'art de la guerre*. Grenoble: Éditions Philosophie, 2008.

Tai En Sai. *Treaty Ports in China: A Study in Diplomacy*. New York: Columbia University Press, 1918.

Tawney, Richard Henry. *Land and Labor in China*. London: Allen and Unwin, 1932.

Tenney, Charles. "Experiences in China" and "Li Hung Chang." Papers of Charles Daniel Tenney, Dartmouth College Library, 1919–1925.

Valli, Mario. *Gli avvenimenti in Cina nel 1900*. Milan: Urico Hoepli, 1905.

Verdross, Alfred. *Fondements du droit international*. Recueil des cours, Académie de Droit International de la Haye, vol. 16 (1927).

Verne, Jules. *Claudius Bombarnac*. Paris: Hetzel, 1892.

——. *Les tribulations d'un chinois en Chine*. Paris: Arvensa, 2014.

Villetard de Laguérie, Raoul Charles. "En Chine: La physionomie de Tien-Tsin." *L'Illustration*, December 15, 1900.

——. "Tien-Tsin après la défaite des Boxeurs (Voyage exécuté en 1900)." *Le tour du monde: Nouveau journal des voyages* 7, no. 41 (October 12, 1901): 490–92.

Voyron, Régis. *Rapport sur l'expédition de Chine, 1900–1901*. Paris: H. Charles-Lavauzelle, 1904.

Weber, Max. *La Ville*. Paris: Aubier Montaigne, 1982.

——. *Religions of China: Confucianism and Taoism*. Glencoe, IL: Free Press, 1951.

Weulersse, Georges. *Au Petchili et sur les frontières de Mandchourie*. Paris, 1900.

——. *Chine ancienne et nouvelle: Impressions et réflexions*. Paris: Armand Colin, 1902.

Williams, E. T. "Taxation in China." *Quarterly Journal of Economics* 26, no. 3 (May 1912): 482–510.

Secondary sources

Adshead, S. A. M. "Un cycle bureaucratique: L'administration du sel en Orient et en Occident." *Annales: Économies, sociétés, civilisations* 38, no. 2 (1983): 221–33.

Allee, Mark A. *Law and Local Society in Late Imperial China: Northern Taiwan in the Nineteenth Century*. Stanford, CA: Stanford University Press, 1994.

Alvin, Mark. "Mandarins and Millenarians: Reflections on the Boxer Uprising of 1899–1900." Lecture delivered at the School of Oriental and African Studies, June 6, 1979.

Anderson, Warwick. "Excremental Colonialism: Public Health and the Poetics of Pollution." *Critical Inquiry* 21, no. 3 (Spring 1995): 640–69.

Arnold, Dana. "Construire la modernité urbaine: la concession britannique à Tianjin, 1860–2013." *Outre-Mers: Revue d'histoire* 382–383 (June 2014): 89–102.

Baark, Erik. *Lightning Wires: The Telegraph and China's Technological Modernization, 1860–1890*. Westport, CT: Greenwood Press, 1997.

Badel, Laurence, and Stanislas Jeannesson. "Une histoire globale de la diplomatie?" *Monde(s)* 5 (May 2014): 6–26.

Badie, Bertrand. *L'état importé: L'occidentalisation de l'ordre politique*. Paris: Fayard, 1992.

Balazs, Etienne. *Chinese Civilization and Bureaucracy: Variations on a Theme*. New Haven, CT: Yale University Press, 1964.

Baur, Georg. *China um 1900: Aufzeichnungen eines Krupp-Direktors*. Cologne: Böhlau Köln, 2005.

Bergère, Marie-Claire. *Histoire de Shanghai*. Paris: Fayard, 2002.

Bernstein, Lewis. "After the Fall: Tianjin Under Foreign Occupation, 1900–1902." In *The Boxers, China, and the World*, ed. Robert Bickers and R. G. Tiedemann. Lanham, MD: Rowman & Littlefield, 2007.

——. "A History of Tientsin in Early Modern Times, 1800–1910." PhD dissertation, University of Kansas, 1988.

——. "Tianjin (Tientsin), China, Battle and Siege." In *The War of 1898 and U.S. Interventions*, ed. Benjamin R. Beede. New York: Routledge, 1994.

Besse, Jean-Marc. "Catoptique: Vue à vol d'oiseau et construction géométrique." Paper given at the conference "La Vue Aérienne: Savoirs et Pratiques de l'Espace," Paris, CNRS-British Academy, June 9, 2007.

Bickers, Robert. *The Scramble for China: Foreign Devils in the Qing Empire, 1832–1914*. London: Penguin Books, 2012.

Bickers, Robert, and R. G. Tiedemann, eds. *The Boxers, China, and the World*. Lanham, MD: Rowman & Littlefield, 2007.

Bin, Li. "La protection de la propriété en Chine: Transformation du droit interne et influence du droit international." Doctoral thesis, Université Paris-1 Panthéon-Sorbonne, 2009.

Bland, John Otway Percy. *Li Hung-chang*. Charleston, SC: Bibliobazaar, 2009.

Bodde, Derk, and Clarence Morris. *Law in Imperial China: Exemplified by 190 Ch'ing Dynasty Cases (With Historical, Social, and Juridical Commentaries)*. Cambridge, MA: Harvard University Press, 1967.

Bodin, Lynn E., and Chris Warner. *The Boxer Rebellion*. Oxford: Osprey Publishing, 1979.

Boulanger, Philippe. "Les espaces coloniaux dans la géographie militaire française (1871–1939)." In *L'empire des géographes: Géographie exploration et colonisation (xixe–xxe s.)*, ed. Pierre Singaravélou, 135–46. Paris: Belin, 2008.

Bourdelais, Patrice, ed. *Les hygiénistes: Enjeux, modèles et pratiques, xviiie–xxe siècles*. Paris: Belin, 2001.

Bourdelais, Patrice, and Jean-Yves Raulot. *Une peur bleue: Histoire du choléra en France 1832–1854*. Paris: Payot, 1987.

Bourdieu, Pierre. *Sur l'état: Cours au Collège de France (1989–1992)*. Paris: Seuil, 2012.

Bourgon, Jérôme. "La coutume et le droit en Chine à la fin de l'empire." *Annales: Histoire, sciences sociales* 54, no. 5 (1999): 1073–1107.

——. " 'Sauver la vie': De la fraude judiciaire en Chine à la fin de l'empire." *Actes de la recherche en sciences sociales* 133 (June 2000): 32–39.

Bouvier d'Yvoire, Vincent. "Les concessions françaises en Chine, 1916–1929: Canton, Shanghai, Hankeou, Tientsin." Thesis, Université Paris-1 Panthéon-Sorbonne, 1988.

Boyd, Julia. *A Dance with the Dragon: The Vanished World of Peking's Foreign Colony.* London: I. B. Tauris, 2012.

Brizay, Bernard. *La France en Chine: Du xviiie siècle à nos jours.* Paris: Plon-Perrin, 2013.

Brook, Timothy, Jérôme Bourgon, and Gregory Blue. *Death by a Thousand Cuts.* Cambridge, MA: Harvard University Press, 2008.

Brun, Jean-François. "Intervention armée en Chine: L'expédition internationale de 1900–1901." *Revue historique des armées* 258 (2010): 14–45.

Buck, David D. *Urban Change in China: Politics and Development in Tsinan, Shantung, 1890–1949.* Madison: University of Wisconsin Press, 1978.

Cahen, Michel. *Africando: Bilan 1988–2009 et projets 2010–2018,* vol. 1. Report, Ecole des Hautes Etudes en Sciences Sociales (EHESS), 2010.

Cassel, Pär Kristoffer. *Grounds of Judgment: Extraterritoriality and Imperial Power in Nineteenth-Century China and Japan.* Oxford: Oxford University Press, 2012.

Cavallarin, Marco, Barbara Henry, Aglaia De Angeli, Ludovica De Courten, and Jérôme Pauchard, eds. *Gli ebrei in Cina e il caso di Tien Tsin: Convivenze in Cina.* Livorno: Belforte Editore, 2012.

Chabaille, Fleur. "La présence française en Chine (1916–1951), la politique de l'extension à 'petits-pas.' " Thesis, Université Paris-1 Panthéon-Sorbonne, 2010.

Charle, Christophe. *Discordance des temps: Une brève histoire de la modernité.* Paris: Armand Colin, 2011.

——. *Paris fin de siècle: Culture et politique.* Paris: Seuil, 1998.

——. *Paris 1900: La capitale des capitales?* Paris: Petit-Palais, July 4, 2014.

Charle, Christophe, ed. *Le temps des capitales culturelles xviiie–xxe siècles.* Seyssel: Champ Vallon, 2009.

Chemouilli, Philippe. "Le choléra et la naissance de la santé publique dans le Japon de Meiji. 1: Modernité, choléra et pensée hygiénique." *Médecine sciences* 20, no. 1 (January 2004): 109–14.

——, "Le choléra et la naissance de la santé publique dans le Japon de Meiji. 2: Forces et faiblesses d'une politique de santé publique." *Médecine sciences* 20, no. 2 (February 2004): 236–40.

Chen, Cai. *A Pictorial Record of the Qing Dynasty: Business Documents.* Singapore: China Renmin University Press, 2009.

Chen, Bofeng. "Excessive Litigation, *Xinfang* and Legal Traditions of New China." *Peking University Law Journal* (Zhongwai Faxue) 16, no. 2 (2004).

Ch'en, Jerome. "The Nature and Characteristics of the Boxer Movement: A Morphological Study." *Bulletin of the School of Oriental Studies* 23 (1960): 20–26.

——. *Yuan Shih-k'ai.* Stanford, CA: Stanford University Press, 1972.

Chen, Ke. "Nongovernmental Organizations and the Urban Control and Management System in Tianjin at the End of the 19th Century." *Social Sciences in China* 11, no. 4 (1990).

Chen, Li. "Legal Specialists and Judicial Administration in Late Imperial China, 1651–1911." *Late Imperial China* 33, no. 1 (June 2012): 1–54.

Chenevix Trench, Charles. *The Road to Khartoum: A Life of General Charles Gordon.* New York: Dorset Press, 1988.

Chevrier, Yves. "La question de la société civile, la Chine et le chat du Cheshire." *Études chinoises* 14, no. 2 (Fall 1995): 153–251.

Chien, Po-tsan et al., eds. *I ho t'uan* (The Boxers). Shanghai: Shen-chou kuo-kuang she, 1951.

Ch'ü T'ung-tsu. *Local Government in China Under the Ch'ing.* Stanford, CA: Stanford University Press, 1969.

Chung Yam Po. *Westerners in Li Hongzhang's Mufu: With References to Gustav Detring and Hosea Ballou Morse.* Hong Kong: Hong Kong Baptist University, 2010.

Cicchiti-Suriani, Arnaldo. "La concessione italiana di Tient Tsin (1901–1951)." *Rassegna Italiana di Politica e Cultura* 31 (October 1951): 563.

Clifford, Nicholas R. *Spoilt Children of Empire: Westerners in Shanghai and the Chinese Revolution of the 1920s.* Middlebury, NH: University Press of New England, 1991.

Cohen, Paul A. *China Unbound: Evolving Perspectives on the Chinese Past.* London: Routledge, 2003.

——. *Discovering History in China: American Historical Writing on the Recent Chinese Past.* New York: Columbia University Press, 1985.

——. *History in Three Keys: The Boxers as Event, Experience, and Myth.* New York: Columbia University Press, 1997.

Cohen, William B. *Empereurs sans sceptre.* Paris: Berger-Levrault, 1974.

Coleman, Maryruth. "Municipal Politics in Nationalist China: Nanjing, 1927–1937." PhD dissertation, Harvard University, 1984.

Cook, James A. "Bridges to Modernity: Xiamen, Overseas Chinese and Southeast Coastal Modernization, 1843–1937." PhD dissertation, University of California San Diego, 1998.

Craft, Stephan. *V. K. Wellington Koo and the Emergence of Modern China.* Lexington: University Press of Kentucky, 2004.

Crouch, Archie R., ed. *Christianity in China: A Scholar's Guide to Resources in the Libraries and Archives of the United States.* Armonk, NY: M. E. Sharpe, 1989.

Curti, Merle, and John Stalker. " 'The Flowery Flag Devil': The American Image in China 1840–1900." *Proceedings of the American Philosophical Society* 96, no. 6 (December 1952): 663–90.

Debelle, Daisy. "Les nouvelles dynamiques du tourisme et de la patrimonialisation en Chine: Étude des anciennes concessions et du quartier français de Tianjin en particulier." Thesis, Université Paris-1/Université de Tianjin, 2015.

Deluermoz, Quentin, and Pierre Singaravélou. *A Past of Possibilities: A History of What Could Have Been*. Trans. Stephen W. Sawyer. New Haven, CT: Yale University Press, 2021.

Denison, Edward, and Yu Ren Guang. *Building Shanghai: The Story of China's Gateway*. Chichester: Wiley, 2006.

Dibner, Bern. "Hoover and Agricola." *Technology and Culture* 13, no. 3 (July 1972): 421.

Dikötter, Frank. *Crime, Punishment and the Prison in Modern China*. New York: Columbia University Press, 1992.

——. *Exotic Commodities: Modern Objects and Everyday Life in China*. New York: Columbia University Press, 2013.

Dong, Wang. *China's Unequal Treaties: Narrating National History*. Lanham, MD: Lexington Books, 2005.

Dong, Yue. "Memories of the Present: Vicissitudes of Transition in Republican Beijing, 1911–1937." PhD dissertation, University of California San Diego, 1996.

Drayton, Richard. "Masked Condominia: Pan-European Collaboration in the History of Imperialism, c. 1500 to the present," *Global History Review* 5 (2012): 308–31.

——. *Nature's Government: Science, Imperial Britain and the "Improvement" of the World*. New Haven, CT: Yale University Press, 2000.

Drévillon, Hervé. *Batailles: Scènes de guerre de la table ronde aux tranchées*. Paris: Seuil, 2007.

Dryburgh, Marjorie. "Japan in Tianjin: Settlers, State and the Tensions of Empire Before 1937." *Japanese Studies* 27, no. 1 (May 2007): 19–34.

Duchesne, Albert. "Les aspects diplomatiques du projet d'expédition belge en Chine en 1900." *Revue belge de philologie et d'histoire* 32, no. 1 (1954): 77–96.

Dunstheimer, Guillaume G. H. "Le mouvement des Boxeurs: Documents et études publiés depuis la deuxième guerre mondiale." *Revue historique* 470 (April–June 1964): 387–416.

——. "Religion et magie dans le mouvement des Boxeurs d'après les textes chinois." *T'oung Pao* 47 (1959): Books 3–5.

Dussart-Desart, Roland. *Les tramways de Tientsin*. Brussels: Tramania, 2017.

Dutton, Michael. *Policing and Punishment in China: From Patriarchy to "The People."* Cambridge: Cambridge University Press, 1992.

Edgerton, Robert B. *Warriors of the Rising Sun: A History of the Japanese Military*. New York: W. W. Norton, 1997.

Eisenstadt, Shmuel N., and Wolfgang Schluchter. "Introduction: Paths to Early Modernities—A Comparative View." *Daedalus* 127, no. 3 (1998): 1–18.

Elleman, Bruce A. *Modern Chinese Warfare, 1795–1989*. London: Routledge, 2001.

Elliott, Jane E. *Some Did It for Civilisation, Some Did It for Their Country*. Hong Kong: The Chinese University Press, 2002.

Elvin, Mark. "The Gentry Democracy in Shanghai, 1905–1914." Doctoral thesis, Cambridge University, 1968.

——. "Mandarins and Millenarians: Reflections on the Boxer Uprising of 1899–1900." Lecture delivered at the School of Oriental and African Studies, June 6, 1979.

Elvin, Mark, and G. William Skinner, eds. *The Chinese City Between Two Worlds*. Stanford, CA: Stanford University Press, 1974.

Esherick, Joseph. *The Origins of the Boxer Uprising*. Berkeley: University of California Press, 1987.

Esherick, Joseph, ed. *Remaking the Chinese City: Modernity and National Identity, 1900–1950*. Honolulu: University of Hawaii Press, 1999.

Esherick, Joseph, and Mary Backus Rankin, eds. *Chinese Local Elites and Patterns of Dominance*. Berkeley: University of California Press, 1990.

Esselstrom, Erik. *Crossing Empire's Edge: Foreign Ministry Police and Japanese Expansionism in Northeast Asia*. Honolulu: University of Hawaii Press, 2009.

Fairbank, John K. "Patterns Behind the Tientsin Massacre." *Harvard Journal of Asiatic Studies* 20, nos. 3–4 (December 1957): 480–511.

Fairbank, John K., ed. *The Cambridge History of China: Late Ch'ing 1800–1911*, vol. 1. Cambridge: Cambridge University Press, 1978.

Fairbank, John K., Martha Henderson Coolidge, and Richard J. Smith. *H. B. Morse, Customs Commissioner and Historian of China*. Lexington: University Press of Kentucky, 1995.

Fang, Qiang. "A Hot Potato: The Chinese Complaint Systems from Early Times to the Present." PhD dissertation, SUNY Buffalo, 2006.

——. "Hot Potatoes: Chinese Complaint Systems from Early Times to the Late Qing (1898)." *Journal of Asian Studies* 68, no. 4 (November 2009): 1105–35.

Fang Zhiqin and Sifen Liu, eds. *Liang Qichao shiwen xuan*. Guangzhou: Guangdong Renmin Chubanshe, 1983.

Fei, Hsiao-t'ung. *China's Gentry: Essays on Rural-Urban Relations*. Chicago: Margaret Park Redfield, 1953.

Feuerwerker, Albert. *The Chinese Economy, ca. 1870–1911*. Ann Arbor: University of Michigan Press, 1969.

Fichter, James R. *So Great a Profit: How the East Indies Transformed Anglo-American Capitalism*. Cambridge, MA: Harvard University Press.

Ford, Christopher. *The Mind of Empire: China's History and Modern Foreign Relations.* Lexington: University Press of Kentucky, 2010.

Gabbiani, Luca. "À la recherche du lustre d'antan: La réhabilitation de la voirie de Pékin pendant la première décennie du xxe siècle." *Études chinoises* 23 (2004): 181–271.

——. "Les origines de la santé publique à Pékin, 1901–1911: Influences et conséquences." In *Les hygiénistes: Enjeux, modèles et pratiques, xviiie–xxe siècles*, ed. Patrice Bourdelais, 373–92. Paris: Belin, 2001.

——. *Pékin à l'ombre du Mandat Céleste: Vie quotidienne et gouvernement urbain sous la dynastie Qing (1644–1911).* Paris: Éditions de l'EHESS, 2011.

Ged, Françoise. "Shanghai: Habitat et structure urbaine 1842–1995." Doctoral thesis, Paris, École des Hautes Études en Sciences Sociales, 1997.

Gipouloux, François. *La Méditerranée asiatique: Villes portuaires et réseaux marchands en Chine, au Japon et en Asie du Sud-Est, xvie–xxie siècle.* Paris: CNRS Éditions, 2009.

Gobille, Boris. "Usurpation de fonction et appropriation du pouvoir selon différents types de situations de crise: Éléments de discussion." In *Usurpations de fonction et appropriations du pouvoir en situation de crise (xixe–xxe siècle)*, ed. Quentin Deluermoz and Jérémie Foa, Conference Proceedings, January 16, 2010. Paris: Centre d'Histoire du XIXe Siècle, 2012.

Goerg, Odile, and Xavier Huetz de Lemps. *La ville coloniale, xve–xxe siècle.* Paris: Seuil, 2012.

Goodman, Bryna. *Native Place, City, and Nation: Regional Networks and Identities in Shanghai, 1853–1937.* Berkeley: University of California Press, 1995.

Goodman, Bryna, and David S. G. Goodman, eds. *Twentieth-Century Colonialism and China: Localities, the Everyday, and the World.* London: Routledge, 2012.

Grousset, René. *Histoire de la Chine.* Paris: Fayard, 1942.

Grove, Linda. "International Trade and the Creation of Domestic Marketing Networks in North China, 1860–1930." In *Commercial Networks in Modern Asia*, ed. Linda Grove and Shinya Sugiyama. London: Routledge, 2013.

Grove, Richard. *Green Imperialism: Colonial Expansion, Tropical Island Edens and the Origins of Environmentalism, 1600–1860.* Cambridge: Cambridge University Press, 1995.

Guttmann, Allen. *Sports: The First Five Millennia.* Amherst: University of Massachusetts Press, 2007.

Haag, Michael. *Alexandria: City of Memory.* New Haven, CT: Yale University Press, 2004.

Hao, Yen-p'ing. *The Comprador in Nineteenth Century China: Bridge Between East and West.* Cambridge, MA: Harvard University Press, 1969.

Harrington, Peter, and Frederick A. Sharf. *The Boxer Rebellion: China 1900, the Artist's Perspective.* London: Greenhill Books, 2000.

Hays, J. N. *Epidemics and Pandemics: Their Impacts on Human History*. Santa Barbara, CA: ABC-CLIO, 2005.

Henriot, Christian. *Belles de Shanghai: Prostitution et sexualité en Chine aux xixe–xxe siècles*. Paris: CNRS Éditions, 1997.

——. *Shanghai 1927–1937: Élites locales et modernisation en Chine nationaliste*. Paris: Éditions de l'École des Hautes Études en Sciences Sociales, 1991.

Henriot, Christian, and Geneviève Dubois-Taine, eds. *Cities in the Pacific Rim: Sustainability and Diversity*. Paris: PUCA, 2001.

Henriot, Christian, and Catherine Yeh. *Chinese Urban History Workshop: A Reader*. Lyon: Institut d'Asie Orientale, 1996.

Hershatter, Gail. *Dangerous Pleasures: Prostitution and Modernity in Twentieth-Century Shanghai*. Berkeley: University of California Press, 1997.

——. *The Workers of Tianjin, 1900–1949*. Stanford, CA: Stanford University Press, 1986.

Hevia, James. "Loot's Fate: The Economics of Plunder and the Moral Life of Objects." *History and Anthropology* 6, no. 4 (1994).

Hocquet, Jean-Claude. "Production du sel et changement technique en Chine." *Annales: Économies, sociétés, civilisations* 46, no. 5 (1991): 1021–39.

Ho-fung, Hung. *Protest with Chinese Characteristics: Demonstrations, Riots and Petitions in the Mid-Qing Dynasty*. New York: Columbia University Press, 2011.

Honglin, Ma. "Lin Hei'er." In *Biographical Dictionary of Chinese Women: The Qing Period, 1644–1911*. Ed. Lily Xiao Hong Lee, A. D. Stefanowska, Sue Wiles, and Clara Wing-chung Ho. London: M. E. Sharpe, 1998.

Hotte, Thomas G. *The China Question: Great Power Rivalry and British Isolation, 1894–1905*. Oxford: Oxford University Press, 2007.

Houdaille, Jacques, and Louis Henry. "Célibat et âge au mariage aux xviiie et xixe siècles en France. II: Âge au premier mariage." *Population* 34, no. 2 (1979): 403–42.

Howarth, Peter. *China's Rising Sea Power: The PLA Navy's Submarine Challenge*. London: Routledge, 2006.

Hsiao Kung-Ch'üan. *Rural China: Imperial Control in the Nineteenth Century*. Seattle: University of Washington Press, 1960.

Huang, Philip. *Civil Justice in China: Representation and Practice in the Qing (Law, Society, and Culture in China)*. Stanford, CA: Stanford University Press, 1996.

Huang, Philip, and Kathryn Bernhardt, eds. *Research from Archival Case Records: Law, Society and Culture in China*. Leiden: Brill, 2014.

Huber, Valeska. "The Unification of the Globe by Disease? The International Sanitary Conference on Cholera, 1851–1894." *Historical Journal* 49, no. 2 (2006): 454–74.

Huetz de Lemps, Xavier. "'À bas les murailles!': Le débat sur le dérasement des fortifications dans les villes espagnoles (xixe–début xxe siècle)." In *Les passions d'un historien: Mélanges en l'honneur de Jean-Pierre Poussou*, 1105–14. Paris: Presses de l'Université de Paris-Sorbonne, 2010.

——. *L'archipel des "épices": La corruption de l' administration espagnole aux Philippines (fin xviiie–fin xixe siècle)*. Madrid: Casa de Velasquez, 2006.

——. "Manille au xixe siècle: Croissance et aménagement d'une ville coloniale (1815–1898)." PhD dissertation, Université de Bordeaux-3, 1994.

Hunt, Michael H. *The Making of a Special Relationship: The United States and China to 1914*. New York: Columbia University Press, 1983.

Hüttner, Johann-Christian. *Voyage à la Chine*. Paris: Pillot Jeune, 1803.

Jennings, Eric T. *À la cure, les coloniaux! Thermalisme, climatisme et colonisation française (1830–1962)*. Rennes: Presses Universitaires de Rennes, 2011.

——. *La ville de l'éternel printemps: Comment Dalat a permis l'Indochine française*. Paris: Payot, 2013.

Jing Li. *China's America: The Chinese View the United States, 1900–2000*. Albany: SUNY Press, 2012.

Kang, David C. "Hierarchy in Asian International Relations, 1300–1900." *Asian Security* 1, no. 1 (January 2005): 53–79.

Kellogg, Vernon. *Herbert Hoover: The Man and His Work*. New York: D. Appleton and Company, 1920.

Ki Che Leung, Angela. "'Variolation' and Vaccination in Late Imperial China, ca. 1570–1911." In *History of Vaccine Development*, ed. Stanley A. Plotkin. New York: Springer, 2011.

Kuhn, Philip. *Rebellion and Its Enemies in Late Imperial China*. Cambridge, MA: Harvard University Press, 1970.

Kurgan-Van Hentenryk, Ginette. *Jean Jadot: Artisan de l'expansion belge en Chine*. Brussels: Académie Royale des Sciences d'Outre-mer, 1965.

——. *Léopold II et les groupes financiers en Chine: La politique royale et ses prolongements*. Brussels: Académie Royale de Belgique, 1972.

Kwan Man Bun. "Order in Chaos: Tianjin's Hunhunr and Urban Identity in Modern China." *Journal of Urban History* 27 (2000): 75–91.

——. *The Salt Merchants of Tianjin: State-Making and Civil Society in Late Imperial China*. Honolulu: University of Hawaii Press, 2001.

Kwong, Luke S. K. "The Rise of the Linear Perspective on History and Time in Late Qing China c. 1860–1911." *Past & Present* 173 (November 2001): 57–190.

LaCouture, Elizabeth. "Modern Homes for Modern Families in Tianjin, China, 1860–1949." PhD dissertation, Columbia University, 2010.

Lai Xinxia. *Tianjin jindaishi* (Contemporary History of Tianjin). Tianjin: Nankai daxue chubanshe, 1987.

Lee Khoon Choy. *Pioneers of Modern China: Understanding the Inscrutable Chinese*. Singapore: World Scientific, 2005.

Lehner, Georg, and Monika Lehner. *Österreich-Ungarn und der "Boxeraufstand" in China*. Innsbruck: StudienVerlag, 2002.

Lemire, Vincent. *Jérusalem 1900: La ville sainte à l'âge des possible*. Paris: Armand Colin, 2013.

Leuchtenburg, William E. *Herbert Hoover: The 31st President, 1929–1933*. New York: Macmillan, 2009.

Li Hongtu. "De 'Sous-le-Ciel' (*tianxia*) à l' 'Outre-océan' (*yang*): Évolution de la représentation du monde extérieur chez les Chinois." *Monde(s)* 3 (2013): 91–112.

Li, Lillian M., and Alison Dray-Novey. "Guarding Beijing's Food Security in the Qing Dynasty: State, Market, and Police Source." *Journal of Asian Studies* 58, no. 4 (November 1999): 992–1032.

Li Rong-Zhi and Huan-yu Xiao. "Introduction of Table Tennis Into Modern China and Its Development." *Journal of Chengdu Sport University* 5 (2012): 1–6.

Li Xiaocong. *A Descriptive Catalogue of Pre-1900 Chinese Maps Seen in Europe*. Beijing: International Culture Publishing Corporation, 1996.

Li Zhaojie and Li James. "Traditional Chinese World Order." *Chinese Journal of International Law* 1 (2002): 20–58.

Lian Hu. "Tianjin, un centre majeur de l'industrie culturelle chinoise?" PhD dissertation, EHESS, 2012.

Liang Yiqun. "Lin Hei'er: 'Hongdengzhao' dashijie." In *Gujin zhuming funü renwu* 1:360–64. Shijiazhuang: Hebei renmin chubanshe, 1986.

Liao Yizhong. " Lin Hei'er." in *Qingdai renwu zhuangao* 3:98–101. Beijing: Zhonghua shuju, 1987.

Lieberthal, Kenneth. *Revolution and Tradition in Tientsin 1949–1952*. Stanford, CA: Stanford University Press, 1980.

Lin Jingneng, ed. *Tianjin renkoushi* (Historical Demography of Tianjin). Tianjin: Nankai daxue chubanshe, 1990.

Lishunde dafandian (The Astor Hotel). Tianjin: Jinguo zhongdian wenwu baohu danwei, 1993.

Liu, Lydia H. *The Clash of Empires: The Invention of China in Modern World Making*. Cambridge, MA: Harvard University Press, 2004.

Liu Haiyan. *Kongjian yu shehui: Jindai Tianjin cheng shi yanbian/Space and Society: Changes in Modern Tianjin*. Tianjin: Tianjin Academy of Social Sciences Press, 2003.

Liu Heung Shing. *China Revolution: The Road to 1911*. Hong Kong: Hong Kong University, 2001.

Lung Chang. *La Chine à l'aube du xxe siècle*. Paris: Nouvelles Éditions Latines, 1962.

Luo Shuwei, ed. *Jindai Tianjin chengshi shi* (Tianjin's Modern Urban History). Beijing: Chinese Academy of Social Sciences Press, 1993.

Machiels, Christine, and Éric Pierre. "La prostitution des mineur(e)s au xxe siècle." *Revue d'histoire de l'enfance "irrégulière"* 10 (2008): 7–12.

MacKinnon, Stephen R. "Police Reform in Late Ch'ing Chihli." *Late Imperial China* 3, no. 4 (December 1975): 82–99.

——. *Power and Politics in Late Imperial China: Yuan Shih-k'ai in Beijing and Tianjin, 1901–1908.* Berkeley: California University Press, 1980.

Mak, Ricardo K. S. "Western Advisers and Late Qing Chinese Military Modernization: A Case Study of Constantin von Hanneken (1854–1925)." *Journal of Northeast Asian History* 2, no. 10 (2014): 47–70.

Malezemoff, Andrew. *Russian Far Eastern Policy, 1881–1904.* Berkeley: University of California Press, 1958.

Mann, Susan. "Urbanization and Historical Change in China." *Modern China* 10, no. 1 (January 1984): 79–113.

Mansel, Philip. *Constantinople: City of the World's Desire 1453–1924.* New York: St. Martin's Press, 1998.

Marinelli, Maurizio. "An Italian 'Neighbourhood' in Tianjin: Little Italy or Colonial Space?" In *Twentieth-Century Colonialism and China: Localities, the Everyday and the World,* ed. Bryna Goodman and David S. G. Goodman, 92–107. London: Routledge, 2012.

——. "Making Concessions in Tianjin: Heterotopia and Italian Colonialism in Mainland China (1860–1945)." *Urban History* 36, no. 3 (December 2009): 399–425.

——. "Projecting *Italianità* on the Chinese Space: The Construction of the 'Aristocratic Concession' in Tianjin (1901–1947)." In *Italy's Encounters with Modern China: Imperial Dreams, Strategic Ambitions,* ed. Maurizio Marinelli and Giovanni Andornino, 1–26. Basingstoke: Palgrave Macmillan, 2014.

Martin, Brian G. *The Shanghai Green Gang: Politics and Organized Crime, 1919–1937.* Berkeley: University of California Press, 1996.

Mazower, Mark. *Salonica, City of Ghosts: Christians, Muslims and Jews 1430–1950.* London: Harper, 2005.

McCord, Edward A. *The Power of the Gun: The Emergence of Modern Chinese Warlordism.* Berkeley: University of California Press, 1993.

Mengin, Christine. "Écrire l'histoire des concessions de Tianjin par l'architecture: État des lieux." *Outre-Mers: Revue d'histoire* 382–383 (June 2014): 13–25.

Metcalf, Thomas. *Imperial Connections: India in the Indian Ocean Arena, 1860–1920.* Berkeley: University of California Press, 2008.

Mingzheng Shi. "Beijing Transforms: Urban Infrastructure, Public Works, and Social Change in the Chinese Capital, 1900–1928." PhD dissertation, Columbia University, 1993.

Monger, George W. "The End of Isolation: Britain, Germany and Japan, 1900–1902." *Transactions of the Royal Historical Society* 5, no. 13 (1963): 103–21.

Murphey, Rhoads. *China Meets the West: The Treaty Ports.* New York: Macmillan, 1975.

———. "The City as a Center of Change: Western Europe and China." *Annals of the American Association of Geographers* 44 (1954): 349–62.
———. *The Outsiders: The Western Experience in India and China.* Ann Arbor: University of Michigan Press, 1977.
———. "The Treaty Ports and China's Modernization." In *A Chinese City Between Two Worlds*, ed. Mark Elvin and G. William Skinner, 17–71. Stanford, CA: Stanford University Press, 1974.
———. *The Treaty Ports and China's Modernization: What Went Wrong?* Ann Arbor: University of Michigan, Center for Chinese Studies, 1970.
Murthy, Viren. "The Democratic Potential of Confucian Minben Thought," *Asian Philosophy: An International Journal of the Philosophical Traditions of the East* 10, no. 1 (2000).
Naquin, Susan. *Peking: Temples and City Life, 1400–1900.* Berkeley: University of California Press, 2000.
Nguyen, Johan. *La réception de l'acupuncture en France: Une biographie revisitée de George Soulié de Morant.* Paris: L'Harmattan, 2012.
O'Brien, Anita M. "Military Academies in China, 1885–1915." In *Perspectives on a Changing China*, ed. Joshua A. Fogel and William T. Rowe. Boulder, CO: Westview Press, 1979.
O'Brien, Phillips. *The Anglo-Japanese Alliance, 1902–1922.* London: Routledge, 2004.
Ono, Kazuko. *Chinese Women in a Century of Revolution, 1850–1950.* Stanford, CA: Stanford University Press, 1989.
Paillette, Céline. "Épidémies, santé et ordre mondial: Le rôle des organisations sanitaires internationales, 1903–1923." *Monde(s): Histoire, espaces, relations* 2, no. 2 (2012).
Pan, Lynn. *Sons of the Yellow Emperor.* New York: Kodansha USA, 1994.
A Panorama of the Historic Architecture in Tianjin. Tianjin: China Architecture and Building Press, 2007.
Peterson, Glen. "Overseas Chinese and Merchant Philanthropy in China: From Culturalism to Nationalism." *Journal of Chinese Overseas* 1 (2005): 87–109.
Pinol, Jean-Luc, and François Walter. *La ville contemporaine jusqu'à la seconde guerre mondiale.* Paris: Seuil, 2003.
Poisson, Emmanuel. "Faux, falsification, pouvoir et société." *Extrême-Orient, Extrême-Occident* 32 (2010): 5–11.
Polumbaum, Judy. "From Evangelism to Entertainment: The YMCA, the NBA, and the Evolution of Chinese Basketball." *Modern Chinese Literature and Culture* 14, no. 1 (2002): 178–230.
Power, Brian. *The Ford of Heaven: A Cosmopolitan Childhood in Tientsin.* Oxford: Signal Books, 2005.
Qin Shao. "Making Political Culture: The Case of Nantong, 1894–1930." PhD dissertation. East Lansing: Michigan State University, 1994.

Quested, Rosemary. *The Russo-Chinese Bank: A Multinational Financial Base of Tsarism in China.* Birmingham: Birmingham University Press, 1977.

Rankin, Mary Backus. *Elite Activism and Political Transformation in China: Zhejiang Province 1865–1911.* Stanford, CA: Stanford University Press, 1986.

——. "Local Elites and Community Affairs in the Late Imperial Period." *Études chinoises* 9, no. 2 (Fall 1990): 13–60.

Reed, Bradly W. *Talons and Teeth: County Clerks and Runners in the Qing Dynasty.* Stanford, CA: Stanford University Press, 2000.

Rhoads, Edward J. M. *Manchu & Han: Ethnic Relations and Political Power in Late Qing and Early Republican China, 1861–1928.* Seattle: University of Washington Press, 2000.

——. *Stepping Forth Into the World: The Chinese Educational Mission to the United States, 1872–1881.* Hong Kong: Hong Kong University Press, 2011.

Rihal, Dorothée. "La concession française de Hankou (1896–1943): De la condamnation à l'appropriation d'un héritage." Thesis, Université Paris-7, 2007.

Roberts, Luke S. "The Petition Box in Eighteenth-Century Tosa." *Journal of Japanese Studies* 20, no. 2 (Summer 1994): 423–58.

Rogaski, Ruth. *Hygienic Modernity: Meanings of Health and Disease in Treaty-Port China.* Berkeley: University of California Press, 2004.

Romanov, Boris Aleksandrovich. *Russia in Manchuria, 1892–1906.* Ann Arbor, MI: J. W. Edwards, 1952.

Roux, Alain. *Grèves et politiques à Shanghai: Les désillusions, 1927–1932.* Paris: Editions de l'EHESS, 1995.

Rowe, William T. *Hankow: Commerce and Society in a Chinese City, 1796–1889.* Stanford, CA: Stanford University Press, 1984.

——. "The Problem of Civil Society in Late Imperial China." *Modern China* 19, no. 2 (1993): 139–57.

——. "The Public Sphere in Modern China." *Modern China* 16, no. 3 (1990): 309–29.

Rozman, Gilbert, ed. *The Modernization of China.* New York: Free Press, 1981.

Rudolph, Jennifer. *Negotiated Power in Late Imperial China: The Zongli Yamen and the Politics of Reform.* Ithaca, NY: Cornell University Press, 2008.

Ruskola, Teemu. "Law Without Law, or Is Chinese Law an Oxymoron?" *William & Mary Bill of Rights Journal* 11 (2002): 655–69.

Sanjuan, Thierry, ed. *Les grands hôtels en Asie: Modernité, dynamiques urbaines et sociabilité.* Paris: Publications de la Sorbonne, 2003.

Saunier, Pierre-Yves, and Shane Ewen, eds. *Another Global City: Historical Explorations Into the Transnational Municipal Moment 1850–2000.* New York: Palgrave Macmillan, 2008.

Schmidt, Vera. *Aufgabe und Einfluss der europäischen Berater in China: Gustav Detring (1842–1913) im Dienste Li Hung-changs.* Wiesbaden: Otto Harrassowitz Verlag, 1984.

Schneer, Jonathan. *London 1900: The Imperial Metropolis.* New Haven, CT: Yale University Press, 2001.

Scott, James C. *Weapons of the Weak: Everyday Forms of Peasant Resistance.* New Haven, CT: Yale University Press, 1985.

Scully, Eileen P. *Bargaining with the State from Afar: American Citizenship in Treaty Port China, 1844–1942.* New York: Columbia University Press, 2013.

Semelin, Jacques. "Analyser le massacre: Réflexions comparatives." *Questions de recherches* 7 (September 2002): 42.

Serodes, Fabrice. *Anglophobie et politique: De Fachoda à Mers el-Kébir.* Paris: L'Harmattan, 2010.

Seyersted, Finn. *Common Law of International Organizations.* Leiden: Brill, 2008.

Sharf, Frederic A., and Peter Harrington. *China 1900: The Eyewitnesses Speak—The Experience of Westerners in China During the Boxer Rebellion, as Described by Participants in Letters, Diaries and Photographs.* London: Greenhill Books–Stackpole Books, 2000.

Sheehan, Brett. "The Currency of Legitimation: Banks, Bank Money and State-Society Relations in Tianjin China, 1916–1921." PhD dissertation, University of California Berkeley, 1997.

——. *Trust in Troubled Times: Money, Banks, and State-Society Relations in Republican Tianjin.* Cambridge, MA: Harvard University Press, 2003.

Sigel, Louis T. "The Diplomacy of Chinese Nationalism, 1900–1911." In *Myth and Reality: Social and Political Change in Modern China, 1860–1949*, ed. David Pong and Edmund Fung, 223–33. Lanham, MD: University Press of America, 1985.

Silbey, David. *The Boxer Rebellion and the Great Game in China.* New York: Hill and Wang, 2012.

Singaravélou, Pierre. "Dix empires dans un mouchoir de poche: Le territoire de Tianjin à l'épreuve du phénomène concessionnaire (années 1860–1920)." In *Territoires impériaux: Une histoire spatiale du fait colonial*, ed. Hélène Blais, Florence Deprest, and Pierre Singaravélou. Paris: Publications de la Sorbonne, 2011.

——. "Les stratégies d'internationalisation de la question coloniale et la construction transnationale d'une science de la colonisation à la fin du xixe siècle." *Monde(s)* 1 (2012): 135–57.

Skinner, G. William, ed. *The City in Late Imperial China.* Stanford, CA: Stanford University Press, 1977.

Spector, Stanley. *Li Hung Chang and the Huai Army: A Study in Nineteenth-Century Chinese Regionalism.* Seattle: University of Washington Press, 1974.

Spence, Jonathan. *The Search for Modern China.* New York: W. W. Norton, 1991.

Spicq, Delphine. "La politique de l'eau et l'hydraulique urbaine dans la plaine du nord de la Chine: Le cas de Tianjin, 1900–1949." PhD dissertation, Paris-7, 2004.

——. *L'avènement de l'eau courante à Tianjin (1900–1949)*. Saarbrücken: Éditions Universitaires Européennes, 2012.

Stanway, Glen. *Fearless: The Story of Chin Woo Kung Fu*. Royston, UK: Gmax Academy, 2013.

Stapleton, Kristin. *Civilizing Chengdu: Chinese Urban Reform, 1895–1937*. Cambridge, MA: Harvard University Press, 2000.

Staunton, George Léonard, and Jean-Henri Castéra. *Voyage dans l'intérieur de la Chine*. Paris: F. Buisson, 1798.

Suzuki, Shogo. *Civilization and Empire: China and Japan's Encounter with European International Society*. New York: Routledge, 2009.

Tait Slys, Mariya. *Exporting Legality: The Rise and Fall of Extraterritorial Jurisdiction in the Ottoman Empire and China*. eCahiers de l'Institut, Graduate Institute, Geneva, February 2014.

Tawney, Richard Henry. *Land and Labor in China*. London: Allen and Unwin, 1932.

Tertrais, Hugues. "Ordre et désordre asiatiques." *Matériaux pour l'histoire de notre temps* 88 (October–December 2007): 3–7.

——. "Une révolution sous influence: La république chinoise face au consortium bancaire." *Matériaux pour l'histoire de notre temps* 109–110 (2013): 25–31.

Thaxton, Ralph, *Salt of the Earth: The Political Origins of Peasant Protest and Communist Revolution in China*. Berkeley: University of California Press, 1997.

Thierry, François. "Fausses dates et vraies monnaies: Rites, information, propagande et histoire dans la numismatique chinoise." *Extrême-Orient, Extrême-Occident* 32 (2010): 41–59.

Thireau, Isabelle, and Linshan Hua. "The Moral Universe of Aggrieved Chinese Workers: Workers' Appeals to Arbitration Committees and Letters and Visits Offices." *China Journal* 50 (2003): 83.

Thiriez, Regine. *Barbarian Lens: Western Photographers of the Qianlong Emperor's European Palaces*. Amsterdam: Gordon and Breach, 1998.

Thompson, Larry Clinton. *William Scott Ament and the Boxer Rebellion: Heroism, Hubris and the "Ideal Missionary."* Jefferson, NC: McFarland, 2009.

Thompson, Roger R. *China's Local Councils in the Age of Constitutional Reform, 1898–1911*. Cambridge, MA: Harvard University Press, 1995.

Tianjin lishi bowuguan (Historical Museum of Tianjin). *Jindai Tianjin tuzhi* (Illustrated History of Contemporary Tianjin). Tianjin: Tianjin guji chubanshe, 1992.

Tong Lam. "Policing the Imperial Nation: Sovereignty, International Law, and the Civilizing Mission in Late Qing China." *Comparative Studies in Society and History* 52, no. 4 (October 2010): 881–908.

Tsin, Michael T. W. *Nation, Governance and Modernity in China: Canton, 1900–1927.* Stanford, CA: Stanford University Press, 1999.

Tsuzuki, J. "Bericht über meine epidemiologischen Beobachtungen und forschungen während der Choleraepidemie in Nordchina im Jahre 1902 und über die im Verlaufe derselben von mir durchgefürhten prophylaktischen Massregeln mit besonderer Berücksichtigung der Choleraschutzimpfung." *Archiv für Schiffs und Tropen-Hygiene* 8 (1904).

Vaicbourdt, Nicolas. "De la 'me too policy' aux ambitions contradictoires: La brève histoire de la concession américaine de Tianjin, 1860–1902." *Outre-Mers: Revue d'histoire* 382–383 (June 2014): 27–46.

Vandermeersch, Léon. "L'institution chinoise de remontrance." *Études chinoises* 13, nos. 1–2 (Spring–Fall 1994): 31–46.

Vié, Michel. "La Mandchourie et la 'question d'extrême-Orient,' 1880–1910." *Cipango* 18 (2011): 19–78.

Wakeman, Frederic, Jr. "Models of Historical Change: The Chinese State and Society, 1839–1989." In *Perspectives on Modern China: Four Anniversaries*, ed. Kenneth Lieberthal, 68–102. Armonk: M. E. Sharpe, 1991.

——, *Policing Shanghai, 1927–1937.* Berkeley: University of California Press, 1995.

Wang Huatang, *Tianjin—yige chengshi de jueqi* (Tianjin: Development of the City). Tianjin: Tianjin renmin chubanshe, 1990.

Weber, Jacques, and François de Sesmaisons, eds. *La France en Chine (1843–1943).* Paris: L'Harmattan, 2013.

Weishuai Tian. "Une institution missionnaire française en Chine: l' Institut des Hautes Études Industrielles et Commerciales (1923–1951)." PhD dissertation, Université Paris-4, 2014.

Weitzel, Thibault. *Le fléau invisible: La dernière épidémie de choléra en France.* Paris: Vendémiaire, 2011.

Westad, Odd Arne. *Restless Empire: China and the World Since 1750.* New York: Basic Books, 2012.

White, Richard. *The Middle Ground: Indians, Empires, and Republics in the Great Lakes Region, 1650–1815.* Cambridge: Cambridge University Press, 1991.

Wilkinson, Endymion. *Chinese History: A New Manual.* Cambridge, MA: Harvard University Press, 2013.

Will, Pierre-Étienne. *Bureaucratie et famine en Chine au xviii*[e] *siècle.* Paris-La Haye: Éditions de l'EHESS–Mouton, 1980.

——. "Ingénieurs, philanthropes et seigneurs de la guerre dans la Chine républicaine, 1911–1935." *Annuaire du Collège de France, 2007–2008.*

———. "Science et sublimation de l'état." *Actes de la recherche en sciences sociales* 133 (June 2000): 13–25.

Wittfogel, Karl. *Oriental Despotism: A Comparative Study of Total Power.* New Haven, CT: Yale University Press, 1957.

Wong Kam C. *Chinese Policing: History and Reform.* New York: Peter Lang, 2009.

———. *Police Reform in China.* Boca Raton, FL: CRC Press, 2011.

Wong, Roy Bin. *China Transformed: Historical Change and the Limits of European Experience.* Ithaca, NY: Cornell University Press, 1997.

Wright, Arnold, ed. *Twentieth Century Impressions of Hongkong, Shanghai, and Other Treaty Ports of China.* London: Lloyds Greater Britain, 1908.

Wu Hung. "Tiananmen Square: A Political History of Monuments." *Representations* 35 (Summer 1991): 84–117.

Xiang Lanxin. *The Origins of the Boxer War: A Multinational Study.* London: Routledge, 2003.

Xiaobo Zhang. "Merchant Associational Activism in Early Twentieth Century China: The Tianjin General Chamber of Commerce, 1904–1928." PhD dissertation, Columbia University, 1995.

Yago, Kazuhiko. "The Russo-Chinese Bank (1896–1910): An International Bank in Russia and Asia." In *The Origins of International Banking in Asia: The Nineteenth and Twentieth Centuries*, ed. Shizuya Nishimura, Toshio Suzuki, and Ranald C. Michie. Oxford: Oxford University Press, 2012.

Yan Yan. "Le protectorat religieux de la France en Chine (1840–1912)." PhD dissertation, Université Paris-1 Panthéon-Sorbonne, 2011.

Yee, Cordell D. K. "Traditional Chinese Cartography and the Myth of Westernization." In *The History of Cartography*, vol. 2, *Cartography in the Traditional East and Southeast Asian Societies*, ed. J. B. Harley and David Woodward. Chicago: University of Chicago Press, 1994.

Yee, Frank Y. C. "Police in Modern China." PhD thesis, University of California Berkeley, 1942.

Yan Xiu. *Yan Xiu xiansheng nian pu.* Jinan: Jilu Press, 1990.

Yongming Zhou. *Historicizing Online Politics: Telegraphy, the Internet, and Political Participation in China.* Stanford, CA: Stanford University Press, 2006.

Young, Ernest P. *Ecclesiastical Colony: China's Catholic Church and the French Religious Protectorate.* Oxford: Oxford University Press, 2013.

Young, L. K. *British Policy in China, 1895–1902.* Oxford: Clarendon Press, 1970.

Yuan Fang. "Influences of British Architecture in China. Shanghai and Tientsin 1843–1943." PhD thesis, University of Edinburgh, 1995.

Yvorel, Jean-Jacques, ed. "Cent ans de répressions des violences à enfants." *Revue d'histoire de l'enfance "irrégulière"* 2 (1999): 9–11.

Zhang Chang and Liu Yue. "International Concessions and the Modernization of Tianjin," In *Harbin to Hanoi: The Colonial Built Environment in Asia, 1840 to 1940,*

ed. Laura Victoir and Victor Zatsepine. Hong Kong: Hong Kong University Press, 2013.
Zhang Zhidong. *Zhang Wenxiang gong quanii* (Complete Works of the Honorable Zhang Wenxiang). Taipei: Wenhai Chubanshe, 1970.
Zhang, Zhongli. *The Chinese Gentry: Studies on Their Role in Nineteenth-Century Chinese Society*. Seattle: University of Washington Press, 1955.
Zhengyuan, Fu. *Autocratic Tradition and Chinese Politics*. Cambridge: Cambridge University Press, 1993.
Zola, Émile. *Rome*. Paris: Bernouard, 1929.

Index

Page numbers in *italics* indicate figures.

Printed and bound by CPI Group (UK) Ltd, Croydon, CR0 4YY

04/06/2025

14683797-0004